MW01193336

THOMISTIC PHILOSOPHY

BY

Rev. HENRI GRENIER, Ph.D., S.T.D., J.C.D.
Professor of Philosophy, Laval University

Translated from the Latin of the original
CURSUS PHILOSOPHIAE (Editio tertia)
by
Rev. J. P. E. O'Hanley, Ph. D.

IN THREE VOLUMES

VOLUME I

GENERAL INTRODUCTION, LOGIC,
PHILOSOPHY OF NATURE

First English Edition

Published by
ST. DUNSTAN'S UNIVERSITY
CHARLOTTETOWN, CANADA

1948

Nihil obstat:

GAVAN P. MONAGHAN, Ph.D., Paed.D.,
Censor deputatus.

Die 20 Januarii, 1948.

Imprimatur:

† JACOBUS BOYLE, D.D.,
Episcopus Carolinapolitanus.

Carolinapoli, die 2 Februarii, 1948.

Des ateliers de L'ACTION CATHOLIQUE, Québec.

To

ST. DUNSTAN

Scholar Statesman Saint

AUTHOR'S PREFACE

Thomistic Philosophy is offered to the English-speaking world in response to numerous requests, especially from teachers throughout Canada and The United States, for an English translation of our *Cursus Philosophiae*.

It was our good fortune to obtain for this work the talented services of Rev. J. P. E. O'Hanley, St. Dunstan's University, who holds the Ph. D. degree from the « Angelicum », world-famous centre of Thomism, and who is a gifted Latinist of many years of teaching experience.

We have read carefully the MS. of *Thomistic Philosophy*, and have found it to be an excellent rendition in English of the original work: not only is the doctrine of Aristotle and St. Thomas, as presented in the Latin work, most faithfully safeguarded, but it is couched in language that is both precise and idiomatic.

We welcome this opportunity to give public expression to our sentiments of profound gratitude to Rev. Dr. O'Hanley for his generous cooperation, and to congratulate him on having carried to successful completion a very difficult assignment.

HENRI GRENIER.

Feast of The Conversion of St. Paul, 1948.

TRANSLATOR'S FOREWORD

« Domestic and civil society even, which, as we all see, is exposed to great danger from the plague of perverse opinions », writes Pope Leo XIII, « would certainly enjoy a far more peaceful and secure existence if a more wholesome doctrine were taught in the academies and schools — one more in conformity with the teaching of the Church, such as is contained in the works of Thomas Aquinas. For the teachings of Thomas on the true meaning of liberty, which at this time is running into license, on the divine origin of all authority, on laws and their force, on the paternal and just rule of princes, on obedience to the higher powers, on mutual charity one towards another — on all these and kindred subjects, have very great and invincible force to overturn those principles of the new order which are well known to be dangerous to the peaceful order of things and to public safety » (1). This momentous papal admonition is certainly as timely in 1948 as it was when it was promulgated to the world of almost seventy years ago; and it is, we are convinced, the only apology — if indeed an apology be necessary, — that need be offered for the appearance of an English edition of Rev. Dr. Henri Grenier's *Cursus Philosophiae*, a work which « breathes the spirit of St. Thomas on nearly every page » (2).

Some few revered and well-intentioned teachers, *laudatores temporis acti*, may object that the study of the philosophy of St. Thomas Aquinas from an English manual is a dangerous innovation, an unwarranted break with scholastic tradition, an imprudent abandonment of the cultural advantages of the Latin tongue, an almost treasonable desertion of the works of the Angelic Doctor, with the original Latin text of which the student should become thoroughly familiar. These objections, though not entirely unfounded, fail to take into account the lamentable fact that, unless the teachings of St. Thomas are made available in the vernacular, they will remain accessible only to the few.

(1) Encyclical Letter *Aeterni Patris*, 4 August, 1879.
(2) Cf. *The Thomist*, July, 1946, p. 466.

The study of Thomistic philosophy is not the exclusive right of the Latinist; but, in the case of the English-speaking peoples of Canada and the U.S.A., it is too often his peculiar privilege, simply because the number of important philosophical works, especially of manuals, in English is meagre indeed. Moreover, in recent years the study of Latin has been so falling into desuetude, even in many Catholic schools, that the standard Latin manuals of philosophy have already become closed books to far too many of our undergraduate students. Therefore, unless textbooks in English *ad Angelici Doctoris rationem, doctrinam et principia* (3) are made available, many students requiring credits in philosophy will be exposed perforce to the subversive doctrines of pseudo-philosophies, or, at best, will have access only to courses that consist in little more than a cursory survey, certainly not an analytical study, of the historical development of philosophical thought. « We exhort you », writes Leo XIII, « . . . to restore the golden wisdom of St. Thomas, and to spread it far and wide for the defence and beauty of the Catholic faith, for the good of society, and for the advantage of all the sciences. . . . But, lest the false for the true, or the corrupt for the pure, be drunk in, be ye careful that the doctrine of St. Thomas be drawn from his own fountains, or at least from those rivulets which, derived from the very fount, have thus far flowed, according to the established agreement of learned men, pure and clear; be careful to guard the minds of youth from those which are said to flow thence, but in reality are gathered from strange and unwholesome streams » (4). Dr. Grenier is ever mindful, and heedful too, of this Leonine warning, for he informs us in the Preface to his French work, *Cours de Philosophie*, that his manual draws its inspiration from sources that are pure: Aristotle, St. Thomas Aquinas, and the great scholastic commentators, Cajetan, John of St. Thomas, and Francis a Silvestris of Ferrara (Ferrariensis) (5). We readily understand, then, why Rev. Ignatius McGuiness, O.P., in his review of *Cursus Philosophiae*, declares: « Abbé Grenier, while he follows

(3) Cf. *Cod. Iur. Can.*, c. 1366 (2).
(4) *Aeterni Patris.*
(5) Avertissement Au Lecteur, p. xii.

the major divisions of philosophy now canonized by usage, includes and arranges matter according to a plan which, however fresh and novel it may appear, has the sanction of Aristotle and St. Thomas. . . . The mind and teaching of St. Thomas are faithfully adhered to, and, wherever possible, any of the Twenty-Four Theses pertinent to the discussion is quoted. The whole course then has a strongly theological slant, and attempts to present not merely a philosophical background to seminarians, but an ambitious and Catholic outlook on life to college students in general » (6). The same reviewer, referring to the English edition in preparation, avers: « when it appears, unless too badly marred by the errors that beset books in English . . . and by the involved Latinisms that obscure vernacular philosophy, *it is to be recommended to those schools in this country that sincerely desire to comply with Church legislation on following St. Thomas* — a desire too frequently hampered by a lack of English manuals other than those whose Thomism is merely nominal or completely and deliberately absent » (7).

The *Cursus* is not an exhaustive work, nor was it intended to be such: it was written primarily for undergraduate students. Indeed an exhaustive work in Thomistic philosophy for undergraduates, whose time is crowded with many other subjects and often with too many campus activities, would defeat its own end. The Horatian admonition in regard to poetry, we maintain, is applicable in its entirety to any textbook, and especially to a manual of philosophy:

> *Quidquid praecipies, esto brevis, ut cito dicta*
> *Percipiant animi dociles teneantque fideles.*
> *Omne supervacuum pleno de pectore manat* (8).

Thomistic Philosophy, the authorized English translation of Dr. Grenier's *Cursus Philosophiae*, is making its debut in

(6) *The Thomist*, July, 1946, pp. 465-466.
(7) *Ibid.* The italics are mine.
(8) *Ars Poetica*, II. 335-338.

an age which has shown a renewed and often an enthusiastic interest in the philosophical teachings of the Angel of the Schools. Perhaps we have good reason to believe that a new Thomistic day is already dawning, for Jacques Maritain, French philosopher of world-wide renown, seems to suggest that this age will witness a rebirth of Thomism: he foresees a new age of Christian culture, the « rehabilitation of the creature in God, . . . an age of theocentric humanism », an age guided by the sure teachings of St. Thomas Aquinas (9).

If *Thomistic Philosophy* can make even the smallest contribution to this « second spring » of Christian thinking, to the realization of the « reconstruction of our cultural and temporal forms of life, forms which have been built up in an atmosphere of dualism and anthropocentric rationalism » (10), the translator will have the consolation of having labored *pro virili parte* in the cause of Christian civilization, *ad instaurandum omnia in Christo.*

The translator makes grateful and fraternal acknowledgment to Rev. Dr. Grenier for having accorded him the privilege and high honor of having had a small part in the production of *Thomistic Philosophy*, for many helpful suggestions, and for permission to use his *Cours de Philosophie* as an aid and guide in the preparation of the present work.

J. P. E. O'Hanley.

---

(9) Cf. *True Humanism*, London, Geoffrey Bles: The Centenary Press, 1938, pp. 64-70.
(10) *Ibid.*, p. 64.

TABLE OF CONTENTS

I

GENERAL INTRODUCTION

II

LOGIC

OR

RATIONAL PHILOSOPHY

FIRST PART OF LOGIC

FORMAL LOGIC

Book I

SIMPLE TERMS

Book II

DISCOURSE AND PROPOSITION

Book III

ARGUMENTATION

SECOND PART OF LOGIC

MATERIAL LOGIC

Book I

NATURE OF LOGIC

Book II

UNIVERSALS

Book III

DEMONSTRATION

Book IV

DIALECTICS AND SOPHISTRY

III

PHILOSOPHY OF NATURE

GENERAL PHILOSOPHY OF NATURE

Book I

MOBILE BEING

BOOK II

PROPERTIES OF MOBILE BEING

BOOK III

GENERATION OF MOBILE BEING

SPECIAL PHILOSOPHY OF NATURE

Book I

ANIMATED MOBILE BEING IN GENERAL

Book II

VEGETATIVE MOBILE BEING

Book III

SENSITIVE MOBILE BEING

BOOK IV

INTELLECTIVE MOBILE BEING

GENERAL INTRODUCTION

NOTION AND ORIGIN OF PHILOSOPHY

1. Nominal definition of Philosophy. — Philosophy, according to its nominal definition, is the love of wisdom.

Wisdom has various meanings.

Sometimes wisdom is used as equivalent to virtue. Thus a man of wisdom signifies a good man.

Sometimes it is used as the name of that gift of the Holy Spirit by which we judge, in virtue of a certain innate endowment, of divine things and find delight in them.

Sometimes it signifies exceptional skill in an art. Thus we speak of a wise architect, i.e., an architect who has great skill in his art.

It is used also to denote a sublime knowledge or science of things.

Philosophy is the love of wisdom, in as much as wisdom means a sublime knowledge or science of things.

From this nominal definition, we can now deduce the following conclusion:

Philosophy is a science which is sought primarily *for its own sake*, and not because of its utility in life. Indeed, the philosopher is a lover of wisdom or science. One who truly loves science seeks it for its own sake, not because of something else.

2. The study of philosophy is not futile. — Since philosophy is sought primarily for its own sake and not because of its utility in life, some may suppose that the study of this science is futile. But such a study is not futile, for it satisfies a desire of our human nature. Man by his very nature desires science for its own sake. Three reasons and a sign [1] may be given in evidence of this natural desire, a desire indeed which may be said to be the first psychological source of philosophy.

a) *First reason.* — All things naturally seek their own perfection. But the perfection of the intellect is knowledge or science. For the intellect of itself is a blank, and receives its perfection in science or knowledge. Hence every being endowed with an intellect, e.g., man, has a natural desire for science.

b) *Second reason.* — Everything is naturally inclined to its own proper operation; v. g., a hot body to heat, a heavy body to fall downwards. But the proper operation of man as man is the operation of his intellect; and in this he differs from all other beings. Hence man naturally desires the operation of his intellect, and consequently he is naturally inclined to knowledge.

c) *Third reason.* — Everything naturally desires to be united to its principle, for in this does its perfection consist. But man is united to his principle only through his intellect: man attains God, Who is the principle of the human intellect, only through knowledge. Hence it follows that man is naturally inclined to knowledge or science.

d) *Sign.* — The senses serve two purposes: knowledge of things and utility in life. But we love our senses not only because of their utility in life, but also for their own sakes, in as much as they are capable of knowledge. This is evident from the fact of our very great love for the sense of sight, which is of great service to us in obtaining knowledge: we love it when it is of service to us, and also when we have no need of its service. Likewise, we love the intellect not only because it is useful to us in life, but also because it enables us to have knowledge of things. In other words, man is naturally inclined to seek knowledge for its own sake.

Question. — Since all men desire knowledge for its own sake, why is it that all men are not interested in the study of science, and especially of philosophy?

(1) *In Metaph.*, l. I, l. 1, nn. 2-5 (Cathala).

Answer. — A man can desire an end, and yet fail to pursue it, either on account of the difficulty of attaining it, or because of his many occupations. Likewise, though all men are naturally inclined to science, yet, because of pleasure, the necessities of life, or even laziness, they do not devote themselves to the study of it.

3. Brute knowledge and human knowledge. — For a more accurate knowledge of the notion of philosophy, which is a human science, we must compare brute knowledge with human knowledge.

All animals have senses; but not all animals have all the senses; only perfect animals are so endowed.

Some animals, as the oyster, have no memory.

Other animals have the sense of memory, and therefore can possess some degree of prudence. For prudence, from a remembrance of the past, makes provision for the future.

The judgment of prudence in these animals is not based, as in man, on the deliberation of reason, but rather on a natural instinct by which they naturally feel that what is beneficial should be sought and what is injurious should be avoided. Thus a lamb naturally follows its mother, but flees from a wolf.

Other animals not only have memory, but can acquire a certain learning from habituation; v.g., the horse, the dog. These are perfect animals.

But man not only has memory and can be taught, but he can *experiment;* even perfect animals can, only to a very small degree, participate in this power. They are said to enjoy a participation of it, in as much as they become accustomed, from numerous experiences they remember and from habitude, to seek or avoid something.

But man experiments in as much as he judges of singular things *by his reason.*

Over and above experiment, man possesses the art or science of discovering by reason the *universal*, that may be predicated of all things that are similar; v.g., when we learn that Peter is a *man*.

Art or science is a perfection proper to man that is in no way participated by other animals. Hence we may state now that philosophy, because it is a science, deals with universals.

4. Comparison between experiment and art. – Human experiment results from the remembrance of many things; and human art or science is the result of many experiments. And because experiment enables a person to function with accuracy and ease, experiment would seem to be similar to art or science, which also enables him to do so. However, art goes farther than experiment: experiment deals with singulars, whereas art is concerned with universals. Example: If I know that a certain medicine has been beneficial to Plato, Socrates, and others suffering from the same malady, my knowledge belongs to the realm of experiment; but if I know that a medicine is universally beneficial to men suffering from a particular disease, my knowledge belongs to the realm of art.

Hence we may compare art and experiment *as regards operation* and *as regards knowledge* (1).

1) *As regards operation.* — Experiment is concerned with singulars, whereas art extends to universals. But, since actions or operations are concerned with singulars, the difference between art and experiment that arises from universals and singulars ceases to exist in the case of operation. For even though art extends to universals, like experiment, it deals with singulars. Hence art and experiment do not differ in their mode of operation. Nevertheless, they differ in the efficacy of their operation: men who experiment make more progress in their operation than they who without experiment depend solely on art.

2) *As regards knowledge.* — Although experiment enjoys a preeminence over art as regards the efficacy of operation, yet art or science is preeminent as regards knowledge.

(1) *In Metaph.*, l. I, l. 1, nn. 20-30 (Cathala).

This is proved from an example, from a sign, and from the nature of the senses.

a) *From an example.* — Let us consider operations in reference to a ship. There are the manual operations of the workmen who prepare the timbers for the construction of the ship; there are the operations of the shipbuilder who constructs a particular design of ship; and there are the operations of the captain who sails the ship when built.

The art of the captain is nobler than that of the shipbuilder, because the latter is subordinate to the former. Similarly, the art of the shipbuilder is nobler than the manual experiment of the workmen, because they prepare the timbers for a particular type of ship. But the captain is distinguished from the builder in as much as the former knows why the ship must be a special type; for the ship must be a special type in order that it may serve the purpose for which it is intended. Similarly, the builder is distinguished from the carpenters, because the former knows why the timbers should be joined in such and such a way; and of this the carpenters who prepare the timbers have no knowledge.

Hence art is distinguished from experiment: **art is knowledge through causes; experiment does not know causes. Art** is nobler to the degree of its greater knowledge of causes.

b) *From a sign.* — Ability to teach is a sign of knowledge. Moreover, persons who have art can teach with certitude, since they know the causes from which they are able to demonstrate. But persons who have only experiment cannot teach with certitude; and the knowledge they impart to others is merely their opinion. Hence it follows that art enjoys a preeminence over experiment as regards knowledge, because art is knowledge that is more certain than experiment.

c) *From the nature of the senses.* — Knowledge of singulars belongs more properly to the senses than to any other faculty, because all knowledge of singulars begins with the senses. Yet no one would say that the knowledge of the senses is wisdom, because the senses have no knowledge of causes. Example: the sense of touch knows that fire is hot, but it does not know the cause of fire's property of heat. But persons who experiment have knowledge of singulars, but no knowledge of causes; persons who have art have knowledge of causes. Hence experiment has no right to be called wisdom; but art approximates wisdom.

In the light of the foregoing observations, we may now state that philosophy, which is wisdom, is concerned with universals, and that it is certain knowledge through causes.

5. Speculative science and practical science. – A speculative science is one whose object is knowledge itself, that is to say, one whose end is the knowledge of truth.

A practical science is one whose object is utility, that is to say, one whose end is not the contemplation of truth, but rather some work; v.g., mechanical arts.

A speculative science is wisdom to a greater degree than is a practical science. The discoverer of an art is considered to be a man of wisdom because he has better judgment and better discernment of causes than other men, not because of the utility of his discovery. Hence those sciences belong to the realm of wisdom which have been discovered on account of knowledge itself, as the speculative sciences; not, however, those whose object is some utility.

Philosophy, which is the same as love of wisdom, must be speculative; nevertheless, one part of philosophy (Moral Philosophy) is practical.

6. Art, science, and wisdom. — We have been using the terms art, science, and wisdom almost indifferently. But art, science, and wisdom are distinct from one another.

Art directs operations which pass into exterior matter; v.g., building, sawing, etc.

Science has a broad meaning and a proper meaning.

Science, in its broad meaning, is any certain knowledge.

Science, in its proper signification, is certain knowledge derived as a conclusion from certain principles.

Wisdom is the study of things through their first causes.

Philosophy is not art, but is both science and wisdom, as we shall see later.

7. Historical origin of philosophy. — Men, moved by natural inclination, first began to philosophize because of their curiosity concerning causes. In considering things that happen in the world, they sought enlightenment regarding them by inquiring into their causes.

At first, men wondered about uncertain things which were quite visible. Later, they proceeded little by little from their knowledge of manifest things to an inquiry into hidden things. Thus they began to inquire about the moon, its eclipses and change of shape, about the sun, the stars and their orderly arrangement, and finally about the orderly arrangement of the whole universe.

Thus the first philosophers among the Greeks, called Ionians, were especially concerned with the question, « From what material is the world made? » Thales (beginning of 6th century, B.C.) thought that the first principle or element from which all things are made is water; Anaximenes (528 B.C.) and Diogenes contended that it is air; and Heraclitus (578-480 B.C.) held that it is fire; Empedocles (5th century B.C.) maintained that there are four elements, namely, fire, air, earth, and water; Anaximander (about middle 6th century B.C.) asserted that the first principle of all things is something infinite and unlimited; Anaxagoras (428 B.C.) maintained that all things are made from infinite principles.

This first problem easily led to another: « What agency effects the generation or changes which take place in the world? » For the wood which becomes a statue is made a statue by another, not by itself. Heraclitus of Ephesus, surnamed the Obscure, (end of 6th century, B.C.) taught that all things are in constant flux, or that all things in their very nature are becoming.

The Eleatic School, on the contrary, affirmed that changes

are only apparent. The chief representatives of the school are Xenophanes (497 B.C.), Parmenides, Zeno, and Melissus.

Other philosophers attempted, in an obscure way, to find out by what agency change takes place. They claimed there were several elements, and to one of them, v.g., fire, they attributed activity; and to the others passivity.

To many this solution appeared insufficient; and, in an effort to find the true solution, they sought to discover whence came the good and the order found in things. Since no one supposed that good and order came from fire or from chance, Anaxagoras maintained that all things have their origin in an intelligence (Deus ex machina).

According to Hesiod and Parmenides, all things have their origin in love. Empedocles, seeing that evil also exists in the world, added a second principle, the principle of hatred. Good, in his opinion, comes from love, and evil from hatred.

8. Later historical evolution of philosophy.— 1° *Socrates.* Socrates (469-399 B.C.), unlike the Sophists, placed special stress on the importance of the right formation of concepts and definitions. Hence he proposed another problem: « What is a thing? » Moreover, he showed that the object of science is something fixed, determinate, and universal.

2° *Plato* (427-348 B.C.), a pupil of Socrates, adopted the teaching of Heraclitus, according to whom everything is in the state of becoming. Hence he had to solve the momentous problem: if everything is in constant flux, how can science arrive at anything fixed and universal? He claimed that there are two real worlds: a world of sensible things that are in constant flux, and a world of ideas which are fixed and determinate; and that singular sensible things are formed by their participation of the latter. Thus above all men there exists the Idea-of-man; and all men are merely participations of this Idea. The same is to be said of the horse, the good, the beautiful, and all other things.

The human intellect, before its union with the body, contemplated these ideas; and now, in perceiving a sensible thing in this world of flux, it recalls the world of ideas.

3° *Aristotle*. Aristotle (384-322 B.C.), the Stagirite, a pupil of Plato, collected the teachings of his predecessors, and showed how they sought the existence of some cause: the earliest philosophers were concerned with material cause (from what matter?); others with efficient cause; Plato, with formal cause. As a result of his study of motion, he added a fourth cause, namely, final cause. For four causes enter into the making of a wooden statue, viz., wood, the material cause; the figure of a statue, the formal cause: a sculptor, the efficient cause; the end intended, the final cause: the agent does not produce a determinate effect unless he has something definite in mind during his work.

Hence Aristotle defined philosophy as: «the knowledge of things through their causes». Since a philosopher is a man of wisdom or a friend of wisdom, he showed how some knowledge is science and wisdom. Knowledge is science when it is through causes; and science is wisdom when it judges inferiors and classifies them in their proper order. In the order of sciences, a superior science has the role of wisdom in respect to an inferior science, in as much as it passes judgment on the principles of the latter.

Furthermore, a science that is knowledge through first and highest causes is wisdom in the strict sense. Today, this science is called Metaphysics; and it deals with being as being.

Wisdom, in the strict sense, is judged by no superior science; it must pass judgment on and defend its own principles, which are the first principles of all human knowledge. Therefore wisdom, according to Aristotle, has to defend the value of all human knowledge against the teaching of Scepticism.

Aristotle deserves the first place among the philosophers of all time, for it was he who first elaborated with great breadth and depth of mind the fundamental points of a philosophy that we call *perennial*.

9. Distinction between philosophy and sacred theology. — When a doctrine of faith is diffused, it exercises an influence on philosophers, even on the faithless.

In the first century, the truths of faith were spread by

preaching. But soon a more detailed and complete exposition of these truths became necessary, in order that the objections of infidels might be refuted.

In the time of the ante-nicene Fathers, this work was done by the great Apologists, as St. Justin Martyr, St. Irenaeus, Tertullian, St. Clement of Alexandria, and Origen, who showed the points of agreement between Greek philosophy, especially Platonic, and the doctrines of Christ; and they attempted to refute the errors of the infidels.

A similar work was done by the great Greek Fathers, Athanasius, Basil, Gregory Nazianzen, Gregory of Nyssa, Chrysostom, and Cyril of Alexandria. These men were theologians; but, in the defense of the truths of Christianity, they gladly made use of the different systems of philosophy, especially Neo-Platonism, whose doctrines they corrected.

St. Augustine (354-430) far surpassed all the other Fathers in breadth and depth of learning. Yet, in dealing with philosophical questions, he never went outside the realm of faith. Hence he does not seem to establish sufficient distinction between philosophy and sacred theology.

The thirteenth century was the Golden Age of Christian philosophy. There were many causes for this:

1) The introduction of the works of the early philosophers, and especially of Plato and Aristotle, in Latin translations.

2) The rise of the universities, of which the University of Paris was the most important.

3) The Mendicant Orders. They were founded shortly before this time, and had many men of great genius.

4) The introduction of the Arabian commentaries on Aristotle: the commentaries of Alfarabi (10th century) and Avicenna (Ibn Sina, 980-1036), who interpreted Aristotle in Neo-Platonic fashion; Averroes (Ibn Rosch, 1126-1198), the Commentator, who, in establishing the relation between faith and reason, made a distinction between a literal sense and an allegorical sense in the Koran; he supposed that the literal sense, the only sense used by philosophers, leads to truth; and

that the allegorical sense of theologians does not of itself lead to truth.

Alexander of Hales (d. 1245) and William of Auvergne (d. 1249) were already beginning to propound certain theses according to the mind of Aristotle.

St. Bonaventure (1221-1275) strongly inveighed against certain teachings of Aristotle, and was rather a follower of Augustine.

St. Albert the Great (1193-1280) wrote commentaries on almost all the works of Aristotle, and tried to reconcile the philosophy of the Stagirite with the teachings of Christianity.

But already, especially in the University of Paris, certain masters, under the leadership of Siger of Brabant (d. 1282), were willing to adopt all the teachings of Aristotle without exception; and indeed they interpreted them in their Neo-Platonic form, as the Arabian commentators, especially Averroes, had done. It was for this reason that their teaching was called Latin Averroism.

The principal point of Latin Averroism was its theory of twofold truth, by which Siger attempted to safeguard the teachings of faith. According to this theory, what is true in philosophy may be false in theology, and vice versa. Such a theory of faith and Christain teaching was very dangerous. St. Thomas Aquinas (1225-1275), the Angelic Doctor and a pupil of St. Albert the Great, pointed out the best way of reconciling philosophy with faith. He taught that there are two modes of truth (1) in matters that we acknowledge as pertaining to God; there are some things true of God that surpass the power of human reason, as the doctrine of the Blessed Trinity; there are other truths that are entirely within the scope and power of natural reason, as the existence of God, the unity of God, and others: these truths philosophers can demonstrate by the light of natural reason.

Moreover, divine truths that can be known by reason are proposed to our belief because of God's goodness towards us:

(1) *Contra Gentes*, l. I, c. 3.

He wills that it be made easily possible for all men to come without doubt or error to a knowledge of God [1].

There is complete harmony between the truths of Christian faith and the truths of reason: the former are firmly held from the light of divine revelation; the latter become evident from the light of natural reason [2]. Hence theology, which is based on principles of faith, is knowledge acquired under the light of divine revelation; and philosophy is the knowledge of things through their causes, acquired under the light of natural reason.

Guided by these principles, St. Thomas in his philosophy followed the teaching of Aristotle, the excellence of which he clearly perceived; but he corrected whatever he discovered in it as opposed to reason or faith. The philosophy of Aristotle and St. Thomas has received the highest commendation from the Church [3]. Therefore our exposition of philosophy in this work is based on the teaching of Aristotle and St. Thomas Aquinas.

10. Principal works of St. Thomas. — The principal works of St. Thomas, in which his philosophy is contained, are the following:

Summa Theologica. — Prima pars (Viterbo, 1266-1268).
Prima-secundae (Paris, 1269-1270).
Secunda-secundae (Paris, 1271-1272).
Tertia pars (Naples, 1272-1273) and supplementum.

Each part is divided into questions, and each question into articles. The development of an article is usually as follows: three objections against the doctrine to be demonstrated, the body of the article, and answers to the objections. It is cited thus: I, q. 16, art. 2, c.; i.e., first part of the *Summa Theologica*, question 16, article 2, in the body of the article.

(1) *Ibid.*, c. 4.
(2) *Ibid.*, c. 7.
(3) *S. Studiorum Congregatio 24 theses, quae doctrinae philosophicae s. Thomae partes fundamentales enuntiant, proposuit.*

Again, I-II, q. 100, a. I, ad 2; i.e., first part of the second part of the *Summa Theologica*, question 100, in the answer to the second objection.

Summa Contra Gentiles (Paris and Anagni, 1258-1260). It is divided into four books; and each book is divided into chapters. Citations from it are made as follows: I Cg. 20, or Contra Gent. l. I, c. 20, that is, Summa Contra Gentiles, book I, chapter 20.

Quaestiones Disputatae.

De Veritate (Paris, 1256-1259).
De Potentia (Italy, 1259-1263, or later).
De Malo (Italy, 1263-1263, or later in Paris).
De Spiritualibus Creaturis (Paris, 1269, or earlier in Italy).
De Anima (Paris, 1269-1270, or earlier in Italy).

Commentaria. — In IV libros *Sententiarum Petri Lombardi* (Paris, 1254-1256).

A book is divided into distinctions, a distinction into questions, a question into articles, an article into little questions, and the solutions follow.

Citation is made in this way: I, dist. 8, q. 2, art. I, sol. I, ad 2; i.e., *Commentarii in Sententiae Petri Lombardi*, book 1, distinction 8, question 2, article I, little question I, solution I, answer to the second little question.

In opera Aristotelis:

In libros *Perihermeneias* (Paris, 1269-1270).
In libros *Posteriorum Analyticorum* (Italy and later Paris, 1268).
In VIII libros *Physicorum* (Italy, 1265 or 1268).
In III libros *De Anima* (Italy and later Paris, 1266).
In XII libros *Metaphysicorum* (Italy and later Paris, 1265).
In X libros *Ethicorum ad Nicomachum* (Italy and later Paris, 1265).

Super Boethium. — *De Hebdomadibus* (1257-1258).
De Trinitate (1257-1258).

The Commentaries on Aristotle are divided into readings. They are cited in this manner: In Phys, l. VI, 1.2, that is, *Commentarium in Physicam Aristotelis*, book 6, reading 2.

Opuscula. — *De Ente et Essentia* (Paris, 1256).
De Unitate Intellectus (Paris, 1270).
Compendium Theologiae (Paris and Naples, 1271-1273).

11. Definition of Philosophy. — We know from what has been already said that philosophers inquire into the causes of things. Moreover, we know that philosophers wish to know the first causes of things, because philosophy means the love of wisdom; and we know too that philosophy and sacred theology are distinct from one another.

Hence philosophy may be defined as follows: *the science of things through their first causes under the light of natural reason.*

a) *Science*, i.e., certain knowledge through causes.

As a science, philosophy is destinguished from art, which directs transitive operation into exterior matter.

As certain knowledge, philosophy is distinguished from modern Mathematics, which does proceed from certain principles, but from principles which are accepted as postulates. Similarly, as certain knowledge, philosophy is distinguished from Physics, which is only probable knowledge.

b) *Of things*, i.e., of all beings, as inorganic beings, plants, irrational animals, men, and God Himself.

c) *Through their first causes*, i.e., ultimate causes. Philosophy inquires also into the proximate causes of things, but always tends to a knowledge of their first causes.

First causes are first or ultimate in a particular order, v.g., in the order of sensible things; or they are absolutely first; v.g., God.

Philosophy is concerned with first causes in a particular order, and also with the absolutely first cause.

d) Under the light of natural reason: Philosophy is thus distinguished from sacred theology, which is a science under the light of divine revelation.

12. Division of Philosophy. – 1° Philosophy is first divided into *speculative philosophy* and *practical philosophy.*

Speculative philosophy is philosophy which considers beings for the sole purpose of acquiring knowledge of them.

Practical or *Moral philosophy* is philosophy which considers how man naturally ought to act to attain his ultimate end.

2° *Speculative philosophy* is divided into Rational Philosophy or Logic, and Real Philosophy.

Rational Philosophy or Logic is a science which considers that being of reason which is the order of concepts and propositions.

Real speculative philosophy is a science which considers real beings, i.e., all beings which have their own nature; v.g., man, God.

3° *Real Speculative Philosophy* is divided into two sciences: *Philosophy of Nature,* which considers mobile being endowed with physical motion, i.e., spatio-temporal being; and *Metaphysics,* which considers being as being.

4° *Practical or Moral Philosophy* is divided into three sciences: *Monastics* or *Individual Moral,* which considers the operations of man acting voluntarily in view of his end; *Economics* or *Domestic Moral,* which considers the operations of domestic society, i.e., of the family; *Politics,* which considers the operations of civil society.

The following is an outline of the division of philosophy:

PHILOSOPHY	*Speculative*	Rational: Logic (I)	
		Real	Philosophy of Nature (II)
			Metaphysics (III)
	Practical or *Moral*	Monastics or Ethics (IV)	
		Economics (V)	
		Politics (VI)	

RATIONAL PHILOSOPHY

OR

LOGIC

INTRODUCTION

13. Nominal definition of Logic. — Irrational animals are moved to their acts by a *determinate instinct* of their nature; man is directed in his acts by the *judgment of reason*. But the judgment of reason is indeterminate as regards the things with which it deals. Therefore man has need of different arts in order that he perform his acts with order and ease. For an art is nothing other than a direction or rule which determines reason and by which reason directs man's acts by determinate means to their proper end.

But reason can direct not only the acts or operations of other faculties, but also its own operations.

Hence, just as reason, in reasoning about manual arts, discovers the art of architecture or the art of carpentry by which man can exercise his acts with order and ease, so also, in reasoning about its own acts, it discovers the art by which man advances with order, ease, and correctness [1] in the very act of reason.

This art is called *Logic*.

Hence Logic may be called the *art of arts*, because it directs us in our acts of reason, from which all arts derive.

Logic is called *rational science* or *science of reason* not only because it proceeds in conformity with reason (this is common to all arts), but because it is concerned with the acts or operations of reason itself as its proper matter.

14. The three operations of the intellect. — Logic deals with the acts or operations of the intellect. To distinguish between the operations of the intellect, we must observe that reason or the human intellect does not come all at once to a perfect knowledge of things, but proceeds little by little from a knowledge of known truths to a knowledge of unknown truths. The operation by which this transition is made is called reasoning.

(1) *In Post. Anal.*, l. I, l. 1.

Example of reasoning:

> Every corporeal being is corruptible.
> But man is a corporeal being.
> Therefore man is corruptible.

But reasoning presupposes another intellectual operation by which the intellect assents to the enunciations or propositions on which the act of reasoning depends; v.g., that the intellect assent to the proposition: *every corporeal being is corruptible*, it must first know what a corporeal being is and what a corruptible being is. This operation is called simple apprehension.

Therefore there are three operations of the intellect:

Simple apprehension,

Judgment,

Reasoning.

These operations are so related to one another that the third presupposes the second, and the second presupposes the first.

15. The operation of the intellect, its products, and the external signs of the products. — Just as in other arts a distinction must be made between operations and the results of these operations, so in Logic a distinction must be made between the operations of the intellect and the results of its operations.

Example: In the building of a house, the vital operations of the builders are distinct from the product of their operations, the house. There could also be a sign to represent the house; v.g., a picture.

Likewise, in the process by which the intellect inquires into and knows truth, a distinction must be made between the operations of the intellect, their products, and the material signs by which these products are externally manifested.

The following table will serve to describe these distinctions:

VITAL OPERATIONS	PRODUCTS	EXTERNAL SIGNS
Simple apprehension	Concepts	Oral and written terms
Judgment	Mental proposition or enunciation	Oral and written propositions
Reasoning	Mental argumentation	Oral and written argumentations

16. Real definition of Logic. — Logic may be defined: *the art which directs the very acts of reason and enables man to advance with order, ease, and correctness in the act of reason itself.*

a) *Art:* a rule of reason by which some of man's acts are directed.

b) *Directs the very acts of reason:* just as the art of architecture directs man's acts in the building of a house, so Logic is the art which directs the very acts of reason, which constitute the matter with which Logic deals.

The acts of reason which Logic directs are reasoning, judgment, and simple apprehension as related to reasoning.

However, Logic does not direct the acts of reason by direct contact with them, but rather by arranging the products of reason, i.e., concepts, propositions, and argumentations as representing known objects, in their proper order.

c) *Enables man to advance with order:* By this art man properly and correctly resolves judgment and reasoning. In order to reason and to pass judgment, reason has recourse to *resolution:* it resolves judgment into its principles and examines the proofs by which it is manifested. Thus reason avers that the *human soul is immortal,* because the human soul is a *spiritual substance.* Therefore the parts of Logic which show how to engender a certain judgmen through reasoning are called Analytics by Aristotle.

17. Division of Logic. — In every art, there are two things which must be given special consideration, namely, the material or matter of which it treats, and the form given to this matter; v.g., in the construction of a house, wood and stone constitute the material; and the assembling of them into a definite structure constitutes the form.

Likewise, in the art of Logic, we must distinguish between its matter and form.

Things or objects of which we wish to have accurate knowledge, i.e., things signified by concepts and propositions, are the matter of Logic.

Its form consists in that disposition of known objects that must obtain in order that true knowledge be attained.

Thus in reasoning, which is the principal consideration of Logic, we distinguish between the form, or disposition of concepts and propositions in virtue of which reasoning is said to be correct or incorrect, and the matter, or the things expressed by the concepts and propositions, in virtue of which the conclusion of the act of reasoning is true or false.

This may be illustrated by the following syllogism:

Man is a donkey.
But Peter is a man.
Therefore Peter is a donkey.

This syllogism is correct as regards its form, because the concepts and propositions are duly related.

But its conclusion is not true, because the syllogism is defective in its matter. It is not true that man is a donkey.

Logic considers both the form and the matter of concepts and propositions. It is therefore divided into:

a) Formal Logic;

b) Material Logic.

Formal Logic is defined: ***the part of Logic which teaches what must be the disposition of concepts and propositions required for correct reasoning.***

Material Logic is defined: *the part of Logic which teaches what the content and mode of expression of concepts and propositions must be, in order that the conclusion of reasoning be true.*

POINTS FOR REVIEW

1. What is art?
2. With what matter does Logic deal?
3. Is Logic necessary? Why is it called the art of arts and rational science?
4. Name the operations of the intellect.
5. Explain the statement: in reasoning and judgment, the reason has recourse to *resolution*.

FIRST PART OF LOGIC

FORMAL LOGIC

Prologue. — Formal Logic sets forth the rules governing the disposition of concepts in reasoning. Since reasoning presupposes judgment and simple apprehension, Formal Logic is divided into three books:

Book I: Simple terms, or what pertains to simple apprehension.

Book II: Discourse and Propositions, or what pertains to judgment.

Book III: Syllogism, or what pertains to reasoning.

BOOK I

THE ONLY CHAPTER

SIMPLE TERMS

Prologue. – The first book of Logic deals with the things that pertain to simple apprehension. Simple apprehension produces concepts. Formal logic deals with concepts in as much as they are *terms*.

Hence we shall first discuss briefly simple apprehension and the concept. Then we shall set forth the notion and division of the term. Finally we shall consider the noun and verb, which are the principal divisions of the term.

Hence there will be four articles in this chapter.

- Simple apprehension and the concept
  - Notion of simple apprehension
  - Notion of the concept
  - The concept and the phantasm
  - Different names of the concept
  - Notes of the concept
  - Comprehension and extension of the concept
- Notion of the term
  - Three ways of considering the concept
  - Definition of the enunciative term
  - Definition of the sign
  - Division of the sign
- Division of the term
  - First division
  - Second division
  - Third division
  - Fourth division
- Noun and verb
  - The noun
  - The verb

ARTICLE I

SIMPLE APPREHENSION AND THE CONCEPT

18. Notion of simple apprehension. — Simple apprehension is defined: *the operation by which the intellect perceives a quiddity without affirming or denying anything about it.*

In this definition two things should be noted:

a) Quiddity signifies anything that can be perceived by the intellect of a thing, and it manifests what the thing is; v.g., man, white, learned man.

b) In as much as nothing is affirmed or denied in simple apprehension, simple apprehension is distinct from judgment.

19. Notion of the concept. — The concept is defined: *the representation which the intellect expresses in itself, and in which we perceive a thing.*

A distinction is to be made between formal concept (subjective, mental, or proper concept) and objective concept (analogical concept).

A formal concept is the image or representation of a thing as it informs the intellect and by means of which we have knowledge of the thing represented.

An objective concept is what the intellect perceives of a thing in its formal concept, or it is the thing as presented to the intellect by means of the formal concept [1].

20. The concept and the phantasm. — We must carefully distinguish between the concept and the phantasm.

(1) On peut dire que l'intelligence atteint la chose tant par le concept mental que par le concept objectif. Mais elle atteint la chose par le concept mental, comme nous saisissons un animal « par nos mains »; elle atteint la chose par le concept objectif, mais comme nous saisissons un animal « par ses pattes ». — MARITAIN, *Petite Logique*, p. 29, note 6, 8e édit.

The phantasm is defined: *the representation of a thing produced by an internal sense in itself (v.g., in the imagination), in which the internal sense has knowledge of the thing.*

Hence *a*) a phantasm is in one of the senses, whereas a concept is in the intellect; a phantasm always represents a material thing, whereas a concept can also represent a spiritual thing; v.g., God, an angel; *b*) a phantasm always represents a singular thing, whereas a concept directly represents a universal; v.g., when I have a concept of man, man is a nature that can belong to many, v.g., to Peter, Paul, etc., and therefore it is a universal.

Neverthless, the phantasm and the concept are intimately associated in human knowledge, because the intellect indirectly attains a singular thing represented by a phantasm, in as much as it always perceives a universal abstracted from material things in a singular thing represented by a phantasm (1).

Example: If we use the term man, we discover at once that we have two representations: an indeterminate representation of man that is infinitely variable — a phantasm; and a concept of man representing what man is, and which, ever remaining the same, may be predicated of any man, v.g., of Peter, Paul, etc.

21. Names of the concept. — A concept is called: An *expressed species*, because it is a representation — species means representation — which is expressed by the intellect.

A *mental word*, because a thing is presented to the mind by that representation, and the mind in a certain way speaks to itself.

An *idea*, although among Scholastics an idea signifies a concept to the likeness or pattern of which an artificer produces an artifact.

A *mental term*, because it is the ultimate element into which a proposition is resolved. In formal Logic, we deal with the concept considered as a term.

(1) I, q. 85, a. 1, ad 5; q. 86, a. 1, c.

22. Notes of the concept. – The notes of a concept are those elements by which an object is known and distinguished from all others; v.g., if man is conceived as a rational animal, then *animality* and *rationality* are the notes of the concept of man; if a man is conceived as an unfledged two-legged animal, in this case *animal, two-legged*, and *unfledged* are the notes of the concept of a man.

23. Comprehension and extension of the concept. – The comprehension of a concept is the *collection of notes which constitute the concept;* v.g., man is an animal, a living being, a body, a substance, a being. The collection of all these notes constitutes the comprehension of the concept of man.

The extension of a concept is defined: *the collection of individuals and objects in general to which a universal concept belongs, or which a universal concept represents;* v.g., man represents all individual beings that have human nature, i.e., Peter, Paul, James, etc.

The relation between the comprehension and the extension of a concept is expressed in the following rule: *as the comprehension of a concept is greater, its extension is less, and vice versa;* in other words, they are in inverse ratio to each other. Thus living being has a greater comprehension than body, because it adds the note of life to body; but its extension is less, because it extends only to living bodies, whereas body extends to both living and non-living beings.

POINTS FOR REVIEW

1. Explain the difference between formal concept and objective concept.

2. What is the difference between the comprehension and the extension of a concept?

3. Has *animal* greater comprehension and extension than *man*? Explain.

4. Classify the following concepts according to their extension: Catholic Christian, Calvinist, Heretic.

ARTICLE II

NOTION OF THE TERM

24. Three ways of considering the concept. — The concept can be considered in three ways: *first*, as it represents simple essences or quiddities; *secondly*, as concepts are parts of an enunciation; *thirdly*, as the order of a syllogism is constituted from concepts [1].

The study of the concept as representing quiddities or simple essences belongs to Material Logic.

The consideration of the concept as constituting the order of a syllogism belongs to the part of Formal Logic that deals with the syllogism.

Here we shall consider the concept as it is a part of an enunciation or as an *enunciative term*. *Man exists* is an enunciation. This enunciation is a whole whose component parts are two concepts, viz., the concept of *man* and the concept of *exists*. Again, if we break up the enunciation, these two concepts remain as the ultimate elements into which the enunciation may be resolved.

Therefore the first component parts of an enunciation are called its terms, because they are the ultimate terms into which an enunciation can be resolved.

25. Definition of the enunciative term. — The enunciative term is mental, oral, or written, as it is a component part of a mental, oral, or written proposition.

The enunciative term, as it comprehends the mental, oral, and written term, is defined: *the sign from which a simple proposition is made.*

(1) *In Periherm.*, l. I, l. 1, n. 5 (Leonina).

a) *Sign:* a concept or mental term is the sign of a thing; an oral term or a written term is *immediately* the sign of a concept, but *principally* the sign of a thing.

b) *From which a simple proposition is made:* a simple proposition, as *man is just*, is distinguished from a compound or hypothetical proposition, as *if man is just, he is pleasing to God.* A term is called a sign from which a *simple* proposition is made, to exclude a proposition itself or discourse, which can be a component part of a compound proposition, but is not the ultimate element into which a proposition can be resolved.

An oral term is defined: *an articulate sound which conventionally signifies that from which a simple proposition or discourse is made.*

a) *Sound:* made with some imagination by the mouth of an animal.

b) *Articulate sound:* thus are excluded inarticulate sounds that have no signification; e.g., coughing.

c) *Conventionally,* i.e., from arbitrary institution. Thus are excluded sounds that have a natural signification, as a groan.

The oral term and the written term, in as much as they have a conventional signification, are distinguished from the mental term, which has a natural signification.

d) *That from which a simple proposition or discourse is made:* as above.

26. Definition of the sign.— Man knows by means of significant concepts, and speaks by means of significant sounds. Therefore all the instruments we use in knowing and speaking are signs. Hence, that a logician have accurate knowledge of his instruments, i.e., terms and discourses, he must first know what a sign is.

The sign is defined: *that which represents something other than itself to a cognitive faculty.*

Since a sign makes known, represents, and signifies, we

must observe the difference in meaning between *to make known*, *to represent*, and *to signify*.

To make known is predicated of everything that contributes to knowledge, and therefore it has a wider extension than to represent. For a cognitive power makes known, but does not represent.

To represent is predicated of everything by which a thing is presented to a cognitive faculty.

To signify is predicated of that which presents to the cognitive faculty something distinct from itself. Thus to represent has a wider extension than to signify, for a known object, which is not a sign, represents itself, not something other than itself, to the cognitive faculty.

The sign represents by signifying, and therefore it is that which represents something other than itself.

Therefore three things are considered in the sign: 1° the thing which signifies: the sign materially understood; 2° the thing which is distinct from the sign but known by means of it: the thing signified; 3° the power of signifying, or the nexus between the sign and the thing signified: the signification.

27. Division of the sign. – The sign is divided both as regards its relation to the cognitive power and as regards its relation to the thing signified.

1° As regards its relation to the cognitive power, it is divided into *instrumental* sign and *formal* sign.

An instrumental sign is *a sign which, from previous knowledge of itself, represents something other than itself;* v.g., a picture of Jupiter is an instrumental sign, because the picture does not represent Jupiter to the cognitive faculty before it is itself known. Similarly smoke does not represent fire to the cognitive faculty, unless the smoke itself is first known. A picture of Jupiter is a sign which is an image; smoke is a sign which is not an image.

A formal sign is *a sign which, without previous knowledge of itself, represents something other than itself.* A concept is a formal sign, for, when we conceive a thing, we know the thing before we know its concept. A formal sign is an image of a thing; but not every image of a thing is a formal sign.

Concepts and phantasms are formal signs. All other signs are instrumental signs.

2° As regards its relation to the thing signified, the sign is divided into *natural* sign, *conventional* sign, and *consuetudinary* sign

A natural sign is *one which of its very nature represents something, without being arbitrarily imposed by public authority or by custom.* Hence a natural sign represents the same thing everywhere. Smoke is a natural sign of fire. A concept is a natural sign of a thing.

A conventional sign is *one which represents something in virtue of an arbitrary disposition of public authority.* The term « man » is a conventional sign.

A consuetudinary sign is *one which represents something because of usage only, without being imposed by public authority.* A tablecloth on a table is a consuetudinary sign that dinner is about to be served.

Cf. JOANNEM A SANCTO THOMA, *Curs. Phil.*, t. I, pp. 7-10 (Reiser)

POINTS FOR REVIEW

1. Is a concept sometimes considered as a syllogistic term and sometimes as an enunciative term? Explain briefly.
2. What is the general definition of oral term?
3. Explain whether or not a sign *represents* and *makes known.*
4. Distinguish between an instrumental sign and a formal sign.
5. Have mental terms and oral terms natural significations? Explain briefly.

DIVISION OF TERMS

28. First division of terms. – 1° The term is first divided into mental term, oral term, and written term.

A *mental term* is a concept from which a simple proposition is made.

An *oral term:* already defined in n. 25.

A *written term* is a conventional graphic sign signifying an oral term.

2° The enunciative term may be divided *essentially* or *specifically*, according to the objects by which the concept is specified. But this division belongs to Material Logic.

The enunciative term may be divided according to its different ways of signifying. This division belongs to Formal Logic.

a) Under this aspect, the mental term is divided into *intuitive concept* and *abstract concept.*

An intuitive concept is a *concept by which the cognitive faculty knows and attains a thing as physically present;* v.g., the concept by which I know that Peter is physically present to me, i.e., in my presence.

An abstract concept is a *concept of a thing that is physically absent;* v.g., the concept that I have of Cicero; the concept that I have of animal as a universal.

b) The mental term is divided secondly into *concept of the thing* and the *concept of the sign* (1).

A concept of the thing is a *concept of the thing signified by*

(1) In Scholastic Latin, they are called *conceptus ultimatus* and *conceptus non ultimatus.* Translator's note.

the term; v.g., the concept of that thing which is man and which is signified by the word « man ».

A concept of the sign is a *concept of the term itself as signifying;* v.g., the concept of the term « man » as signifying.

c) The mental term is divided thirdly into *direct concept* and *reflex concept.*

A reflex concept is a *concept by which we know that we know.* A reflex concept is a concept of another concept, and so its object is an act of cognition, a concept, and whatever in the soul contributes to the concept, as a faculty, habits, and even the very nature of the soul.

A direct concept is a *concept by which we know an object outside our concept, without reflecting on our knowledge;* v.g., the concept by which we have knowledge of a man, a stone, or a plant.

29. Second division of the term. — The second division of the term belongs properly and principally to the *oral* term. Under this aspect, the term is divided into *univocal term, equivocal term,* and *analogous term.*

A univocal term is a *term which signifies things considered divisively according to their strictly one nature,* or *which signifies the things represented by one and the same concept;* v.g., the word « man » signifies all men as identified in one and the same concept of human nature.

An equivocal term is a *term which signifies the things represented, not by one and the same concept, but by several concepts.* In other words, an equivocal term signifies several things, not as they are united under a concept that has a certain unity, — even a unity of proportion — but as they differ; v.g., « dog » as signifying an animal and a star. The concept of an animal and the concept of a star have nothing in common or are in no way similar, but are very different.

An analogous term is a *term which signifies the things represented by a concept that has a unity of proportion;* v.g., « healthy » as referring to an animal and to a herb is an analogous term, because it does not signify the same thing in an animal and in a herb. It is predicated of an animal, because an animal possesses health; of a herb, because it has a relation of proportion to health formally found in an animal, i.e., it is the cause of health in an animal.

30. Third division of the term. — The term is divided thirdly into *categorematic term* and *syncategorematic term.*

A categorematic or significant term is a *term of which the object signified by it is represented as a definite thing, not the mere modification of a thing;* v.g., man, to run, to act, whiteness.

A syncategorematic term is a *term of which the object signified by it is not represented as a definite thing, but as the mere modification of a thing*, that is, by the exercise of the modification of a thing; v.g., speedily, easily, every, some, etc.

31. Fourth division of the term. — The fourth division of the term is the division of the categorematic term into its various subdivisions.

1° *First* the categorematic term is divided into *divisive term* and *collective term.*

A divisive term is a *term which signifies an individual, or several individuals taken separately;* v.g., Peter, Paul, man, animal.

A collective term is a *term which in the singular signifies several individuals taken together*, i.e., collectively, or as a group; v.g., a people, a nation, an army.

To this division of the term is added its division into *common term* and *singular term.*

A common term is a *term which signifies several things taken separately;* v.g., man. A common term signifies several things taken separately in the sense that it signifies something which, either as regards the thing signified or at least as regards our manner of conceiving it, can be perceived as communicable to several. Hence, although there is only one sun, the term sun is a common term, because, as regards our manner of conceiving it, it can be understood as being communicable to several: it could be predicated of several suns, if several suns really existed.

A singular term is a *term which signifies one individual only, for, even as regards our manner of conceiving, it does not signify something communicated to several;* v.g., Peter, this man, this dog, etc.

A common term is *universal* or *distributive*, if its extension is entirely unrestricted, as *every man, every animal;* or *particular*, if its extension is restricted, as *some man, some animal, some ship.*

2° *Secondly*, the categorematic term is divided into *absolute term, connotative term, concrete term*, and *abstract term.*

An absolute term is *one which signifies something after the manner of a substance*, whether it really be a substance, as man, or an accident conceived without a subject, as whiteness, color, created knowledge, the human will.

A connotative term is *one which signifies something after the manner of an accident determining or connoting a subject;* v.g., the term *white* signifies whiteness determining a subject, i.e., whiteness and a subject in which whiteness is found.

Likewise the term *blind* signifies blindness and a subject in which blindness is found.

Hence a connotative term principally and directly signifies its absolute: *white* principally and directly signifies whiteness; indirectly it signifies a subject to which whiteness belongs or in which the thing principally signified is found.

A term which connotes not a subject, but an object, is not a connotative term, but rather an absolute term. Example: the terms science, opinion, faith, which connote their objects, not their subjects, are not connotative but absolute terms.

A concrete term is *one which signifies* THAT WHICH *a thing is;* v.g., man, animal, Peter.

An abstract term is *one which signifies* THAT BY WHICH *a thing is;* v.g., humanity, whiteness, blindness. Humanity is the form by which a man is constituted; whiteness is that by which a thing is white.

3° *Thirdly*, the categorematic term is divided into *term of first intention* and *term of second intention*.

A term of first intention is *one which signifies an object as it exists in reality and in its proper state;* v.g., the term *man* signifies human nature as it exists or can exist in reality, not in the state it has in the intellect, i.e., as conceived by the intellect.

A term of second intention is *one which represents an object as it exists in the intellect,* i.e., *as conceived by the intellect;* v.g., the terms genus, species, etc.

These terms are called *of first intention* and *of second intention* in as much as they represent an object in its first state and in its second state. For what belongs to an object as it exists in reality belongs to it in its first state; and what belongs to it as it exists in the intellect belongs to it in its second state, which supervenes the first state.

4° *Fourthly*, the categorematic term is divided into *complex term* and *incomplex term*.

A complex term is *one whose parts have each their own signification;* v.g., white man, rich miser, learned man, etc.

An incomplex term is *one whose separate parts have not a signification of their own;* v.g., man, animal.

That a term be logically complex, its parts must have and exercise their signification within the complex term which they constitute. It is for this reason that logicians do not regard a term such as *legislator* as a complex term. For the parts of the term, i.e., *legis lator*, have not a meaning of their own within the whole which they compose, i.e., they do not correspond to distinct concepts.

5° *Fifthly*, terms are divided according to their manner of comparison to one another.

According to this division, terms are *disparate* or impertinent and *non-disparate* or pertinent.

Disparate or impertinent terms are *terms which neither include nor exclude one another;* v.g., white and sweet, learned and just, house and horse, etc.

Non-disparate or pertinent terms are *terms which either include or exclude one another.*

Therefore non-disparate terms are *pertinent-of-sequel* or *pertinent-of-repugnance.*

Pertinent-of-sequel terms are *terms which include one another*, or *which follow or accompany one another;* v.g., man and risible, father and son, etc.

Pertinent-of-repugnance terms are *terms which exclude one another*, or *which exclude and are opposed to one another;* v.g., white and black, sight and blindness, hot and cold.

Cf. Joannem a Sancto Thoma, *Curs. Phil.*, t. I, pp. 10-13, 85-112.

ARTICLE IV

NOUN AND VERB

32. Noun. — So far we have dealt with the term in a general way. We have considered it according to the mode of signifying it can have as a part of a discourse.

Now we consider the term according to its role in the composition and construction of discourse. Under this aspect, the term is divided into *noun* and *verb*. The *pronoun* comes under the comprehension of the noun, and the *participle* under the comprehension of the verb. The noun and verb are the two terms which are necessary and sufficient for the composition and construction of an enunciation. Example: In the enunciation: *Peter reads*, *Peter* is the noun, and *reads* is the verb. Thus we see that a noun and a verb are required and sufficient for the construction of the foregoing enunciation.

The noun is defined: *a term which conventionally signifies things as intemporal, is finite and direct, and of which no separate part has a signification* (1).

a) Conventionally signifies: conventional signification is common to all terms.

b) Intemporal. The noun differs from the verb in this: a verb signifies a thing in the mode of movement, i.e., of action or passion. Since action and passion are essentially and immediately measured by time, a verb always signifies a thing as measured by time; v.g., he reads, he loves, etc.

Although a noun can signify time, as *day*, *month*, or can connote time, as *supper*, *dinner*, it does not signify a thing as measured by time, as the verb does; in other words, it does not signify motion, i.e., a thing which primarily and essentially is measured by time.

(1) *In Periherm.*, l. II, l. 4.

c) Finite: a noun is a term which signifies *finite things*, i.e., a term which signifies a determinate nature or a determinate person. Thus is excluded an infinite term, i.e., a term with an indeterminate signification, as *non-man*. Such a term can indeed be a part of an enunciation, but cannot be a noun, because it is destructive of all determinate signification. *Non-man* can be predicated of *chimera*, which does not exist in nature, and of *horse*, which does exist in nature: *a chimera is a non-man; a horse is a non-man.*

Observe that *non-man*, as an infinite term, must be regarded as an incomplex term. In the proposition: *no man is a horse, no man* is not an infinite term, because the negation does not destroy the signification of the noun *man*, but makes the proposition negative.

d) Direct: a noun is a term that signifies direct things, i.e., things in the nominative case; and thus are excluded the oblique cases of the noun, as *of a man, to a man*, etc.

For the logician nouns are enunciative terms. Therefore the oblique cases, though considered as nouns by grammarians, are not considered as nouns by the logician. Although the oblique cases signify the same thing as the nominative case, — *of Peter* signifies the same person as *Peter* — they do not signify a thing as an extreme in an enunciation. Example: the propositions: *Peter exists, Peter does not exist*, are enunciations in which truth or falsity is found; but *of Peter* signifies a thing as belonging to another and in relation to another which is an extreme: *the book of Peter is large*, or *Peter's book* . . .

Certain Latin impersonal verbs in conjunction with oblique cases signify truth or falsity; but in such cases an implied nominative case is easily understood. Example: *poenitet me* is equivalent to: *poenitentia tenet me* (1).

(1) The reader of this explanation is reminded that he is reading the English translation of a Latin work. In Greek and Latin the noun is known as such only in the nominative case. In the genitive, dative, etc., as *Petri* (of Peter, Peter's), *Petro* (to Peter), it is not called a noun. These are oblique cases or terminations of the noun. The oblique cases of the noun signify the same thing as the nominative case, but do not serve to signify a thing as an extreme of an enunciation. When I say *of Peter* (Peter's), *to Peter*, I do not consider *Peter* as something that I can use as an extreme in a proposi-

e) *No separate part has a signification,* i.e., no part separated from the whole. Thus are excluded the discourse, which is not a noun, but is composed of nouns; and the complex term, which is not a noun, but several nouns.

33. Verb. — The verb is defined: *a term which conventionally signifies in a temporal manner, of which no separate part has a signification, is finite and direct, and always signifies the attribution of a predicate to a subject.*

a) *Term . . . of which no separate part has a signification.* Same explanation as that given in the case of the noun.

b) *In a temporal manner:* the verb signifies a thing in the mode of motion, i.e., in the mode of transition, and in relation to the past, present, or future; v.g., the verb *is* (exists) signifies the act of being (existing) in the present and as passing into the past. Hence a verb signifies in a temporal manner, i.e., it always signifies a thing as measured by time.

c) *Finite:* an infinite verb, as *not to run*, is excluded. First, we must observe that *not to run* is an infinite word if regarded as an incomplex term, so that negation renders a verb indeterminate; secondly, we must notice that a verb cannot be rendered infinite in a proposition; for a negative particle affecting a verb in a proposition removes the verb from something and thus makes the proposition negative, but does not make the verb infinite or indeterminate. Thus the proposition, *Peter does not run*, is negative; but the verb is not infinite.

d) *Direct:* oblique verbs are excluded, i.e., all modes and times except the present indicative.

Modes other than the present indicative are excluded: for the conditional, imperative, and optative do not constitute a proposition as required by the logician, that is to say, as signifying truth or falsehood; v.g., Peter *would read*, *let* Peter

tion, but Peter in relation to something else. This short explanation should give us a better understanding of the Latin definition of the noun: *vox significativa ad placitum*, — *sine tempore*, — *cuius nulla pars significat separata*, — *finita*, — *recta*. — Translator's note.

read, that Peter *read,* signify nothing determinately false or determinately true.

All times except the present indicative are excluded, because the past and future strictly do not signify a thing in the mode of action or passion, which is proper to a verb: for to act and to be acted upon strictly mean to act actually and to be actually acted upon, i.e., in the present time.

Besides the past and the future are known only in their relation to the present. The past is what had been present, and the future is what will be present.

e) Signifies the attribution of a predicate to a subject: the verb is always a sign of what is predicated of the noun, either because it signifies the predicate itself, as when we say: *Peter is* (exists), or because it is required to unite the subject and predicate, as when we say: *Peter is white.*

However, we should observe that a verb consists essentially in its signifying a thing in a temporal manner, and in its effecting the composition and union of subject and predicates only as a consequence, though necessarily.

Cf. *In Periherm.,* l. I, l. 4-5; JOANNEM A SANCTO THOMA, *Curs. Phil.,* pp. 13-16, 112-128 (Reiser).

BOOK II

THE ONLY CHAPTER

DISCOURSE AND PROPOSITION

Prologue. — Just as terms pertain to simple apprehension, so the discourse and its species, especially the proposition, pertain to the second operation of the intellect, namely, to judgment.

Hence we shall first discuss judgment and discourse. Secondly, we shall consider *the mode of knowledge*, as it pertains to the discourse. Thirdly, we shall consider the proposition.

Three things will be considered in regard to the proposition: 1) the notion and division of the proposition; 2) the properties of the parts of a proposition; 3) the properties of propositions.

Hence the only chapter in this book is divided into five articles.

Judgment and discourse	Notion of judgment Prerequisites of judgment Definition of discourse Division of the discourse
Modes of knowledge	Notion of the mode of knowledge Division of the modes of knowledge
Notion and divisions of the proposition	Notion of the proposition or enunciation Truth and falsity in the proposition Sources of the division of propositions Division of propositions according to form Division of propositions according to matter Division of propositions according to quantity

Properties of the parts of a proposition	The properties of the parts of a proposition Notion of substitution or substitutive value Division of substitution Rules of substitution Reimposition Amplification, restriction, and alienation or transfer
Properties of propositions	Properties of a proposition Notion of opposition Scheme of the opposition of propositions Different degrees of opposition Notion of equipollence Laws of equipollence Notion of conversion Laws of conversion

ARTICLE I

JUDGMENT AND DISCOURSE

34. Notion of judgment. — Judgment is defined by St. Thomas (1): *the act of the intellect by which it composes and divides by affirming and denying* (2).

When I say: *man is just*, or *man is not just*, my intellect makes a judgment. By affirming, it assents to the composition of the predicate with the subject in the same thing; and by denying, it assents to the division of the predicate from the subject, because the intellect apprehends that the thing represented by the subject and the thing represented by the predicate are different things in reality.

Hence in an affirmative judgment there is only a distinction of reason between the subject and predicate; but they are identified by the intellect in the same thing; v.g., when I say: *man is just*, I say that the thing which I conceive as man is one and the same thing as the thing I conceive as just.

In a negative judgment, there is a real distinction between the subject and the predicate. *Man is not just* signifies that what is conceived as man is really distinct from what is conceived or can be conceived as just.

35. Prerequisites of judgment. – Four things are required for an act of judgment: *a*) the simple apprehension of two terms; *b*) the formation, by means of simple apprehension, of a merely enunciative proposition in which one term is used as subject and the other as predicate; and this is properly composition and division; *c*) a comparison between the

(1) *De Veritate*, q. 14, a. 1.

(2) L'opération de l'intelligence par laquelle elle unit par l'affirmation et sépare par la négation.

subject and the predicate; *d*) a clear knowledge of the conformity or the discrepancy between them.

The perception of the conformity or the discrepancy between the predicate and the subject in the same thing becomes the act of judgment, which consists essentially in *assent* to an enunciative proposition, i.e., *assent by affirming or denying the predicate of the subject.* In is by means of the assent that an enunciative proposition becomes judicative.

Hence we must carefully distinguish an enunciative proposition which precedes judgment from a judicative proposition which is the sign of the assent. The formation of an enunciative proposition necessarily precedes the act of judgment because the act of judgment deals with this proposition. Thus, that the intellect make the judgment: *man is rational*, it must first form this proposition, so that it may be able to pass judgment on it.

Usually the enunciative proposition and the judicative proposition are not distinguished, because they are formed by one and the same act.

NOTE. — The human intellect, on account of its imperfection, judges by composing and dividing: it cannot penetrate into the whole of a thing by a single act, but only by several acts. God and the angels judge, not by composing and dividing, but simply by apprehending. They penetrate into the whole of a thing by a single act.

36. Definition of discourse. – Discourse is defined by Aristotle: *a term which conventionally signifies, whose separate parts signify as terms, not as an affirmation or a negation.*

a) *Term conventionally signifying*, as for the term. Observe that the discourse may be *mental*, *oral*, or *written*. Aristotle begins with the oral discourse, because the oral discourse is better known than the mental discourse. But the discourse, whether oral or written, is defined as a *conventional sign*.

b) *Whose separate parts signify:* thus discourse is distinguished from the incomplex term, as man, legislator; and from the complex term.

Discourse is distinguished from the incomplex term, because the incomplex term corresponds to only one concept, whereas the discourse has parts which correspond to different concepts; and each of the separate parts has a signification.

Discourse is distinguished from the complex term, as *just man*, for, although the complex term, like the discourse, has component parts which correspond to different concepts, it is itself considered as a component part of a discourse, whereas discourse is considered as a whole composed of terms as its parts.

c) *As terms, not as an affirmation or a negation*, i.e., not as an integral proposition.

The compound proposition, as *if Peter runs, Peter moves*, has affirmations or negations as its parts; but these affirmations and negations ultimately are resolved into terms. Therefore in the definition of the discourse in general is found what is common to all kinds of discourse, namely, the having of parts which are simply terms.

37. Division of discourse. – 1° Discourse may be *perfect* or *imperfect*.

a) A *perfect discourse* is one which engenders a complete meaning in the mind of the hearer; v.g., *man is just*. A discourse is not called perfect because it implies the assent of the intellect, but because it does not leave the intellect in suspense and, as it were, awaiting the whole meaning of the discourse, but expresses the whole meaning perfectly and completely [1].

b) An *imperfect discourse* is one which engenders an imperfect meaning in the mind of the hearer; v.g., *Peter while arguing, if he would sleep, when he was crossing over*, etc.

This kind of discourse is called imperfect because it does not present a complete meaning and leaves the mind in suspense.

Observe that terms, such as *Peter while arguing, a just man*, and the like, if considered as component *parts* of a proposition, are complex terms; if considered as forming a *whole*, they are imperfect discourses. This is the formal difference

(1) Joannes a Sancto Thoma, *Cursus Phil.*, t. I, pp. 17-18 (Reiser).

between the imperfect discourse and the complex term. The complex term is formally a part; the imperfect discourse is formally a whole.

2° Perfect discourse may be *ordinant*, *enunciative*, or *argumentative*.

a) An *ordinant discourse* is one which expresses a practicable ordinance of the intellect; v.g., do this.

It may be *vocative*, as *O good Peter; interrogative*, as *What time is it ?; deprecative*, as *Give us, O Lord, the spirit of goodness;* and *optative*, as *May my father be spared his life* (1).

b) An *enunciative discourse* is one which expresses truth or falsity; v.g., man is an animal; a horse is a donkey.

c) An *argumentative discourse* is one by which the intellect acquires a knowledge of an unknown truth from a truth already known; v.g., a syllogism.

Logic does not deal with ordinant discourse, because it is not concerned with the knowledge of truth, but only with enunciative and argumentative discourse.

(1) *In Periherm.*, l. I, l. 7 (Leonina).

POINTS FOR REVIEW

1. What is the difference between a judgment and an enunciative proposition?

2. State (a) the essential constituent of judgment, (b) its prerequisites.

3 Distinguish between an imperfect discourse and a complex term.

4. Enumerate the divisions of perfect discourses. Why is it that a logician does not deal with ordinant discourse?

ARTICLE II

MODES OF KNOWLEDGE

38. Notion of the mode of knowledge. – The mode or means of knowledge is defined: *a discourse which manifests what is unknown.*

To understand this definition we must know the distinction between to *manifest* and to *signify.*

What is manifest may be understood in two ways:

first, as opposed to what is obscure;

secondly, as opposed to what is unknown and not applied to the cognitive power.

What is obscure is made manifest by something better known and clearer, which removes obscurity. And when what is better known and clearer is a discourse, we have a *mode of knowledge.* Hence the mode of knowledge may be defined: *a discourse which manifests what is obscure.*

What is unknown or not applied to the cognitive power is made manifest by a representation or sign that applies the object to the cognitive faculty; and this is properly *to signify*, and does not pertain to the mode of knowledge (1).

39. Division of the modes of knowledge. — To know how the mode of knowledge is divided, we must observe that there are two things which a discourse should manifest, namely, either *an incomplex thing* or *a complex thing*, i.e., *a complex truth.*

An incomplex thing, as *man, living being, animal*, can be manifested to the intellect, i.e., explained,

as regards the obscurity of *its quiddity,*

(1) Joannes a Sancto Thoma, *Cursus Phil.*, t. I, p. 18 (Reiser).

or as regards the confusion of *its parts.*

An incomplex thing is made manifest as regards the obscurity of its quiddity by *definition.*

An incomplex thing is made manifest as regards the confusion of its parts by *division.*

But if a complex truth, as *man is mortal,* is obscure or doubtful, it is made manifest by proof, which pertains to argumentation.

Hence, from the point of view of things that can be made manifest, the modes of knowledge are adequately divided into:

definition,

division,

and argumentation.

We shall deal with argumentation in Book III.

Definition and division, considered as imperfect discourses, — *rational animal, a sentient living being,* — pertain to the second operation of the intellect. But from the point of view of the object manifested, which is an incomplex thing, they belong to simple apprehension. Therefore we shall deal with them in Material Logic when we consider simple essences.

POINTS FOR REVIEW

1. Define mode of knowledge, and state what it signifies.

2. Is it a complex thing or an incomplex thing that is made manifest by definition?

3. Distinguish between definition and division.

ARTICLE III

NOTION AND DIVISIONS OF THE PROPOSITION

40. Notion of proposition or enunciation. — Following the practice of logicians, we shall regard the proposition and the enunciation as meaning the same thing, although an enunciation sometimes is properly called a proposition, namely, when it serves for the construction of an argumentation.

Proposition or enunciation is defined: *a discourse which signifies truth or falsity by indicating*, as when we say: *man is an animal.*

a) *Discourse:* thus enunciation or proposition is distinguished from term, complex or incomplex.

b) *Signifying truth or falsity:* thus enunciation or proposition is distinguished from imperfect discourse, and from perfect but ordinant (vocative, interrogative, imperative, deprecative and optative) discourse, which do not explain truth.

c) *By indicating,* i.e., by asserting the predicate of, i.e., by composing the predicate with the subject; or by dividing the predicate from the subject: *man is just, man is not just.*

41. Truth and falsity in propositions. – Truth obtains when the judgment of the intellect about a thing is in conformity with reality; falsity, when it is not in conformity with reality.

Therefore truth or falsity obtains in an enunciation, i.e., in a composition or division, only after the judgment by which it is declared to be conformed or non-conformed with reality. More briefly, an enunciative proposition becomes true or false when it becomes assertive, i.e., judicative. Example: the intellect can form the following composition: *Paul is sick.*

If the intellect suspends its assent, the composition is neither true or false. But if the intellect assents to the proposition, by judging that it is in conformity with reality, we have a true proposition.

Hence truth and falsity are in judgment (and in the mental proposition) as in their subject; in the judicative proposition (oral or written), as in their sign; and in composition and in division before assent, as in their state of possibility only (1).

42. Sources of the division of propositions. – The division of propositions is derived from three sources:

1° the form
2° the matter } of the proposition.
3° the quantity

43. Division of propositions according to form. – According to the copula or form, the proposition is said first to be simple (categorical) or compound (hypothetical).

1° *A simple* or *categorical proposition* is one whose component parts are a subject, a predicate, and a copula; v.g., *man is an animal.* The subject is that of which something is said. The predicate is that which is said of something. The copula is the verb which unites the subject and predicate.

A *compound* or *hypothetical proposition* is one whose component parts are simple propositions; v.g., *if a man runs, he moves.*

In a compound or hypothetical proposition, not terms but simple propositions are immediately united; and the copula is not a verb, but such particles as *if, and,* etc.

2° The compound proposition is openly compound, or occultly compound.

An openly compound proposition is one whose composition is clearly shown from the structure of the discourse; v.g., if Peter runs, he moves.

(1) Joannes a Sancto Thoma, *Cursus Phil.,* t. I, pp. 144-150 (Reiser).

An occultly compound proposition is one in which the proposition is apparently simple, but, if expounded, is resolved into several propositions. Therefore it is said to be « exponible »; v.g., the proposition: *Christ alone is the Saviour of man*, may be resolved into: *Christ is the Saviour; no other is the Saviour.*

3° The openly compound proposition may be copulative, disjunctive, conjunctive, or conditional.

A *copulative proposition* is one in which several simple propositions, or several subjects, or several predicates are joined by the conjunctive particles *and*, *neither*, etc.; v.g., *the just shall be saved and the unjust shall be lost; Peter and Paul are holy; no one can serve God and mammon.*

But a proposition in which several subjects or several predicates are joined by a particle can be simple, according to the meaning of the proposition; v.g., the proposition, *Peter and Paul are friends*, is a simple proposition, because it cannot be resolved into the following: *Peter is a friend, and Paul is a friend.*

Rule of the copulative proposition: That a copulative proposition be true, all the simple propositions of which it is composed must be true; if one of them is false, the copulative proposition is false; v.g., *the moon moves and the earth does not* is a false proposition, because the second part of it is false.

A *disjunctive proposition* is one in which several simple propositions, or several subjects, or several predicates are joined by the disjunctive particle *or*, etc.; v.g., *he will remain in the place or be killed; the door is open or closed.*

A disjunctive proposition may be properly or improperly disjunctive.

It is *improperly* disjunctive when the particle indicates that at least one of the parts of the proposition is true; v.g., *either Peter or Paul died in Rome.*

It is *properly* disjunctive when the particle indicates that one of the parts of the proposition is true, and excludes the others; v.g., a *body either moves or remains at rest.*

Rule of the disjunctive proposition: That a properly disjunctive proposition be true, it is required that its parts are not at the same time true or at the same time false.

A conjunctive proposition is one that declares that each of two predicates cannot at the same time be attributed to the same subject; v.g., *a man cannot be living and dead at the same time.*

A *conditional proposition* is one in which several simple propositions are joined by the particle *if*; v.g., *if man is an animal, he is a sentient being.*

The proposition to which the conditional particle is prefixed is called the *condition* or *conditional proposition;* the other proposition is called the conditioned proposition; and the nexus between the two propositions is called the *sequence.*

Rule of the conditional proposition: That a conditional proposition be true, it is sufficient that the nexus between the condition and the conditioned proposition be true, even though the propositions themselves be false. Thus the following proposition is true: *if Peter runs without movement, he moves without movement.*

4° The occultly compound proposition may be exclusive, exceptive, or reduplicative.

An *exclusive proposition* is one whose subject or predicate is qualified by the exclusive particle, *alone, only,* etc.; v.g., *God alone is omnipotent.* This proposition can be resolved into the following: *God is omnipotent; no person other than God is omnipotent.*

An *exceptive proposition* is one in which something contained under the extension of the subject is excluded from a participation of the predicate by the exceptive particle, *except, unless,* etc.; v.g., *all beings except God are finite.* This proposition may be resolved into the following: *All beings other than God are finite; God is a being, God is not finite.*

A *reduplicative proposition* is one whose subject is qualified by the reduplicative particle, *inasmuch, as,* etc. (even implied); v.g., *man as an animal is a sentient being.* This proposition may be resolved into the following: *man is an animal; as an animal, he is sentient.*

5° By reason of the copula, a categorical proposition may be affirmative or negative.

An affirmative proposition is one in which the predicate is united to the subject; v.g., *Peter is white.*

A *negative proposition* is one in which the predicate is separated from the subject; v.g., *man is not a stone.*

The proposition, *not to sin is good,* is not a negative proposition, because the negation does not qualify the copula.

6° By reason of the copula, a proposition may be absolute (1) or modal.

a) An *absolute* proposition is one which simply unites a predicate to a subject; v.g., *Peter is running.*

A *modal proposition* is one which states the mode according to which the predicate belongs or does not belong to the subject; v.g., *God is necessarily eternal; to be eternal necessarily belongs to God.*

That a proposition be modal, the mode must determine the composition of the predicate with the subject, not the predicate itself or the subject itself. Thus the proposition: *Peter runs fast,* is not a modal proposition, because it does not signify: *to run belongs fast to Peter.*

In a modal proposition we make a distinction between the *mode* and the *dictum.* The *dictum* states the composition of the predicate with the subject; the *mode* determines the mode or manner of this composition. In the proposition: God is necessarily eternal, *God is eternal* is the dictum, and *necessarily* is the mode.

There are four modes: necessity, impossibility, possibility, and contingency.

b) There are two kinds of modal propositions: divisive and compound.

---

(1) An absolute proposition is also called a proposition *de inesse.*

A *divisive modal proposition* is one in which the mode affects the copula; v.g., *God is necessarily eternal.*

A *compound modal proposition* is one in which the mode is taken as the predicate, and the dictum as the subject; v.g., *That God be eternal is necessary.*

44. Division of propositions according to matter. — By the matter of a proposition we understand the terms of the proposition as related to one another.

1° First, a proposition may be in necessary matter, in impossible matter, or in contingent matter.

A *proposition in necessary matter* is one in which the predicate necessarily belongs to the subject, because it pertains to the essence of the subject, or necessarily results from it; v.g., *man is rational; man is risible.*

A *proposition in impossible matter* is one in which the predicate is necessarily incompatible with the subject; v.g., *the human soul is corporeal.*

A *proposition in contingent matter* is one in which the predicate accidentally belongs or does not belong to the subject; v.g., *man is white.*

A proposition in necessary matter and a proposition in impossible matter are each called an *analytical* proposition by modern philosophers, because the relation between the subject and predicate is known from the notion or analysis of them; a proposition in contingent matter is called *synthetic*, because the relation between the subject and predicate is known by means of experience.

2° Secondly, according to matter, a proposition may be necessary, contingent, or impossible.

A *necessary proposition* is one which states something which cannot be other than it is; v.g., *man is rational.*

Every *affirmative* proposition in necessary matter, and every *negative* proposition in impossible matter is a necessary proposition.

A *contingent proposition* is one which states something which can be other than it is; v.g., *man is just.*

An *impossible proposition* is one which states something which cannot be; v.g., *man is not rational.*

Every *negative* proposition in necessary matter, and every *affirmative* proposition in impossible matter is an impossible proposition.

3° A necessary proposition may be self-evident or non-self-evident.

A *self-evident proposition* is one in which the relation between the subject and the predicate is immediately known from the very notion of them; v.g., *a circle is not a square; the whole is greater than its part.*

A *non-self-evident proposition* is one in which the relation between the subject and the predicate is not immediately known from the notion of them, but is known either from reasoning or from authority; v.g., *the soul is immortal; God is triune.*

A contingent proposition is neither self-evident nor non-self-evident, because the relation between the subject and predicate is not known from the notion of them, but from experience.

A self-evident proposition is called immediate. But a contingent proposition, in which the relation between the subject and predicate is immediately known from experience, is not immediate in the intellect; v.g., *this snow is white; Paul is sick.*

45. Division of propositions according to quantity. – A proposition, according to its quantity, may be universal, particular, singular, or indefinite.

A *universal proposition* is one whose subject is modified by a universal term, as *every, no;* v.g., *every plant is living.*

A *particular proposition* is one whose subject is modified by a particular term, as *some;* v.g., *some man is just.*

A *singular proposition* is one whose subject is a singular term; v.g., *Socrates is a philosopher.*

An *indefinite proposition* is one whose subject is a common term not modified by a sign; v.g., *man is mortal; man is just.*

An indefinite proposition whose predicate necessarily belongs to or necessarily is incompatible with its predicate is universal; an indefinite proposition whose predicate can belong or not belong to its subject is a particular proposition.

———

ARTICLE IV

PROPERTIES OF THE PARTS OF A PROPOSITION

46. Properties of the parts of a proposition. — The parts of a proposition are the extremes or terms. The properties which appertain to the terms, as the parts of a proposition, are the following: substitution, reimposition, amplification, and restriction.

47. Notion of substitution. — The substitution, or substitutive value, of a term is distinct from its signification (1). Both substitutive value and signification are substitutions of a word or name for something. But signification is a representative substitution by which the name represents the thing signified to the mind. Substitution, or substitutive value, is, as it were, an applied substitution by which the intellect, after learning the signification of a name, applies the name in different ways in propositions, that it may serve as a substitute for that to which the intellect wishes to apply something (2). Thus when I say: *this man is white*, man, which signifies human nature, is substituted in the proposition for that to which whiteness ought to be applied by the copula *is*.

Hence substitution, i.e., substitutive value, is defined: *the acceptance of a term for something of which it is verified according to the exigence of the copula* (3).

a) *Acceptance of a term for something*, i.e., the applied substitution of the term for the thing.

b) *Of which it is verified according the exigence of the copula:*

---

(1) I, q. 39, a. 5 ad 5; *De Pot.*, q. 9, a. 4, c. and ad 6.
(2) Joannes a Sancto Thoma, *Cursus Phil.*, t. I, p. 29 (Reiser).
(3) The use of the term. Grenier, in his *Cours de Philosophie* (tome I, p. 32), defines this term as follows: *l'emploi d'un terme pour une chose, emploi qui est légitime eu égard à la copule.*

this substitution must be legitimate according to the kind of existence which the copula signifies. Thus in a proposition in necessary matter, or in a proposition in impossible matter, in neither of which time is considered, the thing for which the term is used must be strictly possible; v.g., *man is a rational animal; a circle is not a square.*

In a proposition in contingent matter, the thing for which the term is used must have actual existence in time, according to the exigency of the copula. In the propositions, *Adam is doing penance, Antichrist was a liar*, the terms, *Adam* and *Antichrist*, have no substitutive value, because Adam no longer exists but did exist, and Antichrist did not exist in the past but will exist in the future.

48. Division of substitution. – Substitution may be divided as regards the thing signified, in its relation to the copula, and as regards its extension (1).

1° *As regards the thing signified*, a proposition may be improper or proper.

a) *An improper substitution* is the acceptance of a term for a thing which it signifies in an improper or metaphorical sense; v.g., *the lion of the tribe of Juda hath prevailed.* The term *lion* is used here for Christ, Whom it signifies in an improper or metaphorical sense.

A *proper substitution* is the acceptance of a term for a thing which it signifies or represents in its proper sense; v.g., *the lion roars.*

b) Proper substitution is material, simple or logical, and personal or real.

A *material substitution* is the acceptance of a term for itself, i.e., for the word itself (2); v.g., *man is a noun; Cicero is a word of three syllables.*

A *simple or logical substitution* is the acceptance of a term for a universal nature which it represents as it is in the intellect; v.g., *man is a species.*

(1) Joannes a Sancto Thoma, *Cursus Phil.*, t. I, p. 31 (Reiser); Maritain, *Petite Logique*, pp. 80-90, 8e édit.
(2) In this case the term represents itself.

A *personal or real substitution* is the acceptance of a term not only as it immediately represents a universal nature, but also as it mediately represents the individuals in which this nature is found; v.g., *man is an animal*, i.e., *this man and that man are animals.*

2° *In its relation to the copula*, substitution may be accidental or essential.

An *accidental substitution* is the acceptance of a term for a thing to which the predicate belongs not intrinsically but accidentally; v.g., *man is white.*

An *essential substitution* is the acceptance of a term for a thing to which the predicate intrinsically and essentially belongs; v.g., *man is an animal.*

3° *As regards its extension*, substitution may be singular or common.

a) A *singular substitution* is the acceptance of a singular term for a singular thing; v.g., *Peter* is arguing; *this man* is just.

A *common substitution* is the acceptance of a common term for its inferiors; v.g., *man* is just; *man* is an animal.

b) Common substitution may be distributive or universal, particular, and copulative or collective.

A *universal substitution* is the acceptance of a common term for all and each of its inferiors; v.g., *man* is mortal, i.e., *individual men are mortal.*

A *particular substitution* is the acceptance of a common term for some of its inferiors taken separately; v.g., *some* man is just.

A *collective substitution* is the acceptance of a common term for all its inferiors not taken separately but collectively; v.g., *soldiers* make an army; the *Apostles* are twelve in number.

Universal substitution may be complete, incomplete, and exceptive.

A *complete universal substitution* is the acceptance of a common term for all the individuals it signifies; v.g., *every man* is mortal.

An *incomplete universal substitution* is the acceptance of a common term for all the genera and species of the individuals to which it extends; v.g., *every animal* was in the Ark, i.e., *every species of animal.*

An *exceptive universal substitution* obtains when one of the inferiors of a common term is excepted; v.g., *every man*, except the Blessed Virgin Mary, *is born in sin.*

Particular substitution may be determinate or indeterminate.

A *determinate substitution* obtains when a particular term is verified in some determinate inferior; v.g., *some man* is running.

An *indeterminate substitution* obtains when a particular term is not verified in some determinate inferior; v.g., *some ship* is needed for sailing; but no determinate ship is necessary.

49. Rules of substitution. — *As regards the subject.* — 1° *The general rule:* The subject has a substitution or substitutive value according to the exigence of the predicate, i.e., according to the meaning of the proposition.

2° There are *three special rules.*

a) A subject modified by a universal sign has a universal or distributive substitutive value; a subject modified by a particular sign has a particular substitutive value; v.g., *every man* is an animal; *some man* is a liar.

A singular term always has a singular substitutive value.

b) A subject (common) modified by no sign with which its predicate is accidentally compatible or incompatible always has a *particular* and *disjunctive* substitutive value; v.g., the proposition: *man is white*, means: *some man*, i.e., *this man or that, is white.*

c) A subject (common) modified by no sign with which its predicate is essentially compatible or incompatible has a *distributive* substitutive value; v.g., the proposition: *man is an animal*, means: *all men taken separately are animals.*

As regards the predicate. — 1° In an affirmative proposition, a predicate never has a *distributive* substitutive value; v.g., the proposition, *man is an animal*, signifies: man is some indeterminate kind of animal, not *this* animal or *that* animal.

2° In a negative proposition, the predicate always has a universal or distributive substitutive value; v.g., *man is not an angel*, i.e., is no angel, neither *this* angel nor *that*.

50. Reimposition. – For the grammarian reimposition is the same thing as denomination, and to reimpose is to denominate. For the logician reimposition imposes on a formality signified by one term the formality signified by another term. Thus understood, reimposition is defined: *the application of the formality signified by one term to the formality signified by another term;* v.g., Peter is a *great* logician. In this example, the term *great*, which is the reimposing term, is not *absolutely* applicable to Peter, but only as regards the notion and formality of logic, i.e., formally in as much as he is a logician. It is in this that reimposition formally consists.

Hence reimposition obtains any time a predicate is not absolutely applicable to a subject, but only in virtue of some formality.

2° Reimposition is divided into *real reimposition* and *logical reimposition* or *reimposition of reason.*

A *real reimposition* obtains when the reimposing term designates a real accident or formality; v.g., Peter is a *great* logician.

A *logical reimposition* or a *reimposition of reason* is one which is made by means of a logical accident (accident of reason); v.g., man is a *species*. Species is not applicable to man considered in himself, but to man conceived in the abstract.

3° There are four *rules of reimposition*, viz., two of real reimposition, and two of logical reimposition.

a) First rule of real reimposition. — When an adjective serves as the predicate and a substantive as the subject, there is no reimposition, that is, there is no application of the predicate to the formality signified by the subject, and the subject has only a material value. Examples: *the doctor is great; this man (Christ) is eternal.* Christ is not eternal because he is a man, or because of his human nature.

When the words, *in as much as* and the like, are used with reference to the subject, there is a reimposition of the predicate on the subject; v.g., *Christ, in as much as he is man, is a creature.*

b) *Second rule of real reimposition.* — When a substantive and an adjective are used as the same extreme, there is a reimposition of the adjective on the formality of the substantive, provided that the adjective can determine the substantive and is not disparate to it. Reimposition thus obtains in the following examples: Peter is a *great* logician; a *great* logician debates.

There is no reimposition in this example: Peter is a *black logician*, because *black* and *logician* are disparate terms.

c) *First rule of logical reimposition.* — A predicate of second intention belonging to the thing signified reimposes, as when we say: *man is a species.*

A predicate of second intention is one which belongs to a thing, not as it is in itself, but as it is in the intellect.

In this case, reimposition obtains because the predicate does not belong absolutely to the subject, but belongs to it as it exists in the state of abstraction.

A predicate of second intention which belongs to the term, but not to the thing signified by the term, does not effect reimposition, as when we say: *man is a noun; Peter is a name, etc.*

d) *Second rule of logical reimposition.* — A term which signifies an interior act of the soul causes reimposition on the object to which it has reference under the proper formality of this act; v.g., *I know a man*, i.e., under the concept of man; *I know the Pope*, i.e., in as much he is the Pope; *I wish to enjoy myself*, i.e., under the formality of enjoyment, not under the formality of evil.

Thus the following sequence is not valid: *I know the man who is approaching; but the man approaching is Peter; therefore I know Peter.*

I can indeed know someone under the concept of one approaching, and not under the concept of Peter.

Rule for the sequences of reimposition: if the reimposition is changed, the sequence is invalid both in real reimposition and in logical reimposition.

51. Amplification, restriction, and alienation or transfer. — 1° Amplification is defined: *the extension of a term from a lesser to a greater substitutive value;* v.g., if I say: *man can be just*, the term *man* is extended to all possible men.

Restriction is defined: *the restriction of a term from a greater to a lesser substitutive value;* v.g., if I say: *a man who is just is wise*, man does not stand for every man, but only for one who is just.

2° A term can be amplified (enlarged) or restricted in two ways:

first, in relation to the more or fewer substitutive values it has;

secondly, in relation to the more or fewer times when it can be verified.

In the first way, amplification and restriction are found only in a common term which has a personal and accidental substitutive value.

For a simple or logical substitution does not designate individuals. We may say that *man is a species*, but not that *Peter is a species.*

A term which has an essential substitutive value is applicable to all individuals; v.g., *man is an animal;* this proposition signifies that all human individuals, as Peter, Paul, etc., are animals. A term which has a singular substitutive value is not applicable to several: *this man is my friend.* Therefore only a common term which has a personal and accidental substitutive value can be restricted or amplified in relation to more or fewer supposits or individuals.

Examples: *every man runs; some man runs;* in the first example, the term *man* is predicated of more individuals than in the second.

In the second way, that is to say, in relation to the more or fewer times when a term can be verified, even a term which has a singular substitutive value can be amplified or restricted.

In logical amplification and restriction, the different times are the present, the past, the future, the possible, and the imaginable.

3° The rules of argumentation in amplification and restriction may be reduced to two.

a) *First rule:* in proceeding from the ample to the non-ample, i.e., from the non-restricted to the restricted, the sequence is valid in *affirmative* propositions, if the ample term is universal or distributive and if the existence of the non-ample term is affirmed; in *negative* propositions, the sequence is valid even if the existence of the non-ample term is not affirmed, provided that the ample term is universal or distributive.

Examples: if we say: *every man is colored,* we may not infer: *therefore this man is colored,* unless the existence of this man is first affirmed or understood.

But, for a negative proposition, the existence of the extremes in not required. Hence if we state: *no man is white,* we may infer: *therefore Peter is not white,* even if the existence of Peter is not affirmed or understood.

b) *Second rule:* from the non-ample to the ample, i.e., from the restricted to the non-restricted, the sequence is valid in the opposite way; hence in *affirmative* propositions the sequence is valid if the ample term is not universal and distributive, even if the existence of the non-ample term is not affirmed; in *negative* propositions, if the ample term is not universal, provided that the existence of the non-ample term is affirmed.

Examples: *man debates, therefore every man debates; some man does not debate, therefore no man debates.* The sequence in these propositions is not valid, because the ample term is universal or distributive.

Peter debates; therefore some man debates. In this case, the sequence is valid.

Peter does not debate; therefore some man does not debate. The sequence is not valid in this example, unless the existence of Peter is affirmed. For if Paul were the only man in the world and he debated, the sequence would not be valid.

4° *Alienation* or *transfer* obtains when we pass from the proper signification of a term to its improper or metaphorical signification; v.g., *man is painted; Peter is a lion.*

It is always the predicate which indicates the alienation or transfer of the subject, because subjects are such as they are permitted to be by their predicates.

But when a term is used as an adjective to modify the subject, it causes not an alienation or transfer of the subject, but a restriction of it. Example: if we say: *a painted man is a picture, painted* does not cause an alienation or transfer of the subject, but restricts it by drawing an analogy with the less principal subject.

POINTS FOR REVIEW

1. State the kind of substitution or substitutive value found in the subject of each of the following propositions: The planets are seven. Animal is a genus. Whiteness is an accident. To love is a verb. An animal is sentient. Man is discursive. Man is black. A ship is a necessity for sailing.

2. Determine the substitution or substitutive value of the predicate in each of the following propositions: No man is a brute. Man is rational. Man is an animal. The human soul is immortal.

3. Show whether or not reimposition is found in the following propositions: Alexander the Great was a pupil of Aristotle. Aristotle was a great philosopher. Christ is eternal. I saw the king of the kingdom of Italy. The doctor sings. An artificer produces an artifact. A credulous prince is cruel.

ARTICLE V

PROPERTIES OF PROPOSITIONS

52. Properties of propositions. — The properties of propositions are *opposition*, *equipollence*, and *conversion*. These properties are relative, because they depend on the relation of one proposition to another.

53. Notion of opposition.—Logical opposition of propositions is defined: *the affirmation and negation of the same predicate of the same subject.*

The subject and predicate in opposed propositions must have the same signification, the same genus of substitution or substitutive value (not necessarily the same species of substitution), and the same time in a proposition in contingent matter. When we say, *Peter is laughing, and Peter is not laughing*, opposition obtains if the subject and predicate have the same time in the two propositions.

The following are the different genera of substitution: proper, improper, material, logical, and personal.

54. Division of opposition. — The opposition of propositions may be contradictory, contrary, or sub-contrary. To these kinds of opposition we add subalternation, which properly is not opposition, but rather a relation of two propositions that are different only in quantity.

1° *Contradictory opposition* is defined: opposition in truth and falsity. Hence two contradictory propositions cannot be at the same time true nor at the same time false.

Contradictory opposition is found *a*) between an affirmative universal proposition and a negative particular proposition, and vice versa; *b*) between a negative universal proposition and an affirmative particular proposition, and vice versa; c) between two singular propositions of which one is affirmative, and the other negative.

Examples: Every man is just. — Some man is not just.
No man is just. — Some man is just.
Peter is wise. — Peter is not wise.

The reason why two contradictory propositions cannot be at the same time true, nor at the same time false, is because the one totally destroys the other.

2° *Contrary opposition* is opposition in truth, but not in falsity. Hence two contrary propositions cannot be at the same time true, but can be at the same time false.

Contrary opposition obtains between two universal propositions of which one is affirmative, and the other negative.

Example: Every man is just. — No man is just.

Two contrary propositions can be at the same time false in contingent matter, but not in necessary matter. In contingent matter, the subject can be applied only to some, not to all the inferiors, of the subject. In this case the two universal propositions are false. Thus in the foregoing example, *every man is just*, and *no man is just*, the two propositions are false.

3° *Sub-contrary opposition* is opposition in falsity, but not in truth. Hence two sub-contrary propositions cannot be at the same time false; but they can be at the same time true.

Sub-contrary opposition obtains between two particular propositions of which one is affirmative, and the other negative.

Example: Some man is just. — Some man is not just.

Sub-contrary propositions can be at the same time true in contingent matter, as in the foregoing example, but not in necessary matter.

4° *Subalternation or subalternate opposition* is a relation between two affirmative propositions of which one is universal and the other particular, or between two negative propositions of which one is universal and the other particular.

Examples: Every man is just. — Some man is just.
No man is just. — Some man is not just.

The universal proposition is called *subalternating*, and the particular proposition is called *subalternated*. In necessary matter, if the subalternating proposition is true or false, the subalternated proposition is necessarily true or false; in contingent matter, even if the subalternating proposition is false, the subalternated proposition can be true (cf. example).

55. Scheme of the opposition of propositions. – The different kinds of opposition are given in the scheme that follows. In the scheme, A designates an affirmative universal proposition; E a negative universal proposition; I an affirmative particular proposition; and O a negative particular proposition.

A. Every man is just— CONTRARIES — No man is just. E

SUBALTERNS —CONTRA-DICTORIES— —CONTRA-DICTORIES— SUBALTERNS

I. Some man is just — SUBCONTRARIES — Some man is not just .O

But modal propositions are opposed to one another in the ways shown in the following scheme:

It is necessary that it be — CONTRARIES — It is impossible that it be

SUBALTERNS —CONTRA-DICTORIES— —CONTRA-DICTORIES— SUBALTERNS

It is possible that it be — SUBCONTRARIES — It is possible that it not be

56. Different degrees of opposition. – The highest degree of opposition is contradictory opposition.

Contradictory propositions are opposed in quantity, in affirmation and negation, and in truth and falsity.

The second degree of opposition is contrary opposition.

Contrary propositions are opposed in affirmation and negation and in truth, but not in quantity, nor in falsity in contingent matter.

The third degree of opposition is *sub-contrary* opposition, which is rather apparent than real: the subject is not really the same in the two propositions, since it designates, i.e., is substituted for, different individuals. When we say: *some men are just, some men are not just, just* is not affirmed and denied of the same men.

Subalternation is not properly opposition.

57. Notion of equipollence. – Equipollence, in general, is the same as equivalence. Here equipollence has a special meaning, and is defined: *the giving the same signification to two opposed propositions by the use of a negative particle.*

Hence two propositions which were first opposed but, later are made equivalent by the use of a negative particle, are equipollent propositions.

58. Rules of equipollence. – The rules of equipollence are more concerned with language than with thought, and, moreover, are applicable to the Latin language rather than to English. Hence we shall omit the study of them in English. However, for the sake of completeness, we shall add the presentation of these in Latin as they appear in the original Latin text of this work, viz., in *Cursus Philosophiae* (Editio tertia), vol. I, pp. 64-65.

Leges aequipollentiae in sequenti versiculo continentur:
Prae *contradic*, Post *contra*, Praeterpostque *subalter*.
1° In *contradictoriis* praepone negationem subjecto (1).

(1) Negatio malignantis naturae, non autem infinitatis naturae. — Joannes a Sancto Thoma, *Cursus Phil.*, t. I, p. 46 (Reiser).

Exemplum: propositio, *omnis homo est justus*, fit aequipollens suae contradictoriae, *aliquis homo non est justus*, hoc modo, *non omnis homo est justus*.

2° In *contrariis*, postpone negationem subjecto.

Exemplum: *omnis homo est justus*, fit aequipollens suae contrariae *nullus homo est justus*, hoc modo, *omnis homo non est justus*.

3° In *subalternatis*, praepone et postpone simul negationem subjecto.

Exemplum: *Omnis homo est justus*, fit aequipollens subalternae, *aliquis homo est justus*, hoc modo, *non omnis homo non est justus*.

NOTA. — In subcontrariis, non datur proprie aequipollentis, sed postponendo negationem subjecto, propositio fit identica.

59. Notion of conversion. — Conversion is *the inversion of the extremes of a proposition from the subject to the predicate, and from the predicate to the subject, without changing the quality and the truth of the proposition* (1).

To make a conversion correctly, there is required: *a*) that the subject have the same extension as predicate that it had as subject, and that the predicate have the same extension as subject that it had as predicate; v.g., *Peter sees a stone*, is thus converted: *someone who sees a stone is Peter; b*) that the same kind of substitution or substitutive value be safeguarded; *c*) that the same quality be safeguarded, i.e., that the copula remain negative or affirmative in both propositions; *d*) that both propositions be true.

There are three kinds of conversion: *a*) *simple*, in which the quantity of the proposition remains the same; *b*) *accidental*, in which the quantity of the proposition is changed; *c*) *by contraposition*, when a negative particle is prefixed to the interchanged extremes.

60. Rules of conversion. — The rules of conversion may be stated as follows:

Simpliciter fEcI convertitur: EvA per accidens;
AstO per contrap: sic fit conversio tota.

The meaningless words fEcI, EvA, AstO, by which logicians sum up the rules of conversion in two mnemonic lines,

(1) Conversion — the reversing of propositions.

have no other object than that of grouping the figurative vowels A, E, I, O.

1° A negative universal and an affirmative particular are simply converted.

Examples: the proposition, *no body is a spirit*, is converted thus: *no spirit is a body;* and the proposition, *some man is white*, is converted thus: *some white (being) is (a) man.*

2° An affirmative universal is converted accidentally (1); a negative universal can also be converted accidentally (2).

Examples: the proposition, *every man is an animal*, is converted thus: *some animal is a man;* the proposition, *no man is an angel*, can be converted thus: *some angel is not a man.*

3° A negative particular can be converted only by contraposition; but an affirmative universal can also be converted by contrasposition.

Examples: the proposition, *some man is not just*, is thus converted: some non-just (being) is not non-man, which is equivalent to: some non-just (being) is a man; the proposition, *every man is an animal*, may be converted thus: *every non-animal is non-man* (3).

---

(1) The rules of conversion are derived from the substitutive value of the subject and predicate. Therefore A is converted accidentally, because the predicate of proposition A always has a particular substitutive value. In definitions, proposition A could, because of its matter, be converted simply: Every man is a rational animal; every rational animal is man.

(2) In this case, the second proposition expresses the same truth as the first proposition, but in a partial manner.

(3) On a souvent dit que cette théorie de la conversion est une subtilité inutile. Cependant un logicien anglais, M. Bain, en fait bien voir l'utilité pratique. La source la plus féconde des sophismes, dit-il, est la tendance de l'esprit à convertir les affirmations universelles sans limitation. Lorsqu'on dit: « Tous les esprits puissants ont de larges cerveaux » l'auditeur passe facilement à la proposition convertie: « Tous les larges cerveaux indiquent de puissants esprits ». Cette erreur de la logique est une des plus fréquentes: il y a donc intérêt à appliquer la forme logique pour se mettre en garde contre elle. — PAUL JANET, *Logique*, chap. IV. Quoted by Hugon, *Logica Minor*, p. 160.

BOOK III

Argumentation

Prologue. — The third operation of the intellect is concerned with argumentation as its product. But argumentation is either deductive or inductive. Deductive argumentation is either categorical or hypothetical. Hence there will be three chapters in this book.

CHAPTER I

ARGUMENTATION IN GENERAL

Prologue. — There will be only one article in this chapter; it is divided as follows:

Argumentation:
- Notion of reasoning
- Antecedent and consequent
- Inference and sequence
- Division of sequence
- Notion of argumentation
- Laws of argumentation
- Division of argumentation

THE ONLY CHAPTER

ARGUMENTATION

91. **Notion of reasoning.**—Argumentation is the product of reasoning. Reasoning is defined: ***the act by which the mind acquires knowledge of a new truth by means of truths already known.***

a) *Act of the mind*, just as simple apprehension and judgment are acts of the mind.

b) *By means of truths already known:* truths can be known independently of each other, or because of their coordination and subordination.

Reasoning proceeds from coordinated and subordinated truths, as when we say: *Everything material is corruptible. But a body is material . . .*

c) *The mind acquires knowledge of a new truth:* Because the mind coordinates and subordinates several truths, it is moved at the same instant to a new truth [1]. Reasoning consists essentially in this movement or discursive operation.

Thus from the truths stated in *b*), the mind is moved to this truth;

---

(1) « In eodem instanti quo minor cognoscitur ut minor, deducitur assensus conclusionis, ut asseritur a D. Thoma (1, Post., lect. 2), quia posita cognitione minoris formaliter ut coordinata et subordinata majori, atque adeo supponendo cognitam bonitatem consequentiae, hoc ipso ponitur lumen sufficiens et necessitans ad manifestandam conclusionem. » JOANNES A SANCTO THOMA, *Cursus Phil.*, t. I, pp. 764-765 (Reiser).

« En résumé donc, l'acte de raisonner suppose que certaines propositions ont déjà été construites par l'esprit. Considérant ces propositions dans un certain ordre et les percevant comme vraies, l'esprit dans un acte simple (acte d'« inférence ») qui constitue l'essentiel du raisonnement, perçoit que par là même, à cause de cette vérité présupposée une autre proposition est vraie qu'il a construite, et à laquelle il ne peut pas refuser son assentiment s'il l'a donné aux propositions précédentes. » JACQUES MARITAIN, *Petite logique*, p. 185, 8e édition.

Therefore every body is corruptible.

Hence in reasoning there is a discursive operation not only as regards pure succession, as when we turn to a thing after we have perceived it in act (1), but also as regards causal succession (2).

62. The antecedent and the consequent. — The two truths from which the intellect proceeds are called *the antecedent.*

The truth (or proposition) to which another truth is subordinated is called *the major.*

The truth which is subordinated is called *the minor.*

The truth in which the act of reasoning is terminated is called *the consequent.*

63. Inference and sequence. — Inference is the antecedent's property of inferring the consequent.

Sequence is the statement of an inference, or the nexus which the intellect places between the antecedent and the consequent, which denotes an inference (3).

64. Division of the sequence. — 1° The sequence may be valid or invalid.

A *valid sequence* is one which denotes a real inference; that is to say, a sequence is valid when the antecedent really infers the consequent.

An *invalid sequence* is one which denotes not a real but only an apparent inference; that is to say, a sequence is invalid when the antecedent appears to infer the consequent, but does not reallv do so (4).

2° Valid sequence may be material or formal.

A *material sequence* is one which is valid only as regards some determinate matter; v.g., if we say: *some man is rational;*

(1) I, q. 14 a. 7.
(2) We know a new truth by means of others.
(3) Joannes a Sancto Thoma, *Cursus Phil.*, t. I, p. 22 (Reiser); Maritain, *op. cit.*, p. 189: « La conséquence est l'énoncé d'une inférence ».
(4) Joannes a Sancto Thoma, *op. cit.*, p. 59 (Reiser).

therefore every man is rational, the sequence is valid in that matter. But if we change the matter and say: *some man is good; therefore every man is good*, the sequence is invalid.

A *formal sequence* is one which is valid as regards its form.

Form is defined: *the disposition of propositions and terms according to quantity, quality, and other logical properties, so that a consequent may be inferred from an antecedent.*

Formal logic treats only of the formal sequence.

65. Notion of argumentation. — Just as we made a distinction between the act itself and its product in simple apprehension and in judgment, so also do we do so in reasoning; we distinguish between the act of reasoning and its artifact, — mental argumentation, — and oral expression, oral argumentation.

Argumentation in general is defined: *a discourse in which, one thing being given, another follows:*

a) *one thing being given*, i.e., the antecedent, or rather the minor being subordinated to the major;

b) *another follows*, i.e., the consequent.

66. Laws of argumentation. — 1° *It is impossible that a false consequent follow from a true antecedent.* This is so because the consequent is contained in the antecedent. Therefore, if we have a true antecedent and a false consequent, we have an antecedent that is partially false. What is partially false is not absolutely true. If this were not so, an antecedent could be true and false at the same time, which is indeed a contradiction.

2° *It is possible that a true consequent follow from a false antecedent.* Something which is false cannot of itself either manifest or cause truth. But truth can result accidentally from something false, in as much as the consequent which is connected with a false antecedent is true, not because it follows from the antecedent, but for some other reason [1]. **Example:** *Every man is a stone. But every stone is living. Therefore every man is living.*

3° *The conclusion always follows the weaker part*, i.e., if a proposition of the antecedent is negative or particular, the consequent cannot be affirmative or universal. The antecedent causes the consequent.

4° *The antecedent must be better known to us than the consequent.* This is so because the antecedent manifests the consequent.

67. Division of argumentation. — Argumentation is divided essentially into two genera of argumentation, namely, deductive argumentation and inductive argumentation.

Deductive argumentation, which is properly called the *syllogism*, is that which proceeds from universals to a lesser universal.

Example:

Every animal is a substance.
But every man is an animal
Therefore every man is a substance.

Inductive argumentation, which is called induction, is that which proceeds from singulars perceived by the senses.

Example:

Body A, body B, body C . . . are heavy.
Therefore every body is heavy.

Observe that the word *syllogism* may have a wide meaning. As such it may be used to designate both deductive and inductive argumentation. Thus some speak of the *inductive syllogism*. But properly the word syllogism is used only of deductive argumentation.

(1) « Solum ergo dicitur verum sequi ex falso quatenus supposita admissione praemissae falsae, adhuc potest stare connexio cum conclusione vera. » JOANNES A SANCTO THOMA, *Cursus Phil.*, t. I, p. 19 (Reiser).
Therefore in this case the antecedent really causes a true consequent, but not as true.

CHAPTER II

THE CATEGORICAL SYLLOGISM

Prologue. — In this chapter we shall consider the nature, laws, figures, and moods of the categorical syllogism. Hence there will be four articles in this chapter.

Nature of the categorical syllogism	Notion Matter and form Principles
Laws of the categorical syllogism	Eight laws of the syllogism Statement and explanation of the laws of the terms Statement and explanation of the laws of the propositions
Figures of the categorical syllogism	Notion Number Direct conclusion, indirect conclusion Indirect first figure Comparative value of the figures Laws of the individual figures Principles of the individual figures
Moods of the categorical syllogism	Notion Possible moods Useful moods Perfect moods, imperfect moods Reduction of imperfect moods to perfect moods

ARTICLE I

NATURE OF THE CATEGORICAL SYLLOGISM

68. Notion of the categorical syllogism. — The categorical syllogism is defined: *an argumentation in which is inferred, from an antecedent that unites two terms to a third, a consequent that unites these two terms to each other.*

Example:

Antecedent	Every body is a substance. But every man is a body.
Consequent	Therefore every man is a substance.

In the antecedent the terms *man* and *substance* are united to the term *body;* in the consequent the two terms *man* and *substance* are united to each other.

69. Matter and form of the categorical syllogism. — It is clear from the foregoing definition that a syllogism is made up of three terms, and that these terms constitute three propositions.

The three terms, which may be complex or incomplex, constitute the *remote matter* of the syllogism; the three propositions constitute its *proximate matter.*

The first two of the three propositions, which are inferring propositions, are called the *premises*, or the *antecedent;* the third, which is the inferred proposition, is called the *conclusion*, or the *consequent.*

The three terms, considered as constituting the matter of the syllogism, are called the syllogistic terms.

The *syllogistic term* is defined: *the subject and predicate into which the proposition is resolved.*

a) *subject and predicate:* the copula, or the verb as containing the copula, is not the syllogistic term. The reason is this: the syllogism is not a statement of truth, as the proposition is; it consists essentially in the union of the three terms used as subject and predicate. The copula, or the verb which contains the copula, is the connection between syllogistic terms (1);

b) *proposition*, i.e., the premises and conclusion.

The terms of a syllogism are three in number, viz., the major term, the minor term, and the middle term.

The *major term* is the term that becomes the predicate in the conclusion; it is also called the *major extreme.*

The *minor term* is the term that becomes the subject in the conclusion; it is also called the *minor extreme.*

The *middle term* is the term to which the extremes are united in the premises.

The predicate of the conclusion is called the major term, and the subject of the conclusion is called the minor term, because the predicate essentially has a greater extension than the subject.

One of the propositions of the premises is called the *major,* and the other is called the *minor.*

The *major proposition* is the proposition in which the major extreme is united to the middle term.

The *minor proposition* is the proposition in which the minor extreme is united to the middle term.

Example:

No animal is a plant.
But every man is an animal.
Therefore no man is a plant.

Plant is the major extreme; *man*, the minor extreme; *animal*, the middle term. — *No animal is a plant*, the major proposition; *every man is an animal*, the minor proposition; *no man is a plant*, the conclusion.

The *form* of the syllogism is the disposition of its matter so as to infer its conclusion. Therefore the form affects both

(1) Joannes a Sancto Thoma, *Cursus Phil.*, t. I, p. 63 (Reiser).

the remote matter of the syllogism, i.e., the terms, and in this case is called the *figure* of the syllogism; and the proximate matter, i.e., the propositions, and in this case is called the *mood* of the syllogism.

The figures and moods of the syllogism will be discussed in separate articles later.

70. Supreme principles of the categorical syllogism. — The categorical syllogism depends on the principle of triple identity and the separating third. This principle may be stated thus: *two things identical with a same third thing are identical with each other* (principle of triple identity); *two things, one of which is identical, the other not identical with a same third thing, are not identical with each other* [1] (principle of the separating third).

In a syllogism two terms are compared with a third, and their identity is affirmed or denied according as both are united to a third, or as one is separated from it.

The principle of identity and the separating third is immediately evident, and may be immediately reduced to the principle or contradiction, the first of all principles: « A thing is or is not, or it is impossible that the same thing be and not be ».

But the principle of triple identity and the separating third cannot of itself be applied in a syllogism, because the middle term to which the extremes are united is a universal [2]; it can be applied only by means of two other principles which Aristotle calls the *dictum de omni* and the *dictum de nullo.*

Dictum de omni: Everything which is affirmed distributively or universally of a subject is affirmed of all its inferiors.

Dictum de nullo: Everything which is denied distributively

(1) Cf. I, q. 28, a. 3, ad 1, ubi S. Thomas sic explicat hoc principium: quae sunt eadem uni tertio, sunt eadem inter se, « si tertium sit unum re et ratione », idest non virtualiter aut formaliter multiplex. Nam si tertium sit formaliter multiplex, duo possunt esse ei eadem sub duplici formalitate diversa; et tunc non sunt eadem inter se.

(2) In the expository syllogism the middle term is singular; but the expository syllogism is not really a syllogism.

or universally of a subject is denied of all its inferiors [1].

Example: whatever is affirmed or denied of man is affirmed or denied of all the inferiors of man, v.g., of Peter, Paul, etc.

(1) *In Post Anal.*, l. I, l. 9. Principia « dictum de omni », « dictum de nullo » sumuntur ex extensione subjecti. Nonnulli syllogismi principia ex comprehensione petere volunt. Et *ibid.*, nota y. MERCIER, *Logique*, pp. 179 ss., 8e édit.; MARITAIN, *op. cit.*, pp. 217 ss., 8e édit.

ARTICLE II

LAWS OF THE CATEGORICAL SYLLOGISM

71. Eight laws of the syllogism. — Logicians have given us eight laws to guide us in the correct application of the supreme principles of the syllogism, the *dictum de omni* and the *dictum de nullo* (1).

The first four laws are concerned with the *terms* of the syllogism; the last four with its *propositions*. They may be stated as follows (2):

1. Let there be three terms: the Major, the Middle, and the Minor.
2. Let them not have a greater extension in the Conclusion than in the Premises.
3. Let not the Middle Term enter the Conclusion.
4. Let the Middle Term be universal at least once.
5. If both Premises are negative, no Conclusion follows.
6. If both Premises are affirmative, the Conclusion cannot be negative.
7. No Conclusion can follow from two particular Premises.
8. The Conclusion always follows the weaker part.

72. Statement and explanation of the laws of the terms. — *First law.*—Let there be three terms: the Major, the Middle, and the Minor.

This law results from the very essence of the categorical syllogism, which identifies two terms with a third. And the

(1) Ces huit règles . . . dérivent de la nature même du syllogisme, comme des déterminations plus particulières du principe suprême . . . « d'identité » . . . et des deux principes (dictum de omni et dictum de nullo) qui lui sont joints.

Elles n'ajoutent à ces principes aucun principe nouveau, mais elles sont pratiquement utiles, parce qu'elles règlent de plus près le travail syllogistique. MARITAIN, *op. cit.*, p. 223.

(2) Logicians usually present these laws in the traditional Latin formulation of them in metrical verses:

Terminus esto triplex, major, mediusque, minorque.
Latius hos quam praemissae conclusio non vult.
Nequaquam medium capiat conclusio oportet.
Aut semel aut iterum medius generaliter esto.
Utraque si praemissa neget, nihil inde sequetur.
Ambae affirmantes neqeunt generare negantem.
Nil sequitur geminis ex particularibus unquam.
Pejorem sequitur semper conclusio partem.

same term, taken twice, must have the same substitutive value *a*) as to mode of existence, *b*) as to genus of substitution (not necessarily as to species of substitution). Example: a universal substitution can be changed into a particular, but not a personal into a logical. Otherwise it would be equivalent to two terms. Hence the following syllogism is invalid:

> Animal is a genus.
> But man is an animal.
> Therefore man is a genus.

Animal has a logical substitutive value in the major, and a real substitutive value in the minor. Therefore there are four terms.

Second law. — Let them not have a greater extension in the Conclusion than in the Premises; that is to say, the terms must not have a greater extension in the Conclusion than in the Premises. This law is violated when a term has a particular substitutive value in the premises and a universal substitutive value in the conclusion.

This law derives from the fact that the premises cause the conclusion. Therefore what is not in the premises cannot be in the conclusion.

Therefore the conclusion of the syllogism that follows is invalid:

> Every man is an animal.
> But no horse is a man.
> Therefore no horse is an animal.

The term *animal* has a *particular* substitutive value in the major, and a *universal* substitutive value in the conclusion.

Third law. — Let not the Middle Term enter the Conclusion. It is of the very nature of a syllogism that the middle term be united to the extremes in the premises.

The following syllogism violates this law:

> Napoleon was a general.
> But Napoleon was small.
> Therefore Napoleon was a small general.

The conclusion should be: some small (man) was a general.

Fourth law. — Let the Middle Term be universal at least

once, that is to say, let the *middle term* have a *universal* or *distributive* substitutive value in at least one of the premises.

If the middle term is used twice as a *particular* term, it can be substituted for different inferiors; and in that case it will be equivalent to two terms. It is for this reason that the following syllogism is invalid:

> Every man is an animal.
> But every brute is an animal.
> Therefore every brute is a man.

The term *animal* has a particular substitutive value in both the major and minor.

NOTE. — A singular term, in its *logical function*, is equivalent to a universal term.

73. Statement and explanation of the laws of the propositions. — *Fifth law.*— If both Premises are negative, no Conclusion follows; that is to say, no conclusion can be inferred from two negative premises.

In this case the premises state that the extremes have no relation of identity with the middle term. Hence we cannot know whether or not they have a relation of identity to each other. The syllogism that follows is a violation of this law:

> No stone is an animal.
> But no man is a stone.
> Therefore no man is an animal.

That the premises be negative, the negation must be applied to the *copula*, and not merely to the subject or predicate.

> What has no parts cannot perish by the dissolution of its parts.
> But the human soul has no parts.
> Therefore the human soul cannot perish by the dissolution of its parts.

In this syllogism, the minor, *the human soul has no parts*, is an affirmative proposition. The middle term in the major is: what has no parts, i.e., a (being) *not having parts*. Therefore the minor is: But the human soul is a (being) not having parts. The negation is applied to the predicate, but not to the copula.

Sixth law. — If both Premises are affirmative, the Conclusion cannot be negative.

This law obtains in virtue of the principle: *two things identical with a same third are identical with each other.*

Seventh law. — No Conclusion can follow from two particular premises. If both premises are negative, there will be no conclusion, as stated in the fifth law. If both premises are affirmative, the middle term will always be particular; and this is a violation of the fourth law.

Example:

I. Some man is an animal.
I. But some animal is irrational.
I. Therefore some man is irrational.

The term *animal* twice has a particular substitutive value.

If one premise is *affirmative*, and the other *negative*, only one term in the premises has a universal substitutive value. This term, according to the fourth law, is the middle term; and hence the syllogism violates the second law, for the major term has a particular substitutive value in the premises, and, as predicate of a negative conclusion, a universal substitutive value in the conclusion.

Or a universal term is the major term, and then the syllogism violates the fourth law: the middle term twice has a particular substitutive value.

Examples:

I. Some man is learned.
O. But some wise (being) is not learned.
O. Therefore some wise (being) is not a man.

The term *man* has a particular substitutive value in the premises, and, contrary to the second law, a universal substitutive value in the conclusion.

O. Some learned (being) is not wise.
I. But some man is learned.
O. Therefore some man is not wise.

The middle term, in violation of the fourth law, twice has a particular substitutive value.

Eight law. — The Conclusion always follows the weaker part.

The weaker part is the *negative part* in relation to an *affirmative part*, and the *particular part* in relation to a *universal part*. Therefore this law has two parts:

1° If one premise is negative, and the other affirmative, the conclusion will be negative in virtue of the principle: *two things, one of which is identical, the other not identical with a same third thing, are not identical with each other.*

2° If the premise is particular, and the other universal, the conclusion will be particular.

For *a*) either both premises are *affirmative*, *b*) or one is *affirmative* and the other is *negative.*

a) *If both premises are affirmative*, there will be only one universal term in the premises, i.e., the subject of the universal proposition, and this term, according to the fourth law, will be the middle term; and the minor term, the particular in the premises, will be, according to the second law, particular in the conclusion.

Example:

I. Some man is learned.
A. But every man is an animal.
I. Therefore some animal is learned.

b) *If one premise is affirmative, and the other negative*, there are two universal terms in the premises, viz., the subject of the universal proposition and the predicate of the negative proposition. That the fourth law be safeguarded, one of these terms will be the middle term; and that the second law be safeguarded, the other will be the major term; for the conclusion will be negative, and its predicate or major term will have a universal substitutive value. Hence the minor term has a particular substitutive value in the premises, and therefore, according to the second law, must have a particular substitutive value in the conclusion.

Hence the conclusion of the following is invalid:

O. Some man is not learned.
A. But every man is an animal.
E. Therefore no animal is learned.

The correct conclusion: *therefore some animal is not learned.*

ARTICLE III

FIGURES OF THE CATEGORICAL SYLLOGISM

74. Notion of the syllogistic figure. — The figure of the syllogism is, as we have already said, the form of the syllogism as affecting its remote matter.

It is defined: *the disposition of the terms as subject and predicate* (1) *such as can infer the conclusion.*

75. Number of figures. — The figures of the syllogism derive from the various dispositions of the middle term (m) in relation to the major (T) and minor extreme (t). There are three possible dispositions of the middle term: 1° it may be the subject in the major and the predicate in the minor; 2° or it may be predicate in both premises; 3° or it may be the subject in both premises. Hence there are three figures, and they are expressed by logicians in the following manner:

Sub prae., prima; sed altera *bis prae.*, tertia *bis sub.* This logical formula is explained as follows:

sub prae prima: middle term subject in the Major and predicate in the Minor (first figure);

sed altera bis prae: middle term the predicate twice (second figure);

tertia bis sub: middle term the subject twice (third figure).

The different figures are presented schematically in the following table:

First figure	Second figure	Third figure
m T	T m	m T
t m	t m	m t
t T	t T	t T

(1) « The disposition of the terms according to which one is the subject and the other is the predicate. »

76. The conclusion, direct and indirect. — A direct conclusion is the conclusion of a syllogism in which the extremes have the same disposition in the premises as they have in the conclusion, that is to say, in which the minor extreme is the subject of the minor, and the major extreme is the predicate of the major.

An indirect conclusion is the conclusion of a syllogism in which the minor extreme, or the major extreme, or both, have not the same disposition in the premises as they have in the conclusion.

In the first figure the conclusion is direct; in the second and third it is indirect.

77. The indirect first figure. — Some logicians, headed by Galen (131-200), introduce a fourth figure, called the *Galenic* figure. In this figure the middle term is predicate in the major, and subject in the minor.

Example:

T m Every man is living
m t But every living (being) is a substance.
t T Therefore some substance is a man.

This figure, according to Aristotle, does not differ *logically* from the first figure, but is merely the first figure as it indirectly concludes, because of the *grammatical* disposition of the terms, especially of the middle term. The conclusion, *some substance is a man*, has the same signification as the proposition, *man is some substance* (1).

Thus the indirectly-concluding first figure becomes directly-concluding by the transposition of the minor extreme and the major extreme, and vice versa. Such a transposition in the foregoing syllogism is made as follows:

Every living being is a substance.
But every man is living.
Therefore every man is a substance.

(1) On voit par là que si la 4e figure est une figure *grammaticale*, elle n'est pas une figure *logique* distincte: *pour la pensée*, le prédicat grammatical de la conclusion y est en réalité *sujet*. — Jacques Maritain, *op. cit.*, p. 226, note 24.

But observe that a syllogism of the directly-concluding first figure in which the major comes second must not be confused with a syllogism of the indirectly-concluding first figure.

Example:

Every man is living.
But every living (being) is a substance.
Therefore every man is a substance.

This syllogism is merely a syllogism of the directly-concluding first figure, in which the major is not in its proper place.

78. Comparative value of the figures. — The figure in which the middle term is subject and predicate must be given first place, because in this case the middle term partakes of the nature of both extremes, and therefore is really the middle term. Therefore this figure is called the first figure.

In the second place comes the figure in which the middle term is predicate twice, because the role of predicate is nobler than that of subject. It is for this reason that this figure is called the second figure.

In the third place comes the figure in which the middle term is subject twice; it is called the third and last figure (1).

79. Laws of the individual figures. — Special laws of the figures are derived from the application of the general laws of the syllogism to individual figures.

Hence, by the very fact that these special laws are observed, the general laws are observed.

First figure. — Let the minor be affirmative, and the major universal.

1° *Let the minor be affirmative.* If the minor is negative, the conclusion will be negative, and the major affirmative; the major term will be particular in the premises, and universal in the conclusion, contrary to the second law of the syllogism.

2° *And the major universal.* Otherwise the middle term, already a particular term in the minor as predicate of an affirmative proposition, will also be particular in the major

(1) Opusculum 48 inter opera s. Thomae.

as subject of a particular proposition; and thus it will be a particular term twice, in violation of the fourth law of the syllogism.

Second figure. — Let one premise be negative, and let not the major be particular.

1° *Let one premise be negative.* In the second figure the middle term is predicate twice; hence, if one premise is not negative, it will be a particular term twice, in violation of the fourth law of the syllogism.

2° *And let not the major be particular.* Since one premise is negative, the conclusion will be negative, and the major extreme will be a universal term in the conclusion. Therefore, to avoid violating the second law of the syllogism, the major extreme must be a universal term in the major. But the major extreme in the second figure is the subject of the major. Therefore the major must be universal.

Third figure. — Let the minor be affirmative, and the conclusion particular.

1° *Let the minor be affirmative.* As for the first figure.

2° *And the conclusion particular.* The minor extreme, the subject of the conclusion, is predicate of an affirmative minor, that is to say, it is a particular term in the premises. Therefore, if the conclusion is not particular, the minor extreme, in violation of the second law of the syllogism [1], will be a universal term in the conclusion.

In this figure the middle term is predicate in the major and subject in the minor. Hence, when the major is affirmative, the middle term is particular in the major, and, if the minor is not universal, the middle term, in violation of the fourth law of the syllogism, is a particular term twice.

Thus, when the minor is negative, the minor extreme, which is its predicate, is a particular term in the premises. According to the second law of the syllogism, it must be a particular term in the conclusion, and then the conclusion is particular.

---

(1) The following are the laws of the indirect first figure:
If the major is affirmative, let the minor be universal.
If the minor is affirmative, let the conclusion be particular.
If one premise is negative, let the major be universal.

When one premise is negative, the conclusion is negative, and therefore the major extreme in the conclusion will be a universal term. Therefore, according to the second law of the syllogism, the major extreme must be a universal term in the premises. But the major extreme is the subject of the major. Therefore the major must be universal.

80. Principles of the individual figures. — The general principles of the categorical syllogism *dictum de omni* and *dictum de nullo* are not applied in their whole universality except in the direct first figure.

In all the other figures they are applied in a determinate manner.

Their special application in the second figure is called the *dictum de diverso*. If an attribute can be predicated affirmatively or negatively of a member of some species (genus), every individual (species) of which that attribute cannot be predicated (affirmatively or negatively) does not belong to this species (genus).

Example:

All fortitude is a virtue.
But no temerity is a virtue.
Therefore no temerity is fortitude.

M, *a virtue*, is affirmed of T fortitude, but it cannot be affirmed of t (temerity). Therefore t (temerity) is not T (fortitude).

Its special application to the third figure is called the *dictum de parte*. Two terms which contain a common part are partly identical; if however one contains a part that the other does not, they are partly different.

Example:

Man is just.
But man is an animal.
Therefore some animal is just.

T, *just* and t *animal* have a particular substitutive value and contain M *man* as their common part, and therefore they are partly identical: some animal is some just (being).

ARTICLE IV

MOODS OF THE CATEGORICAL SYLLOGISM

81. Notion of the mood of a syllogism. – The mood of a syllogism is its form as it affects its proximate matter or propositions. It is defined: *the disposition of propositions according to their essential quality*, i.e., affirmation and negation, *and according to their quantity.*

82. Possible moods of the syllogism. – Sixteen moods are possible in each figure: for the quantity of propositions can have four different moods. The premises are: 1° both universal; 2° or both particular; 3° or the major is universal and the minor is particular; 4° or the major is particular and the minor is universal. Similarly the quality of propositions can have four different moods. The premises are: 1° both affirmative; 2° or both negative; 3° or the major is affirmative and the minor negative; 4° or the major is negative and the minor affirmative.

Since the four dispositions according to quality are possible in each of the four dispositions according to quantity, there are sixteen possible moods in each figure: 4 x 4 = 16. But there are four figures of the syllogism (1); 16 x 4 = 64. Therefore there are sixty-four possible moods of the syllogism.

83. Useful moods of the syllogism. – Since quality and quantity in propositions are signified by the vowels A, E, I and O, the sixteen possible moods in each figure may be expressed thus:

AAA — AEE — AII — AOO
EEE — EAE — EIO — EOO
III — IAI — IEO — IOO
OOO — OAO — OEO — OIO

(1) The first figure as it concludes directly and indirectly is equivalent to two figures.

That a mood be useful, it must follow the general laws of the syllogism as well as the special laws of each figure (1). If we apply these laws, we shall discover that there are only nineteen useful moods, namely:

In the direct first figure:
4 — AAA, EAE, AII, EIO

In the indirect first figure:
5 — AAI, EAE, AII, AEO, IEO

In the second figure:
4 — EAE, AEE, EIO, AOO

In the third figure:
6 — AAI, EAO, IAI, AII, OAO, EIO

Logicians have grouped these nineteen useful moods of the syllogism in four mneomic verses composed of conventional words. The first three vowels of these conventional words represent in order the Major, the Minor, and the Conclusion, under the symbols A, E, I, or O. The verses are as follows:

Direct first figure: Barbara, Celarent, Darii, Ferio.
Indirect first figure: Baralipton, Celantes, Dabitis, Fapesmo, Frisesomorum.
Second Figure: Cesare, Camestres, Festino, Baroco.
Third Figure: Darapti, Felapton, Disamis, Datisi, Bocardo, Ferison.

84. Perfect and Imperfect moods. — *Perfect moods* are moods in which the conclusion is direct. Only the moods of the direct first figure are perfect moods.

Imperfect moods are moods in which the conclusion is not direct. The moods of the indirect first figure, of the second figure, and of the third figure are imperfect.

Indirect reduction or reduction to the impossible is indicated by the consonant C in Baroco and Bocardo (2). It is made

(1) Thus, according to the fifth law, the following are useless moods: EEE, EOO, OOO, OEO; according to the seventh law: III, IOO, OIO, OOO; etc...

(2) Hence we have the following Latin verses:
S vult simpliciter verti; P vero per accidens.
M vult transponi; C per impossibile duci.

thus: the major (in Bocardo) or the minor (in Baroco) is omitted and is replaced by the contradictory of the conclusion.

Example:

	Every virtue is pleasing to God.	A Ba —
Second figure.	But some emulation is not pleasing to God.	O ro —
	Therefore some emulation is not a virtue.	O co.

It is reduced thus:

	Every virtue is pleasing to God.	A Bar —
First figure.	But all emulation is a virtue.	A ba —
	Therefore all emulation is pleasing to God.	A ra.

Reduction to the impossible is made against an adversary who, after admitting the premises, denies the conclusion. After admitting the contradictory of the denied conclusion, he infers a conclusion which is the contradictory of one admitted premise. Hence the adversary is forced to admit that two contradictory things can be true at the same time, which is impossible. Then he must admit that the first conclusion is true.

85. Reduction of imperfect moods to perfect moods. — In perfect moods the consequent is clearly evident, but not so clearly evident in the imperfect moods. Hence it is useful to reduce the latter to the former.

The laws by which this reduction is made are indicated in the symbols of each imperfect mood:

a) An imperfect mood may be reduced to the perfect mood of the first figure which begins with the same consonant.

Example: Celantes, Cesare, Camestres may be reduced to Celarent; Fapesmo and Festino to Ferio.

b) There are two types of reduction: 1) direct; 2) indirect or to the impossible.

Direct reduction is made according to the moods indicated by the three consonants s.p.m., which follow the first three vowels, and which signify the three propositions of a syllogism.

The letter (s) indicates that the proposition symbolized by the preceding vowel should be converted *simply;* the letter (p) that it should be converted *accidentally;* and the letter (m) that the premises should be transposed, that is to say, that the major become the minor, and that the minor becomes the major.

Example:

	All fortitude is a virtue.	A Ca —
Second figure.	But no temerity is a virtue.	E mes —
	Therefore no temerity is fortitude	E tres.

C indicates that this mood ought to be reduced to Celarent; M indicates that the premises should be transposed; and S (mestres) indicates that the minor and conclusion should be converted simply. Example of reduction:

No virtue is temerity.	E Ce —
But all fortitude is a virtue.	A la —
Therefore no fortitude is temerity.	E rent.

Exercises. — In what figure are the following syllogisms? Are they correct or not? If they are not correct, what rules do they violate?

The powerful are not merciful.
But the poor are not powerful.
Therefore the poor are not merciful.

Every man is an animal.
Every sentient being is an animal.
Therefore every sentient being is a man.

Every animal is a substance.
No stone is an animal.
Therefore no stone is a substance.

Every animal is a substance.
No animal is a stone.
Therefore no stone is an animal.

Some animal is not a stone.
No animal is inorganic.
Therefore some inorganic (being) is not a stone.

Some animal is rational.
But every horse is an animal.
Therefore some horse is rational.

Some animal is not rational.
But no ape is an animal.
Therefore an ape is not rational.

A house is not an animal.
But man is not a house.
Therefore man is not an animal.

A horse is black.
But some ape is not a horse.
Therefore some ape is not black.

No house is an animal.
But no house is rational.
Therefore no rational (being) is an animal.

Some men are holy.
But sinners are men.
Therefore sinners are holy.

Every vegetal being is living.
But every sentient being is living.
Therefore every vegetal and every sentient being are living.

A spirit is immaterial.
But matter is not a spirit.
Therefore matter is not immaterial.

Some substance is not rational.
But some man is rational.
Therefore some man is not a substance.

CHAPTER III

THE HYPOTHETICAL SYLLOGISM

Prologue. — The deductive syllogism is essentially divided into the categorical syllogism and the hypothetical syllogism. Hence we shall now consider the hypothetical syllogism. Moreover, there are other accidental divisions of the syllogism in general, of which we shall deal in this chapter. Hence there will be two articles in this chapter:

- Hypothetical syllogism
  - Notion
  - Division
    - Conditional
    - Disjunctive
    - Conjunctive
  - Laws of the conditional syllogism
  - Figures of the conditional syllogism
  - Laws of the disjunctive syllogism
  - Figures of the disjunctive syllogism
  - Laws and figure of the conjunctive syllogism

- Other divisions of the syllogism
  - According to the integrity of propositions
    - Complete
    - Incomplete or Enthymeme
  - According to absolute or modal propositions
    - Absolute
    - Modal
  - According to the terms
    - Direct
    - Oblique
  - According to the simplicity or complexity of the propositions
    - Epicheirema
    - Polysyllogism
    - Sorites
    - Dilemma

ARTICLE I

THE HYPOTHETICAL SYLLOGISM

86. Notion of the hypothetical syllogism. — The hypothetical syllogism is defined: *a syllogism is which the major is a hypothetical proposition, and the minor posits or destroys one of the parts of the major;* v.g., if Peter studies, he learns. But he studies. Therefore he learns.

The hypothetical syllogism depends on the connexion between the propositions, and not merely on the connexion between its terms; and thus it is essentially different from the categorical syllogism. Therefore any syllogism that proceeds from the connexion of its terms, even though it may contain hypothetical propositions, is categorical; v.g., if A is, B is. If B is, C is. Therefore if A is, C is, when equivalent to: A is B. But B is C. Therefore C is A.

87. Division of the hypothetical syllogism. — The hypothetical syllogism is conditional, disjunctive, or conjunctive, according as its major is a conditional proposition, a disjunctive proposition, or a conjunctive proposition.

88. Laws of the conditional syllogism. — The supreme principles of the conditional syllogism are the general principles of all argumentation: *only a true consequent can be derived from a true antecedent; both a true consequent and a false consequent can be derived from a false antecedent* (Cf. N. 66).

From the foregoing general principles are derived the special laws of the conditional syllogism:

First law. — To posit the condition is to posit the conditioned; but to posit the conditioned is not to posit the condition [1].

Example:

> If Peter runs, Peter moves.
> But Peter runs.
> Therefore Peter moves.

But we may not argue:

> But Peter moves.
> Therefore Peter runs.

Second law. — To destroy the conditioned is to destroy the condition; but to destroy the condition is not to destroy the conditioned. Thus:

> If Peter runs, Peter moves.
> But Peter does not move.
> Therefore Peter does not run.

But we may not argue:

> But Peter does not run.
> Therefore Peter does not move.

89. Figures of the conditional syllogism. — There are two figures, and they may be tabled schematically: *in positing posits*, i.e., to posit the condition in the minor is to posit the condition in the conclusion; *in destroying destroys*, i.e., to destroy the conditioned in the minor is to destroy the condition.

According to affirmation or negation in the two parts of the major there are four moods for each of the two figures, and they may be tabled schematically as follows:

First figure: *in positing posits*

1) If A is, B is. But A is. Therefore B is.
2) If A is, B is not. But A is. Therefore B is not.
3) If A is not, B is. But A is not. Therefore B is.
4) If A is not, B is not. But A is not. Therefore B is not.

Second figure: *in destroying destroys*

1) If A is, B is. But B is not. Therefore A is not.
2) If A is, B is not. But B is. Therefore A is not.
3) If A is not, B is. But B is not. Therefore A is.
4) If A is not, B is not. But B is. Therefore A is.

---

(1) We say *to posit*, not *to affirm*, because sometimes a condition is negative and then it is posited, not affirmed, in the minor. For a similar reason we say *to destroy*, not *to deny*.

90. Laws of the disjunctive syllogism. — *First law.* Let the disjunctive major be true, that is to say, let its members be completely enumerated, and let them not be true and false at the same time. The syllogism that follows sins against this law:

Peter is a Catholic or a pagan.
But Peter is not a Catholic.
Therefore Peter is a pagan.

The disjunctive major is not true, since Peter can be a heretic or a schismatic.

Second law. — *a*) If the major is *properly* disjunctive and has two members, to posit one member is to destroy the other member, and to destroy one member is to posit the other member.

Example:

Peter is either at rest or in motion.
But Peter is at rest.
Therefore Peter is not in motion.

or:

But Peter is not at rest.
Therefore Peter is in motion.

b) If there are more than two members in the disjunctive major, 1° if one is destroyed, the others are affirmed disjunctively; v.g.,

Peter's house is larger, or smaller,
or the same size as Paul's house.
But it is not the same size.
Therefore it is larger or smaller.

2° or if one is posited, the others are destroyed; v.g.,

But Peters house is larger.
Therefore it is neither smaller nor the same size.

3° or if all except one are destroyed, that one is posited; v.g.,

But it is neither larger nor smaller.
Therefore it is the same size.

c) If the major is *improperly* disjunctive and has two members, at least one of which is true, to destroy one member is to posit the other, but to posit one member is not to destroy the other.

The following syllogism violates this rule:

Either Peter or Paul died in Rome.
But Paul died in Rome.
Therefore Peter did not die in Rome.

91. Figures of the disjunctive syllogism.

There are two figures, according as one member of the major is posited or destroyed in the minor.

In each figure there are four moods just as for the conditional syllogism.

92. Laws of the conjunctive syllogism. — *First law.* To posit one member is to destroy the other. Example: Peter is not in Lyons and in Rome. But he is in Lyons. Therefore he is not in Rome.

Second law. — To destroy one member is not to destroy the other member. The following syllogism is false: Peter is not in Lyons and in Rome. But he is not in Rome. Therefore he is not in Lyons.

NOTE. — If the two members of the major are contradictorially opposed according to matter, to destroy one member is to posit the other; v.g., the human soul is not material and immaterial. But it is not material. Therefore it is immaterial.

The figure of the conjunctive syllogism: There is only one figure (in positing destroying), and in it there are four moods.

ARTICLE II

OTHER DIVISIONS OF THE SYLLOGISM

93. Preliminary remarks. — The divisions of the syllogism that follow are not essential but *accidental* divisions. Though they are found in the hypothetical syllogism, they are first and foremost divisions of the categorical syllogism.

94. Division of the syllogism according to the integrity of its propositions.—According to this division we have the complete syllogism and the incomplete syllogism, or the enthymeme.

A *complete syllogism* is one in which all the premises are explicity formulated.

An *incomplete syllogism* or an *enthymeme* is one in which one premise is omitted; v.g., *God is the supreme good. Therefore God ought to be loved.*

95. Division of the syllogism according to absolute or modal propositions. — According to this division we have the absolute syllogism and the modal syllogism.

An *absolute syllogism* is one in which the premises are absolute propositions.

A *modal syllogism* is one in which either one or both of the premises are modal propositions.

Example:

> Every animal is necessarily a substance.
> But every man is necessarily an animal.
> Therefore every man is necessarily a substance.

96. Division of the syllogism according to its terms.— According to this division we have the direct syllogism and the oblique syllogism.

A *direct syllogism* is one in which all the syllogistic terms are direct.

An *oblique syllogism* is one in which one syllogistic term (or several) — Tt M — is oblique.

Example:

> Christ is God.
> But Mary is the Mother of Christ.
> Therefore Mary is the Mother of God.

M (Christ) is oblique in the minor; T (God) is also oblique in the conclusion.

97. Division of the syllogism according to the simplicity or the complexity of the argumentation. — According to this division we have the epicheirema, the polysyllogism, the sorites, and the dilemma.

1° An *epicheirema* is a syllogism in which the proof is conjoined to one or to both of the premises. Example: *Every man is corruptible, because he has a composite essence. But Peter is a man. Therefore Peter is corruptible.*

2° A *polysyllogism* is an argumentation that links together several syllogisms in such a way that the conclusion of one becomes a premise of the one that follows. Example: *A spirit has no matter. But the human soul is a spirit. Therefore the human soul has no matter. But what has no matter is incorruptible. Therefore the human soul is incorruptible.*

3° A *sorites* is an argumentation made up of several propositions that are connected in such a way that the predicate of the first becomes the subject of the second, and the predicate of the second the subject of the third, and so on, until a conclusion is reached that is made up of the subject of the first proposition and the predicate of the last. Example: *An avaricious man longs for much goods; a man who longs for much goods needs much goods; a man who needs much goods is not happy; therefore an avaricious man is not happy.*

Such is the definition of the Aristotelian sorites.

Goclenius (1598) proposed another sorites (the Goclenian),

and it is defined thus: an argumentation made up of several propositions that are connected in such a way that the subject of the first becomes the predicate of the second, and the subject of the second the predicate of the third, and so on, until a conclusion is reached that is made up of the subject of the last proposition and the predicate of the first. Example: *All bodies are perishable; plants are bodies; the oak is a plant; therefore the oak is perishable.*

That the argumentation of a sorites be valid, two conditions are required:

a) The individual propositions must be strictly and absolutely true.

b) The terms which enter the sorites must retain, on being repeated, exactly the same substitutive value.

There is one practicable rule for discovering the truth of the sorites, which Cicero called the most deceptive type of reasoning: resolve the sorites into simple syllogisms. There will be as many simple syllogisms less one as there are premises; and any error there may be will appear at once.

4° A *dilemma* (or two-horned syllogism) is an argumentation whose antecedent presents a disjunction of such kind that, whether one or other of its parts be posited, the same conclusion follows.

Therefore the dilemma differs from the disjunctive syllogism, in which the minor posits or destroys only *one part* of the major.

If the major has two parts, the argument is called a dilemma; if it has three parts, the argument is called a trilemma, etc. . .

Tertullian's dilemma against the decree of Trajan is famous: *The Christains are either guilty or innocent. If they are guilty, why do you prohibit search for them? If they are innocent, why do you punish those who are denounced?*

Rules of the dilemma: a) The disjunction must be complete. *b*) The consequent, which is deduced from each of the parts of the major, must follow *legitimately* (in valid sequence) and *exclusively* from each member of the disjunction, so that the dilemma cannot be *retorted*.

Against this rule sins the following dilemma proposed to a person, to prevent him from undertaking the administration of public affairs. *You will administer public affairs either honestly or dishonestly; if honestly, you will displease men; if dishonestly, you will displease God. Therefore.*

To this argument one may reply as follows: *I shall administer public affairs either honestly or dishonestly; if honestly, I shall please God; if dishonestly, I shall please men. Therefore.*

———

CHAPTER IV

INDUCTIVE ARGUMENTATION

Prologue. – There will be only one article in this chapter, and it is divided as follows:

Induction
- Three meanings of induction
- Definition of induction
- Comparison of induction and the deductive syllogism
- The movement of descent in induction
- Function of the movement of descent in induction
- Division of induction
- The supreme principle of induction
- Force and certitude of induction
- Sufficient enumeration of individuals
- Analogy and example

INDUCTION

98. Three meanings of induction. – Induction has three meanings:

a) It may signify the abstraction of a universal concept from a singular; v.g., when I conceive Peter as *man*. This kind of induction pertains to simple apprehension.

b) It may signify the formulation of a self-evident universal proposition, i.e., of a principle, which presupposes experience. In this case the concepts of the subject and predicate are drawn from experience, and the nexus or relation between the subject and predicate is immediately known from the concept or notion of them; nevertheless the intellect *is induced*, — and this is why we speak of an induction, — or *is led by way of manuduction* by sensible experience to unite the predicate to the subject and to perceive the immediate nexus between them (1).

This kind of induction pertains to judgment.

c) It may signify an argumentation in which the relation between the subject and predicate of a universal conclusion is manifested by the enumeration of several singulars and by experience.

This kind of induction is identified with the inductive syllogism, and it pertains to the third operation of the intellect.

---

(1) Fonseca, *In Metaph.*, c. 1, q. 4, s. 4.

Note the teaching of Cajetan: « . . . Principia sunt evidentia ex propriis terminis, sic jam compositis, vel (et idem est) si taliter componantur eorum termini ab intellectu: sed taliter componi nequeunt absque experimento determinativo intellectus ad hoc, etc. Unde quando dicitur quod principia ex solis terminis lumine intellectus cognoscuntur, non excluditur adminiculum sensus, sed tantummodo termini medii, sic enim principia cognoscimus in quantum terminos cognoscimus; quia absque alio medio termino complexum illud, quod principium est, evidens est: et non quia absque experimentali complexione compositio intellectus fiat, etc. » *In II Post.*, c. XIII.

It is with this kind of induction that we are concerned in the present chapter.

99. Definition of induction. — Induction, as an operation of reason, is defined: *a progression from sufficiently enumerated singulars to a universal.*

a) *Progression,* i.e., a movement by which the human intellect proceeds from singular data.

b) *To a universal,* that is to say, to a conclusion whose subject does not represent a group of individuals, or all the individuals of a group, but something one (i.e., one nature) that may be communicated to several (1); v.g.,

Peter, Paul, James, etc. . . are mortal.
But Peter, Paul, James, etc. . . are men.
Therefore man is mortal.

100. Comparison of induction and the deductive syllogism. — Induction, as a kind of argumentation, and the deductive syllogism(2) are essentially different. Moreover, induction, as a mode of knowledge, cannot be reduced to the deductive syllogism.

a) The deductive syllogism is founded on the connexion of its three terms (concepts or notions), and therefore belongs entirely to the purely intelligible plane.

Induction, on the contrary, proves that a predicate is identified with a universal subject, because it is identified with the singulars of an enumeration, and therefore it passes from the sensible order to the intelligible order.

b) Hence in a deductive syllogism there is a middle term in the premises that unites the minor and major extremes.

In induction the *enumeration of singulars or individuals* takes the place of the middle term.

---

(1) Disons que l'induction ne fait pas passer de *quelques uns* à tous, — à tous les individus d'une collection pris comme tels, — mais bien de quelques uns à *tout,* — à tout l'objet de concept universel qui se réalise en chaque individu. — Maritain, *op. cit.,* p. 320.

(2) The categorical deductive syllogism.

From these differences arise differences between the syllogism and induction as regards the premises and the conclusion. These differences may be illustrated by the examples that follow:

Deductive syllogism	Induction
An animal is sentient.	Bodies a, b, c, . . . conduct electricity.
But man is an animal.	But bodies a, b, c, . . . are metals.
Therefore man is sentient.	Therefore metal conducts electricity.

1° *Differences as regards premises.* — *a*) The major of a syllogism expresses a conformity between two concepts, because the intellect perceives that one is included in the comprehension of the other: *sentient* is included in *animal.*

The major of an induction expresses a conformity between a predicate and several singulars, because this is known from experience.

b) The minor of a deductive syllogism states the conformity of the two concepts to each other, because the intellect perceives that one is extended to the other in whose comprehension it is included: *animal* is extended to *man,* because *animal* is included in the comprehension of man.

The minor of an induction states that the several singulars or individuals are the terms for which a universal term is substituted, or that the several singulars are subjective parts whose potential whole is this universal. Briefly, there is only a *generalization* of singulars in the minor of an induction.

2° *Differences as regards conclusion.* — The conclusion of a deductive syllogism is a proposition in which the intellect perceives, by means of premises, an intelligible nexus between the subject and predicate. The conclusion of an induction is a proposition in which the intellect affirms a predicate of a universal subject, not because it perceives an intelligible nexus between the subject and predicate, but because the predicate is identified with the singulars of the enumeration.

Briefly: The conclusion of a deductive syllogism expresses a truth that is known from principles.

The conclusion of an induction expresses a law

of nature or a law that is known from experience.

Hence the deductive syllogism is a scientific process, and induction is a process proper to experimental knowledge.

101. The movement of descent in induction.—Induction, in its principal function, ascends from singulars to a universal. But, if the conclusion which is found by ascending induction is accepted as the major, induction can descend from a universal to singulars. Induction is this case, though it seems to be the same materially as the syllogism, is entirely different from it.

Example:

Man is mortal.
But Peter is a man.
Therefore Peter is mortal.

If the major is accepted as a proposition in which the intellect sees the intelligible nexus between the subject and the predicate, (man is mortal, because, being essentially composed of a soul and matter, he is corruptible), then we have a syllogism. If, however, the major states that man is mortal, because, as shown by experience, all men die, then we have an induction which descends.

In the conclusion of the syllogism, *mortal* is identified with Peter, because in the premises the intellect sees that mortality is included in the very notion of man. In the conclusion of the induction, mortal is identified with Peter, because Peter is one of those individuals for whom the term *man* has a substitutive value; the individuals are mortal, as is evident from ample experience.

Many authors erroneously confuse the movement of descent of induction with the syllogism.

102. Function of the movement of descent in induction.—The principal function of the movement of descent in induction is to judge a conclusion or law of nature known by ascending induction as legitimate or not.

For a law of nature that is induced from only some experiments is nothing more than a hypothesis. It is by descending from a universal to singulars that the intellect can best show whether the hypothesis is legitimate or not. It should be noted that the intellect does not immediately descend to singulars from a hypothesis, but rather it passes from a universal hypothesis to another hypothesis that is less universal, and gradually it reaches the singulars (1).

103. Division of induction. — a) From the point of view of the enumeration of its parts, an induction may be complete or incomplete.

A *complete* induction is one that is made after the complete enumeration of the singulars contained under a universal.

An *incomplete* induction is one which is made after an incomplete enumeration of these singulars (2).

b) An incomplete induction is sufficient or insufficient according as the enumeration of the singulars is sufficient or insufficient to admit a universal.

Insufficient induction is not true induction, and it can lead only to a hypothesis that is slightly probable.

Complete induction is always sufficient.

104. Principle of induction. — It is clear from what has been said that induction depends on the following principle: *what is affirmed or denied of several sufficiently enumerated singulars is affirmed or denied of the whole universal of which these singulars are inferiors.*

---

(1) Ainsi Pascal ne peut vérifier directement l'hypothèse de Torricelli, sur la pression atmosphérique et l'ascension de l'eau dans les pompes; mais si elle est vraie, un liquide plus dense montera moins haut et au sommet d'une montagne l'ascension sera plus faible. Les faits vérifièrent ces secondes hypothèses et indirectement la première.

(2) The adjective incomplete can easily be misleading. It does not signify that the induction is badly executed. It might be well to adopt the terms: *induction by complete enumeration* and *induction by incomplete enumeration* instead of *complete induction* and *incomplete induction*. — Translator's note.

105. Force and certitude of induction. – Inference, as it obtains in virtue of the form or disposition of the propositions in induction, is not *necessary*, as it is in the syllogism in which there is a *process* in virtue of the connexion of concepts, but only *sufficient* for the admission of a universal from the enumeration of the singulars (1).

Hence the conclusion of an induction of itself is only probable. However, it can become certain if some other kind of proof is brought into the induction. It is in this way that the conclusion of a complete induction is certain: it is such in virtue of another kind of reasoning. But complete induction is not pure induction, but an argument from equivalent to equivalent (2).

Example:

Sight, touch, taste, hearing, and smell are organic powers.
But sight, touch, taste, hearing, and smell are senses,
i.e., they are equivalent to every sense.
Therefore every sense is an organic power.

106. Sufficient enumeration of singulars. – The whole force of and difficulty with induction consists in the sufficient observation and enumeration of the singulars. If the conclusion of an induction is already certain from some other source, more than one singular need not be enumerated: one is sufficient; v.g., we may say: *Peter is mortal. Therefore man is mortal.* Otherwise diligent investigation is required.

There are certain rules, laid down by Bacon and Stuart Mill, according to which an enumeration can be made sufficient. These rules or canons are called the method of agreement, the method of difference, the method of concomitant variations, and the method of residues.

Canon of the *method of agreement:* if all the cases of a phenomenon always and everywhere have the same common antecedent, that antecedent may be regarded as the explanation of that phenomenon.

Canon of the *method of difference:* if to remove one antecedent is to remove the phenomenon, that antecedent may be considered as the explanation of the phenomenon; v.g., if F is produced with ABCD, and not with BCD, the antecedent A is the explanation of the phenomenon F.

---

(1) Joannes a Sancto Thoma, *Cursus Phil.*, t. I, p. 198 (Reiser).

(2) A hypothesis becomes a law or a fact in experimental science, when it is proved from experience by induction of descent. Thus the proposition: All metals conduct electricity, is *certain* today, because it is clear from experience that all metals conduct electricity. This is a case of argument from equivalent to equivalent.

Canon of the *method of residues:* if the antecedents which explain some phenomena are removed, the residue of phenomena which remains is explained by some other common circumstance.

107. Analogy or example. — An analogy or example is a progression from one singular or particular to another singular or particular.

Example:

Paul the sinner asked God's pardon.
Therefore Peter the sinner will ask God's pardon.

Analogy is reducible to induction as the imperfect to perfect; and it leads only to a conclusion that is slightly probable.

NOTE. — Example, as imperfect induction, must be distinguished from the kind of example by which a truth already known is illustrated.

SECOND PART OF LOGIC

MATERIAL LOGIC

Prologue. — Formal or minor logic deals with the form of the syllogism, that is to say, it sets forth the rules for the correct disposition of the terms and propositions in a valid syllogism.

Material or major logic deals with the matter of the syllogism, that is to say, with the content of concepts and propositions. In a word, it is concerned principally with the conditions of true and certain reasoning.

There are three processes by which reason acquires knowledge of a new truth by means of truths already known: 1° a process involving necessity in which error is impossible and by which certain knowledge is acquired; this process is called *demonstration;* 2° a process that does not involve necessity and whose conclusion is only probably true; this is the probable or *dialectic* syllogism; 3° a process in which reason always fails to arrive at a true conclusion; this process is called the *sophism* (1).

In this second part of logic, we deal first with the nature of logic — this will serve as an introduction to the whole of material logic; secondly, we deal with universals; and thirdly, we deal with dialectics and sophistry.

---

(1) *In Post. Anal.*, l. I, l. 1, n. 5 (Leonina).

Therefore there will be four books:

Book I: Nature of Logic.

Book II: Universals.

Book III: Demonstration.

Book IV: Dialectics and Sophistry.

BOOK I

Nature of logic

Prologue.— In this first book, we shall discuss Logic in itself, and also the formal object of Logic. Hence there will be two chapters in this book:

CHAPTER I

LOGIC IN ITSELF

Prologue.— In this chapter, we shall deal first with the necessity of Logic in the acquisition of knowledge. The question of the necessity of Logic is the same as the question of the existence of Logic. Logic is an instrument used in the acquisition of knowledge; and if it is neither necessary nor useful in the acquisition of science, it does not exist.

Later Logic will be considered as it is a science.

Hence there will be two articles in this chapter.

Necessity of Logic
- Statement of the question
- Thesis: Logic is not strictly necessary for the acquisition of knowledge in the imperfect state; Logic is strictly necessary for the acquisition of knowledge in the perfect state

Logic as a science
- Statement of the question
- Thesis: Logic is a science and at the same time a liberal art
- Difficulties
- Logic is a strictly speculative science
- Difficulties

ARTICLE I

NECESSITY OF LOGIC

108. Statement of the question. — 1° A distinction must be made between natural Logic and artificial Logic.

Natural logic is nothing other than the aptitude or disposition of the human intellect to reason.

Artificial logic is the art of reasoning superadded to that natural disposition of the reason.

At present we are concerned with artificial Logic, not with natural Logic. Indeed, natural Logic is not properly Logic, but rather the beginning of Logic.

2° Science is *certain and evident knowledge through causes*, A distinction must be made between science in the imperfect state and science in the perfect state.

Science in the imperfect state is science by which the intellect has certain and evident knowledge, as results from a first demonstration.

Science in the perfect state is science by which the intellect not only has certain and evident knowledge, but by which it can deal with all that pertains to a full knowledge of the object of a science,and can defend itself from opposing errors or attacks.

3° We are concerned here with the question of whether or not Logic is necessary for the acquisition of science.

We must distinguish between what is *absolutely necessary* and what is *relatively necessary.*

A thing is said to be absolutely necessary *when its necessity derives from its very essence, or from an intrinsic cause.* Thus it is absolutely necessary that man be rational and mortal.

A thing is said to be relatively necessary when it is *necessary for the attainment of an end.*

A thing that is necessary for the attainment of an end may be *strictly necessary* or only *useful*, i.e., necessary in a certain respect.

A strictly necessary thing is *one without which the attainment of an end is utterly impossible*, as respiration is necessary for life.

A useful thing, i.e., a thing necessary in a certain respect, is *one without which an end can be attained, but not well attained.* Good food is useful, or necessary in a certain respect, for life, because without good food life cannot be well supported, though it can be supported.

109. Opinions. — *a*) Some philosophers, as Epicurus and Peter Gassendi, claim that Logic serves no purpose; others, as the Donatists and Luther, consider that it is deleterious.

b) Others, as the Conimbricenses, affirm that Logic is useful, but not necessary.

c) Others, as de Aguirre (†1699), contend that Logic is strictly necessary for the acquisition of science in both the perfect state and in the imperfect state.

d) The common opinion, and the one we adopt, asserts that Logic is strictly necessary for the acquisition of knowledge in the perfect state, but not strictly necessary for the acquisition of knowledge in the imperfect state.

110. Statement of the thesis.

THESIS. — LOGIC IS NOT STRICTLY NECESSARY FOR THE ACQUISITION OF KNOWLEDGE IN THE IMPERFECT STATE; LOGIC IS STRICTLY NECESSARY FOR THE ACQUISITION OF KNOWLEDGE IN THE PERFECT STATE.

First part. — *Logic is not strictly necessary for the acquisition of knowledge in the imperfect state.*—The art of reasoning is not strictly necessary for the production of every demonstration whatsoever. But Logic is the art of reasoning. Therefore Logic is not strictly necessary for the production of every demonstration whatsoever, or for the acquisition of knowledge in the imperfect state.

The minor is the definition of Logic.

The major. — The art of reasoning, like every other art, is acquired from acts, for one who learns an art performs the operations of that art without art. Hence one who has not the art of reasoning can perform the actions of this art, i.e., can produce or posit demonstration, but only in an imperfect manner: otherwise one could not acquire the art of reasoning. Therefore the art of reasoning is not strictly necessary for the production of every demonstration whatsoever.

Second part. — *Logic is strictly necessary for the acquisition of science in the perfect state.*—The art of reasoning is strictly necessary for the acquisition of knowledge in the perfect state. But Logic is the art of reasoning. Therefore Logic is strictly necessary for the acquisition of knowledge in the perfect state.

The minor is the definition of Logic.

The major. — Science in the perfect state is acquired only by perfect discourses [1]. But the art of reasoning is strictly necessary for perfect discourses: reason is not determined to perfect discourses merely by the inclination of its nature, but must needs be determined and perfected by art. Therefore the art of reasoning is strictly necessary for the acquisition of science in the perfect state.

Cf. *De Trinitate*, q. 6, a. 1. — *In Metaph.*, L. II, l. 5, n. 335 (Cathala).— JOANNEM A SANCTO THOMA, *Cursus Phil.*, t. I, pp. 251-256 (Reiser).

(1) Observe that *discourse* is used here in the sense of *thought-discourse*, of which oral discourse is the expression (cf. 36). Translator's note.

POINTS FOR REVIEW

1. Explain the difference between: 1° what is absolutely necessary and what is strictly necessary; 2° what is strictly necessary and what is necessary in a certain respect, i.e., useful; 3° science in the imperfect state and science in the perfect state; 4° artificial Logic and naturel Logic.

2. What is the teaching of the Conimbricenses on the necessity of Logic?

ARTICLE II

LOGIC AS A SCIENCE

111. Statement of the question. – 1° Science is certain and evident knowledge acquired through demonstration.

2° In the thesis, we state that Logic is a science and at the same time a liberal art.

Art is defined : *a virtue of the intellect which inclines it to do its work easily and well.*

a) *Virtue :* a stable disposition which inclines a faculty to do its work easily and well.

b) *Of the intellect :* a virtue which is in the intellect as in its subject.

c) *Inclines . . . to do its work easily and well :* art is thus distinguished from prudence. Prudence not only gives facility in acting, but also regulates that facility. Art gives facility for the performing of a work, but it does not regulate that facility. In other words, prudence gives a well-regulated use of a faculty, whereas art gives only facility for the execution of a work. Example : art gives a shipbuilder the facility to construct a ship well ; but prudence teaches him when and how, in view of liberty and the end of human acts, he ought to use that facility.

3° Two things are to be considered in art : the matter and the form or directive rule.

a) There are two things to be considered in the matter of an art, namely, the action of the artificer which is directed by the art, and the work on which his art is exercised (1). The matter with which art is concerned must not be wholly determinate, but must have some indifference or indetermina-

(1) *In Ethic.*, l. VI, l. 3, n. 1154 (Pirotta).

tion in virtue of which it can be regulated by reason. Example : if the operations of a house-builder were wholly determined by nature, the art of house-building would serve no purpose. Similarly, if the timber used in the construction of a house did not have some indifference or indetermination as regards the form of the house, no art wou'd be required for the building of a house.

b) The form of an art serves as a directive rule or rules. The direction given by art must be given according to certain and determinate methods, or by certain and determinate means. Indeed, if direction is varied according to circumstances, then it is not art but prudence that is required.

Hence two things are required for art : *indetermination* of matter, and *determination* of form, i.e., of directive rules.

4° Art is an intellectual virtue that is concerned with the performing of a work.

A work may be *external* or *internal.*

An external work is one that is produced in exterior matter by means of transitive action ; v.g., a house, a statue, a picture.

An internal work is a work of reason, i.e., a work which not only is regulated by reason, but is wrought in the intellect; v.g., an enunciative discourse, a syllogism, a work of counting and measuring, a poetical work, a rhetorical discourse.

5° The distinction between a mechanical or servile art and a liberal art follows the distinction between an external work and an internal work.

A mechanical or servile art is one which is concerned with external work ; v.g., the art of painting, the art of house-building, etc.

A liberal art is concerned with internal work ; v.g., poetry, rhetoric, grammar, logic, etc.

112. Statement of the thesis.

THESIS.—LOGIC IS A SCIENCE AND AT THE SAME TIME IS A LIBERAL ART.

First part. — *Logic is a science.* — All certain and evident knowledge acquired by means of demonstration is science. But Logic is certain and evident knowledge acquired by means of demonstration. Therefore Logic is a science.

Major is the definition of science.

Minor. — Logic does not set forth in an indeterminate manner the rules for discoursing, but proves them by demonstration, discusses them in a scientific manner, and clearly explains their nature. Hence Logic is certain and evident knowledge acquired by means of demonstration.

Second part. — *Logic is at the same time a liberal art.* A science which directs by certain and determinate rules the operations of the intellect in forming definitions, divisions, and argumentations is a liberal art. But Logic is a science which directs by certain and determinate rules the operations of the intellect in forming definitions, divisions, and argumentations. Therefore Logic is as the same time a liberal art.

Major. — All the requirements of a liberal art are found in this science : *a*) certain and determinate rules ; *b*) an indetermination of matter, because the intellect, in forming definitions, divisions, and argumentations, can proceed with or without error.

The *minor* is clear, because Logic directs the intellect in the knowledge of truth.

113. Difficulties. — 1° *Logic is not a science.*

a) A mode of knowledge is not a science. But Logic is a mode of knowledge. Therefore Logic is not a science.

Major. — A mode of knowledge, *let it go;* a discipline which is called a mode of knowledge because it deals with modes of knowledge, *I deny.*

Minor. — Logic is a mode of knowledge, *I deny;* is called a mode of knowledge because it deals with modes of knowledge, *I concede.*

Logic deals with modes of knowledge, i.e., with definition, division, enunciation, and argumentation. Therefore it may be called a mode of

---

Cf. *De Trinitate*, q. 5, a. 1, ad 3. — *In Metaph.*, l. IV, l. 4. — I-II, q. 57, a. 3, ad 3 and a. 6, ad 3. — II-II, q. 47, a. 2, ad 3. — *In Post Anal.*, l. I, l. 1. — JOANNEM A SANCTO THOMA, *Cursus Phil.*, t. I, pp. 256-259 (Reiser).

knowledge from the point of view of its object. And thus it is distinguished from other sciences which deal with things.

b) An instrument of other sciences is not a science. But Logic is an instrument of other sciences. Therefore Logic is not a science.

Major.— What is primarily an instrument of other sciences, *let it go;* what is primarily an instrument of the intellect in the acquisition and direction of other sciences, *I deny.*

Minor.— Logic is primarily an instrument of other sciences, *I deny;* Logic is primarily an instrument of the intellect in the acquisition and direction of other sciences, *I concede.*

Logic is primarily an instrument which the intellect uses for the direction of other sciences.

But, even though Logic were primarily an instrument of sciences, it could still be a science. Indeed it is not repugnant that an instrument be of the same nature as the thing it produces, although this is not necessary, as when a hammer is made by means of another hammer.

2° *Logic is not an art.*

A science cannot be an art. But Logic is a science. Therefore Logic cannot be an art.

Major. — A science cannot be at the same time a mechanical or servile art, *I concede;* it cannot be a liberal art, *I deny.*

Minor. — Logic is a science but not a liberal art, *I deny;* but not a mechanical art, *I concede.*

When a mechanical art is employed in the production of an external work, it is not a science, because it is not concerned with the knowledge of truth.

But it is not repugnant that a liberal art, while concerned with speculation, be at the same time a science, although not every liberal art is a science.

114. Logic is a purely speculative science. - 1° First we must note the difference between the speculative and the practical.

The speculative and the practical are formally distinct according to their ends.

The speculative is that whose end is truth, or the knowledge of truth.

The practical is that whose end is the production of a work. Hence, though the practical can know truth, it does not stop in the knowledge of truth, but directs it to the performing of work.

2° From this distinction between the end of the speculative and the end of the practical, it follows that a speculative science and a practical science are essentially distinguished *according to their mode of considering.*

A speculative science considers what a thing is ; a practical science considers how a thing is effected.

Hence, *in the first place*, a speculative science either deals with non-operable matter, as God, the angels, heaven, etc.; or, if concerned with operable matter, as a house, a picture, etc., it does not consider how the thing is produced, but what it is ; v.g., what a house is.

A practical science deals with operable matter, as a house a picture, and all works of mechanical art, and it considers them in as much as they are operable things.

Secondly, the principles used by a speculative science manifest *only*, and, as it were, illuminate truth ; v.g., it is impossible that a thing be and not be at the same time and under the same respect.

The principles used by a practical science not only manifest, but also reduce to practice, that is to say, they direct that a thing be made and be constituted in its being ; v.g., good is to be done.

3° Suarez and Vasquez contend that Logic is both a speculative and a practical science.

St. Albert the Great and the Conimbricenses affirm that Logic is a practical science.

Thomists do not deny that Logic has a certain mode of the practical, in as much as it gives order to and directs the knowledge of truth, and therefore directs it to the mode of a work; but they teach that Logic is a purely or essentially speculative science. Scotus and his school follow this opinion.

115. Statement of the thesis.

THESIS. — Logic is a purely speculative science

1° *From the definition of a speculative science.* — A science which seeks science for its own sake is a purely speculative science. But Logic seeks science for its own sake. Therefore Logic is a purely speculative science.

The *major* is the definition of a speculative science.

Minor. — A science which was invented so that reason would not proceed in ignorance or in error, but could have correct knowledge of things, seeks science for its own sake; for the only object of this science is the avoidance of ignorance, and therefore it seeks knowledge for its own sake. But Logic was invented so that reason would not proceed in ignorance or in error, but could have correct knowledge of things. Therefore Logic seeks science for its own sake.

2° *According to its principles.* — A science which uses principles that are entirely speculative is a purely speculative science. But Logic is a science which uses principles that are entirely speculative. Therefore Logic is a purely speculative science.

The major is clear from the statement of the question.

Minor. — The two principles which Logic uses in the construction of syllogisms, the *dictum de omni* and the *dictum de nullo*, are entirely speculative, as are all the other principles it uses for the other modes of knowledge.

3° *According to its matter.* — A science which is directly and essentially concerned with known objects in as much as they are known, i.e., as they are knowledge, is a purely speculative science. But Logic is a science which is directly and essentially concerned with known objects in as much as they are knowledge. Therefore Logic is a purely speculative science.

Major. — Because such a science is not concerned with operable matter, but with cognoscible matter only (see the statement of the question).

Minor. — The principles by which Logic discourses are essentially and directly concerned with known objects as known; such principles are the following: « things identical with a same third are identical with each other »; the « dictum de omni » and the «dictum de nullo »; the rules of amplification and of restriction, of substitution, etc. Hence Logic is directly and essentially concerned with known objects as known.

To understand this last conclusion, we should note that Logic is concerned both with operations of the reason and with known objects, as its matter.

The operations of the reason have a natural tendency to objects, for every kind of knowledge is knowledge of some object. Under this aspect, Logic does not direct the operations of the intellect or reason.

But the operations of the reason can tend to their objects with or without error, and, under this aspect, they need the direction of Logic.

But Logic does not direct the operations of the intellect by acting directly on these operations and subjective concepts, but by placing in order and artificially disposing the objects to which these operations tend.

Hence Logic is concerned directly and essentially with known objects as known, which it places in order; from this placing in order, Logic directs the operations of the intellect (and formal concepts) in as much as they are concerned with objects thus known. Therefore the operations of the intellect constitute only the remote matter with which Logic is concerned.

Cf. I-II, q. 57, a. 3, ad 3 and q. 51, a. 2, ad 3. — Joannem a Sancto Thoma, *Cursus Phil.*, t. I, pp. 271-277 (Reiser).

116. Difficulties. — 1° A science which has a work is a practical science. But Logic has a work; v.g., the work of forming definitions, enunciations, and syllogisms. Therefore Logic is a practical science.

Major. — A science which has a work distinct from speculation, *I concede;* a work not distinct from speculation, *I deny.*

Minor. — Logic has a work distinct from speculation, *I deny;* not distinct from speculation, *I concede.*

Logic regards speculation as a kind of work, in as much as speculation can be directed and regulated by certain rules. Therefore, though Logic has a certain practical aspect, it is a purely speculative science.

2° A science which directs operations is a practical science. But Logic is a science which directs operations. Therefore Logic is a practical science.

Major. — A science which directs operations as operable and to be constituted in existence, *I concede;* a science which directs the operations of the intellect, in as much as this science places known objects in order and disposes them as known, to which these operations tend, *I deny.*

Minor. — Logic directs operations as operable and to be constituted in existence, *I deny;* Logic directs the operations of the intellect, in as much as it places known objects in order and disposes them as known, to which these operations tend, *I concede.*

Logic does not direct the operations of the intellect by direction that derives from operations as operable. For the intellect produces its operations and constitutes them in being by a tendency of its nature, and without art. But Logic in an artificial way places known objects in order and disposes them, as known, to which the operations of the intellect tend naturally. Therefore it does not direct the operations of the intellect as operable and to be constituted in existence, but in as much as they know the objects. Therefore it is a purely speculative science.

3° A science which speculates in order that it may direct and regulate is a practical science. But Logic speculates in order that it may direct and regulate. Therefore Logic is a practical science.

Major. — A science which speculates in order that it may direct and regulate something operable, *I concede;* that it may direct and regulate speculation, *I deny.*

Minor. — Logic speculates in order that it may direct and regulate something operable, *I deny;* that it may direct and regulate speculation, *I concede.*

Note the formal difference between something speculative and something operable or practical. Every operation of the intellect that tends to truth and rests therein is speculation. Only an action which is not concerned with the contemplation of truth can be practical.

Likewise, a work of the intellect contemplating truth is speculative. An action that is not concerned with the contemplation of truth and its work are *operable* or practical.

POINTS FOR REVIEW

1. Explain the difference between an internal work and an external work.

2. What is the difference between a liberal art and a mechanical art? Are a picture, architecture, poetry, grammar, and rhetoric liberal arts or mechanical arts?

3. What is the formal distinction between the speculative and the practical?

4. Distinguish between a speculative science and a practical science as regards their matter and their principles.

CHAPTER II

FORMAL OBJECT OF LOGIC

Prologue. — The formal object of Logic is being of reason, as we shall see. Hence we shall deal first with being of reason in general, and, secondly, with the formal object of Logic. Therefore there will be two articles in this chapter.

Being of reason	Notion of being of reason Division of being of reason Extrinsic denomination Distinction Division of distinction Comparison between being of reason reasoning and being of reason reasoned.
The formal object of Logic	Statement of the question Thesis: The formal object of Logic is second intentions Kinds of second intention.

ARTICLE I

BEING OF REASON

117. Notion of being of reason. – A being of reason, according to its etymology, is a being that depends in some way on reason.

A thing can depend on reason as an effect on its cause, or as an object on a cognitive faculty.

A thing can depend on reason as an effect on its cause in two ways : either as an effect on its efficient cause ; and it is in this way that works of art depend on reason ; or as an effect on a subject and material cause ; and it is in this way that the operations of the intellect and the intellectual virtues depend on reason.

Things which depend on reason in these two ways are real beings, not beings of reason ; v.g., works of art, though constituted by reason, have real existence. Similarly acts of the intellect and intellectual virtues, even though they exist only in reason, have real existence in reason.

A thing that depends on reason as an object on a cognitive faculty is properly called a *being of reason.* Such a thing does not exist in nature, — it is not an object which exists in reality, — but is only conceived and known. Hence a being of reason may be defined : *a being which has objective existence in reason, and can have no existence in reality.*

a) *Being which has existence:* The definition of every being derives from its relation to existence.

b) *Objective existence in reason :* a being of reason is considered a being or an object in reason.

c) *Can have no existence in reality :* being of reason is thus distinguished from real being. A real being is an object of knowledge which has real existence ; a being of reason has no real existence, but existence only in as much as it is considered an object of knowledge.

From this definition we can deduce three things:

a) The *sign* which manifests a being of reason obtains when the intellect forms a proposition regarding an object which has no real existence; v.g., when we say: *a square circle is impossible*, we consider a square circle, which has no real existence, as object, that is to say, we conceive a real non-being after the manner of a being, because to it we apply a copula which signifies being, i.e., existence.

b) The *formation* of a being of reason properly obtains when the intellect conceives a non-being, or a thing that has no real existence, after the manner of a real being. If the intellect did not conceive non-being after the manner of a being, it could not apply to it a copula which signifies existence.

c) A *distinction* must be made in the twofold function of knowledge as regards being of reason.

Knowledge makes a being of reason known.

Knowledge also conceives real non-being as having the nature and mode of being.

The first function of knowledge presupposes being of reason already constituted. Thus, when we speculate on a species, which is a being of reason, the formation of the being of reason is a prerequisite of this speculation.

The second function of knowledge properly forms and constitutes the being of reason.

118. Division of being of reason. - There are three things that we may consider in a being of reason :

a) the *subject* to which being of reason is attributed, as when we say : *man is a species;*

b) *real being after the manner of which* being of reason or non-being is conceived ; v.g., quantity after the manner of which a vacuum, which is not a real being, is conceived;

c) *the thing which* is conceived after the manner of being, i.e., non-being.

a) *From the point of view of the subject to which being of reason is attributed*, being of reason is divided into being of reason with foundation in reality and being of reason without foundation in reality ; v.g., if we say : *man is a species*, species is a being of reason which has a foundation in reality, since all men have the same nature as regards essential predicates. But if we way: a mountain of gold is a *chimera*, chimera is a being of reason which has no foundation in reality, because a mountain of gold has no real existence.

b) *From the point of view of being after the manner of which being of reason is conceived*, being of reason may be divided into all the genera of things ; v.g., a chimera may be conceived after the manner of *substance*, a vaccum after the manner of *quantity*, blindness after the manner of *quality*, etc.

c) *From the point of view of a thing which is not being in reality, but which is conceived after the manner of real being*, being of reason has its essential division. Under this aspect, being of reason can only be *negation* or *relation*.

Let us prove that this is the essential division of being of reason.

Being of reason, from the point of view of a thing which is conceived after the manner of real being, derives from its opposition to real being, and it consists essentially in its incapacity for existence in reality.

What is incapable of existence in reality may be something positive or non-positive.

If it is something non-positive, then it is a negation, by which we understand a *privation*. Certainly negation is not real being, because negation has not real existence, but destroys existence.

If it is something positive, then it is a substance or an accident. But what is a substance is conceived as existing *in itself* ; v.g., man ; and what is an accident is conceived as having existence *in another;* v.g., whiteness. In these cases, we have not non-being, but rather something conceived as having existence.

But the accident of relation is conceived not only as having existence *in* a subject, but as having reference *towards* a term ; v.g., paternity in Peter is a real accident which exists in Peter as its subject ; and it also has reference to Paul as son. Therefore relation has two aspects or two kinds of existence : *existence in* and *existence towards*.

Now if we conceive a relation only according to its reference to a term, that is to say, according to its "existence towards", with the negation of existence in a subject or with the negation of "existence in", then we have a non-being conceived after the manner of a being; in other words, we have a being of reason; v.g., if we say: *Peter is known*, we posit a relation between Peter and knowledge. But that relation posits nothing real in Peter; in other words, it is not a real accident in Peter, but merely a relation of reason.

Hence being of reason is adequately and essentially divided into *negation* and *relation*.

119. Extrinsic denomination. — Denomination is the application of a form to a subject.

Denomination may be *intrinsic* or *extrinsic.*

Intrinsic denomination obtains when the form is inherent in the subject; v.g., man is denominated white from the whiteness which is inherent in man.

Extrinsic denomination obtains when the form does not exist in what it denominates, but in another; v.g., a wall is denominated *seen* from vision which does not exist in the wall, but in the eye.

Some philosophers think that extrinsic denomination is either something real, or a being of reason of a genus all its own, distinct from both relation and negation.

To solve this problem, we must make a distinction between the form by which a thing is denominated, and the application of this form to the thing denominated.

The form by which a thing is denominated can be something real; v.g., a wall is denominated seen from vision which really exists in the one seeing.

But the application of this form to the subject denominated is a being of reason, because it posits nothing in the subject denominated.

The application of the form to the subject denominated refers the thing denominated to the thing from which the denomination derives. An since *reference* is a relation, we must conclude that extrinsic denomination is not a being of reason of a genus all its own, distinct from the relation of reason, but that it is reducible to the relation of reason.

120. Distinction. — Just as there is being of reason, so too there is distinction of reason. Indeed, distinction follows the order and nature of being.

First, we must find out the meaning of distinction in general.

Distinction is *plurality* or *multitude*. It signifies nothing other than remotion or lack of unity of identity. Things are distinct which are not the same.

Distinction must be distinguished from *division*, *diversity*, and *difference*.

Division is separation. Division is not formally opposed to unity or identity, but to union and continuity.

Diversity signifies distinction with the exclusion of anything in common.

Things are diverse which have nothing in common. Hence diversity is total distinction. Example : man and color are diverse.

Difference signifies distinction with the inclusion of something in common. Things are different which are identified as regards something and distinguished as regards something else; they are partially distinct; v.g., intellectual virtue and moral virtue are not absolutely diverse, but yet they are different.

121. Division of distinction. — Just as there are only two genera of beings, namely, *real being* and *being of reason*, so also there are only two kinds of distinction, namely, *real distinction* and *distinction of reason*.

1) Real distinction is *the remotion or lack of identity which obtains in reality, independently of the consideration of the intellect;* v.g., the distinction between a man and a house.

Distinction of reason or logical distinction is *the remotion or lack of identity which is made by the intellect, but which does not obtain in reality;* v. g., the distinction between justice and mercy in God.

2) Real distinction is divided into *absolute real distinction* and *modal* or *formal real distinction.*

Absolute real distinction is the *distinction between two or more things;* v.g., the distinction between Peter and Paul, between quantity and quality, etc.

Modal or formal real distinction is the *distinction between a thing and its mode;* v. g., the distinction between the nose and its curvature; or *the distinction between two or more modes of one and the same thing;* v.g., the distinction between the curvature and straightness of a body.

3) Distinction of reason is divided into *distinction of reason reasoning* and *distinction of reason reasoned.*

Distinction of reason reasoning is the *distinction which is made by the intellect, without foundation in reality,* or it is merely *distinction as regards the mode of signifying and understanding;* v.g., when I say: *Peter is Peter,* Peter is only distinguished from himself, for first Peter is conceived as subject, and then as predicate.

Distinction of reason reasoned is *distinction which is formed by the intellect, with foundation in reality;* v.g., the distinction between mercy and justice is God.

122. Comparison between distinction of reason reasoning and distinction of reason reasoned. – Comparison between distinction of reason reasoning and distinction of reason reasoned should be made both as regards identity, and as regards foundation. Indeed, on the one hand, every kind of distinction is a lack of identity; on the other, distinction of reason is divided according as it has or has not foundation in reality.

1° *As regards identity.*— Identity may be formal or material.

Formal identity is *identity in the same proper nature, or in the same definition.* Therefore things are formally distinct which are distinct according to their nature, or definitions.

Material identity is *identity in entity or reality.* Therefore things which are really distinct are materially distinct.

If we say: man is a *rational animal,* there is no formal identity between *animal and rational,* because the definition of animal is different from the definition of rational; but there is material identity in this case, because man is an *animal* and *rational* by the same entity or nature.

Distinction of reason reasoning does not destroy identity as regards the object: it does not destroy the material identity or the formal identity of the object.

Distinction of reason reasoning consists solely in the diverse mode of signifying and conceiving the same object. To have this distinction, it is not sufficient that the intellect simply conceive or know the same object twice; it must conceive the same object as two things, not according to different notions founded in the object,— this would be a distinction of reason reasoned,— but by making a comparison between two concepts of the same thing, as when we say: *Peter is Peter.*

Distinction of reason reasoned leaves intact the material identity of the object,— otherwise it would be a real distinction, — but it destroys its formal identity; v.g., the distinction between animal and rational as predicated of man.

Hence the distinction of reason reasoning is less than the distinction of reason reasoned, because it destroys identity to a lesser degree.

2° *As regards foundation.*— *a)* The foundation of the distinction of reason reasoning derives from the intellect only.

Hence if the intellect makes a distinction, *only* because it knows some object after the manner of things that are distinct, this distinction is not a distinction of reason reasoned, but rather a distinction of reason reasoning. Example: we make a distinction between God's intellect and His intellection. We make this distinction only because we know God by comparison to creatures, in which the intellect is distinguished from intellection, as a faculty from its operation or act. But this distinction has no foundation in the object known. i.e., in God. God is pure act or absolutely simple, and therefore in Him there can be no foundation of distinction between a faculty and its operation.

b) The foundation of the distinction of reason reasoned derives both from the object known and from the intellect knowing.

As regards the object known, the foundation of the distinction of reason reasoned is a virtual distinction contained in the object itself. Virtual distinction is defined: *the eminent perfection of a thing which in its one simple entity contains two or more aspects, each of which has its own definition.*

It is in this way that a distinction of reason reasoned is said to have a foundation *in reality.*

As regards the intellect knowing, the foundation of the distinction of reason reasoned is the imperfection of the intellect itself, which does not adequately attain these natures or aspects of its object by a single concept, but which can attain them only by diverse concepts.

Thus the divine attributes, each of which has its own proper definition, are the same divine entity. But the human intellect cannot adequately attain the divine entity by a single concept; it knows it only after the manner of or by comparison to creatures. Therefore we know God only by diverse concepts, one of which explains a divine perfection not explained by another. Hence the distinction between the divine perfections, as they are conceived by us, is a distinction of reason reasoned.

POINTS FOR REVIEW

1. State whether or not the following are beings of reason: a picture, simple apprehension, judgment, a genus.

2. Define being of reason. Is it mere non-being?

3. Under what aspect is being of reason divided into being with a foundation and without a foundation in reality? Under what aspect can being of reason be divided into all the genera of things?

4. Why is it that negation and relation are the essential divisions of being of reason?

5. Does distinction of reason reasoning destroy formal identity as regards the object? Define formal identity as regards the object.

6. In what does distinction of reason reasoning consist? What is a virtual distinction?

7. State the twofold foundation of distinction of reason reasoned.

8. Is extrinsic denomination a being of reason?

9. What kind of distinction exists between: *a*) the divine intellect and divine volition; *b*) the divine will and divine volition; *c*) being, substance, living thing, animal and rational as predicated of man?

Article II

THE FORMAL OBJECT OF LOGIC

123. Statement of the question. – 1° In general, the object of a science is everything the science considers, or the things with which it deals. 2° The object of a science may be *material* of *formal*.

The material object is everything with which the science deals.

The formal object is that formality or determination in virtue of which a science attains its material object.

The faculty of sight provides a good example. This faculty attains the thing seen as its material object; but it attains the thing seen under the aspect of something colored, which is the formal object of sight.

3° It is certain that Logic deals with operations of reason, things known, and beings of reason, called *second intentions*, such as the intentions of genus, species, and so on.

We must find out which of these three is the formal object of Logic.

4° Intention, in its present meaning, does not signify the act of the will which is distinguished from the act of election, but rather it pertains to knowledge. Knowledge tends to an object, and therefore in a general way it may be called *intention*.

Intention may be understood with reference to concepts — or knowledge, and as such it is called formal intention; or with reference to objects, and as such it is called objective intention.

Here we are concerned with intention as referring to objects, that is to say, with objective intention.

5° An object may be considered in two states:
first, as it is in reality;
secondly, as it is in knowledge.

The state of being of an object in knowledge is second with respect to its state of being in reality, which is first.

This is the foundation of the distinction between first and second intentions.

6° First intentions are the formalities which are proper to a thing as it exists in itself; v.g., *man is an animal.*

Second intentions are the formalities which are proper to a thing as they exist in the state of knowledge, i.e., in the intellect; v.g., *man is a species.*

7° A second intention is a being of reason; it does not exist in reality, but is formed by the intellect; it is not *a negation* or a *privation*, but rather it is *a relation of reason*, because it consists in the order and the comparison of things as known.

8° A second intention has its proximate foundation in things as known, and its remote foundation in the things themselves.

Hence, when the intellect establishes mental relations or order between real things as known, the second intention is a being of reason or a relation of reason with a foundation in reality; v.g., when we say: *man is a species.*

But when the intellect establishes mental relations or order between beings of reason as known, the second intention is a being of reason without a foundation in reality; v.g., when we say: *a relation of reason is a genus which is divided into diverse species.*

9° A second intention is that relation of reason which is proper to a thing as known. The relation of reason which is proper to a thing as it exists in reality is not a second intention. Example: if we say *God is the creator*, creator can signify either the creative action of God, and then it expresses something real; or the relation of God to the creature whose « producer » He is; and in this case it expresses a relation of reason, because in God there is no real relation. But that relation of reason is not a second intention, because it is proper to God, not absolutely as He is in the state of knowledge, but as He is in the state of being in reality.

10° All admit that Logic directs the acts of reason.

According to Suarez, Logic directly attains the acts of the reason. Hence the formal object of Logic is something real, namely, the acts of the reason as dirigible.

According to the Thomists, Logic directs the acts of the reason, not by directly and essentially attaining the acts of the reason, but by directly and formally establishing mental relations between objects as they exist in the state of knowledge.

Therefore, according to them, the acts of the reason, formal concepts, and things known are the material objects of Logic. Indeed, the formal object of Logic is the order or mental relations between known objects as known, or it is second intentions which are relations of reason.

The Thomistic opinion is certain.

124. Statement of the thesis.

THESIS.— THE FORMAL OBJECT OF LOGIC IS SECOND INTENTIONS.

1° Definition, enunciation, and argumentation are second intentions. But the formal object of Logic is definition, enunciation, and argumentation. Therefore the formal object of Logic is second intentions.

Major.— Definition, enunciation, and argumentation consist formally in an artificial disposition of terms as noun and verb, subject and predicate. But this artificial disposition is a disposition of things as they exist in the state of knowledge, or it is a second intention. Therefore . . .

Minor.— Logic is the art of defining, enunciating, and arguing. Hence its formal object is definition, enunciation, and argumentation.

2° Logic does not direct the intellect by positing a real and intrinsic rectitude in its acts, but rather by artificially disposing things as known. But the formal object of Logic is that formality in virtue of which Logic directs the intellect.

Therefore the formal object of Logic is the disposition of things as known, or it is second intentions.

Major.— For when objects are correctly disposed by the art of Logic, the act of the intellect, naturally and without any other direction, is drawn to them. For knowledge by its nature is knowledge of an object.

Minor.— It is clear, for Logic is a scientific art which scientifically directs the intellect in the acquisition of knowledge of truth.

125. Kinds of second intention. - Every relation is divided in virtue of its proximate foundation. Second intention is a relation of reason whose proximate foundation is a thing as known, or a thing as it exists in the state of apprehension. Hence second intention is divided according to the relation between the thing known and knowledge, in as much as the thing known determined by diverse mental relations and knowledge is directed in diverse ways.

Because the relations established by the intellect are different in the first, second, and third operations of the intellect, second intention is first divided according to these three operations.

In the first operation, second intention is divided into the intention of term, which is a part of the enunciation and the syllogism, and into the intention of universality in as much as the superior universal is predicated of the inferior.

Intention of term is divided into intention of noun, verb, and the other terms.

Intention of universality is divided into the various modes of universality, as genus, species, etc.

In the second operation, we have the intention of discourse, which is divided according to the various modes of perfect and imperfect discourse, and according to the divisions of the proposition, which is one of the perfect discourses.

The proposition itself establishes other second intentions which are properties of the proposition and properties of the parts of a proposition.

In the third operation, we have the intention of sequence or argumentation, which is divided according to the division of induction and the syllogism properly so-called.

The syllogism is divided into various moods and figures; induction into the movements of ascent and descent.

POINTS FOR REVIEW

1. What is the difference between formal intention and objective intention?

2. What is a second intention? Why is it called *second*?

3. Is a second intention a being of reason? a negation or relation of reason?

4. Are all relations of reason second intentions?

5. What is the teaching of Suarez in regard to the formal object of Logic?

BOOK II

Universals

Prologue. - We have already studied the nature of Logic. We must now consider the requisites, as regards matter, of a scientific demonstration.

The matter of a scientific demonstration, as it pertains to the first operation of the intellect, is the universal.

Hence in Book II we deal first with the universal in general.

Secondly, we coordinate universals, i.e., superior and inferior predicates in each genus or class. These classes of predicates are called predicaments.

Thirdly, we discuss definition and division. For predicaments have reference to the definitions of things.

Therefore there will be three chapters in this book.

Chapter I. The universal.

Chapter II. The predicaments.

Chapter III. Definition and division.

CHAPTER I

THE UNIVERSAL

Prologue. - In this chapter, we first consider the universal in itself; secondly, the predication of the universal, or the attribution of the universal to another; thirdly, the division of universals, or the predicables.

Hence there will be three articles in this chapter.

The universal	Meanings of the universal
	Definition of the universal
	Metaphysical universal and logical universal
	Foundation of the logical universal
	The constituent of the logical universal
	The formation of the logical universal
	Predicability is a property of the logical universal
	Distinction between metaphysical degrees.
Predication of the universal	Notion of predication
	Predication does not destroy universality
	The superior universal must have the signification of a whole in relation to the inferior to be predicated of it.
	Division of predication
	Verification of predication
Division of the universal	Notion of the predicables
	Number of the predicables
	Definition of each of the predicables

ARTICLE I

THE UNIVERSAL IN GENERAL

126. Meanings of universal. — The universal is opposed to the singular, which is incommunicable to several. Hence, etymologically, the universal signifies something which has reference or connotes a relation to several things.

But something can be related to several things by its signification, by its causality, or by its being or predicability, i.e., by its being able to exist in its inferiors and be attributed to them as predicate. Hence we may distinguish between three kinds of universal:

a) the universal as sign;

b) the universal as cause;

c) the universal as predicable.

A universal as sign is a sign which signifies universality in being, or it is a sign that can be universally applied to several things; v.g., common terms, as man and animal, which signify something common (in common) and can be applied to several things.

A universal as cause is a cause that can produce several essentially distinct effects; v.g., God.

A universal as predicable is a thing that can exist in several inferiors and can be attributed to them as predicate; v.g., human nature, which is expressed by the universal term *man*, is found in all men and can be predicated of them. Peter, Paul, John, etc., are men.

Here we deal with the universal as predicable.

NOTE. — Although a universal is common, everything common is not a universal. Thus a house can be common to many in as much as it is owned by many, but it is not a universal.

127. Definition of the universal. — The universal may be defined: *a thing apt to exist in several and to be predicated of them.*

In this definition three things are expressed: the foundation of a relation, the relation itself by which the universal is constituted, and the property of the universal.

a) *Foundation:* « a thing apt to exist in », that is to say, one nature which has unity as separated from many and communicable to them.

b) *Relation:* « in several »; thus is indicated the term to which the universal is related. Therefore a universal connotes a relation, or it is a relation to several in as much as it can be identified with them. Thus we may say: Peter is a man, Paul is a man, etc.

c) *Property of the universal:* « to be predicated of them »; for since a universal can exist in many, or can be identified with many, it can be predicated of them. Therefore predicability is the property of the universal, because it results from the relation by which the universal is constituted, namely, the relation by which the universal can be in many as identified with them.

128. Metaphysical universal and the logical universal. — From the foregoing definition we can understand the division of the universal into two kinds of universal, namely, *metaphysical universal* and *logical universal.*

The metaphysical universal is *a thing* or *a nature abstracted from several.* In this kind of universal, it is with nature that we are directly and principally concerned. Abstraction or universality is regarded as a condition. It is because the metaphysician is concerned principally with natures that this kind of universal is called the metaphysical universal.

The logical universal is *a thing* or *nature considered formally and principally according to its relation to several as inferiors.* In other words, it is an abstracted nature considered formally in its relation of universality to singulars. This relation is a second intention, because it appertains to a thing as it exists in the state of knowledge. It is because the logician is concerned principally with second intentions that this kind of universal is called the logical universal.

The metaphysical universal is the proximate foundation of the relation of reason by which the logical universal is constituted.

Hence, to understand the logical universal, we must consider its foundation, the relation of reason by which the logical universal is constituted, and its property, which is predicability.

129. Foundation of the logical universal. – 1° The foundation of the logical universal is a thing or nature which has unity separated from many and communicable to them.

A thing or nature may be considered in three states:

in the state of nature as such, in as much as a nature is considered only as regards essential predicates; v.g., when we consider man as rational, an animal, living, a body, a substance;

in the state of singularity, that is to say, according to the existence which a nature has in singulars;

in the state of abstraction, according to the existence a nature has in the abstraction of the intellect.

In like manner, unity, which is the lack of division, is of three kinds: *formal unity*, or the unity of nature as regards essential principles; *material unity*, or individual, numerical unity; *universal unity*, or formal unity — unity of nature as separated from many and communicable to them.

2° *a*) If nature is considered in the first state, i.e., as regards itself, in the state of nature, nature is not universal, nor singular, but rather is indifferent to the state of universality and to the state of singularity. Indeed, if nature in itself were universal, it could never be singular; and if it were essentially singular, it could never be found as universal.

Therefore, in the first state, nature has *negative formal unity*. It has formal unity, because it is one nature; it has negative formal unity, because it does not positively exclude plurality, but is indifferent to it.

b) If nature is considered in the second state, i.e., in the state of singularity, it has *material unity*, i.e., numerical or individual unity.

Hence, in this state, nature is not universal, nor has it the aptitude to be in many. Therefore its *formal unity is a unity identified with its numerical unity.*

c) If nature is considered in the third state, or in the state of abstraction, nature has *formal unity common to many.*

In reality there are many singular things which are similar in some formality or nature. The intellect abstracts this formality or nature from singulars, i.e., it separates it from singulars. Therefore the intellect forms a concept which directly and *immediately* represents one formality or nature in which many inferiors are identified, and which *mediately* represents the inferiors to which this formality or nature appertains. Hence nature in the state of abstraction has formal unity, because it is conceived as one thing or nature; it has formal unity *common to many*, because it has the capacity of being in inferiors and of being predicated of them.

Nature in the state of abstraction, or nature as capable of being in many, is the metaphysical universal, and it is the proximate foundation of the logical universal.

130. Constituent of the logical universal. — The universal is defined: *a thing apt to exist in several and to be predicated of them.*

This aptitude may be considered in two ways: *formally and positively*, and *fundamentally.*

The aptitude understood formally and positively is *the relation to inferiors.*

The aptitude fundamentally understood is *the capacity or non-repugnance to receive this relation.*

Aptitude fundamentally understood precedes aptitude

formally understood as its proximate foundation, and constitutes the metaphysical universal.

The logical universal is formally constituted by the aptitude formally and positively understood, or by the positive relation of nature in the state of abstraction to its inferiors. This relation is a second intention, because it is formed by the intellect and appertains to nature only in the state of knowledge.

131. The formation of the logical universal. — 1° The logical universal is one thing or nature as related to many. Hence it must be constituted by a comparative act of the intellect, i.e., by knowledge comparing one thing to many.

The comparative act of the intellect may be understood in two ways: as pertaining to *judgment* — and reasoning — and to *simple apprehension*.

The comparative act of the intellect, as pertaining to judgment, compares one thing to another by composition and division, or it attributes one thing as predicate to another as its subject.

The comparative act of the intellect, as pertaining to simple apprehension, is the contrary of the absolute act.

The absolute act of simple apprehension is an act which does not compare one thing to another and establish a mental relation or order between them, but rather which knows the thing in itself.

The comparative act of simple apprehension is the act which knows one thing or nature not absolutely in itself, but in its relation to another as term; v.g., the act by which we know a relation of one subject to another as its term.

2° Having made these preliminary observations and distinctions, we may now set forth the following conclusions in regard to the formation of universals:

a) The metaphysical universal is constituted by the absolute act of simple apprehension.—A metaphysical universal is nothing other than a thing or nature as separated, i.e., abstracted, by the intellect from individuals, which has no repugnance to existing in them. But when the intellect by its absolute act simply apprehends a nature without giving any consideration to its state of singularity in which it exists in reality, we have a nature as separated or abstracted from individuals. Hence a metaphysical universal is constituted by an absolute act of simple apprehension.

b) *The logical universal is not constituted by an act of judgment.* — By an act of judgment a universal is identified with its inferiors: v.g., when we say: *Peter is a man.* This identification presupposes a relation which the universal has to its inferiors and by which it can be identified with them. A logical universal consists in this relation. Hence an act of judgment by which something is predicated of another, or by which something is attributed to another, presupposes a logical universal as already constituted.

c) *The logical universal is constituted by the comparative act of simple apprehension.*— A logical universal is a nature with relation to its inferiors, in as much as it has a positive aptitude of being or existing in them. But this relation of a nature to its inferiors is constituted by a comparative act of simple apprehension, in as much as the intellect simply compares the nature in its state of abstraction to its inferiors as the terms to which it is related. Hence a logical universal is formed by a comparative act of simple apprehension.

3° We can therefore understand how the universal is constituted.

a) Outside the intellect and in reality, nature exists only as singular.

b) But nature in itself is indifferent both to the state of singularity and to the state of universality. The intellect, by an absolute act of simple apprehension, abstracts nature from singulars. It is thus that the metaphysical universal is constituted.

c) Later, the intellect, by a comparative act of simple apprehension, perceives that the universal has an aptitude to exist in its inferiors. It is in this way that the logical universal is constituted.

132. Predicability is a property of the logical universal.— 1° Predicability is the aptitude by which a universal can be attributed as predicate to another as subject.

2° A property is an attribute which necessarily results from a nature that is already constituted, as from its source.

3° Predicability is not the formal constituent of the logical universal, but it is its property. When the intellect attributes a predicate to a subject, it merely affirms the identity of that subject and predicate. Example: if we say: *Peter is a man*, we posit that that thing which is Peter is the same as that thing which is a man. Hence a universal can be predicated of its inferior because it can be identified with it, or because it is capable of existing in it. In other words, in the logical universal the relation of being in many precedes predicability. The relation of being in many is the formal constituent of the logical universal; predicability results from this relation as a property of the logical universal.

133. Distinction between the metaphysical degrees. — Metaphysical degrees are the superior and inferior predicates which are essentially attributed to a subject; v.g., the predicates man, animal, living, body, and substance are essentially attributed to Peter.

These predicates are called metaphysical degrees because one is more universal than and superior to another, and in knowing them we, as it were, ascend and descend.

2° The distinction that obtains between metaphysical degrees is not a real distinction, but a distinction of reason reasoned (nn. 120-121).

The is no real distinction between them, because they express not different entities, but the same entity. Peter by the same entity or nature is man, animal, living (being), body, and substance.

The distinction that obtains between them is a distinction of reason reasoned, because metaphysical degrees are not formally identified. Each metaphysical degree has its own proper concept, so that the concept of one degree is not the concept of another degree; v.g., the concept of animal is not the same as the concept of living being.

Cf. *De Ente et Essentia.* — CAJETANUM, *Comment.* in De Ente et Essentia. — JOANNEM A SANCTO THOMA, *Cursus Phil.*, t. I, pp. 313-354 (Reiser).

POINTS FOR REVIEW

1. What is a universal as predicable?

2. Distinguish between a metaphysical universal and a logical universal.

3. In what states may nature be considered? In what state has nature (*a*) negative formal unity, (*b*) numerical unity, (*c*) formal unity common to many?

4. What is (*a*) the proximate foundation of the logical universal, (*b*) its formal constituent?

5. By what act of the intellect is the logical universal formed?

6. State whether predicability is the formal constituent or merely a property of the logical universal. Give reasons for your answer.

7. Why is the distinction between metaphysical degrees not a real distinction? Explain why it is a distinction of reason reasoned.

ARTICLE II

PREDICATION OF THE UNIVERSAL

134. **Notion of predication.** — A thing is predicated, i.e., is a predicate, when it is said of another, i.e., when it is attributed to another. Hence predication formally understood is defined: *the union of predicate and subject by way of attribution.*

But a union or conjunction is a relation. Moreover, every relation has a foundation. The foundation of predication, or predication fundamentally understood, is the *material identity of subject and predicate*, if the predication is affirmative; or the *disparity of subject and predicate*, if the predication is negative. In other words, in affirmative predication, the subject and predicate signify something which is materially the same in each, —which has material identity, — but formally different. In negative predication, the subject and predicate signify things which are distinct in reality, i.e., materially different.

It is to be observed that, in affirmative predication, there must be identity of subject and predicate not only as regards the thing signified, but also as regards the mode of signification. For if one and the same thing is conceived as a whole and as a part, there can be no predication. Example: we may not say: *man is humanity*, even though man and humanity signify the same thing, which is human nature. Humanity has the signification of a part, namely, that by which man is man. Therefore it cannot be predicated of man, because the part is not predicated of its whole.

135. **Predication does not destroy universality.** — The problem is this: when a universal is predicated of a singular, it is identified with this singular. Hence we may ask whether in this case the universal becomes the singular, or, in other words, whether predication destroys universality.

The problem is solved as follows: predication does not destroy universality; in other words, a universal, even when predicated of a singular, remains a universal; v.g., when we say: *Peter is a man, man* remains a universal, for otherwise the meaning of the proposition would be: *Peter is this man.*

There are two reasons which we may offer in support of this solution.

First, predication is nothing other than the exercise of a property which appertains to the universal, namely, the exercise of predicability. But a property and its exercise do not destroy the universal, but presuppose it.

Secondly, when a universal is predicated of a singular, it is not universality that is predicated, but rather nature as it exists in the state of universality, so that universality is merely a condition of predicability. A universal nature can be predicated of a singular, or identified with a singular, because it is the same nature which exists in the state of singularity and in the state of universality.

The following is a schematic explanation of what we have just said:

In the state of singularity　　In the state of universality

Thus we can see that predication does not destroy universality, but presupposes it. Indeed, if nature did not exist in the intellect in the state of universality, it could not be predicated of itself as it exists in the state of singularity.

136. The superior universal must have the signification of a whole in relation to the inferior to be predicated of it. — We may say: man is an *animal,a living being* a body. An animal *is a living* (*being*). A living (being) is a *body.* Animal, living, and body are superior predicates in relation to man. Similarly, living and body are superior predicates as regards animal, and body is a superior predicate with reference to living (being).

The difficulty is this: a superior predicate or universal seems to be a part in relation to an inferior predicate; v.g., animal seems to express only a part of man, and living (being) only a part of animal. But the part is not predicated of the whole, because it is not identified with it. The part is distinct from the whole.

The solution of the difficulty lies in the fact that a superior predicate or universal contains a determinate element and an indeterminate element.

If we consider only what is explicitly contained in the superior predicate, i.e., the determinate element, or the formality expressed by the superior predicate, then the superior predicate is only a part in relation to the inferior predicate, and cannot be predicated of it; v.g., man is not only animal; and if we consider only the formality of animal, animal cannot be predicated of man.

If we consider what is contained indeterminately in the superior predicate, i.e., the indeterminate element, then the superior predicate does not signify a part in relation to the inferior predicate, but rather it signifies a whole. And, in this case, it can be predicated of the inferior, for under this aspect it signifies the nature or thing to which it (the superior predicate) belongs; v.g., animal designates the thing of which animal can be predicated, and, although it expresses only the formality of animal, it nevertheless contains indeterminately all the formalities which can be identified with the thing it signifies. The thing which is animal can be rational, living, etc.

Hence a superior universal is predicated of its inferior when it has the signification of a whole and not a part.

137. Division of predication. — 1° Predication is first divided into *direct predication* and *indirect predication*.

Direct predication is *predication in which what really is the subject is posited as subject*, as when a superior is predicated of its inferior, a definition of the thing defined, an accident of a subject; v.g., *man is an animal; man is risible; man is white*.

Indirect predication is *predication in which what is really the predicate is posited as subject*, as when an inferior is predicated of its superior—*some animal is man;* a thing defined of its definition — *rational animal is man;* a subject of an accident—*some risible being is man, some white being is man.*

But we must nóte that a genus, if qualified by an individuating particle, is posited as subject. Hence, if we say: *this animal is a man*, direct predication obtains. If we say: *man is this animal*, we have indirect predication. But if we say: *man is some animal*, we have direct predication. If we say: *some animal is man*, indirect predication obtains. The particle *some* does not render a genus individuated, as does the particle *this*.

2° Direct predication may be *essential* or *accidental.*

Essential predication is *predication in which the predicate belongs intrinsically to the subject*, i.e., it designates the very essence of the subject, or it designates a property which necessarily results from the subject; v.g., *man is rational; man is risible.*

Accidental predication *is predication in which the predicate does not appertain intrinsically ot the subject;* v.g., *man is white.*

3° Predication may be *disparate* or *identical.*

Disparate predication is *predication which depends on terms that cannot be identified with each other;* v.g., *man is not a stone.*

Identical predication is *predication which depends on terms which can be identified with each other*; v.g., *man is rational.*

4° Identical predication may be *formally identical* or *materially identical.*

Formally identical predication is *predication which depends on terms which have the same signification;* v.g., *man is man.*

Materially identical predication is *predication which depends on terms which have different significations, but which designate one and the same thing;* v.g., *man is an animal; divine justice is divine mercy; white is pleasing.*

138. Verification of predication. — 1° In order to know the rules by which predication is verified, we must make a distinction between the abstract and the concrete, and between substance and accident.

An abstract thing is a form without a subject; v.g., *whiteness, humanity.*

A concrete thing is form with a subject; v.g., *a white thing, a man.*

Substance is being which exists in itself; v.g., *man.*

Accident is being in another; v.g., *whiteness.*

2° Having made these distinctions, we may lay down the following rules:

1) *The concrete is directly predicated of the concrete both in substances and in accidents.*

a) We must observe that in the accident concretely understood there is *a subject* which receives an accidental form and which is denominated by this form; *a form* which is received in the subject and which determines the subject; and *a compound* which results from the union of the subject and form.

The concrete of accident, v.g., *a white thing*, does not directly signify a compound of subject and accident which has not one quiddity but which is an accidental being; it formally signifies an accidental form with the connotation of the subject of this form, as the abstract of accident; v.g., *whiteness* signifies an accidental form without the connotation of its subject. Thus the proposition: *man is white*, does not signify that man is *man and whiteness*, but rather it signifies that *man is a subject which has whiteness.*

b) The concrete of accident can be predicated of a thing because it is identified with it either in virtue of its form, as when we say that *a white thing is colored*, or in virtue of its subject, as when we say that *man is white.*

In the first case, the predication is essential; in the second, it is accidental.

2) *The superior abstract is directly predicated of the inferior abstract in two cases:*

a) *In accidents*, because an accident of itself is merely a form; hence the abstract of accident signifies its whole essence and can be directly predicated of its inferior. Thus we may say that *whiteness is a color, whiteness is a quality.*

b) *In substances*, if the abstract of substance is not *understood reduplicatively.* Thus we may say that humanity is animality; but we may not say that *humanity, as humanity, is animality.*

3) *The concrete is not directly predicated of the abstract, nor the abstract of the concrete.*

This is so because the concrete signifies a whole, whereas the abstract signifies a part. Certainly the part is not predicated of the whole, nor the whole of the part.

However, exception must be made for three cases in which the concrete may be directly predicated of the abstract, and the abstract of the concrete.

a) *In the Divine:* God is the Deity, and the Deity is God. In like manner, the Father is Paternity, and Paternity is the Father.

b) *In being and things convertible with being,* as the one, the good, and the true. Entity is being, and being is entity, for otherwise entity would not be being, and being would not be entity. Similarly, the one is unity, etc.

c) *In quantity:* quantity is *quantified.*

Cf. Joannem a Sancto Thoma, *Cursus Phil.*, t. I, pp. 354-375 (Reiser).

POINTS FOR REVIEW

1. Define predication. What is its foundation? When does a superior universal signify a whole in relation to an inferior universal?

2. Distinguish between direct and indirect predication. What is accidental predication? Distinguish between identical and formal predication.

3. When is the concrete directly predicated of the abstract, and the abstract of the concrete?

ARTICLE III

DIVISION OF THE UNIVERSAL

139. Notion of the predicables. - The predicables are nothing other than the members into which the universal is divided.

But there are two things which we must note.

First, the universal that is divided into the predicables is a univocal universal, not an analogous universal; v.g., being.

Secondly, the predicables are divisions of the universal formally as a logical universal, or in virtue of the second intention by which a universal is positively related to its inferiors as capable of existing in them, But a second intention is a relation whose proximate foundation is an abstracted nature, or a metaphysical universal. Moreover, every relation is divided by its foundations. Therefore, in the division of the universal into the predicables, it is the logical universal that is formally divided; but at the same time the metaphysical universal is divided in as much as it is the proximate foundation of the logical universal.

Hence the predicables may be defined: *the diverse modes of universality,* or *the different modes according to which a universal can exist in many.*

But if the universal is considered as regards its predicability, then the predicables, according to their descriptive definition, are *the modes of predicability,* or *the diverse modes of univocally predicating one thing of another,* i.e., of attributing a predicate to a subject.

140. The number of the predicables.— The predicables are five in number, and only five. A universal can designate either the essence or quiddity of the subject of which it is predicated, or something which is not the quiddity or essence.

1° If it designates the essence, *a*) it expresses the whole integral essence, and as such is called *species:* man is a species in relation to his inferiors; or *b*) it expresses a part of the essence as determinable, and in this case it is called *genus:* animal is a genus in relation to its inferiors; or *c*) it expresses a part of the essence as determining and contracting, and then we have what is called *differentia:* rational is a differentia because, by contracting and determining the genus which is animal, it constitutes a species (1): man is a *rational* animal.

2° If it designates something which is not the essence of the subject, *a*) it expresses something that has a necessary connection with the essence of the subject, and thus we have *the property:* risibility is a property of man; or *b*) it expresses something which has not a necessary connection with the essence of the subject, but which may pertain to it in a contingent manner; in this case we have *the predicable accident*, as when we say: man is *white.*

141. The definitions of each of the predicables. — 1° Genus is defined: *a universal which is predicated of several specifically distinct subjects and which incompletely expresses their essence.*

a) *A universal which is predicated of several subjects:* this is common to all predicables or universals.

b) *Specifically distinct subjects:* because the genus is immediately related to things that are different is species as its term.

c) *Incompletely expresses their essence:* the genus is a substantive and essential predicate which expresses not the whole essence, but only a constituent part of it.

2° Species is defined: *a universal which is predicated of*

---

(1) Thus it may be described as the *differentiating* part of the essence. Translator's note.

several numerically distinct subjects and which completely expresses their essence.

We should note carefully the difference between the definition of genus and the definition of species.

Genus is related to things that are specifically distinct as its inferiors; species is related to things that are numerically distinct as its inferiors.

Genus incompletely expresses an essence, because it is a substantive predicate that expresses a part of an essence or quiddity; species completely expresses the whole of an essence.

3° Differentia is defined: *a universal which is affirmed of several subjects as an essential and qualifying predicate.*

As an essential and qualifying predicate: the differentia is a predicate which expresses a part of an essence as determining or qualifying, and therefore in an adjectival manner.

The differentia is related to three things: *a*) to genus which it determines; *b*) to species which it constitutes by determining genus, and of which it is an actually constituent and more determinate part; *c*) to the inferiors of species.

The differentia is formally a logical universal as regards the inferiors contained under species, and therefore it is only in relation to them that it is one of the predicables. This is so because the differentia is a superior predicate only in relation to the inferiors contained under species. In relation to species, the differentia is not superior, but is equal to it; and it is inferior to genus.

Hence when we say: Peter is *rational*, rational is formally understood as one of the predicables, and, moreover, is an essential and qualifying predicate. If we say: man is *rational*, rational is not formally understood as one of the predicables. Man is not inferior to rational: the correlatives of a predicable or a universal are formally inferiors.

4° Property is defined: *a universal which is affirmed of several subjects as a qualifying and necessary accidental predicate.*

a) *Affirmed as a qualifying predicate:* as a quality and in an adjectival manner.

b) *Necessary predicate:* a predicate expressing something which has a necessary connection with the essence of its subject.

c) *Accidental predicate:* a non-essential predicate, i.e., a predicate that does not express the essence of its subject.

Property is used by Porphyry as having four significations:

a) *First,* a property is a universal which appertains only to species, not to every individual of a species, just as to be a grammarian or a doctor appertains to man.

Secondly, a property is a universal which appertains to every individual of a species, but not to a species alone, just as to be bipedal appertains to man.

Thirdly, a property is a universal which appertains to a species alone and to every individual of this species, but not always, as to actually laugh appertains to man.

Fourthly, a property is a universal which always appertains to a species alone and to every individual of the species, just as to be risible appertains to man.

Property, in this fourth meaning, is the fourth predicable.

A property is formally a property, not in reference to a species to which it is equal, but in reference to the individuals of a species to which it is related as a universal is related to its inferiors.

5° Accident is defined: *a universal which is affirmed of several subjects as a qualifying contingent predicate;* v.g., man is *white;*

a) *Affirmed as a qualifying predicate:* as a quality and in an adjectival manner.

b) *Contingent predicate:* it can be identified or not identified with the subject without detriment to the essence or quiddity of its subject, which remains the same in its essential predicates.

A predicable accident is predicable of the inferiors of the

subject which it connotes, not of the inferiors of the form which it signifies; v.g., the inferiors of *white*, as a predicable accident, are not the inferiors of whiteness itself, but those things which accidentally participate whiteness, as a *stone*, *a plant*, *a brute*, *a man*, etc.,

POINTS FOR REVIEW

1. Of what are the predicables divisions? State the essential definition of *the predicables*.

2. Compare the following predicables as regards the superiority or inferiority of their universality: genus, species, differentia, property.

3. What are the different meanings given to property by Porphyry?

CHAPTER II

THE PREDICAMENTS

Prologue. — In the preceding chapter, we considered the logical universal in general, its property, which is predicability, and its division into the five predicables. In the present chapter, we shall consider universals under another aspect.

To understand the work with which we are at present concerned, we must note that the intellect, by simple apprenhension, knows things as they are presented to it by the senses, according to the axiom: *all knowledge begins with the senses.* Though simple apprehansion does not seem to require regulation, yet it does demand a great deal of regulation as regards its object, i.e., as regards the presentation of its object.

Let us consider an example. A colored thing is seen by the eyes. But in the colored object there are many things which are presented to the intellect, as *figure, quantity, relation, substance, motion, existence in place, posture,* etc.

In order that simple apprenhension proceed correctly and that the way be prepared for definitions and demonstrations, the intellect must separate these quiddities or things into different genera, and coordinate them according to superior and inferior genera. Thus it is that we have the predicaments or categories.

Therefore the predicaments are the *coordinations of superior and inferior predicates in each genus.*

But certain distinctions are prerequisite for these coordinations of superior and inferior predicates. Thus it is that we have what are called the *antepredicaments.*

Moreover, there are certain distinctions and coordinations of superior and inferior predicates which result as corollaries common to all or several predicaments; and these are called the *postpredicaemnts*.

Hence there will be three articles in this chapter.

The antepredicaments	Notion of the antepredicaments First antepredicament Second antepredicament Third antepredicament Fourth antepredicament Conditions that a thing be in a predicament
The predicaments	Notion of the predicament Metaphysical and logical predicament Number of the predicaments Notion of each of the predicaments Predicamental accident and predicable accident
The postpredicaments	Notion and number of the postpredicaments Notion of opposition Notion of priority Notion of simultaneity Having, i.e., attributes expressed by the verb *to have*

ARTICLE I

THE ANTEPREDICAMENTS

142. Notion of the antepredicaments. – The antepredicaments are defined: *conditions prerequisite for the constituting and the discerning of the coordination of the predicaments.*

The antepredicaments are four in number.

First, we shall state the notion of each antepredicament, and later, we shall explain why there is such an antepredicament.

143. First antepredicament. - 1° The first antepredicament is the distinction between *univocals, equivocals, analogues*, and *denominatives.*

We have already dealt in Formal Logic with univocal, equivocal, and analogous terms, which are called univocating univocals, equivocating equivocals, and analogating analogues (n. 28).

In our present work in Material Logical, we are dealing with the things which are signified by these terms. These things are called univocated univocals, equivocated equivocals, and analogated analogues.

a) Univocals are defined: *things that have a common name, and whose objective concept* — i.e., *quiddity*, — *signified by the name is absolutely the same.*

Thus Peter, Paul, John are univocals in reference to man; man, donkey, cow are univocals as regards animal, because they participate in the same way what is signified by these names.

b) Equivocals are defined: *things that have a common name, but whose objective concept signified by the name is entirely dif-*

ferent. In other words, equivocals have the same name, but in reality are entirely different. Thus fish, star, and domestic animal are equivocals as regards the name « dog ».

c) Analogues are defined: *things that have a common name, but whose objective concept or formality signified by the name is entirely different, but in a certain respect the same*, i.e., *the same according to a certain proportion.*

Hence analogues are a mean between univocals and equivocals: they are not entirely the same, nor are they entirely different, but are in a certain way proportionate to one another. Thus pulse, color, medicine, and animal are analogues in regard to « health », because they are described as healthful or healthy for different reasons. An animal is described as healthy, because an animal has health; the others are said to be healthful, because they are signs or a cause of health.

d) Denominatives are defined: *things which receive the reimposition of a name from another* (from a denominating form) *which is accidentally and non-essentially related to them;* v. g., a man is described as just from justice, brave from bravery, etc.

2° *The reason of the first predicament.*— The reason of the first predicament, i.e., of the distinction between univocals, equivocals, analogues, and denominatives is this: in the classification of the predicaments, we must consider:

a) what are not placed in a predicament, but are beyond the predicaments;

b) what are placed in a predicament;

c) the relation of what are in one predicament to what are in another predicament.

Things which are not placed in a predicament are analogues and equivocals. Thus being is an analogue. Likewise accident, which is being in another, is an analogue. Hence they are beyond the predicaments.

Things which are placed in a predicament are univocals.

The relation of one predicament to another obtains by way of denomination. Thus substance is denominated *quanti-*

tative from quantity, *qualitative* from quality, an *agent* from action, etc.

144. Second antepredicament. - 1° The second antepredicament is the distinction between the complex and the incomplex.

A complex thing is defined: *a thing that has several quiddities or essences in its comprehension;* v.g., a white man, which has the essence of man and the essence of whiteness in its comprehension.

An incomplex thing is defined: *a thing that signifies only one essence or quiddity*, as man, virtue, science, etc.

2° *The reason of the second predicament.*— The reason of the distinction between the complex and the incomplex is this: the only thing placed in one predicament is an incomplex thing, i.e., a thing which has one quiddity and only one definition. In other words, predicaments are coordinations of incomplex things, not of complex things.

145. Third antepredicament. — 1° The third antepredicament is the distinction between existence in a subject and predication of a subject. It is to be observed that existence in a subject pertains to something real which *inheres*, that is to say, to an accident as a being in another; and predication of a subject pertains to something intentional, that is to say, to a predicate which is attributed to another. By subject we understand first subject, i.e., substance.

Four combinations are possible.

a) Some things are predicated of a subject, but do not exist in that subject.

Thus universal substances are predicated or said of inferiors, but they do not inhere in inferiors as beings in another. They are in inferiors as identified with them.

b) Some things exist in a subject, but are not predicated of a subject.

Singular accidents, as, v.g., this whiteness, this quantity

inhere in substance as their subject, or they are beings in another, but are not predicated of a subject, because they are not superiors.

c) *Some things are neither predicated of nor exist in a subject.* Such are singular substances, as Peter, Paul.

d) *Some things exist in and are predicated of a subject.* Such are universal accidents; v.g., whiteness. To be white is predicated of Peter, and whiteness exists in Peter.

2° *The reason of the third antepredicament.*— In the third antepredicament, a distinction is made between two classes of beings, namely, between substance and accident. Likewise a distinction is made between the singular and the universal.

Hence the way is prepared for the distinction between the predicament of substance and the predicaments of the accidents, and for the coordination of the predicaments according to universality and singularity.

146. Fourth antepredicament. – 1° The fourth antepredicament is the distinction of species and genera from their differentiae.

There are two rules.

a) First rule: *whatever are predicated of the predicate of a subject are predicated of the subject itself.* We are concerned here with real and essential predicates, not with predicates of second intention. Example: animal is predicated of man as subject. Everything that really belongs to animal belongs also to man, as to be sensitive, animated, material.

b) Second rule: *the essential differentiae of non-subalternate genera* (genera of which one is not placed under the other) *are not the same.*

Example: the essential differentiae of substance and quality, though sometimes designated by the same name, are not the same. Thus substance may be divided into material substance and immaterial substance. Similarly, quality may be divided into material quality and immaterial quality. The differentiae of substance and quality according to materiality and immateriality are not the same, because the nature of substance is not the same as the nature of quality.

When genera are subalternated, whether one be placed under another, or both be placed under a third, they have the same essential differentiae, because the differentiae which constitute a superior genus descend to its inferiors. Example: animal is placed under the genus of living being. The differentiae of living being descend to animal. Animal and inorganic being are two genera of which one is not placed under the other, but which are placed under the genus of body. Hence the differentia which constitutes a body as a genus descends to animal and to inorganic being. A body is a *material* substance An animal and an inorganic being are *material* substances.

2° *The reason of the fourth antepredicament.*—The predicaments are classifications of genera and species. Because the essential differentia determines genus, it is not placed under the predicament in the direct line, but rather in the lateral line (first rule). But differentiae which determine non-subalternating genera are placed in distinct predicaments (second rule).

147. Conditions of a thing's being in a predicament. — That a thing be in a predicament, it must be:

a) *Real being*, for natures or quiddities are classified in predicaments (cf. prologue of this chapter), and being of reason has no nature or quiddity.

b) *Finite being*, because God, Who is infinite being, is placed under no genus.

c) *Univocal*, because analogues and equivocals have diverse natures, not one nature (cf. n. 143, the first antepredicament).

d) *Incomplex*, because a complex thing has more than one quiddity (cf. n. 144, the second antepredicament).

e) *Complete being*, i.e., a being which has the mode or nature of a whole.

Thus genus and species are placed under a predicament, because they are conceived as a whole. But differentia, because it determines a genus to constitute a species, has not the nature of a whole, but the nature of a part. Therefore it is not placed under a predicament directly, but indirectly, i.e., in the lateral line (cf. n. 146, the fourth antepredicament).

The physical parts of a nature, as, v.g., matter and soul, are not placed directly under a predicament, but *by reduction* only, that is to say, they are reduced to the whole which is placed under a predicament, as part of it.

Being in the imperfect state and still tending to a term, as an embryo in relation to a perfect animal, is placed *by reduction* in the predicament of their term. Thus a human embryo is placed *by reduction* in the predicament in which man is placed.

POINTS FOR REVIEW

1. Distinguish between univocals and analogues.
2. When are univocals called univocating and univocated ?
3. State the reason of each of the antepredicaments.
4. What are the conditions of a thing's being placed in a predicament ?

ARTICLE II

THE PREDICAMENTS

148. Notion of predicament. — If we consider the universal formally as a logical universal, i.e., in virtue of its relation of universality to its inferiors, we divide it into the five predicables (nn. 139-141).

Here we consider the universal as a nature which has the intention of universality. Finite natures, which exist or can exist, do not all have the same supreme univocal predicate, that is to say, they are not placed in the same supreme genus. Example: man and brute have in common the supreme predicate of substance, because man is a substance and brute is a substance. But color and virtue have not, in common with man and brute, the supreme predicate or genus of substance, because color and virtue are not substances. Therefore, *first*, we divide real finite natures according to their supreme genera. *Secondly*, after determining their supreme genus, we classify under it all superior and inferior predicates, i.e., all other genera and species, down to the individual which is the subject to which the supreme genus and the other superior and inferior predicates are attributed.

Thus it is that we have the predicaments.

Therefore the predicament is defined: *the orderly classification of genera and species under one supreme genus.* Or: *the orderly classification of all the essential predicates which are attributed to the individual.* Or more briefly: *the orderly classification of the metaphysical grades.*

149. Metaphysical predicament and logical predicament. — The genera and species which are given orderly classification in the predicaments may be considered under the aspect of the thing which they express, or they may be considered formally under the aspect of their orderly classification.

A predicament, considered under the aspect of what it expresses, is called a metaphysical predicament, because the consideration of things properly appertains to the metaphysician.

Under the aspect of its orderly classification, which is a second intention, a predicament, because of its being the orderly classification of things as they exist in the intellect, is called a logical predicament, for the consideration of second intentions properly appertains to the logician.

Hence the metaphysical predicament is defined: *the real modes of finite being.*

The logical predicament is the *orderly classification of genera and species.*

150. Number of the predicaments. – In order to find out how many predicaments or supreme genera there are, we shall consider what may be predicated of a subject, that is to say, of an individual which is a substance, for only a substance is properly a subject (cf. n. 145, the third antepredicament).

What may be predicated of a subject.

either belongs to its essence,

or does not belong to its essence.

1° If it belongs to the essence of the subject, we have the supreme genus of *substance.*

2° If it does not belong to the essence of the subject,

either it inheres in the subject *independently* of anything extrinsic by which it is denominated;

or it inheres in the subject *dependently* on something extrinsic by which it is denominated.

1) If something inheres independently of something extrinsic, then we have the supreme genera of *quantity*, *quality* and *relation.*

For what thus inheres,
either is *absolute*,
or is *relative*.

If it is absolute,

a) either it results from matter, and then we have *quantity* which extends material parts;

b) or it results from form, and then we have *quality*, which in qualifying and determining has the mode of form.

If it is relative,

c) we have *relation*, which relates the subject to a term,

2) If something inheres in a subject dependently on some extrinsic thing by which it is denominated, then we have six other supreme genera: *action*, *passion*, *where*, *posture*, *when*, and *habit*.

For that extrinsic thing is
either a cause (or an effect);
or a measure;
or neither a cause nor a measure.

a) If it is a *cause*, then we have *passion*, for something is a patient in as much as it is changed by an efficient cause.

b) If it is an *effect*, then we have *action*, for a subject is called an agent in as much as it produces an effect.

If that extrinsic thing is a *measure*, then it is
either a place,
or a time.
If it is a place,

c) either *only the existence* of the subject in place is considered, and then we have *where*,

d) or the *order of the parts* of the subject in place is considered, and then we have *posture*.

If it is a time,

e) we have *when*.

3) If that extrinsic thing is *neither a cause nor a measure*, then we have *habit*, by which one is said to be dressed, armed, adorned, etc.

Therefore there are ten supreme genera, and hence ten predicaments. The Latin distich that follows will serve as an aid in remembering them.

Arbor	sex	servos	ardore	refrigerat	ustos
Substance	*quantity*	*relation*	*quality*	*action*	*passion*
Ruri	cras	stabo	sed tunicatus ero		
where	*when*	*posture*	*habit*		

151. Notion of each of the predicaments. — 1° **Substance** derives its name from the Latin *stare sub* (to stand under), because it *stands under*, i.e., supports accidents. It is defined: *a thing or quiddity to which it appertains to exist in itself, and not in another as in its subject of inherence.*

a) *To exist in itself*: it is opposed to *existence in another*, which is proper to accidents.

b) *In its subject of inherence*, i.e., in a subject already determined in its first existence, i.e., in a substance already constituted. Hence, if something is in another as a constituent of substance, it is not an accident; v.g., a soul in matter.

The predicament of substance is shown in the following scheme, known as the Tree of Porphyry, because Prophyry is the author of it.

	Substance	
corporeal	Body	incorporeal (angel)
organic	Living Being	inorganic (mineral)
sentient	Animal	non-sentient (plant)
rational	Man	irrational (animal)
	Paul, Peter, James, Henry, etc.	

The classification of genera, species, and differentiae is clear from this outline. A genus is *supreme* if it has no other genus above itself: substance. It is *lowest* if it has no genus below itself: animal. It is *intermediate*, if it has a genus above itself and also another below itself: living being.

Likewise, species is *supreme*, *intermediate*, and *lowest*, as it immediately results from a supreme, an intermediate, or a lowest genus.

So too differentia is called *supreme*, *intermediate*, or *lowest* (specific, ultimate), as it determines a supreme, an intermediate, or a lowest genus.

2° **Accident**, as distinguished from substance, is called *predicamental*, and, though not a supreme genus, is common to the nine predicaments other than substance.

It is defined: *a thing or quiddity to which it appertains to exist not in itself, but in another as in its subject of inherence.*

An accident implies two things: (*a*) it presupposes a subject of inherence,i.e., a subject already constituted in its primary existence, to which it gives a secondary existence; (*b*) it depends on a subject of inherence for its existence.

Quantity is defined: *an accident which extends a subject (substance) into parts.* It is immediately divided into discrete quantity and continuous quantity, as its two species. *Continuous* quantity is magnitude, length, and depth ; *discrete* quantity is number.

Quality is defined: *an accident which modifies a substance in itself;* v.g., science.

a) As an accident, quality is distinguished from substantial essential differentia; (*b*) as a modifier of substance, it is distinguished from quantity, which properly does not modify substance, but extends it into parts and renders it determinable; (*c*) as a modifier of substance *in itself*, it is distinguished from relation, which determines substance in its order or relation to a term, and from the last six predicaments, which determine it in its relation to something extrinsic, by which they are denominated.

Quality is divided into four species: habit and disposition, potency and impotency, passion and patible quality, form and figure.

Habit is a quality by which a subject is well or badly disposed in itself either as regards its being or as regards its operation.

A habit that disposes a subject as regards its being is called an *entitative* habit; v.g., beauty, health. A habit that disposes a subject as regards its operation is called an *operative* habit; v.g., virtue, vice.

When a habit is so perfectly in a subject that it cannot easily be lost, it is properly or specifically called *habit;* it is called *disposition*, when it can easily be lost.

Potency is a quality which disposes a subject simply for operation — not for good or bad operation. *Strong* potency is properly called potency; *weak* potency is called impotency; v. g., weak sight is called impotency.

Passion is a quality according to which alteration takes place; v.g., color, odor, taste, etc. If the altération takes place quickly, as redness from shame, it is properly called *passion;* if it is permanent, as redness from temperament, it is called *patible quality.*

Figure is an accident which results from the termination of quantity considered according to the diverse disposition of its parts. Figure is applied properly to natural things; v.g., the figure of a lion, of a man; and is called form when applied to artificial things v.g., the form of a house.

Relation, in its widest meaning, is defined: *the order which obtains between one thing and another.* Relation, in its widest sense, is either transcendental, i. e., *secundum dici*, or *secundum esse.*

a) *Transcendental* relation is the relation to another that is included in an absolute essence. Hence a transcendental relation is not an accident distinct from the thing which is referred to another; v.g., the soul is of itself, not in virtue of an accident, related to another, i.e., to the body.

b) Relation *secundum esse* is either a relation *of reason;* v.g., a reflex universal; or a *real* relation; v.g., paternity.

c) Real relation *secundum esse* is a predicamental relation, and it is defined: *a real accident whose whole existence consists in its being referred to another.*

Action, in its widest sense, is any kind of operation, and it is defined: *any actuality of power, that is, of operative power.*

Action, in this sense, is divided into immanent action, which is action in a wide sense, and transitive action, which is action in the strict sense, i.e., predicamental action.

a) Immanent action is action which is not destined to produce an effect, but which consists wholly in its being a perfection of an agent, as his disposition; v.g., intellection, volition. Of itself intellection is not the production of a term, but rather it is a disposition of the intellect in relation to an object. Therefore immanent action, as a disposition, belongs to the predicament of quality.

b) Transitive or predicamental action is *action which is destined to produce an effect;* v.g., the building of a house.

Passion is the *accident by which a subject is constituted as the actual recipient of the action of an agent;* v.g., to be sawn.

Where is the *accident arising in a subject from its circumscription of place.*

Posture is the *accident which results in a body from the disposition of the parts of the body in place;* v.g., when a person sits or lies down, he has a special posture.

When is *the accident which results in a subject from the time by which it is measured;* today, tomorrow, etc.

Habit is *the accident which results in a body from the adjuncts of clothing, arms, or ornaments.*

152. Predicamental accident and predicable accident. — The predicamental accident is entirely distinct from the predicable accident.

a) The predicable accident is one of the members into which the logical universal is divided. Therefore it is formally a second intention, or it is the relation of contingency which a thing in the intellect has to the inferior of which it is predicated.

The predicamental accident may be considered either logically or metaphysically.

Accepted in its logical meaning, it is a being-in-another as an analogous predicate which the last nine predicaments, i.e., *quantity, quality, relation*, etc., have in common.

In its metaphysical meaning, it is a being-in-another accepted as a real nature.

b) The predicable accident is opposed to *property;* the predicamental accident is opposed to *substance.*

c) Finally, a thing can be at the same time both a predicable and a predicamental accident, according to the manner in which it is considered; v.g., if we say: man is just, *just* is predicated contingently of man, and thus is used as a predicable accident; *just* signifies justice, which is a being-in-another, and thus it is used as a predicamental accident. A predicamental accident may be predicated as a property; v.g., man is *risible.*

POINTS FOR REVIEW

1. Under what aspect is the universal divided into the predicaments?
2. Explain the difference between metaphysical predicament and logical predicament.
3. Are the last six predicaments mere extrinsic denominations?
4. Is property opposed to predicamental accident?
5. Define each of the ten supreme genera.

ARTICLE III

THE POSTPREDICAMENTS

153. Notion and number of the postpredicaments. — The postpredicaments are certain modes which result from all the predicaments or from several of them, as their common properties.

For, from the distinction and coordination of the predicaments, results *opposition* which is the foundation of distinction. Likewise, from the coordination of genera, result *priority* and *simultaneity*, at least in nature. Again, *to have* results from the derivation of accidents from substance.

Hence there are four postpredicaments which result from all the predicaments, namely ; opposition, priority and posteriority, simultaneity, and to have.

There is a fifth postpredicament : *motion*, which results from only four of the predicaments, viz., *substance, quality, quantity*, and *place*. We shall deal with motion in Philosophy of Nature.

154. Notion of opposition. — Opposition is the repugnance between several things in virtue of which the same things cannot be identified as regards the same thing at the same time and under the same respect.

Opposition may be contradictory, privative, contrary, and relative.

Contradictory opposition is the repugnance between being and non-being.

Privative opposition is the repugnance between form and the lack of form in a subject capable of it ; v.g., between blindness and sight in a man.

Contrary opposition is the repugnance between two positive things which belong to the same genus, but which mutually exclude each other from the same subject ; v.g., virtue and vice, love and hatred.

Contrary opposition may be mediate or immediate.

Mediate opposition is the opposition which exists between two things between which there can be a mean ; v.g., indifference can obtain between love and hatred.

Immediate opposition is the opposition which exists between two things between which there can be no mean ; v.g., between materiality and spirituality.

Relative opposition is the repugnance between things which are mutually related to each other ; v.g., between father and son.

155. Notion of priority. — Priority is the precedence of one thing over another. There are five kinds of priority : of time, nature, consequence, dignity, and order.

Priority of time is priority in duration ; v.g., adolescence comes before manhood.

Priority of nature is priority according to the causality which exists between cause and effect. Priority of nature does not necessarily presuppose priority of time; v.g., the priority of the sun in regard to light.

Priority of consequence is the priority of one thing over another resulting from the fact that the first is inferred from the other, but not vice versa ; v.g., he is a man, therefore he is an animal. But we do not say : he is an animal, therefore he is a man. Therefore animal is prior to man.

Priority of dignity is the priority of one thing over another because of excellence, office, merit, etc.; v.g., a king has priority over his subjects.

Priority of order is priority in the disposition of things ; v.g., Logic enjoys priority of order in the parts of Philosophy.

156. Notion of simultaneity. — Simultaneity is the negation of priority and posteriority, and therefore it has as many modes as priority.

157. To have. — To have is the mode by which one thing is said to have another. The modes of having may be reduced to five : 1° by inherence, as science is had by man : 2° by containing, as wine is had in a cask ; 3° by possession, as a field is had by a man ; 4° by relation, as a son is had by a father ; 5° by juxtaposition, as a garment is had by a man.

CHAPTER III

DEFINITION AND DIVISION

Prologue. - We have already dealt with the distinction and separation of things according to their supreme genera. Now we shall deal with definition and division, that is to say, with the modes by which we have knowledge of essences. There will be three articles in this chapter.

Definition
- Notion
- Kinds
- Laws
- What can be defined

Division
- Notion
- Kinds
- Laws

Methods of finding the definition
- Two methods
- Way of descent
- Way of ascent

ARTICLE I

DEFINITION

158. Notion of definition. — To define, according to its etymology, means to set bounds or limits.

In reality, a definition is a discourse which explains the nature of a thing, or the signification of a term.

Definition is called a discourse, i.e., an imperfect discourse, because it must be a complex term. Since the function of a definition is to make a thing more clearly manifest, it states what the thing defined has in common with other things and in what it is distinct from them. Hence a definition must be be made up of at least two terms, one of which expresses what it has in common with other things, and another which expresses its differentia.

159. Kinds of definition. — 1° A definition may be an explanation of the meaning of a word, and is called a *nominal* definition ; or it may be an explanation of the nature of a thing, and is called a *real* definition.

A *nominal definition* is one which explains the meaning of a word, and is either a mere explanation of its etymology, i.e., of the origin of the word, v.g., philosophy is the *love of wisdom ;* or it declares the commonly accepted meaning of the word; v.g., God is the *first cause of all things.*

A *real definition* is one which explains the nature of the thing signified ; v.g., man is a *rational animal.*

2° *Real* definition is divided into essential definition, descriptive definition, and causal definition.

An *essential definition* is one which explains a thing by means of its parts or essential predicates.

An essential definition is *physical*, if it explains a thing through the really distinct physical parts of its essence ; v.g., man is a substance composed of matter and a rational soul.

An essential definition is *metaphysical*, if it explains an essence through its metaphysical parts, namely, genus and differentia ; v.g., man is a rational animal.

A *descriptive definition* is one which explains a thing through its proper or common accidents ; v.g., man is a risible animal (proper accident) ; man is a bipedal animal (common accident).

A *causal definition* is one which explains a thing through its extrinsic causes, namely, efficient and final causes ; v.g., the soul is a form created by God for beatitude.

The *genetic definition*, which may be reduced to the causal definition, explains a thing by explaining how it is produced ; v.g., an eclipse of the moon is a failing of its light on account of the interposition of the earth between it and the sun.

The most perfect definition is the metaphysical essential definition.

160. Rules of definition.— *First rule:* A definition must be clearer than the thing defined, for it must manifest the thing defined. Therefore, according to this rule,

a) the defined thing must be excluded from the definition, for otherwise the definition would not be clearer than the thing defined. Hence the following definition is a violation of this rule : Logic is a science which sets forth the rules of Logic.

b) the definition must not be metaphorical. A metaphor does not lead to a clear notion of a thing ; v.g., man is an inverted tree.

Second rule: A definition must contain the genus and differentia of the thing defined. Genus and differentia must be *properly* found in a metaphysical essential definition; in other definitions, something must be given in place of genus and differentia, namely, something the thing defined has in common with other things, and something distinctive by which it differs from other things.

Third rule: A definition must be convertible with the thing defined, i.e., it must be neither wider nor narrower than the thing defined, but coextensive with it. If it were wider, it would add to the thing defined something which did not belong to it ; if it were narrower, it would take away from the thing defined something which belonged to it ; v.g., an animal is *a corporeal substance ;* an animal is *a rational sentient being.*

Fourth rule : A definition must not be negative, for a negative definition does not explain what a thing is.

Yet there are some things that can be defined only negatively, because, on account of the feebleness of our intellect, we can have only a positivo-negative concept of them.

Fifth rule: **A definition, for the sake of clarity, must be brief.**

161. What can be defined. — That a thing be definable, *a*) it must be essentially one, i.e., it must have one essence. If it has several essences, each essence must have its own definition. If several things exist as one, there is no repugnance in their being comprehended by a single definition; *b*) it must be universal, for a singular as such is not the object of scientific knowledge, *c*) it must be a species, in order that it may be properly defined. Things which are not species, as the supreme genera, being as such, and the things that result from being, are declared rather than defined.

ARTICLE II

DIVISION

162. Notion of division. — Division is defined: *a discourse which distributes a thing or a noun into its parts.*

In this definition, *a*) *discourse* is used as the genus which division and definition have in common ; *b*) *which distributes into its parts* is used as the differentia by which division is distinguished from definition. For, whereas a definition manifests the thing defined by showing how it is constituted, as when we say : man is a rational animal, a division manifests the thing as divided, i.e., it destroys the confusion of the thing divided by distributing it into parts, as when we say : one kind of animal is rational, the other is irrational.

163. Kinds of division. - Division is either proper (per se) or accidental.

A. — Proper division is the division of the noun, or the division of the thing signified.

1. A division of a noun is the division of a significant word in regard to its significations.

2. There four kinds of proper division of the thing signified :

a) The division of a thing according to its integrant parts, as when we say : a human body is divided into *head*, *thorax*, and *feet* ; the universe is divided into *spirits* and *bodies*.

b) The division of a thing into its constituent parts, i.e., essential division.

Proper division is physical, if division is made into really distinct parts, as when we say : *The soul is one part of man, matter the other ;* or metaphysical, if division is made into genus and differentia, as when we say : *Animal is one extreme of man, rational the other.*

c) Division of a thing into its powers or functions; v.g., *the intellect is one part of the human soul, the will the other.*

d) Division of a genus into its species, or division of a universal or logical whole into the subjective parts of which it is predicated ; v.g., *one kind of animal is man, the other is the brute ; one kind of animal is rational, the other is irrational.*

B. — There are three kinds of accidental division :

a) Division of a subject into its accidents ; v.g., *one kind of animal is white, another black,* etc.

b) Division of an accident into its subject ; v.g., *one kind of white thing is snow, another milk,* etc.

c) Division of an accident into its accidents ; v.g., *one kind of white thing is sweet, another bitter,* etc.

The kind of division with which Logic is principally concerned is the division of genus into its species, i.e., the division of the universal or logical whole.

164. Rules of division. —*First rule:* A division must be adequate, i.e., all the parts taken together must equate the whole. Otherwise a division would sin by excess or defect. Therefore the division of living being into man and brute is incorrect, because living being extends to plant.

Second rule: No member of a division may equal or exceed the whole ; if it did, the division would sin by excess. Therefore the division of animal into living being, sentient being, and rational being is incorrect, because living being has a greater extension than animal, and sentient being has an extension equal to that of animal.

Third rule: The members of a division are formally opposed, so that one does not include, but rather excludes, the other ; v.g., the division of animal into brute and horse is incorrect.

Fifth rule: A division must be brief, for otherwise confusion is engendered.

ARTICLE III

METHODS OF FINDING THE DEFINITION

165. Two methods. — Aristotle proposes two methods of finding a definition : the way of descent and the way of ascent. These two methods, though not infallible, are, nevertheless, very useful.

166. Way of descent. — The procedure in this method is as follows :

1) By means of our confused or obscure knowledge of the thing to be defined, we first look for its supreme genus.

2) After finding this supreme genus, we continue our search for the definition by making a division of the thing to be defined.

3) This division is made according to the rules of division, namely, *a*) the division must be essential, not accidental : it must be made according to the formal notion of the genus; *b*) it must be immediate and orderly, descending step by step from the supreme genus through the intermediate species and the intermediate differentiæ until it reaches the ultimate species. Thus the supreme genus of man is substance. Substance is immediately divided into *body* and *spirit*. *Man is a body. A body is a living being or a non-living being. A living being is sentient or vegetative. A sentient being is rational or irrational. Man is a living, sentient, rational being.* Hence man is defined : a rational animal.

It is by this method that we can best show that the coordination of predicaments and the rules of division are designed for the finding of definitions.

167. Way of ascent. — 1) We determine the object to be defined by its nominal definition.

2) Then we consider the things that fall under this nominal definition, and we investigate what they have in common. If several common notes are found in them, then we must find out, in so far as possible, what is their dominant common note, i.e., the note that explains the others.

Thus in Peter, Paul, and John, all of whom are men, we find imputability, docility, liberty, risibility, and that intellective operation by which they reason from a known truth to a new truth. The dominant common note which explains the others is the last, namely, the operation of reason.

Next we must examine the class of beings which, according to the common estimation of men, are most closely allied to the class under consideration, and, as before, look for their common or characteristic note. In regard to man, for example, we may consider the monkey, which, according to materialists, is man's ancestor. All monkeys are found to be *imitators*.

4) After that we compare the notes of the two classes under consideration, and find out whether they can be reduced to the same formal constituent, i.e., whether they necessarily have in their concept an intelligible nexus with the same nature.

If they have, then these two classes have the same specific nature ; if they have not, then each has its own specific nature, i.e., the two classes are specifically distinct. In the second case, we examine, according to the same procedure, whether the notes that are common to both classes can be reduced to the same generic nature. Thus we find their proximate genus.

Example : the dominant note common to all men is rational operation, i.e., the operation of reason. But the operation of the reason in its concept connotes and requires a rational nature. Hence man is *rational*. The dominant note common to all monkeys is the gift of imitation. But the intellect cannot perceive an intelligible nexus between the gift of imitation and a specific nature which would be found in monkeys. The gift of imitation requires only a nature that is capable of the knowledge of singulars, i.e., a sentient nature, which is found also in men. Hence both man and the monkey have a sentient nature, which is found also in men. Hence both man and the monkey have a sentient nature, i.e., they are *animals*. Thus we determine their proximate genus.

Man has a rational nature. Thus is determined his species. Hence man is defined : *a rational animal.*

The monkey is not rational, and therefore is called an irrational animal. But the monkey's specific nature cannot be determined by his gift of imitation. Hence *an animal that imitates* is not the essential definition of the monkey, but merely a description derived from one of its accidents.

BOOK III

Demonstration

Prologue. — In the second book, we dealt with universals, which appertain to the first operation of the intellect. Now we shall discuss the demonstration. In dealing with the demonstration, which appertains to the third operation of the intellect, we shall treat of the *prerequisites* of a demonstration, that is to say, of foreknowledge and premises, which appertain to the second operation of the intellect.

The effect of the demonstration is science. Hence, after discussing the nature of the demonstration, we shall deal with science.

Therefore there will be two chapters in this book.

Chaper I. The demonstration.

Chaper II. Science.

CHAPTER I

THE DEMONSTRATION

Prologue. — In this chapter, we shall deal first with the foreknowledge required for a demonstration; secondly, we shall discuss the demonstration. Hence there will be two articles in the chapter the divisions of which are as follows :

- Foreknowledge
  - All doctrines and intellective disciplines depend on preexisting knowledge
  - Foreknowledge required for a demonstration
  - Self-evident propositions
  - Universal, essential, and reduplicative premises

- Demonstration
  - Demonstration defined according to its end
  - Demonstration defined according to its matter
  - Division of demonstration
  - Circular demonstration

ARTICLE I

FOREKNOWLEDGE

168. All doctrines and intellective disciplines depend on preexisting knowledge.— 1° We do not say that all knowledge always depends on previous knowledge, because this would require an infinite regression. In this case, the existence and possibility of all knowledge would be destroyed, for thus knowledge could not have a beginning.

2° It is certain that our intellective knowledge depends on our sensuous knowledge according to the axiom: *all knowledge begins with the senses.* Likewise the knowledge of a proposition depends on the knowledge of simple apprehension, i.e., on the knowledge of terms.

But we are not concerned with these problems here, because we, like Aristotle [1], are dealing at present with doctrine and intellective discipline.

3° The terms, doctrine and discipline, have reference to the acquisition of knowledge.

Doctrine is knowledge which is possessed by a teacher and which makes us know, i.e., provides us with knowledge.

Discipline is the reception of knowledge by another.

Hence we are speaking of every kind of probative knowledge, i.e., of knowledge by which the intellect proceeds from one thing to another by demonstration, by probable syllogism, by induction, by enthymeme, or from singular to singular by example.

Therefore expressly do we say that all doctrines and *intellective* disciplines depend on preexisting knowledge, for *it*

(1) *Post. Anal.*, l. I, c. 1.

appertains to the intellect alone to proceed in knowledge from one thing to another.

4° In the light of these distinctions, the proposition stated above becomes evident. For, if the intellect proceeds in knowledge from one thing to another, there must be foreknowledge of the former.

169. Foreknowledge required for demonstration. — 1° We can have the following knowledge of a thing :

knowledge of its *nominal definition ;*
knowledge of *whether it exists ;*
knowledge of its *quiddity* or *real definition.*

To know the name of a thing is the same to know its nominal definition.

To know *whether* a thing *exists*, is applicable to both a proposition and to an incomplex thing.

To know *whether a proposition exists* is the same as to know *whether it is true.*

To know *whether an incomplex thing exists* is the same as to know if the thing, whether it be an existing being, a possible being, or a being of reason, can exist in a genus.

To know the *quiddity of a thing* is to know its essential definition, at least as regards one essential predicate.

2° In a perfect demonstration, the conclusion affirms a property of a subject, as shown in the example that follows :

A rational animal is risible.
But man is a rational animal.
Therefore man is risible.

Therefore there are three things that must be foreknown for a demonstration :

principles, i.e., *premises ;*
subject ;
property.

This is evident : on the one hand, a demonstration proceeds from principles to a conclusion, as from something known to something that before was unknown ; and, on the other hand, the subject and property are compared with the middle term in the premises.

3° The required foreknowledge of principles, subject, and property is as follows :

Of principles : we must have foreknowledge of *whether they are true.*

Of subject : we must have foreknowledge not only of its *nominal definition* and its *existence* (*whether it exists*), but also of its *quiddity* (*what it is*). For the middle term, with which the subject and property are compared in the premises, is the definition of the subject, i.e., an essential predicate of the subject (*rational animal*, in the foregoing example).

Of property : we must have foreknowledge only of its *nominal definition.*

For the conclusion shows that the property is identified with the subject, and consequently that it exists in it (*whether it exists*). Hence knowledge of *whether a property exists* and *what it is* according to its essential predicates is not a prerequisite of a demonstration.

170. Self-evident propositions.— Although every demonstration is not immediately formed from self-evident, i.e., immediate, propositions, yet every demonstration depends on them, and ultimately is resolved into them. Otherwise a demonstration would be an infinite process.

1° *A self-evident proposition* is one in which the relation between the subject and predicate can be immediately known from the very terms ; v.g., man is an animal.

The relation between the subject and the predicate can be immediately known from the very terms, when the predicate is included in the notion of the subject ; and this happens when the predicate *a*) is the definition of the subject, or *b*) is its first property ; v.g., the proposition : *a body has figure*, is not a self-evident proposition, because figure, which is the termination of quantity, appertains to a body in virtue of its quantity [1].

2° A self-evident proposition may be affirmative or negative.

An affirmative self-evident proposition is one in which the predicate is included in the notion of the subject.

A negative self-evident proposition is one in which the predicate is immediately opposed to what is essential to the subject, namely, to its definition, or to its first property ; v.g. *a circle is not square.*

3° A self-evident proposition may be either self-evident in itself only, or self-evident to us.

A proposition self-evident in itself only is one in which the predicate is included in the notion of the subject, but this is not known by us, because we have not sufficient knowledge of what the subject and predicate are ; v.g., *God exists.* This proposition is self-evident in itself, because God's existence is His essence ; but since we do not know what God's essence is, the proposition is not self-evident to us.

A proposition self-evident in itself is, therefore, a proposition which can be immediately known, but is not immediately known.

A proposition self-evident to us is one in which the predicate is included in the notion of the subject, and this is known to us, because we have sufficient knowledge of what the subject and predicate are.

4° *A proposition self-evident only to the wise* is a proposition self-evident in itself which becomes self-evident to us only by discourse. A proposition self-evident in itself, in which the predicate is a first property, becomes self-evident to the wise by means of an a priori demonstration (demonstration by proper cause), in which the middle term is the definition of the subject. A proposition self-evident in itself, in

(1) I, q. 2, a. 1, c. — *De Veritate*, q. 10, a. 12.

which the predicate is the definition of the subject, becomes self-evident to the wise by their search for the definition.

A proposition self-evident to all is one in which the relation between the subject and predicate is immediately known from the terms as apprehended without discourse by sensuous experience.

5° Self-evident propositions are called principles, because it is from them that our knowledge of other things first derives.

Propositions self-evident to all are called *axioms*, or most common principles, because they are taken for granted in all sciences.

Propositions that are self-evident to the wise are called particular principles, because they are different in every science.

6° The first proposition self-evident to all, i.e., the most common first principle, is the principle of contradiction : *nothing can be and not be at the same time and under the same respect* (being is not non-being). This principle cannot be directly proved.

171. Universal, essential, and reduplicative premises (1). — 1° Premises are universal when the predicate has a distributive application to a universal subject, and therefore is applicable to all inferiors of this subject ; v.g., *risible* is predicated distributively of man, and therefore is predicated of Peter, Paul, John, etc.

If we consider the syllogism as regards its form only, as we do in Formal Logic, it is sufficient that the subject be distributively applicable to the universal subject either necessarily, or contingently, or probably. In other words, if the predicate is probably applicable to the universal subject, the syllogism is correct, because in this case it is probably applicable to all the inferiors of this subject. The conclusion of such a syllogism is probable.

(1) In scholastic Latin, they are called *praemissae de omni, per se and secundum quod ipsum*. — Translator's note.

But the conclusion of the demonstration is certain. Therefore the premises of a demonstration are called universal, only when the predicate is *necessarily* applicable to a universal subject.

2° Sometimes the premises of a demonstration are not only universal, but also **direct** (per se).

There are four modes of attributing directly (by itself: per se) a predicate to subjet.[1]

a) The first mode obtains when the predicate belongs to the essence of the subject ; v.g., man is *rational*, man is an *animal*, man is a *substance*.

b) The second mode obtains when the predicate is a property of the subject ; v.g., man is *risible*.

c) The third mode is not a mode of predication, but rather a mode of existence, and it obtains when a thing is said to exist *solitarily*, i.e., of itself. Thus a substantial individual, as, v.g., Peter, is said to exist of itself. Whiteness does not exist of itself, but in another. A white object, a musician, etc. are not said to exist of themselves, but signify a form inhering in a subject.

d) The fourth mode is neither a mode of predication, nor a mode of existence, but rather a mode of causing; and it obtains when the predicate signifies an operation proper to the subject ; v.g., a *builder builds*, a *singer sings*.

When the predicate is applied to a subject according to the first or second mode of predication, **we have the modes of essential predication.**

Any predicate which is predicated according to the first or second mode of essential predication is universal ; but not every universal predicate is predicated according to the first or second mode of essential predication.

Thus, if we say man is a *quantum* (*is quantitative*), we have a universal predicate, but not a predicate which is predicated according to the first or second mode of essential predica-

(1) *Quatuor modi dicendi per se.*

tion. If we say : man is *risible*, we have a predicate which is universal and which is predicated according to the second mode of essential predication.

3° Reduplicate premises are propositions in which the predicate belongs to the subject reduplicatively, that is to say, appertains to the subject as such; in other words, the propositions are convertible. A predicate which belongs to a subject reduplicatively is a predicate of the subject according to the first or second mode of predication ; but every predicate which essentially belongs to a subject does not belong to it reduplicatively Thus when we say : man is an *animal*, the predicate is applicable to the subject according to the first mode of predication, because it is an essential predicate ; but it is not a reduplicative predicate, because every animal is not a man. But when we say : man is *rational*, the predicate is applicable to the subject both according to the first mode of predication and reduplicatively, because every rational being is man.

The most perfect kind of demonstration is that in which all the propositions are reduplicative, i.e., convertible.

Example :

Every rational animal is risible.
But man is a rational animal.
Therefore man is risible.

The three terms, and therefore the three propositions, are convertible. Hence the demonstration is most perfect.

ARTICLE III

DEMONSTRATION

172. Demonstration defined according to its end. — From the point of view of the effect which it causes, which is also its end, the demonstration is defined : *a syllogism that engenders science.*

a) *Syllogism :* a syllogism in the proper sense of the word, i.e., a deductive syllogism, not an enthymeme, nor an induction.

b) *Engenders* : a demonstration is the cause of science.

But science can be understood as meaning actual science, that is, scientific assent, which is the very act of knowing ; or it may be used to designate habitual science, i.e., a habit of science, which is produced from actual science.

In the case of actual science, or scientific assent, the premises only, not the whole demonstration, are the cause of science.

But in the case of habitual science, or a habit of science, the whole demonstration, with the scientific assent of the conclusion, is the cause of science. For a habit is engendered by acts similar to those to which it tends. And science, as a scientific habit, tends to scientific assent to a conclusion derived from premises. Hence it is caused by scientific assent to a conclusion derived from premises, i. e., from the whole demonstration.

c). *Science*, i.e., certain knowledge of the conclusion derived from certain premises.

173. Demonstration defined according to its matter. — From the point of view of the matter from which it results, the demonstrationis defined : *a syllogism composed of premises* *that are true, first, immediate, and prior to, better known than, and causes of the conclusion.*

a) Syllogism : a syllogism properly so-called, i.e., a deductive syllogism, not an enthymeme, nor an induction.

d) True, first, immediate : these three adjectives indicate quasi-absolute conditions of the premises.

A demonstration results from *true* premises, for, although truth may result from a false antecedent, it is proved only from true premises.

A demonstration is the effect of *first* and *immediate* premises, that is to say, of self-evident propositions. These propositions are called *immediate,* because they have no middle term to prove them ; and *first,* because they enjoy a certain primacy in regard to other propositions which they can demonstrate.

c) Prior to, better known than, and causes of the conclusion : these words indicate quasi-comparative conditions of the premises, that is to say, conditions destined to produce the conclusion.

For the middle term, by which the premises are united and manifest the conclusion, is the *cause of the conclusion,* at least in the act of knowledge. Therefore the premises must be *prior to* the conclusion, just as every cause is prior to its effect.

The premises must be *better known* than the conclusion, because in a demonstration the intellect acquires knowledge of a new truth by means of truths already known.

174. Divisions of demonstration. — 1° Demonstration is essentially divided into *demonstration by proper cause,* and demonstration of *the mere existence of truth.* (1)

A demonstration by proper cause is one which shows not only that the conclusion is true, but also the cause or proximate reason why the predicate is identified with the subject in the

(1) Demonstration by proper cause and demonstration of the mere existence of truth are called *demonstratio propter quid* and *demonstratio quia* respectively in scholastic Latin. — Translator's note.

conclusion ; v.g., *rational animal is risible. But man is a rational animal. Therefore man is risible.*

A demonstration of the mere existence of truth is one which proves that the conclusion is true, without showing the proximate cause of the truth of the conclusion. A demonstration of the mere existence of truth proceeds either from effect to cause, or from remote cause, or from something else with which a truth has an essential connexion ; v.g., *I see a stone ; therefore a stone exists.*

Example :

The only difficulty presented in these definitions is the distinction between proximate cause and remote cause.

A proximate cause or reason is one which, formally speaking and essentially, is convertible with its effect. Hence to posit the cause is to posit the effect, and to remove the cause is to remove the effect.

Example:

A rational animal is risible.
But man is a rational animal.
Therefore man is risible.

The middle term (rational animal) signifies the essence of the subject (which is the minor term) and is the proximate cause of the major term (risible), for risibility is the first property of a rational animal, so that all rational animals are risible, and all risible beings are rational animals.

A remote cause is such only in predication, or because of its order or position.

A cause that is remote in virtue of predication belongs to the logical order and is a genus or quasi-genus to the effects of the species; v.g., animal, which is the genus of man, is a remote cause in virtue of predication, in relation to risibility, which is a property or an effect of man.

To posit a remote cause in virtue of predication is not to posit an effect. Thus we may not say: *it is an animal; therefore it is risible.* But if the remote cause is denied in virtue of its predication, the effect is denied. We may say: *it is not an animal; therefore it is not risible.*

Hence the chief function of a remote cause as predicate is to infer a negative conclusion in a demonstration *of the mere existence of truth.*

But a cause that is remote in virtue of its order of position belongs to the real order, and, if it is convertible with its effect, it can produce a more perfect knowledge of the proper cause. Example: we say that *God is eternal, because He is absolutely immutable*, and thus His immutability is the proximate reason of His eternity. But God is *absolutely immutable, because He is absolutely simple or pure act*, so that pure act is the proximate reason of immutability and the remote reason of eternity, with which it is convertible: *eternal being is pure act; pure act is eternal.* Hence in this case we must ascend to pure act, in order to reach a perfect knowledge of why eternity is identified with God.

A demonstration by proper cause is most perfect when all its propositions are convertible or reduplicative.

Example :

Every rational animal is risible.
But every man is a rational animal.
Therefore every man is risible.

A demonstration by proper cause is less perfect when all its propositions are not convertible. Such is the case when we prove that a predicate which is convertible with a genus is applicable to a species (or to an individual of a species), or to a superior genus understood in a particular sense.

Example :

Every animal has senses.
But man is an animal.
Therefore man has senses.

To have senses is convertible with animal, i.e., is a reduplicative predicate, and is attributed to man who is a species of animal.

Every animal has senses.
But every animal is a living being.
Therefore some living being has senses.

To have senses, which is convertible with animal, is attributed to some living being, i.e., to a superior genus of animal in a particular sense.

To have senses, which is convertible with animal, is attributed to some living being, i.e., to a superior genus of animal in a particular sense.

2° Demonstration is divided, secondly, into *a priori demonstration*, *a posteriori demonstration*, and *a simultaneo demonstration*.

An *a priori* demonstration is a demonstration which proves effects from their cause ; v.g., *the order of the world is proved from God's wisdom.*

An *a posteriori demonstration* is a demonstration which

proves a cause from its effect ; v.g., *the existence of God is proved from creatures.*

An *a simultaneo demonstration* is a demonstration which proves by means of something concomitant, as a correlative, or by means of anything else ; v.g., *he is a father; therefore he has a son ;* or, *I see a stone ; therefore a stone exists.*

A demonstration by proper cause is always a priori.

A demonstration of the mere existence of truth may be either a priori (by means of a remote cause), or a posteriori, or a simultaneo.

3° Demonstration is divided *thirdly* into *direct demonstration* and *indirect demonstration.*

A *direct demonstration* (called also ostensive) is a demonstration which positively demonstrates a thing from true and necessary principles ; v.g., *God's eternity is demonstrated from His immutability.*

An *indirect demonstration* (called also *reduction ad absurdum* or *ad impossible*) is a demonstration which proves the truth of a conclusion from the absurdities which would result from the denial of this conclusion ; v.g., *the human soul is immortal, because otherwise God would not be just.*

An indirect demonstration can be a demonstration of the mere existence of truth, if from effects it makes a reduction to the impossible ; or a demonstration by proper cause, if from the causes of impossibility it makes a reduction to the impossible.

Example of demonstration of the mere existence of truth, which is indirect : *if a horse discoursed, he would be rational.*

Example of demonstration by proper cause, which is indirect : *if a stone were living, it would follow that it moved itself.*

175. Circular demonstration. – 1° A circle in a demonstration is a progression from principles to conclusions and a regression from these conclusions to their principles.

2° There are two kinds of circle : uniform and deform.

a) A *uniform circle* is a regression to principles from a conclusion known by means of these principles. Example : man is rational because he is risible, and risible because he is rational. This kind of uniform circle in a demonstration is unlawful, because it proves the conclusion by means of principles, and the principles by means of the conclusion.

b) A *deform circle* is a regression to principles from their conclusion, but not formally from a conclusion as known from these principles, but known by some other means.

This kind of deform circle is lawful and perfectly unites a demonstration of the mere existence of truth to a demonstration by proper cause. Philosophers use this kind of demonstration. Thus, from an imperfect knowledge of the properties of things, we can have an imperfect knowledge of their essence. A perfect knowledge of their essence is obtained by further speculation ; and from this perfect knowledge of their essences, the philosopher descends to a perfect knowledge of their properties.

Similarly, the philosopher ascends from creatures to God, and again descends from God to a more perfect knowledge of creatures.

CHAPTER II

SCIENCE

Prologue. – In this chapter, first, we shall consider the nature of science ; secondly, the specification of sciences ; thirdly, the subalternation of sciences. Hence there will be three articles in the chapter, and they will be divided as follows:

ARTICLE I

NATURE OF SCIENCE

176. Notion of science. - Science has three meanings: *a*) an act or operation ; *b*) a habit ; *c*) a system.

Science, as an act, is defined : *certain knowledge through causes.* There are three requisites for this kind of knowledge: *a*) knowledge of the cause of the affirmation, in a demonstration of the mere existence of truth; *b*) knowledge of the proper cause formally as such (or of the proper effect of this cause in an a posteriori demonstration); *c*) a necessary nexus between the cause and the effect (or between the effect and the cause).

Science, as a habit, is defined : *a stable disposition acquired by means of demonstration which has as its object scientific assent by means of premises.* This disposition is acquired imperfectly by a first demonstration, and is completed or made stable by subsequent demonstration.

Science, as a system, is defined : *a logical artifact which consists in an orderly classification of concepts which constitute the definitions, divisions, and argumentations of some scientific matter.*

177. Division of science. — 1° Science is analogously divided into *speculative science* and *pratical science.*

A speculative science is a science whose end is the contemplation of truth ; v.g., Metaphysics.

A practical science is a science whose end is practice, i.e., which does not rest in the contemplation of truth, but seeks truth for the purpose of directing and regulating practice ; v.g., Ethics.

A practical science is not a science which is a perfect habit, i.e., an intellectual virtue. Only a speculative science can be an intellectual virtue or perfect habit, as a science.

2° Science is also divided into *perfect science* (scientia propter quid) and *imperfect science* (scientia quia).

Perfect science deals with a properly scientific object, that is to say, with quiddity and the resultants of quiddity, as its properties.

Imperfect science deals with the fact of truth (« whether it is »), but without reaching the root and cause of that truth.

Perfect science is engendered by *demonstration by proper cause*, and imperfect science by *demonstration of the mere existence of truth*.

The division of demonstration into demonstration by proper cause and demonstration of the mere existence of truth is an essential or univocal division. A demonstration of the mere existence of truth, though not a most perfect demonstration, as a demonstration by proper cause is, has the proper nature of demonstration, i.e., is properly demonstration, because it concludes with certitude and evidence. Thus, for example, the existence of God is demonstrated with certitude and evidence from creatures.

But the division of science into perfect science and imperfect science is not an essential or univocal division of science. For imperfect science, from the point of view of the object it attains, has not the proper nature of science, because it does not attain *quiddity*, but only the fact of truth. Therefore it is not a science that is specifically distinct from perfect science, i.e., from a science properly so-called, but is, as it were, science in embryo. Hence, when perfect science and imperfect science treat of the same object, imperfect science is reduced to perfect science, as the imperfect to the perfect. In other words, an imperfect science deals only with the preambles of science, not with the proper object of science, which is quiddity.

3° Sciences are divided *essentially* according to the different formal objects by which they are specified ; and *accident-*

ally, in virtue of subordination, into subalternating science and subalternate science.

We shall treat of these division later.

178. Object of science. — Since perfect science is certain knowledge derived from a demonstration which proves the property of its subject, science cannot deal with :

First, a self-evident proposition which is not demonstrable ;

Secondly, contingent matter: otherwise science would not be certain knowledge.

1) A self-evident proposition is one which has no intrinsic middle term, i.e., one in which the connexion between the extremes is made known only by the explanation of them, and without proof.

Hence every proposition in which an essential predicate is attributed to the subject in self-evident.

However, it is not repugnant that a self-evident proposition be demonstrated by an extrinsic middle term, that is to say, by means of effects, or by an extrinsic cause, efficient or exemplar, or by reduction to the impossible.

Demonstration by effect, or by extrinsic cause, does not engender perfect science, because it does not attain a quiddity as the source and cause of the truth of the conclusion.

A proposition in which a first property is predicated of its subject, though lacking a real middle term, — because a first property immediately results from the essence of a thing, — can be demonstrated by a definition, which is distinguished by reason from the subject. Thus we can demonstrate that man is risible, because he is a rational animal.

2) Science cannot deal with contingent matter, for its object must be necessary. But the object of science is called necessary, not positively as it exists, but as it establishes truth that does not depend on a mutable connexion. Thus man is contingent : he can exist or not exist. Science attains man as regards his essential predicates and his properties, which

have a necessary connexion with one another; v.g., man, whether he exists or not, is necessarily a rational animal, is free, is risible, etc.

Therefore a science is said to be concerned with *universals*, because the essential predicates and the properties which flow from them are universals; and with *perpetuals*, because necessary things are perpetually true.

179. Science, intelligence, and wisdom. — Science, intelligence, and wisdom are used here as meaning perfect speculative habits, i.e., speculative intellectual virtues.

A speculative intellectual virtue is defined: *a right disposition by which the intellect is always disposed to speculative truth.*

1° *Science*, as an intellectual virtue, is a right disposition of the intellect as regards conclusions which are derived from certains principles.

2° *Intelligence*, as an intellectual virtue, — not as an intellective faculty, — is a right disposition of the intellect in regard to certain and indemonstrable principles.

There are three things that should be noted in regard to this definition:

a) Indemonstrable principles are principles that are immediately known from the knowledge of their terms; v.g., *every whole is greater than its part.*

b) Indemonstrable principles can be considered in themselves, without consideration of their conclusions. They can also be considered together with their conclusions, as conclusions deduced from principles. The consideration of principles in the second way pertains to science, which also considers conclusions, But the consideration of principles in themselves appertains to intelligence [1].

c) In addition to certain indemonstrable principles, there are also probable indemonstrable principles. If, for example,

(1) I-II, q. 57, a. 2, ad 2.

we say : *all mothers love their children*, we have a probable indemonstrable principle, because it can happen that some mother does not love her children.

Hence, just as there is the habit of indemonstrable principles which are certain and evident, so there are habits of indemonstrable principles which are probable. However, these habits are not, like intelligence, intellectual *virtues*, but remain *imperfect habits*, because they do not *always* dispose the intellect to truth.

3° *Wisdom*, as an intellectual virtue, is a right disposition of the intellect in regard to truth, in as much as it judges of all things according to their first principles and ultimate causes.

Wisdom attains the first principles of beings, i.e., whatever pertains to being as being. It also attains the first cause of beings, which is God.

Since wisdom is most certain knowledge, it must know truth not only as regards what is concluded from principles, but also as regards first principles, not indeed for the purpose of demonstrating them, but that it may explain and defend them.

Hence wisdom is not distinguished from science and intelligence, as opposite from opposites. Wisdom is most perfect science which extends even to first principles, the habit of which is called intelligence.

But wisdom as it extends even to first principles is distinct from intelligence. For it has greater firmness than intelligence in regard to these principles, because it explains and defends them.

180. Art, prudence, and practical science. — 1° Art, in the strict sense, i.e., mechanical art, is an intellectual virtue which directs actions which pass into exterior matter, as, for example, the actions of building, sawing, etc.

Art may be considered in two ways :

a) as applied to operation ;

b) as setting forth rules of operation in the universal and in the abstract [1].

Art, considered as setting forth rules of operation, has the mode of speculation, and, in a wide sense, may be called science. But it is not science in the strict sense of the term.

For art, as setting forth the rules of operation in the universal and in the abstract, is not a habit distinct from art applied to operation. This is so because art arrives at its end by determinate ways. Hence the application of rules to operation does not constitute a new and special difficulty, which would require a habit distinct from the habit which knows artificial rules. Example : a person who possesses the art of music, by following the precepts of this art, can apply his fingers to a musical instrument.

However, in the application of art to an external work, there can be a special difficulty as regards members and muscles. Thus a person who possesses the art of music may have great difficulty or only little difficulty in the use of his fingers.

To overcome this difficulty a new art is not required, — for art is an intellectual virtue, — but merely bodily exercise, or something similar, by which the impediment to the exercise of the art can be removed [2].

A liberal art, which is an art by similitude, can be a science; v.g., Logic.

2° **Prudence is an intellectual virtue which directs actions, i.e. human acts as free and related to the end of human life.**

Prudence applies moral rules to human acts, considered in the concrete. And since human acts, considered as free acts, are contingent and variable, prudence must be a habit distinct from the habit which sets forth moral rules in the universal, i.e., from the science of moral. For the application of moral rules to matter so contingent as a free act provides

---

(1) Joannes a Sancto Thoma, *Curs. Theol.*, t. III, p. 350a (Solesmensium).

(2) Joannes a Sancto Thoma, *Curs. Phil.*, t. I, pp. 281b, 282a (Reiser).

a special difficulty to which there must correspond a special and distinct habit.

3° A practical science, v.g., Moral Philosophy, is a science which deals with how a thing operates, and not with what it is. Since a practical science does not deal with what a thing is, it is not a perfect science which is concerned with quiddity and its resultant properties ; but it is an imperfect science. Therefore it is not a perfect habit, i.e., an intellectual virtue, but, as science, remains an imperfect habit.

181. Opinion and created faith. — 1° For a more perfect understanding of what a science is, we must compare it with inevident habits.

The inevident acts of the intellect are opinion, suspicion, doubt, and faith.

Opinion is assent to something on account of a probable reason and motive, with the fear of the opposite. The following is an example : *tomorrow the sun will shine, or it will not shine.* A man can assent from a probable motive to the first part : *tomorrow the sun will shine,* with fear of the opposite part : *tomorrow the sun will not shine.*

Suspicion is assent which inclines to something from some unimportant sign. It is not essentially different from opinion, but pertains to opinion as something imperfect in the same genus.

Doubt is knowledge without determinate inclination in any direction. There is no assent in doubt, but rather a suspension of judgment.

Faith is thought with assent on account of the authority of the speaker.

Three things are to be noted in this definition.

First, faith is called thought, a movement or act of reason discoursing.

In the understanding of principles, there is no thought,

i.e., discourse ; but the intellective faculty immediately sees the truth from the mere explanation of the terms.

There is discourse or thought in science ; but, on the completion of the demonstration, discourse terminates on the appearance of the conclusion, because the conclusion is proved from principles which are self-evident.

In faith, discourse does not terminate on the appearance of the truth. Therefore faith is called thought, and not *vision.*

Secondly, faith is called thought with *assent,* i.e., with *determinate judgment.* Nevertheless, this judgment is not caused by the appearance of truth, i.e., by evidence, but by the election of the will which determines the intellect to adhere to truth, because this adherence seems good to it.

Thirdly, faith is called assent on account of the authority of the speaker, that is to say, on account of the knowledge and truthfulness of the witness. Truth does not become known or seen on account of the authority of the speaker, but is made credible.

When the speaker or witness is God, we have *divine faith;* when he is a creature, we have *created faith.*

Here we are speaking of created faith.

2° There is no habit of doubt, because doubt is not assent, but the negation of assent.

Suspicion is reduced to opinion or to created faith.

Opinion and created faith imply assent. There are habits of both of them. The habit of opinion and the habit of created faith are essentially different, for the formal constituent of the act of knowledge in opinion is very different from the formal constituent of the act of knowledge in human faith.

Opinion is based on probable reasons which have a verisimilar connexion with opined truth.

Created faith is founded only on the authority of the witness.

3° Science is certain knowledge from self-evident principles.

Certitude is the determination of the intellect to one thing.

Hence science is distinct from and opposed to both opinion and created faith.

We have both vision and certitude of a thing known from science. We have vision, because the intellect reduces the conclusion to self-evident principles ; and we have certitude, because the intellect becomes fully convinced by its object, so that it is free from all fear.

We have inevidence or obscurity and incertitude or fear in the case of a thing that is opined or believed.

Hence science is opposed to opinion and created faith, as vision is opposed to non-vision, and as certitude is opposed to incertitude.

4° Our only remaining difficulty concerns truths that are either held on opinion or are believed without any fear of their being untrue. Thus a man who never saw Rome can believe without doubt or fear that Rome exists.

To solve this difficulty, we must state that there are two kinds of incertitude in opinion and in human faith :

a) incertitude of the thing held on opinion or believed ;

b) incertitude in regard to the motives that lead to probability or credibility.

The first kind of incertitude can never be removed, because the thing held on opinion or believed always remains obscure, and is never seen by the intellect.

But the second kind of incertitude can be removed, when motives make credibility or probability evident.

182. Opinion and faith are incompatible with science. — Three kinds of comparison are possible:

1° First, a comparison can be made between either the act of opinion or the act of faith and the act of science.

Conclusions :

a) It is impossible to posit an act of science and an act of faith concerning the same thing considered from the same point of view. This is so, because science deals with things that are seen, whereas faith is concerned with things that are not seen[1]. Moreover, it is impossible that a thing be seen and not seen from the same point of view.

b) It is impossible to posit an act of opinion and an act of science concerning the same thing considered from the same point of view. This is so, because opinion is assent with the fear of the opposite, whereas science is free from such fear[2]. Moreover, it is impossible that assent be given with fear and without fear to the same thing considered from the same point of view.

Nevertheless, a person, after having demonstrated a conclusion, can prove the same conclusion by means of probable or opinionative data. But in this case he does not prove the proposition from opinionative data for the purpose of forming an opinion, but rather for the purpose of obtaining a better knowledge of the probative power of the probable motives or signs of the conclusion[3].

2° Secondly, a comparison can be made between the habit of opinion or the habit of faith and the habit of science.

Conclusions :

a) The coexistence of a habit of opinion and a habit of science of the same thing considered from the same point of view is impossible[4]. This is so, because habits are inclinations to acts. But the act of opinion and the act of science are in mutual opposition to each other. Hence a habit of opinion and a habit of science are in mutual opposition to each other, i.e., they are contraries, because they tend to acts that are in opposition to each other. Therefore they cannot coexist as regards the same thing considered from the same point of view in the same subject, just as virtue and vice cannot coexist in the same subject as regards the same thing.

(1) II-II, q. 1, a. 5, ad 4.
(2) *De Ver.*, q. 14, a. 9, ad 6. — *In Post. Anal.*, L. I, l. 44. — II-II, q. 1, a. 5, ad 4.
(3) I-II, q. 67, a. 3. — III, q. 9, a. 3, ad 2.
(4) *In Post. Anal.*, L. II, l. 20.

b) *The coexistence of a habit of faith and a habit of science of the same thing considered from the same point of view is impossible.* This is so, because an act of faith and an act of science are in mutual opposition to each other.

3° Thirdly, a comparison can be made between the habit of science and the act of opinion, and also between the habit of opinion and the act of science.

Conclusions :

a) *It is possible to have a habit of science and at the same time to elicit an act of opinion in regard to the same thing.* This is so, because a habit is only an inclination to something, whereas an act is an actual tendency to something. But there is no repugnance in having at the same time an inclination to one thing and a tendency to its opposite ; v.g., a stone which has an inclination downwards can actually tend upwards by means of a violent impulse. Likewise, a person who has a habit of virtue can actually sin.

b) *It is impossible to retain a habit of opinion, if a demonstrative act is elicited concerning the object of that habit.* This is so, because a demonstrative act engenders a habit of science. But a habit of science destroys a habit of opinion.

ARTICLE II

SPECIFICATION OF SCIENCES

183. A science of the natural order cannot be at the same time practical and speculative. — 1° We are concerned here with a science which is specifically one ; v.g., Logic, Philosophy of Nature, Metaphysics, Ethics, Economics, Politics.

Philosophy is not a science that is one in species, but comprises several specifically distinct sciences.

2° A science of the natural order is a science which is acquired by the natural light of the intellect. It is distinct from a sacred science, as sacred theology. Sacred theology is both speculative and practical, for the light of faith, from which it proceeds, attains God, not only as the *first truth to be contemplated* (to which all matters of speculation are subordinate), but also as the *absolutely ultimate end* (to which all practical things are directed).

3° We are speaking of *human* science of the natural order, and are not concerned here with the science of the angels.

4° The explanation of why a human science of the natural order cannot be at the same time speculative and practical is found in the very nature of human knowledge, because it is abstractive, as is clear from the proof that follows.

5° We shall now prove that *a science of the natural order cannot be at the same time speculative and practical.*

A speculative science and a practical science attain truth in opposite ways. But a science of the natural order cannot attain truth in opposite ways. Therefore a science of the natural order cannot be at the same time speculative and practical.

Major. — A speculative science attains truth not as applicable to operation, but as regards its formal principles, and without reference to existence. Thus we say : man is *risible*, because he is a *rational animal.* A practical science attains truth as applicable to operation, and does not abstract from existence. Thus man may be considered as a person *to be cured.* But to attain truth as not applicable to operation and applicable to it, without reference to existence and with reference to it, is to attain truth in opposite ways[1]. Therefore.

Minor.— To attain truth in opposite ways is to attain it by means of distinct lights. But where there are distinct lights, there are distinct sciences. Therefore a science of the natural order cannot attain truths in opposite ways.

184. Practical sciences are specified by their end. — 1° A practical science is a science whose end in not the contemplation of truth, but operation.

2° An end is that for the sake of which something is done.

3° In science we distinguish between the material object, the formal object *quod,* and the formal object *quo.*

The *material object* is everything with which a science deals ; v.g., the material object of sight is everything with which sight is concerned.

The *formal object « quod »* is that by which the material object is rendered determinate, so that it may be attained by science, or, in other words, that which is first attained by science in its material object; v.g., a thing as colored is the formal object *quod* of sight, because a body is rendered determinate by color so that it may be seen, and a body is seen in as much as it is colored.

The *formal object « quo »* is the ultimate formality which renders the formal object *quod* determinate, so that it can be

(1) Joannes a Sancto Thoma, *Curs. Phil.*, L. I, pp. 270-271 (Reiser).

attained by science ; in other words, the ultimate formality under which a science attains things, a formality which adapts things to knowledge, i.e., renders them knowable ; v.g., light is the formal object *quo* of sight, for it is the ultimate formality under which a body is rendered visible and seen.

Hence, as the formal object *quod* determines material objects, so the formal object *quo* determines the formal object *quod*, and is that under which all the things with which a science deals are classified and from which they have their unity.

4° Practical science deals with operables, i.e., with operations and works. Operation is on account of an end, i.e., of its very nature has reference to an end.

Hence the operables with which a practical science deals constitute its material object ; these operables as directed to an end constitute its formal object *quod ;* and the end itself is the formal object *quo*, for a practical science deals with things subordinated to an end from which they have their unity.

5° Proof of thesis.

THESIS. — PRACTICAL SCIENCES ARE SPECIFIED BY THEIR END.

Sciences which have their unity from their end are specified by their end. But practical sciences have their unity from their end. Therefore practical sciences are specified by their end.

Major. — The principle from which a thing has its unity is its principle of specification.

Minor. — Because all the things that are considered by a practical science are reduced to unity in as much as they have reference to the same end.

NOTE. — Moral philosophy, which is a practical science, is divided into three specifically distinct sciences :

a) *Monastics* or Ethics, which considers human acts as related to the end of individual man.

b) *Economics*, which considers human acts as related to the end of domestic society.

c) *Politics*, which considers human acts as related to the end of civil society.

185. Speculative sciences are specified by their degree of immateriality. — 1° Speculative sciences are sciences which have truth, as it is knowable, as their end ; or, in other words, sciences whose end is the contemplation of truth.

2° Since knowledge for its own sake is the end of the speculative sciences, these sciences deal with *things* which are *determinate things*, and which are *knowable* in a determinate way. Thus, a body (a thing) can be considered by the intellect as a *quantum* (a particular knowable thing) and as a *universal* (a thing knowable in a determinate way).

Hence the material object of a speculative science is the things with which this science deals.

The formal object *quod* is that which is first attained in the material object.

The formal object *quo* is that by which the formal object *quod* is rendered knowable in a determinate way, i.e., the formality by which the formal object *quod* is rendered proportionate to the human intellect in a determinate way.

3° Since the intellect is an immaterial faculty, a thing cannot be rendered knowable in a determinate way or proportionate to the human intellect in a determinate way, unless it is rendered immaterial in a determinate way. Hence the formal object *quo* of every speculative science is the determinate immateriality of its formal object *quod*, i.e., the degree of immateriality of its formal object *quod*.

Here immateriality is used as meaning denudation of corporeal matter, i.e., of corporeity.

4° Again, since a speculative science (human) is demonstrative, its formal object *quo* is a determinate kind of immateriality, not any kind whatsoever, but such as proceeds to conclusions from principles.

5° Proof of thesis.

THESIS. — SPECULATIVE SCIENCES ARE SPECIFIED BY THEIR DEGREE OF IMMATERIALITY.

An object is knowable in such or such a way from its degree of immateriality. But speculative sciences are specified by an object as knowable in such or such a way. Therefore speculative sciences are specified by their degree of immateriality.

The *major* is clear from what has been already said.

Minor. — Every science is specified by the object to which it is essentially related. But a speculative science, whose object is knowledge itself, is essentially related to an object that is knowable in such or such a way. Therefore (1).

186. The generic degrees of immateriality are derived from the three ways of abstracting from matter. — 1° The generic degrees of immateriality are the general modes of spirituality of an object under which are contained special modes of spirituality.

2° Abstraction means the abandonment or forsaking of matter.

Abstraction may be understood *formally* and *fundamentally.*

In its formal signification, abstraction is an act by which the intellect abstracts from matter.

In its fundamental signification, abstraction is objective abstractability, in as much as there is in the object the foundation for the establishing of different kinds of immateriality.

When we speak of different ways of abstracting from matter, we are speaking primarily of different modes of objective

(1) *De Trin.*, q. 5, a. 1. — CAJETANUS, *In I*, q. 1, a. 3. — JOANNES A SANCTO THOMA, *Curs. Phil.*, t. I, pp. 818-830.

abstractability, and only as a consequence of the different modes of abstraction on the part of the intellect.

4° Again, abstraction may be *total* or *formal*.(1)

Total abstraction is that by which the *superior* abstracts from the inferior, the *common* from individuals.

Formal abstraction is that by which a *form*, a *quiddity*, abstracts from, i.e., is purified of, singular matter at least.

Total abstraction is a condition common to all sciences which deal not with singulars, but with universals. Total abstraction of itself does not render an object more immaterial and more knowable, but only more common.

The generic degrees of immateriality are derived from the different modes of formal abstraction by which an object is stripped of its matter.

5° Matter is of three kinds :

a) *singular matter*, as this flesh, these bones ;

b) *sensible matter*, as flesh and bones in general ;

c) *intelligible matter*, that is to say, quantity, not as it inheres in a sensible being, but considered in itself, as founding proportions and measures. Quantity considered in this way is called *intelligible matter*, for, though it results from matter, it is regarded as abstracted from sensible matter. Example : a mathematical number of itself is not colored, nor is it subject to motion.

---

(1) Some examples will aid in our arriving at a better understanding of the difference between total abstraction and formal abstraction.

When we say: *The African is black*, African is a concept in relation to its inferiors.

But African does not represent one quiddity abstracted from singular matter, concerning which the intellect can speculate.

Hence African is not abstracted with formal abstraction.

But if we say: *Peter is a man*, man is not only a common and superior predicate of its inferiors, but represents one *quiddity* abstracted from all singular matter, concerning which the intellect can speculate. Hence man is abstracted with total abstraction and also with formal abstraction.

If we say: Peter is a *man*; man is an *animal*, man and animal are in the same degree of formal abstraction, for man and animal are *quiddities* which abstract from all singular matter, not from sensible matter. For *man* and *animal* have not this flesh and these bones, but flesh and bones in general. Nevertheless, animal is more common according to total abstraction than man, because animal is a *genus*, and man is a *species*.

6° Hence the generic degrees of immateriality are derived from the three ways of abstracting from matter, i.e., from the three degrees of abstraction.

The first degree of abstraction is that in which an object abstracts from singular matter, but not from sensible matter ; v.g., man abstracts from this flesh and these bones, but not from flesh and bones in general.

The *second degree of abstraction* is that in which an object abstracts from both singular and sensible matter, but not from every condition of matter ; v.g., mathematical quantity.

The *third degree of abstraction* is that in which an object abstracts from all matter. Such is the case when we consider things which do not exist in matter, as God or an angel ; or when we consider things which, though sometimes existing in matter, can exist without matter, as being as being, substance, quality, the good, the true, the beautiful, etc. as such.

187. The specific degrees of immateriality are derived from the terms reached by abstraction. — 1° The specific degrees of immateriality are the special modes of spirituality of objects, each of which specifies one science.

2° Abstraction is a quasi-movement in which a term-*from-which* and a term-*to-which* are considered. Both terms are *formally* in the act of the intellect which abstracts, and *fundamentally* in the abstractable object.

3° In abstraction, the term-*from-which* is the abandonment of matter. Thus we have generic degrees of immateriality according to the three degrees of abstraction, as we have already said.

The term-*to-which* is the determinate degree of immatiality the abstracted thing acquires; v.g., the object of Logic and the object of Metaphysics are in the same generic degree of immateriality as regards the term-*from-which*, because both abstract from all matter ; but the immateriality of the object of Metaphysics and the immateriality of the object of Logic differ as regards the term-*to-which*. For the immateriality of the object of Metaphysics is the positive immateriality which is proper to real being; the immateriality of the object of Logic is the negative immateriality which appertains to being of reason, i.e., to second intention as founded in things known by the intellect.

The determinate degrees of immateriality which an abstracted thing acquires are determinate modes of knowableness, and therefore are the specific degrees of immateriality by which sciences are specified.

188. Division of speculative philosophy. — Speculative philosophy is divided into three specifically distinct sciences, namely, Philosophy of Nature, Metaphysics, and Logic.

Philosophy of Nature is specified by the immateriality of mobile being as it perfectly abstracts from singular matter, but not from sensible matter.

Metaphysics is specified by the positive immateriality of real being, as real being abstracts from all matter.

Logic is specified by the negative immateriality of second intention.

189. Modern mathematics. — The early philosophers regarded Mathematics as a science in the strict sense, that is, as a science which proceeds from certain principles to certain conclusions, and they held that its object, which is quantity in itself, is in the second degree of abstraction.

They divided Mathematics into two specifically distinct sciences, namely, Geometry and Arithmetic. For discrete quantity, as number, which is the object of Arithmetic, is more immaterial than continuous quantity, as lines and superficies, which is the object of Geometry. For the former is less dependent on place than the latter, which unites its parts in place.

But modern Mathematics is very different from ancient Mathematics.

First, modern Mathematics does not proceed from certain principles, but from *data* which are received not as true, but as verisimilar — *given one thing, another follows*. Therefore modern Mathematics is not a science in the strict sense, for, though it may correctly deduce conclusions from its *data*, it does not proceed from true and certain principles.

Secondly, modern Mathematics deals with symbols, and thus, so it seems, with a being of reason of a class all its own.

Thirdly, when modern Mathematics deals with quantity in itself, it seems to deal with an object in the second degree of abstraction.

190. Modern physics. — 1° Physics is used here not only in its strict sense, but also in a wide sense as including all experimental science, even experimental Psychology.

2° Modern Physics deals with sensible beings or bodies, not only as attained by experiment, but also in accordance with principles borrowed from Mathematics. Therefore modern Mathematics is called physico-mathematical.

3° Physics attains sensible things both by principles that are properly its own and also by principles borrowed from Mathematics.

In attaining sensible things by its own principles, Physics proceeds by means of experience and incomplete induction. From this point of view, the object of Physics does not reach the first degree of abstraction, but remains in total abstraction, because it does not perfectly abstract from singular matter[1]. Example : when we say : *all metals conduct electricity*, we do not know whether this physical property belongs to metal in virtue of its specific nature, or in virtue of singular matter only.

In attaining sensible things by principles borrowed from Mathematics, it proceeds by means of deduction, but from hypothesis. From these point of view, Physics is *hypothetico-deductive*.

(1) « Experimentalis autem cognitio non dicit abstractionem intelligibilem, qua cognoscitur res per suam quidditatem, praesertim quia apud nos experientia semper dependet ab aliquibus sensibilibus. Et sic est diversa abstractio a scientia quae procedit a priori, quantum est ex se. » JOANNES A SANCTO THOMA, *Curs. Phil.*, t. I, p. 828b (Reiser).

4° Though the object of Physics remains in total abstraction, yet it partakes of the abstraction of Mathematics(1). Therefore its immateriality is of a class all its own.

5° Modern Physics is not a science in the strict sense. For, in as much as it is *inductive*, it has only probable conclusions, and is a posteriori. As *hypothetico-deductive*, its conclusions are likewise only probable, because the principles it borrows from Mathematics are not certain.

191. Sciences of the supernatural order. — Sciences of the supernatural order are sciences which are had through participation and derivation from the light of divine science ; v.g., Sacred Theology. Hence these sciences are not specified by the immateriality which results from abstraction from matter, but from different modes of participation of divine science. Thus Sacred Theology, which considers God as virtually revealed, is one science ; infused science, which has knowledge of supernatural quiddities, is another science ; and the science of the blessed, which clearly attains God in Himself, is another science.

192. Methods of defining in sciences. — Since the objects of sciences are knowable in different ways, they are definable in different ways. In other words, each science has its own proper method of defining ; v.g., an object which contains sensible matter in its concept cannot be defined as an object which excludes this kind of matter. Thus Philosophy of Nature defines quantity in one way, and Mathematics defines it another way.

Cf. *De Trinitate*, q. 5, aa. 1, 2, 3, 4. — Joannem a Sancto Thoma, *Curs. Phil.*, t. I, pp. 818-830 (Reiser).

POINTS FOR REVIEW

1. Explain why a human science of the natural order cannot be speculative and practical at the same time.

(1) *Ibidem*, p. 827.

2. Define the following objects of a science: material object, formal object *quod*, and formal object *quo*.

3. Explain why practical sciences are specified by their end.

4. What is abstraction as regards the object?

5. Explain why speculative sciences are specified by the immateriality of their object.

6. Enumerate and define the generic degrees of immateriality or abstraction.

7. From what are the specific degrees of immateriality derived?

8. Distinguish between the immateriality of the object of Logic and the immateriality of the object of Metaphysics.

9. From what point of view is modern Physics *a*) inductive, *b*) deductive? Classify the immateriality of its object.

10. How are sciences of the supernatural order specified?

11. Why has each science its own proper method of definition?

ARTICLE III

SUBALTERNATION OF SCIENCES

193. Definition of the subalternation of sciences. – The subalternation of sciences in general is the dependance of one science upon another science.

One science can depend upon another science in virtue of its end only, as happens in some practical sciences. Thus equestrian knowledge is subject to military knowledge, and military knowledge to political science. But there is not a true subalternation of sciences in this case.

True subalternation of sciences is defined : *the dependence of an inferior science on a superior science in the manifestation of truth.* Hence there is true subalternation of sciences when an inferior science receives the principles from which it proceeds from a superior science.

194. Kinds of subalternation of science. — 1° True subalternation (or proper mode of subalternation) of sciences is divided into *relative subalternation* and *absolute subalternation.*

Relative subalternation obtains when a science, which resolves its conclusions into self-evident principles, receives principles from another science. Thus Philosophy of Nature, which has self-evident principles of its own, is subalternate to Metaphysics, because it sometimes borrows a self-evident principle from Metaphysics.

In this manner also Monastics and Economics are subalternate to Politics. Monastics and Economics are not subalternate to Politics in virtue of their end only, but also in the manifestation of truth, in as much as the common good, which is the proper end of Politics, is sometimes assumed as a principle to clarify and prove the conclusions of Monastics and Economics.

Absolute subalternation obtains in the case of a science that has no principles except those manifested by another science, that is to say, when a science has not self-evident principles of its own, but borrows them from another science.

2° Absolute subalternation of sciences is divided into *proper subalternation* and *most proper subalternation.*

Proper subalternation obtains when a science has no principles except those manifested by another science, with the result that it does not of itself resolve its conclusions into self-evident principles. This kind of subalternation is found in Sacred Theology which, in virtue of evidence and principles, is subalternate either to the science of the blessed or to Divine science. For by faith Sacred Theology believes what is clearly seen in the science of the blessed and in Divine science.

Most proper subalternation is subalternation in virtue of a subject, and obtains when the subject of an inferior science adds an accidental differentia to the subject of a superior science, with the result that the inferior science borrows principles from the superior science.

The following observations should be made in regard to this definition :

a) An essential or specific differentia and a property can be added to a subject. But in this case we have not a subalternation, but rather the same science. For the same science deals with genus and species, with essence and its properties ; v.g., Philosophy of Nature deals with motion and also with the kinds or species of motion.

b) One science can add an accidental differentia to the subject of another science, without being subalternate to it ; v.g., Medecine deals with bodies as curable, and yet is not subalternate to Philosophy of Nature, which deals with mobile being.

c) In order that there be most proper subalternation, the subject of the inferior science must add to the subject of the superior science an accidental differentia which is the principle of special truths whose manifestation or explanation depends on principles borrowed from the superior science.

It is in this way that modern Physics is subalternate to Mathematics.

The early philosophers gave as an example of most proper subalternation a conclusion considered in Medicine to which the principles of Geometry are applicable. That conclusion is as follows: *circular wounds are difficult to cure.* A physician, as such, knows this conclusion only from experience. But, to explain it, he has to make use of principles borrowed from Geometry. For a circular wound is difficult to cure, because the parts of a circular wound do not approximate each other, and therefore are not easily joined. This is so, because a circle is a figure without angles.

d) A subalternate science borrows from its subalternating science not principles of the subalternating science, but conclusions which become principles of the subalternate science.

e) Experimental knowledge, which is subalternate to a superior science in as much as it attains sensible things by its own motion, has its own proper principles, and is *inductive;* but such knowledge does not become *explanatory*, except in so far as it borrows principles from its subalternating science.

This is the reason why nowadays experimental « science » which is not physico-mathematical is called merely *descriptive*, and not *explanatory*.

f) Sacred Theology and the science of the blessed or divine science have the same subject, which is God in His inner life. They differ only as regards evidence : the principles which Sacred Theology receives on faith are clearly seen in the science of the blessed or Divine science. This is the reason why the subalternation of Sacred Theology to the science of the blessed or Divine science is called proper, and not most proper. For, as regards their subject, there is no subalternation, but rather identity.

195. Relation of subalternate science to subalternating science.—1° A subalternate science is specifically distinct from its subalternating science.

2° The question of the relation of a subalternate science to its subalternating science may be stated thus : is a subalternate science the same habit of science when it is united and when it is not united with its subalternating science ?

3° A subalternate science is connected with a subalternating science, when he who has the subalternate science has at the same time the subalternating science from which principles are provided for the subalternate science.

When he has not a subalternating science, the subalternate science is not united with a subalternating science.

4° The point of difficulty is this : a subalternate science when not united with a subalternating science only believes the principles borrowed from its subalternating science. In this case. it does not resolve its conclusions into self-evident principles, and does not seem to be a science.

5° Nevertheless, we must point out that a subalternate science is the same habit of science when it is united and when it is not united with a subalternating science ; but when it is not united, it has an imperfect state of science as regards the person possessing it.

The reason is this : a subalternate science of its very nature requires that it be united with a subalternating science. Hence, when it is not united, it is in a state of imperfection; when it is united, it is not destroyed, nor is a new habit of science engendered, but the imperfect habit is brought to its connatural perfection.

Cf. *Post Anal.*, L. I, l. 25. — JOANNEM A SANCTO THOMA, *Curs. Phil.* t. I, pp. 795-803.

POINTS FOR REVIEW

1. What is true subalternation of sciences ?

2. Distinguish between *a*) absolute and relative subalternation, *b*) proper and most proper subalternation.

3. Does subalternation obtain between the following: Monastics and Politics, Medicine and Philosophy of Nature, Theology and the science of the blessed or Divine science as regards the subject? Give reasons for your answers; and explain what you mean by subalternation as regards the subject.

4. When is a subalternate science united or not united with a subalternating science?

5. Why does a subalternate science remain the same habit of science when it is united and when it is not united with a subalternating science?

———

BOOK IV

THE ONLY CHAPTER

DIALETICS AND SOPHISTRY

Prologue. — After having studied demonstration and its effect, which is science, we shall now deal with the probable or dialectical syllogism and with sophisms. The divisions of the only chapter in this book are as follows :

Dialectics
- Notion of dialectics
- Doctrinal dialectics and applied dialectics
- Probability
- Division of dialectical argumentation
- Dialectical proposition
- Dialectical definition
- Dialectical term
- Instruments of dialectics
- Utility of dialectics for philosophy
- Modern mathematics and physics are dialectical

Sophistry
- Notion of sophistry
- Notion of sophism
- Division of sophisms
- Dictional sophisms
- Extra-dictional sophisms

ARTICLE I

DIALECTICS

196. Notion of dialectics. — Dialectics is defined: *that part of Logic which establishes a method of arguing on all problems from probable principles.*

Dialectics has something in common with demonstrative logic, and something in which it differs from it.

Dialectics, like demonstrative logic, directly deduces its conclusions from premises.

But it differs from demonstrative logic as follows : demonstrative logic deduces its conclusions from certain principles, whereas dialectics deduces its conclusions from probable principles ; demonstrative logic engenders science, whereas dialectics engenders only opinion.

197. Doctrinal dialectics and applied dialectics. — Dialectics may be *pure* or *doctrinal*, or it may be *applied.*

Doctrinal dialectics sets forth the rules by which any science can infer conclusions from probable principles. Thus, like Logic, of which it is a part, it is a science.

Applied dialectics makes use of the rules set forth by doctrinal dialectics, but reaches conclusions in the sciences it serves that are only probable.

This is another way in which dialectics differs from demonstrative Logic. For, in demonstrative Logic, it is only the doctrine that appertains to Logic; the application of rules belongs to real philosophy or to the particular sciences in which demonstration takes place. This is so, because demonstration results from the proper principles of the things with which a science deals.

But in dialectics the application of rules appertains to Logic, i.e., to dialectics, because probable argumentation does not proceed from the principles of the things with which a science deals, but from logical intentions which are extraneous to the things with which it deals.

198. Probability. — Probability is opposed to what is certain or determinate.

There are two kinds of probability : *real* probability and *logical* probability.

Real probability is found in things independently of knowledge ; v.g., the probability of an occurence which is not completely predetermined in its causes. In this sense, we may say that the proposition, *the sun will rise tomorrow*, is probable. This kind of prabability can cause certitude. For it can be certain that an event not completely predetermined in its causes is really and actually probable, even though it will never take place.

Logical probability has no foundation in things, but depends solely on an intellect which is not perfectly determined by things. In other words, it depends solely on the indetermination of the human intellect, which passes from potency to act.

Such probability keeps the intellect in the logical order, although it always tends, by means of this probability, to draw nearer to the real order, but never reaches it.

The proposition, *the human soul is probably immortal*, will serve as an example. This proposition remains in the logical order, for, in reality, the human soul is either immortal or not immortal. But, admitting the immortality of the human soul, the foregoing proposition leads the intellect in the direction of the reality, for it is truer than either of the propositions: *it is false* that the human soul is immortal ; *it is doubtful* that the human soul is immortal.

2° There are two kinds of logical probability : *direct* probability and *indirect* probability.

Direct probability affects only the manner in which the predicate is united to the subject, as in the following proposition : the human soul is *probably* immortal.

Indirect probability is probability which affects the very terms of a proposition.

This kind of probability obtains when common and indeterminate terms are used as if they were proper and determinate; v.g., the term « intelligence » in experimental Psychology ; the terms « matter » and «energy » in Physics. For, on the discovery of new theories, these terms are given new meanings.

Dialectics infers its conclusions from logical probabilities.

199. Divisions of dialectical argumentation. – Dialectical argumentation is divided into the *deductive syllogism* and *induction.*

The *dialectical syllogism* infers its conclusion from probable premises by means of a middle term.

The dialectical syllogism proceeds, i.e., infers its conclusion, in virtue of the connexion of terms. Although the conclusion of this kind of syllogism is only probable because the premises are only probable, yet it necessarily follows from the premises.

Dialectical induction does not proceed from the connexion of terms, but makes use of a sufficient enumeration of singulars instead of a middle term. Induction leads to a universal, but it does not necessarily infer a conclusion from singulars. Its conclusion always remains probable (n.105).

200. Dialectical proposition. – The dialectical proposition is the opposite of the scientific proposition.

A proposition is scientific when it is certain, that is, when it completely excludes its opposite.

A proposition is dialectical when it is probable, that is, when the affirmation it posits does not exclude its negation, and vice versa ; v.g., the proposition, *the human soul is probably immortal*, does not completely exclude the proposition, *the human soul is mortal.*

201. Dialectical definition. — Definitions are essential, descriptive, or causal.

A descriptive definition is one that explains a thing either through its proper or common accidents.

A dialectical definition is one that explains a thing through its common accidents ; v.g., man is defined : an *unfledged bipedal animal.*

202. Dialectical term. — A dialectical term is one that signifies a thing by a common accident conceived as a proper accident.

Although a dialectical term leads in the direction of the real order, it remains in the logical order ; v.g., *non-man* is a dialectical term, because it signifies a non-being and a being in a certain logical unity. A non-being is a non-man, but a tree is a non-man.

In like manner, every common term that is used as a proper term is dialectical, because it signifies things as having a certain unity, which remains logical, which they have not in nature.

By a dialectical term the intellect tends towards reality, but never attains it in its proper principles. Moreover, with dialectical terms the intellect can form propositions in regard to reality that are never certain, but which are probable.

203. Instruments of dialectics. — 1° The instruments of dialectics are instruments that are used for the forming of dialectical argumentation.

They are four in number :

a) *the choice and statement of probable propositions.*
b) *the distinction of the divers significations of a term.*
c) *the investigation of similarities or resemblances ;*
d) *the investigation of dissimilarities or differences.*

The last three instruments are subservient to the first,

that is to say, to the choice and statement of probable propositions.

2° *The distinction of the divers signification of a term.* Since the dialectician knows neither the essence nor the properties of things, he must choose the common term that seems to him best suited to designate their essence and properties.

3° *The investigation of similarities and differences.* The discovery of similarities provides an opportunity of arguing from similarity, and the discovery of differences, of arguing from contrariety : contraries have different natures.

204. Utility of dialectics for philosophy.—1° Probable arguments, whether for the affirmative side or for the negative side, are instruments which make us better able to discover the truth and to detect errors.

2° Probable arguments are helpful especially in explaining the first principles of a science. For first principles cannot be explained from the properties of a science, for not only are they the first principles of the science in question, but they explain all the other principles of that science ; but they can be explained by probable opinions.

205. Modern Physics and Mathematics are dialectical.—This is evident from what has been already said. For modern Mathematics proceeds from data which are accepted not as true, but as verisimilar.

Modern physics is *inductive* and *hypothectico-deductive.*

Hence modern Mathematics and Physics approach more and more closely to reality, but never fully reach it.

ARTICLE II

SOPHISTRY

206. Notion of sophistry. — Sophistry is that part of Logic whose object is the apparent syllogism or sophism.

Sophistry, like dialectics, is divided into *pure* or *doctrinal sophistry* and *applied sophistry.*

Doctrinal sophistry shows how to construct a sophism and how to refute it. Doctrinal sophistry is a true science.

Applied sophistry seems to reach conclusions from probable premises, but in reality does not do so. Like applied dialectics, applied sophistry can argue on all problems, but is not a true science.

207. Notion of sophism. — A sophism, in general, is an apparent syllogism which seems to infer a conclusion from probable premises, but in reality does not do so.

An apparent syllogism which proceeds from probable premises may be invalid either as regards its *matter*, in as much as its premises seem to be probable, but in reality are not; or as regards its *form*, in as much as it seems to infer a conclusion in virtue of the disposition of its terms and propositions, but in reality does not do so.

An apparent syllogism that is invalid as regards its matter is a true syllogism which proceeds from premises which are only apparently suited to the question under consideration.

Its refutation appertains to the science which deals with this question.

An apparent syllogism which is invalid as regards its form is a sophism. It is with this kind of syllogism that Logic deals.

Therefore a sophism may be defined : *a syllogism which seems to infer a conclusion from probable premises, but in reality does not do so, because it is invalid as regards its form.*

The sophism is the argumentation of one who is not wise, but who wishes to be considered as wise. Therefore sophistry is a source of intentional deception.

208. Division of sophisms. — Sophisms are *dictional* or *in language*, and *extra-dictional* or *in matter*, according as they infer a false conclusion either from the abuse of terms, or from sources other than this abuse.

According to Aristotle, there are six kinds of dictional sophism, and seven kinds of extra-dictional sophism.

209. Dictional sophisms. – Dictional sophisms are divided into the following kinds: sophisms of *equivocation*, *amphibology*, *composition*, *division*, *accent*, and *figure of speech.*

1° Sophism of *equivocation* is the deception that arises from the ambiguity of a term ; v.g., *the dog barks ; but the Dog is a star ; therefore a star barks.*

2° Sophism of *amphibology* is the deception that arises from the ambiguity of a discourse ; v.g., *this is Aristotle's book ; but what is Aristotle's belongs to Aristotle ; therefore this book belongs to Aristotle.*

3° Sophism of *composition* or *composite meaning* is the deception arising from the understanding as true in a composite sense a proposition that is true only in a divided sense ; v.g., *the blind see, said Christ ; but Paul is blind ; therefore Paul sees.* — The word *blind* signifies a subject capable of seeing and the privation of sight. The proposition, *the blind see*, is true if understood of the subject only, i.e., of the subject in a divided sense, not in a composite sense : of the subject which had been blind, not of the subject with the actual privation of sight.

4° Sophism of *division* or *divided sense* is the deception arising from the understanding as true in a divided sense a proposition that is true only in a composite sense ; v.g., *a man in good health cannot be sick ; but Peter is in good health; therefore Peter cannot be sick. A man-in-good-health* signifies a subject and good health. The proposition, *a man in good health cannot be sick,* is true if it is understood in a composite sense : a man in good health is not sick, when he is in good health ; but it is false if understood of the subject only, i.e., in a divided sense : a subject which is in good health can become sick. Compositions and divisions are solved by making a distinction between their composite sense and their divided sense.

5° Sophism of *accent* (sophism possible especially in Latin and Greek) is the deception arising in the case in which a word has different meaning according as a different syllable is accented ; v.g., *occídit* and *óccidit, lepóres* and *lépores.* The following sophism is an example of sophism of accent : v.g., *qui lépores quærit, canibus indiget ; atqui oratores lepóres quærunt ; ergo oratores canibus indigent.*

6° Sophism of *figure of speech* is the deception arising from the use of similar words with different meanings, as if they had one and the same meaning ; v.g., *you ate whatever you bought ; but you bought raw meat ; therefore you ate raw meat.*

210. Extra-dictional sophisms. — Extra-dictional sophisms are divided into : sophisms of *accident, confusion of absolute and qualified statement, refutation of the wrong point, begging the question, consequent, false cause,* and *many questions.*

1° Sophism of *accident* is the deception arising from the use of an accidental predicate as an essential predicate ; v.g., *man runs ; but Socrates is a man ; therefore Socrates runs.*

2° Sophism of *confusion of absolute and qualified statement* is the deception arising from the assumption that what is true in a particular case is absolutely true ; v.g., *arms should be restored to their owner ; but enraged Charles is the owner of these arms ; therefore arms ought to be restored to enraged Charles.*

3° Sophism of *refutation of the wrong point* is the deception arising from a person's thinking, that he is leading his adversary into a contradiction when he is not doing so, because he is arguing beside the point, i.e., becauses he does not know how the refutation should be made ; v.g., *a human soul has never been found in performing surgical operations on cadavers ; therefore it does not exist.*

4° Sophism of *begging the question* is the deception arising from presupposing in the antecedent the conclusion which has to be demonstrated by means of that same antecedent. In this case the conclusion begs the premises, and a vicious circle results ; v.g., *air is heavy ; therefore it has weight.*

5° Sophism of *consequent* is the deception arising from assuming that the antecedent and consequent are convertible, when they are not convertible ; v.g., *a man who is running is moving ; but Peter is moving ; therefore Peter is running.*

6° Sophism of *false cause* is the deception arising from assuming something as the cause of an effect which in reality is not its cause. What is assumed as a cause may be : *a*) something prior in time (after this, therefore on account of this) ; *b*) something contemporaneous (with this, therefore on account of this) ; *c*) an occasion ; *d*) a condition ; *e*) an empty name ; v.g., *there is no thought without the brain ; therefore the brain is the cause of thought.*

7° Sophism of *many questions* is the deception arising from asking several questions as a single question, so that a single answer involves error ; v.g., *are virtue and vice to be avoided or not ?* A single answer to this question involves error.

PHILOSOPHY OF NATURE

GENERAL INTRODUCTION

211. Origin of Philosophy of Nature. — Philosophy of Nature, or Natural Philosophy, had its beginning when the first philosophers began to inquire into the generation and corruption of things, and, in general, into motion which is perceived by the senses. Since the intrinsic principle of motion and rest is called nature, these philosophers were called *natural* philosophers, for they inquired into things that have a nature, i.e., into things that are mobile. Because things which exist are called beings, we may say that natural philosophers deal with mobile beings, i.e., natural beings.

212. Object of Philosophy of Nature. — In view of what has been said earlier, we are now able to determine the object of Philosophy of Nature. The object of any science, as we know from Logic, is threefold, namely, *material object*, *formal object « quod »*, and *formal object « quo »*.

1) The material object of Philosophy of Nature is all natural bodies that are sensible, i.e., subject to motion. Hence Philosophy of Nature is distinct from Mathematics, which deals with mathematical bodies, i.e., abstract quantities; and from Metaphysics, the object of which abstracts from all matter.

2) The formal object *quod* of Philosophy of Nature is mobile being, i.e., natural being.

There are several things of which we must take note.

a) Mobile being, as we understand it here, is being endowed with motion properly so-called, i.e., sensible and successive motion, or physical motion, v.g., the motion of the sun, the motion of a man walking.

Motion, in general, is the transition from potency to act. There are two kinds of motion: physical and metaphysical.

Physical motion is a transition from potency to act with succession and continuity, as the motion found in quantity.

Metaphysical motion is a simple transition from potency to act, without succession or continuity in the transition. This kind of motion is found in immaterial substances; v.g., in an angel. Philosophy of Nature deals with mobile beings endowed with physical motion, not with beings endowed with metaphysical motion.

b) Mobile being, as the object of Philosophy of Nature, does not signify something composed of being and mobility (being + mobility), but rather being as it is the foundation or source of mobility. In other words, a mobile being is a quiddity which is the first source, i.e., first principle, of mobility. Quiddity may be substantial or accidental. Since accident is radicated in substance, mobile being is used here to designate substance, not as formally distinct from accidents, but as the first source of both substantial mobility, — v.g., when a man dies,— and of accidental mobility, — v. g., when a man walks.

c) Although a mobile being is a body, the formal object *quod* of Philosophy of nature is not a body, but mobile being. For body and mobile being have not the same formal constituent.

Body is formally the root of quantity, and hence is defined in relation to divisibility.

Mobile being is formally the root of change which takes place with succession and continuity. Thus mobile being requires divisibility as a condition, but is not formally defined in relation to it. Therefore motion is the proper passion of mobile being, but not of bodies.

In reality every mobile being is a body. But if by impossible hypothesis some mobile being were not a body, such a mobile being would be, nevertheless, the object of Philosophy of Nature.

A similar case is found as regards the object of sight.

The material object of sight is a body, and the formal object *quod* is a colored object. If by impossible hypothesis a colored object were not a body, such a colored object would be, nevertheless, the object of sight.

d) The formal object *quod* of Philosophy of Nature is not nature, but natural or mobile being.

Nature, in Philosophy of Nature, signifies an essence which is the principle of successive and continuous motion, not any essence of any being.

Philosophy of Nature deals with things or quiddities which have such a principle of motion in themselves, i.e., a nature. Hence the formal object *quod* of Philosophy of Nature is not nature itself, but being endowed with a nature, that is to say, natural or mobile being.

Since all physical motion is in space and time, the formal object *quod* of Philosophy of Nature may be said to be spatio-temporal being.

3) The formal object *quo* of Philosophy of Nature is that immateriality which results from abstraction from all singular matter, but not from sensible matter. For mobile being, as it is considered by Philosophy of Nature, abstracts from singular matter, not from sensible matter ; v.g., man is a mobile being, and includes in his concept flesh and bones in general. but not this flesh and these bones.

213. Modern Physics is distinct from Philosophy of Nature. — Physics is used here not in the strict sense, but in a wide sense as signifying all experimental sciences, including Experimental Psychology.

1° Physics thus understood is distinguished from Philosophy of Nature *in virtue of its object.*

The formal object *quod* of Physics, as it is subalternate to Mathematics, is measurable being ; v.g., Physics deals with heat as measured by the thermometer.

The formal object *quo* of Physics is an inferior kind of immateriality which is proper to a thing as measurable or measured.

Such a thing, as we have already said (n.190), does not attain the first degree of abstraction, but remains in total abstraction. Nevertheless, in as much as it is measured, it partakes to some extent of the immateriality which is proper to Mathematics.

2° Again, **Physics is distinguished from Philosophy of Nature *in virtue of its method* of dealing with things.**

Philosophy of Nature immediately abstracts its object, which is mobile being, from experience, and later studies it in regard to its *proper principles*. Hence Philosophy of Nature is *demonstrative*, and is a science in the strict sense of the term.

Physics attains its object, which is constituted by nature, only by means of art. For the application of a measure to measurable being, — and it is in this that scientific experiment consists,— is a work of art. Moreover, the instruments which a physicist uses are instruments of art.

Physics makes scientific experiments, and, in the light of its findings, establishes laws and theories. Moreover, the laws of Physics express algebraic relations between different variable measures, as, for example, the following law : *when the temperature remains the same, the volume of a given mass of gas varies inversely as its pressure* (1).

Theories explain laws not by causes, but by measures which are regarded as ultimate and irreducible to other measures.

Hence **Physics, from the point of view of its method of dealing with things, is not *demonstrative*, but *inductive*, in as much as it proceeds from experiments ; and is *hypothetico-deductive*, in as much as it is subalternate to Mathematics.**

Therefore all laws and theories of Physics are *physico-mathematical*.

214. Atomism and Dynamism. — 1° Atomism is a theory which teaches that the first principles of bodies are atoms,

(1) This principle is known as Boyle's Law, and is applicable to all gases. If the volumes of a same mass of gas are expressed by the symbols V and V_1 and the pressures by the symbols P and P_1, the law may be expressed algebraically thus:

$$\frac{V_1}{P_2} = \frac{P_2}{P_1} \text{ or } P_1 V_1 = P_2 V_2$$

which are described as minute, extended, indivisible, or at least undivided, substantially immutable corporeal particles.

There are two kinds of Atomism : pure and dynamic.

Pure Atomism teaches that all atoms have the same specific nature, and that they have no intrinsic activity.

Dynamic Atomism teaches that atoms are endowed with forces.

2° Dynamism is a theory which teaches that the first principles of bodies are unextended forces only. Further, according to some, a body, i.e., matter, is energy.

3° Modern Scholastics reject these systems for two reasons : *first*, because Atomism (especially pure Atomism) teaches that all changes may be explained solely by local motion, and that matter is *homogeneous*, i.e., that all bodies are of the same species ; *secondly*, because, according to Dynamism, forces exist without a subject, that is to say, accidents exist without substance ; and because unextended forces cannot be the constituents of an extended body.

4° *Judgment on Atomism and Dynamism.* — *a*) Atomism and Dynamism are theories which explain the metric structure of bodies, but not the first principles of which mobile being as such is constituted. Hence Atomism and Dynamism belong to the realm of Physics, not to Philosophy of Nature. Nevertheless, there are many who hold that they are philosophical systems.

b) Each science has its own proper method of definition. Therefore the terms used by physicists must not be accepted in their philosophical signification.

Hence Atomism can explain all phenomena or changes solely by local motion, because it can consider all things in relation to local motion in as much as It is measurable. It is a fact that local motion enters into all changes that take place in the world, even into qualitative changes.

The object of Physics is measurable being. From this

point of view, matter may be called *homogeneous*. Example : a stone and a man are measured in the same way.

Forces are not conceived by physicists as accidents, but as the ultimate metrical elements into which matter can be resolved. Hence the distinction between substance and accidents is not destroyed by Dynamism. Physicists do not arrive at this distinction.

Finally, the existence of unextended forces, in the sense proposed by Dynamism, is a mere theory useful in explaining the metrical structure of bodies. And unextended forces are perhaps nothing more than forces that cannot be measured.

215. Relation between Physics and Philosophy of Nature. — 1° Physics and Philosophy of Nature are entirely distinct. Physics is not subalternate to Philosophy of Nature, because it does not borrow its principles from it, but has its own proper principles.

2° Philosophy of Nature does not require either Physics or scientific experiments for the statement of its principles or for the development of its demonstrations. For, given motion, whose existence is known with certainty from daily experience, it establishes the first principles of mobile being by means of a posteriori demonstration. From these principles it deduces, by means of demonstration by proper cause, all the properties of mobile being.

3° Nevertheless, since Philosophy of Nature is a science, it must exercise the function of *wisdom* in relation to Physics, in as much as it must reflect on the principles, method, and theories of experimental science, so that it may pass judgment on them and make use of them.

Thus is constituted Philosophy of sciences, which is a part of Philosophy of Nature.

When Philosophy of Nature exercises its function of wisdom, it compares its conclusions with the affirmations of experimental science, in order that it may explain both more fully. But such an explanation remains valid for a time only, because all scientific theories are subject to change. Hence, from this point of view, Philosophy of Nature is only materially, i.e., as regards its matter, not formally, i.e., as regards its principles, dependent on experimental science. **Therefore a strictly philosophical conclusion must not be rejected because it is at variance with some scientific theory.**

4° Philosophy of Nature and Physics, though distinct as regards their formal object, have the same material object, namely, bodies. Hence neither Philosophy of Nature alone, nor Physics alone, is sufficient to give us a complete knowledge of bodies, in as far as this is possible ; both are required.

216. Division of Philosophy of Nature. — Philosophy of Nature is a science that is specifically one. It is divided into two parts by Aristotle : *general* Philosophy of Nature and *special* Philosophy of Nature.

General Philosophy of Nature deals with spatio-temporal being in general, i.e., mobile being as such. Aristotle presents this part in the eight books of his *Physica Auscultatio.*

Special Philosophy of Nature has three divisions, according to the three different kinds of motion, viz., local motion, motion of generation and corruption, and motion of augmentation which is proper to living beings.

Aristotle treats the first part in his books *De Coelo* and *De Mundo ;* the second part, in his books *De Generatione et Corruptione ;* and the third part, in his books *De anima.*

Later Philosophers divide Philosophy of Nature into General Philosophy of Nature and Special Philosophy of Nature.

In General Philosophy of Nature, which they call Cosmology, they deal with mobile being in general, and also with local motion and motion of generation and corruption. In Special Philosophy of Nature, which they call Psychology, they deal with being endowed with vital motion.

We have adopted this modern division, for it is more suitable for our purpose.

POINTS FOR REVIEW

1. Define physical motion, and show how it is distinguished from metaphysical motion.

2. Distinguish between body and mobile being. Is there any difference between mobile being and natural being?

3. Is nature the formal object *quod* of Philosophy of Nature? What is the formal object *quod* of Physics?

4. May matter be called homogeneous in Physics?

5. Explain whether or not Physics is subalternate to Philosophy of Nature. Is it an introduction to Philosophy of Nature?

GENERAL PHILOSOPHY OF NATURE

Prologue. – In general Philosophy of Nature, we shall deal, first, with mobile being, secondly, with its properties, and thirdly, with its generation. Hence there will be three books in general Philosophy of Nature.

Book I: Mobile being.

Book II: Properties of mobile being.

Book III: Generation of mobile being.

BOOK I

Mobile being

Prologue. — First, we shall consider the principles of mobile being. And since mobile being is natural being, i.e., being which has a nature, secondly, we shall deal with nature.

Therefore there will be two chapters in this book.

CHAPTER I

PRINCIPLES OF MOBILE BEING

Prologue.— In this chapter, we shall first consider physical principles in general. Secondly, we shall demonstrate that first matter and substantial form are the constituent principles of mobile being. Thirdly, we shall discuss first matter; fourthly, substantial form; fifthly, substantial composition. Therefore there will be five articles in this chapter.

Principles in general
- Notion and division of principle
- Number of physical principles
- Contrariety of physical principles
- Definition of physical principles

Constituent principles of mobile being
- Statement of the question
- Thesis: The essential constituents of mobile being are first matter and substantial form
- First matter and substantial form do not exist of themselves

First matter
- Negative definition of first matter
- Positive definition of first matter
- First matter is pure potency
- Answer to an objection
- It is absolutely repugnant that first matter exist without form
- The potency of first matter is purely passive
- First matter has an innate appetite for form
- First matter has an appetite for all forms, but in different ways
- Appetite of first matter for the human soul
- First matter cannot be engendered and corrupt negatively
- First matter had its beginning through creation
- Unity of first matter
- First matter of itself is absolutely unintelligible

Substantial form	**Notion and division of form in its widest meaning** **Definition of substantial form** **Substantial form is the principle of specification, the principle of being, and the first principle of operation** **Substantial form is material or immaterial** **In the engendering of compounds, material forms are not produced by infusion into matter, but by eduction from matter** **Unity of substantial form in mobile being** **Substantial forms are like numbers** **Permanence of the elements in a compound**
Substantial compound	**Matter and form are the essential parts of a natural compound** **Matter and form are immediately united to each other** **A natural compound is not something distinct from its united parts** **The intelligibility of the essence of mobile being is proportionate to the perfection of its substantial form**

ARTICLE I

PRINCIPLES IN GENERAL

217. Notion and division of principle. — 1° A principle is *that from which a thing in any way proceeds.*

2° A thing can proceed from another either as regards knowledge or as regards reality. Hence we have the principle of knowledge and the principle of reality.

3° The principle of a thing may be extrinsic, as an efficient cause ; or it may be intrinsic.

Intrinsic principles are of two kinds, viz., metaphysical and physical, i.e., natural.

Metaphysical principles are principles which are common to every genus of being, that is to say, principles which are the constituents of every kind of finite being, namely, potency and act.

Physical or natural principles are principles from which mobile being is first made or constituted. By mobile being we understand any being that is subject to sensible and corporeal motion.

218. Number of physical principles. — 1° The earliest philosophers taught that all things were made from a single material principle. This principle, they claimed, was either fire, or air, or water, or some mean between them.

Empedocles contended that there were four physical principles : fire, air, water, and earth.

Anaxagoras maintained that there were an infinite number of physical principles.

2° In reality, there are only three physical or natural principles. This is clear from the very notion of motion, i.e., of becoming. For, that anything be made, three things are required and sufficient : *a*) a *subject* in which a new *determination* or *actuality* takes place ; *b*) a *term* which is this determination, i.e., a *form; c*) *a privation* of this determination, i.e., a *privation* of the form in the subject. Example : the production of a wooden statue requires: wood, which is the *subject*, in which there is the *privation* of the figure of the statue, and the production of the figure of the statue, i.e., the production of the *form* in the wood. Hence there are three physical or natural principles : *subject, form*, and *privation*.

219. Contrariety of physical principles. — 1° All the philosophers of antiquity recognized some contrariety among natural principles. Those who claimed that there was only one material principle recognized tenuity and density as constituting its contrariety, for these seemed necessary in order that other things be made from this single material principle. Others held that contrariety derived from emptiness and fulness, strife and friendship, etc. These philosophers recognized a certain contrariety of principles, because forced to do so by the evidence of truth. For physical principles are the principles of mutable things as mutable. And every mutation requires contrariety between the term-from-which and the term-to-which, as is clear from proof.

2° But physical principles may be considered in two states :

a) as principles of a thing in its state of *becoming*, i.e., as principles of the generation of a thing ;

b) as principles of a thing in its state of *actual existence*, or as principles of the composition of a thing, i.e., as the component parts of a thing.

Physical principles, as the principles of the generation of a thing, are three in number : *subject, form* and *privation*.

Physical principles, as the principles of the composition of a thing, are two in number : *subject* and *form*. Although a thing is made from a subject in which there is the *privation* of the form of the thing to be made, *privation* does not constitute the thing as made.

3° Some of the philosophers of old affirmed that the physical principles of a thing are in opposition not only as the principles of generation, but also as the component parts of a thing.

Marx, Engels, and their followers, who teach *dialectical materialism*, maintain that there is opposition in the very essence of things, and hence that all the progress and evolution of things depend on the conflict between the principles of nature.

Hence, according to them, physical principles, as the intrinsic component parts of a thing, are opposite, and indeed contradictory.

4° According to Aristotle, physical principles are contrary in as much as they are the principles of a thing in its state of becoming or generation, not in as much as they are principles of a thing in the state of actual existence.

The contrariety that obtains between physical principles is not contrariety in the strict sense, but rather privative opposition.

5° The foregoing remarks have prepared us for the proof of the propositions that follow.

a) Physical principles, as the component parts of a thing, are not contraries.—Things which are united to each other are not contraries. But physical principles, as the component parts of a thing, are united to each other. Therefore physical principles, as the component parts of a thing, are not contraries.

Major. — Contraries exclude one another. But things which are united to one another do not exclude one another. Therefore . . .

The *minor* is clear.

b) Physical principles, as the principles of a thing in its state of becoming, are contraries. — Things which exclude one another in a subject are contraries. But physical principles, as the principles of a thing in its state of becoming, exclude one another in a subject. Therefore physical principles, as the principles of a thing in its state of becoming, or as principles of generation, are contraries.

The *major* is clear.

Minor. — In the state of becoming or generation, form is produced as the term-to-which, and the *privation* of form is lost as the term-from-which. Hence *form* and *privation* exclude one another in the same subject.

Therefore we should note that contrariety obtains between *form* and its *privation*. A *subject* of itself is not in contrary opposition to its *form*; it is such only in as much as it is a subject in which there is *privation* of form.

220. Definition of physical principles. — Physical principles, as we understand them here, are principles from which a mobile being is *first* made or constituted.

Hence they are *first* principles, and as such are distinguished from all secondary principles.

Aristotle gives the following definition of physical first principles : *things which are not made from others, nor from one another, but from which all things are made* (1).

a) First principles are not made *from other things*, because otherwise they would not be *first* principles, but would be the results or products of principles.

b) First principles are not made *from one another*, because principles are not only *first*, but contrary first. And contrary principles do not mutually aid one another, but exclude one another.

There are two ways in which we may understand that first principles are not made from one another:

1) one is not composed of another ;

(1) *Phys.*, l. I, c. 5 (188 a 27).

2) one is not made from another, another being understood formally and in the abstract, as term-from-which. But this must be understood formally and in the abstract, and not as regards subject, i.e., materially. Thus whiteness is not made from blackness, nor is cold made from heat. But a black object may become white, and a hot object may become cold. Similarly, form is not formally made from privation ; but a form is educed from a subject of *privation*, and thus privation is only accidentally or materially the term from which form is produced.

c) All things are made from *first principles*, that is to say, all mobile beings are constituted or are engendered from them.

POINTS FOR REVIEW

1. What in general do you understand by a physical or natural principle ?
2. Define physical first principles.
3. Briefly explain when physical principles may be said to be in contrary opposition to one another.
4. What kind of contrariety obtains between first principles ?

ARTICLE II

CONSTITUENT PRINCIPLES OF MOBILE BEING

221. Statement of the question. — 1° We have already considered physical principles in general. We must now consider these principles in particular, as constituting the essence of mobile being.

We are here confronted with the problem of the constituent principles of mobile being, a problem arising chiefly from the difficulty of reconciling being as stable and determinate with motion by which a being becomes another being, i.e,, of reconciling the state of existence with the state of becoming. For being, as *stable* and *mutable*, seems to include opposition in its very motion : mutability is opposed to stability.

The early philosophers proposed this difficulty as follows : *being is not made from being, because it is already being, as*, v.g., *from a statue actually existing is not made the same statue. On the other hand, nothing is made from nothing.*

Influenced by this argument, some philosophers, as Heraclitus, denied the existence of determinate and stable being. They held that motion is the only reality, and hence that all reality is a flowing or flux which is continually evolving. In recent times, this same opinion was proposed by Bergson.

Others, as Parmenides, for the same reason, denied all change, and taught that being is one and immutable.

Aristotle solved the difficulty by making a distinction between the principles of mobile being, i.e., between subject and form. He taught that every mobile being has two essential constituent principles : a material or potential subject, which he calls *first matter*, and perfection or act, i.e., *substantial form.*

His teaching is called *hylomorphism* (ὕλη, matter; μορφή, form).

2° *Essence* is that by which a thing is what it is, or that by which a thing is constituted in a determinate species. Since a thing can be constituted in a determinate species as a substance or as an accident, essence may be substantial or accidental. Here we are concerned with substantial essence, i. e., with the substance of mobile being. For mobile being is the formal object *quod* of Philosophy of Nature, as regards its substance, in as much as this substance is the first source of both substantial and accidental mobility, as we have already said.

3° *First matter* is the first substantial subject from which every mobile being is made or is. This subject is called *first matter*, to distinguish it from mobile being already constituted, which we call *second matter*; v.g., wood from which a statue is made is called second matter.

4° *Substantial form* is perfection, determination, or act by which mobile being is essentially constituted. This kind of act is called *substantial*, to distinguish it from *accidental* form, which is required by a being which is already constituted in its first existence; v.g., operation, which is added or supervenient to a being that is already constituted, is an accidental form.

Substantial form is defined: *the first act of first matter.* As opposed to form, first matter is called *potency* or potentiality.

5° First matter and substantial form are principles which are united as the constituent or component parts of mobile being. But yet they are principles which are really distinct from each other.

The principles of the generation of mobile being are *first matter*, *substantial form*, and *privation*.

222. Statement of the thesis.

THESIS. — THE ESSENTIAL CONSTITUENTS OF MO-

BILE BEING ARE FIRST MATTER AND SUBSTANTIAL FORM.

1° Everything that changes is composed of a subject, which is in potency to act, and act. But the essence of mobile being really changes. Therefore mobile being is essentially composed of a subject or potency, which is called *first matter*, and act, which is called *substantial form* (1), i.e., the essential constituents of mobile being are first matter and substantial form.

Major. — Everything which changes acquires or loses some perfection or act. But everything which acquires or loses act is composed of that act, and of a subject which can be made determinate by that act, i.e., potency. Therefore everything which changes is composed of a subject, i.e., potency, and act.

Minor. — Really distinct and opposite properties derive from distinct essences, for essence is the source of properties. But sometimes the properties of mobile being, before and after change, are really distinct and opposite ; v.g., when a living being becomes a non-living being, or when a non-living being, by means of assimilation, becomes a living being, i.e., a part of a living being. Therefore, in such cases, the essence of mobile being really changes.

2° Substantial being which is multiplied *numerically* in the *same species* is essentially composed of first matter and substantial form. But mobile being is substantial being, and is multiplied *numerically* in the *same species*. Therefore mobile being is essentially composed of first matter and substantial form.

Major. — Substantial being is multiplied numerically in the same species in as much as the act by which its essence is determined is multiplied either in itself or by reception into a subject. But act cannot be multiplied in itself: if it could, act in itself would not be the same in this individual and that,

(1) Creatura vero corporalis est quoad ipsam essentiam composita potentia et actu; quae potentia et actus ordinis essentiae, materiae et formae nominibus designantur. — *Thesis VIII* s. Thomae.

and thus it would constitute distinct essences. Therefore it follows that substantial being is multiplied numerically in the same species only in as much as the act by which its essence is determined is received into a substantial subject, which together with act constitutes the essence of substantial being. In other words, substantial being which is multiplied in the same species is composed of first matter and substantial form.

The truth of the *major* may be seen also from an example of an artificial thing. The figure by which a statue of Mercury is constituted is not multiplied in itself, but rather receives its multiplication from reception into different subjects, v.g., into this piece of wood and into that piece. In like manner, the act by which the essence of a mobile being is constituted is multiplied only be reception into a subject.

The *minor* is evident. Peter, Paul, John, etc. are mobile beings which are multiplied numerically in the same species.

223. First matter and substantial form do not exist of themselves. — 1° Existence is defined: *the act or formality that constitutes a thing outside of all causes and outside of nothing.* For, *first*, what exists only in its cause does not yet exist; v.g., a statue, as it exists in the power of the statuary, does not yet exist ; *secondly*, what exists has existence in reality and is outside of nothing.

2° A thing exists of itself when it has its own proper existence. Thus all complete substances, as Peter, Paul, have their own proper existence.

Although all accidents exist in another as subject, and although the proper existence of an accident is a *secondary* existence of the subject in which it exists, nevertheless, all accidents have their own proper existence. Example.: when we say : *Peter is white*, we speak of two entities : a substance or subject, which is Peter, and an accident, which is whiteness. Whiteness has existence in Peter, but the existence of whiteness is not the existence of Peter, for Peter can continue in his existence even when he loses his whiteness, as would happen if Peter became black. Nevertheless, the existence of whiteness is a secondary existence of Peter, for Peter, by means of whiteness, exists *as white*.

3° We say that first matter and substantial form do not exist of themselves, because neither of them has its own proper existence. But first matter and substantial form exist by the existence of the whole which results from them, i.e., by the existence of the mobile being. In other words, although first matter and substantial form belong to the genus of substance, neither the one nor the other may be said to be *that which* exists.

First matter exists only as the subject *by which* that *which is*, i.e., mobile being, is constituted. In like manner, substantial form exists only as the perfection or act *by which* is constituted mobile being *which* exists by its own proper existence.

Briefly, first matter and substantial form exist only as the principles *by which* mobile being is constituted ; mobile being is that *which* exists, i.e., *which* has existence of itself.

4° Since first matter and substantial form have not their own proper existence, they are not complete quiddities, i.e., complete beings, but only the principles of a complete being. Therefore they do not belong directly to the predicament of substance, but come under that category by reduction, as substantial principles (1).

5° We shall now prove that *first matter and substantial form do not exist of themselves*.

1) The first principles of mobile being do not exist of themselves. But first matter and substantial form are the first principles of mobile being. Therefore first matter and substantial from do not exist of themselves.

Major. — Things which have their own proper existence are not the first principles of being, but are beings, for being is denominated from existence. In other words, the first principles of mobile being do not exist of themselves.

The *minor* is evident.

---

(1) Earum partium neutra per se esse habet, nec ponitur in praedicamento nisi reductive ut principium substantiale. — *Thesis IX* s. Thomae.

2) Existence is proper to what is made and engendered. But what is properly made and engendered is a compound. Therefore existence properly belongs to a compound, and hence first matter and substantial form exist only by the existence of a compound [1].

Major. — The proper termination of becoming and generation is existence. Hence existence corresponds to generation.

Minor. — What is made and engendered is the compound itself ; v.g., man, i.e., the complete substance of man, is engendered. First matter and substantial form are only the principles by which that which is engendered is constituted.

POINTS FOR REVIEW

1. Name and define the principles of the generation of mobile being.

2. Define essence.

3. Are the constituent principles of mobile being substantial? Explain.

4. Prove that the essence of mobile being really changes.

5. Define existence, and explain what is meant by saying that a thing exists of itself.

6. Have first matter and substantial form their own proper existence? Explain how they exist.

7. Describe briefly how first matter and substantial form may be placed in the predicament or category of substance.

(1) I, q. 45, a. 4 and a. 8; q. 65, a. 4; q. 75, a. 1; and q. 90, a. 2.

ARTICLE III

FIRST MATTER

224. Negative definition of first matter. — Since first matter is an incomplete being, it has no proper genus nor a proper differentia. Therefore it cannot be properly defined[1]. Nevertheless, both a positive and a negative improper definition of it are possible.

Aristotle gives the following *negative* description of first matter : « First matter is not a particular thing, nor the quality of a thing, nor its quantity, nor is it assigned to any of the other categories which render being determinate »[2].

The meaning of this description is as follows : first matter has not of itself a determinate essence in the genus of substance, in the genus of quantity, or in any other genus.

225. Positive definition of first matter. — Aristotle gives the following positive definition of first matter : « The first subject of which a thing is made, and not in an accidental manner.»

Subject : thus is excluded a form which is not a subject; it is a determination which is added to a subject.

First : thus is excluded a subject of accidental and artificial form, which is not a first subject, but is a compound substance that supports accidents, which is made from a prior subject, and thus is not first matter, but rather second matter.

Of which a thing is made : thus other causes are excluded ; for the efficient cause is that by which a thing is made ; the end is that on account of which a thing is made ; the exem-

(1) *De Ente et Essentia*, c. 2.
(2) *Metaph.*, L. VII, c. 3 (1029 a 20).

plar cause is that to whose likeness a thing is made ; the form is that through which a thing has existence. Matter alone is that *from which* a thing is made.

Not in an accidental manner : thus is excluded privation, i.e., the term-from-which, for privation does not enter into the composition of a thing as a constituent part, as matter does ; a thing is constituted from privation only in the sense that privation is that from which the production of the thing begins — what is left behind. And thus privation is accidental in relation to the thing as existing or constituted (1).

226. First matter is pure potency.— 1° *Preliminaries.* 1) First matter of itself is an indeterminate subject, but can be made determinate by form. Therefore it is potency, i.e., a capacity (understood in the concrete) for some act.

2) Pure potency is potency which has neither formal act, nor entitative act of its own, i.e., which has no determination of its own.

Formal act is form which with first matter constitutes something else, i.e., mobile being.

Entitative act is existence by which a thing is formally placed outside of its causes and outside of nothing.

3° All Scholastics, since the time of Aristotle, conceive first matter as a real entity which is potency.

Yet there are some who cannot see that what of itself is not in some way in act can be a real entity. Therefore they understand that first matter is in potency, only because it lacks formal act or an informing form, but not because of itself it lacks entitative act or existence. Such is the opinion of Henry of Ghent, Durandus(2), and Suarez(3).

4) St. Thomas and his followers affirm that between actual being and mere nothing there is a real entity which is potency. And this potency is first matter. Hence they conceive first

(1) Joannes a Sancto Thoma, *Cursus Phil.*, t. II, p. 58 b 10-40 (Reiser).
(2) *In I*, dist. 8, q. 2, n. 15, seq.
(3) *Metaph.*, disp. 31, sect. 4 et seq.

matter as an entity which of itself is in no way in act, that is to say, which has neither formal act, nor entitative act or existence, and which receives existence only in so far as it is determined by form. Therefore they call it *pure potency* (1).

2° We shall use two arguments to prove that *first matter is pure potency.*

1) First matter has the same relation to substantial form that second matter has to second matter. But second matter has not artificial existence before it is determined by artificial form, and it receives its artificial existence only by means of its artificial form ; v.g., wood receives the existence of a statue when it is determined by the form of the statue, and by means of the artificial form by which it becomes a statue. Therefore first matter has no substantial existence, i.e., no entitative act, before it is determined by substantial form, and receives existence only by means of substantial form. In a word, first matter of itself is pure potency.

2) The subject of substantial form is pure potency. But first matter is the subject of substantial form. Therefore first matter is pure potency.

Major. — A first subject, which is not pure potency, already has its own substantial existence. But every form which is added to a subject which already has its own substantial existence is a form which gives secondary existence, i.e., is an accidental form. Hence the subject of substantial form is pure potency.

The *minor* is clear from the very notion of first matter.

227. Answer to an objection. — Our adversaries propose the following objection: Form which gives a partial substantial existence to complete the partial existence of the substantial subject into which it is received is substantial form: for only one complete substantial existence is formed from two partial substantial existences. But first matter of itself has only a partial existence which is completed by the partial existence received from form. Therefore first matter, as having a partial existence, is the subject of substantial form. In other words, the subject of substantial form is not pure potency.

(1) *De Potentia*, q. 4, a. 1, c. — I, q. 7, ad 3, and q. 66, a. 1. — *Contra Gentes*, L. II, c. 43.

This argument must be rejected, because a partial existence is absurd. For either a thing is constituted outside its causes and outside of nothing, and then it has complete existence; or it is not constituted outside its causes and outside of nothing, and in this case it has no existence. Hence existence is either complete, or it simply is not. In other words, existence is indivisible, so that it can in no way be conceived as partial.

228. It is absolutely repugnant that first matter exist without form. — 1° It is certain that first matter participates in existence by means of form, and is naturally dependent on it for its existence, just as an accident is naturally dependent on a substance for its existence.

2° But an accident can, by the absolute power of God, i.e., by a miracle, exist without a subject, as is the case in the Blessed Eucharist. Hence the question arises : it is absolutely repugnant that first matter exist without form, so that not even by a miracle can it exist without form ?

3° All who conceive that first matter of itself is in act, i.e., has a partial existence, affirm that first matter can exist without form.

Nevertheless, they do not claim that that partial existence, which comes from form and is specified by it, can be found in matter without form. But they teach merely that an existence proper to matter itself, in as much as matter is an entity distinct from form, can be found in matter that is separated from all form.

4° St. Thomas teaches that it is absolutely impossible that first matter exist separated from form, and hence that it cannot so exist even by the absolute power of God or by a miracle[1]. And his reason is this : existence, according to its very definition, is essentially an act by which something *determinate* is constituted outside its causes and outside of nothing. But first matter of itself is not *something determinate*, but is pure potency. Hence it is absolutely repugnant that first matter exist without form, for otherwise it would be al-

(1) I, q. 66, a. 1. — *Quodlib.*, 3, a. 1. — *De Potentia*, q. 4, a. 1. — *Contra Gentes*, L. III, c. 4.

ready determinate without form. In other words, of itself it would not be pure potency.

229. The potency of first matter is purely passive. — The potency of first matter is in no way active. This may be proved in two ways.

First, activity is first act, i.e., power to act ; but first matter of itself has no first act, which is form ; therefore first act has no activity whatsoever.

Secondly, existence is a condition necessarily required that a thing operate actively or effectively ; but first matter of itself has no entitative act or existence whatsoever ; therefore first matter of itself is in no way active, but is purely passive.

230. First matter has an innate appetite for form. — 1° *Preliminaries.* — *a*) The appetite is the inclination or relation of a thing to a good suitable to itself(1).

b) The appetite is *innate* or *elicited.*

An innate appetite is an appetite that springs from nature, without knowledge ; v.g., the appetite of a plant for water.

An elicited appetite is an appetite which follows knowledge; v.g., the appetite by which an animal desires food or drink which it apprehends.

c) The innate appetite of first matter for form is not distinguished from the entity of matter, but is the matter itself as it is transcendentally related of itself to a good suitable to itself.

2° *Proof of the proposition.* — First matter is transcendentally related by its whole entity to form by which it is actuated and determined, as to the good most suitable to itself. But this transcendental relation is an innate appetite, and is

(1) I, q. 78, a. 1, ad 3; q. 80, a. 1, ad 6; q. 81, a. 1, c; and q. 87, a. 4, c.

not really distinct from the entity of matter. Therefore first matter has an innate appetite for form(1).

231. First matter has an appetite for all forms, but in different ways. — 1° The following forms may be distinguished :

a) forms which first matter neither has, nor ever had;

b) forms which it has ;

c) forms which it has had, but has no longer.

2° *a*) As regards forms which it neither has, nor ever had, first matter has an appetite by way of tendency and desire.

b) As regards forms which it has, first matter still retains its appetite, not by way of tendency and desire, but by way of possession and rest. Nevertheless, this possession does not satisfy the appetite of first matter, for it still has an appetite for other forms.

c) As regards forms which it has had, but has no longer, first matter still retains its appetite by way of proportion, not however as regards fulfillment, i.e., as regards the production of these forms in itself. The reason is this : when a form is once lost, it cannot be produced again by another agent. For one agent cannot produce a form already produced by another agent; nor can the same agent produce the same form twice.

232. Appetite of first matter for the human soul. — 1° First matter has an appetite for all forms under only one formality, that is to say, in as much as they all have the same mode of completing and actuating matter, as, v.g., sight is concerned with all colors, in as much they all have the same formality of visibleness.

2° Therefore first matter, although informed by a perfect form, always has an appetite for others. Hence, even when it has the most perfect form, which is the human soul, matter does not rest in it as in its end. Moreover, it is better for

(1) *In Phys.*, L. I, l. 15. — I, q. 59, a. 2.

matter to pass on to some other form, no matter how inferior, so that it may satisfy its appetite for all forms(1).

Nevertheless, the human soul is the most perfect form by which first matter can be determined. Although the human soul is not the ultimate end of the appetite of matter, it is, nevertheless, the ultimate end of the agent, i.e., of the active principle of generation. Therefore man is said to be the end of all generation (2).

233. First matter cannot be engendered or corrupt negatively. — *a*) We say it cannot be engendered or corrupt negatively, or positively, for of itself first matter has no existence, not even a partial existence, by which it would be everlasting.

b) If first matter could be engendered, it would be made from a preexisting subject. But first matter is the first subject from which every mobile being is made. Therefore . . .

c) Finally, first matter is incorruptible, because it is the subject of all change or mutation. Hence, if it loses one form, it at once acquires another : the corruption of one is the generation of another.

234. First matter had its beginning through creation. — Since first matter is the first subject from which every mobile being is made, it cannot be produced from another subject, but only from nothing. But production from nothing is creation. Therefore . . .

Nevertheless, since first matter does not exist as *that which*, it is not properly created, but rather it is concreated when the first mobile being composed of first matter and subtantial form is created.

235. Unity of first matter.— *a*) *Specifically*, first matter has negative unity, in as much as first matter under one form

(1) Joannes a Sancto Thoma, *Cursus Phil.*, t. II, p. 79b (Reiser).
(2) *Contra Gentes*, L. III, c. 22.

has, of itself, nothing by which it may be conceived as different from first matter under another form.

b) First matter is also one and the same *successively*, in as much as, of itself, first matter existing under one form remains the same when by generation it is made exist under another form, as, v.g., gold, of itself, remains the same when first it exists in circular form, and later as a square.

236. First matter of itself is absolutely unintelligible. — Nothing is intelligible except in as much as it is some way determinate or in act. But first matter of itself is absolutely indeterminate, and is made determinate only by form. Therefore first matter of itself is entirely unintelligible, and becomes intelligible only by form.

POINTS FOR REVIEW

1. Give the negative definition of first matter.

2. Explain why first matter is called the first subject from which anything is made.

3. How is first matter distinguished (a) from other causes, (b) from privation?

4. Does Suarez teach that first matter is pure potency? What is his teaching in regard to the potentiality of first matter? What is pure potency?

5. Define entitative act; formal act.

6. Explain why the subject of substantial form must be pure potency. Can there be partial existence?

7. Explain why the potency of first matter is purely passive.

8. Define innate appetite.

9. Is the innate appetite of first matter for form distinct from the entity of first matter? Explain.

10. Under what aspect has first matter an appetite for all forms?

11. Explain briefly how first matter has an appetite for forms it once had, but has no longer.

12. When first matter has its most perfect form, does it rest in it, i.e., is its appetite for forms fully satisfied?

13. Why is man said to be the end of all generation?

14. Explain why first matter is not engendered, and why it does not corrupt.

ARTICLE IV

SUBSTANTIAL FORM

237. Notion and division of form in its widest meaning. — 1° Form, in its widest meaning, is that by which a thing is what it is ; v.g., a statue of Mercury becomes a statue of Mercury, provided that the wood has the figure, i.e., the form, of Mercury.

Form was called *perfection* by the Greeks, because all perfection derives from form, just as the capacity for perfection derives from matter.

Form is also called *act*, because it constitutes and determines a thing in a certain mode of being, just as matter is called *potency*, because of itself it is indifferent to any particular mode of being.

2° *a*) Form, in its broadest meaning, is divided, *first*, into *extrinsic form* or exemplar, and *intrinsic form*.

Extrinsic form is *form which a thing imitates :* imitated form ; v.g., an artificer's idea to the likeness of which a house is built.

Intrinsic form is *form which constitutes a thing in its being ;* v.g., the rational soul is the intrinsic form of man.

b) Intrinsic form is divided into *subsisting form* and *informing form.*

Subsisting form is *form which does not exist in a subject ;* v.g., angels are subsisting forms.

Informing form is *form which is received into a subject ;* v.g., the soul of a horse.

c) Informing form is divided into *substantial form* and *accidental form.*

Substantial form is *form which constitutes substance in its being*, i.e., *form which gives first existence, without presupposing any other existence ;* v.g., the soul of a horse gives the horse his substantial being, and first constitutes him in nature.

Accidental form is *form which is added to a thing that is already constituted in its substantial being, and which gives it a secondary existence;* v.g., whiteness, velocity, bravery, quantity, etc.

238. Definition of substantial form. — Substantial form, as we have already said, is properly defined : *the first act of first matter.*

a) It is called *act*, to distinguish it from first matter, which is pure potency.

b) It is called *first*, to distinguish it from existence, which is the ultimate act of a thing, and from accidental forms, which are only secondary acts which presuppose substantial act.

c) It is called the act of *first matter*, to distinguish it from subsisting forms, as angels, which are acts, but which are not received into matter.

239. Substantial form is the principle of specification, the principle of being, and the first principle of operation. — 1° Substantial form, which determines first matter, constitutes complete mobile being in this or that species. Hence it is the *principle of specification.*

2° Substantial form is the principle of being, not in as much as it is the active principle of existence, but in as much as by form substance becomes the proper subject of existence(1). In other words, form is the principle of being, as it is subordinate to an agent : the agent produces the form, and by means of the form, not by means of the matter, produces existence(2).

3° Substantial form is the *first principle of operation.*

(1) *Contra Gentes*, L. II, c. 55.
(2) I, q. 50, a. 5. Cajetanus, *ibidem.* — Joannes a Sancto Thoma, *Cursus Theol.*, t. II, p. 13, n. 13 (Sol.).

For operation follows existence, and a thing operates in as much as it is in act. But substantial form is the first act which gives existence. Hence it is the first and radical principle of operation(1).

240. Substantial form is material and immaterial.— 1° *Preliminaries.* a) That is first called *material* which is perceived by the senses as having quantity. But, in a more general way, anything is called material which depends on matter or on material conditions for its existence, even though of itself it is not perceived by the senses as being quantitative. It is in this sense that substantial form is called material.

b) Material substantial form is form which can exist (as a principle *by which*) only when united to first matter. It is defined : *form which depends on matter intrinsically* (as regards its entity and its existence) *and subjectively* (as on a subject into which it must be received, in order that it exist).

Immaterial substantial form is form which, although it exists in matter, can, nevertheless, exist separated from matter. The human soul is such a form. It is defined : *form which is intrinsically and subjectively independent of matter.*

2° Since substantial form is the first principle of operation, diversity of substantial forms is manifested to us by diversity of operations.

3° We shall now prove that *substantial form is either material, or immaterial.*

Where operation is proper to the compound, there form can exist only when united to matter, i.e., form is material ; and where operation is proper to form only, there form can exist without matter, i.e., form is immaterial. But in certain mobile beings, as plants and brute animals, operation is proper to the compound, as assimilation of food and sensation ; in other mobile beings, i.e., in men, the operations, i.e., intellection and volition, are proper to the form. Therefore substantial

(1) I, q. 76, a. 1.

form is material in plants and brute animals, and immaterial in men.

The *major* is clear from the fact that operation follows existence.

241. In the engendering of compounds, material forms are not produced by infusion into matter, but by eduction from matter. — 1° *Preliminaries.*— *a*) Here we are speaking of the production of forms *in the engendering of a compound ;* for the first substantial form is concreated when the first mobile being is created.

b) We are concerned with *material forms*, because immaterial form, i.e., the human soul, which exists independently of matter, is produced independently of matter : it is not made from matter, but is created.

c) *To be educed* from matter is correlative to *to be contained* in matter : for those things are educed from another which are contained in it. Hence material forms are said to be educed from matter in the same way as they are said to be contained in matter.

d) A thing can be contained in another in two ways : *in act* or actually, and *in potency* or potentially.

A thing is actually contained in another when it is possessed in its entity by the other as *de facto* existing in it : thus a sword is actually contained in its scabbard, water in a dish, etc.

A thing is potentially contained in another, when, though not actually existing in the other, it can be made from it ; thus all kinds of artificial figures are contained in wax, because they can be made from it; similarly, heat is potentially contained in water, because, by the action of fire, heat can be made from water[1].

e) Since first matter is pure potency, material forms are not actually contained in it, hidden as it were, but are con-

(1) I, q. 90, a. 2, ad 2, and q. 45, a. 8. — *De Spiritualibus Creaturis*, a. 2, ad 8. — *Contra Gentes*, L. II, c. 86.

tained in it only potentially. Hence *to be educed from matter* means *to be made by the transmutation of matter*, or *to pass from potency to act*. Extraction from the potency of matter signifies that a thing which was in potency becomes act or in act(1).

f) Therefore the eduction of form is a transmuting production, which has a relation to two causes: *efficient cause*, by which form is produced, and *material cause*, from which and in which form is produced and has its being.

g) Eduction from matter is the opposite of infusion into matter. Infusion of form into matter obtains when form is produced independently of matter, and is united to it from without to inform it. Thus the human soul, as an immaterial form, is not produced dependently on matter, but is created by God, and is united to matter to constitute man.

2° We shall now prove that *in the engendering of compounds, material forms are not produced by infusion into matter, but by eduction from matter.*

The eduction of form from matter means the making of form dependently on presupposed matter in whose potency it is contained. But, in the engendering of compounds, material forms are made dependently on presupposed matter in whose potency they are contained. Therefore, in the engendering of compounds, material forms are made by eduction from matter, not by infusion into matter(2).

The *major* is evident from the preliminary remarks. The *minor* will be proved in parts. *a*) *Material forms which are produced presuppose matter:* for all generation presupposes matter.

b) *Material forms are contained in the potency of matter:* material forms have material existence, and not exceeding the limits of matter.

---

(1) I, q. 90, a. 2, ad 2. — *De Potentia*, q. 3, a. 8, a. 12.

(2) Quidam enim, ut Plato et Avicenna, posuerunt omnes formas ab extrinseco esse . . . sed in hoc videntur fuisse decepti quia attribuebant fieri proprie istis formis, cum tamen fieri non sit nisi compositi, cujus etiam proprie est esse: formae enim esse dicuntur non ut subsistentes, sed ut quo composita sunt, unde et fieri dicuntur non propria factione, sed per factionem suppositorum quae transmutantur transmutatione materiae de potentia ad actum; unde sicut composita fiunt per agentia naturalia, ita etiam formae quae non sunt subsistentes. — *Quodl.*, IX, q. 5, a. 11.

c) *Material forms are made dependently on matter:* becoming follows existence, i.e., is proportionate to it; and, as material form, cannot exist without matter; they therefore depend on matter in their becoming, that is to say, they are made dependently on matter.

242. Unity of substantial form in mobile being. — 1° *Preliminaries.*—a) Substantial form is *one* in the sense that it excludes any other substantial form in the same being.

b) We contend that substantial form is *one*, i.e., that there is only one substantial form in any mobile being that has one substantial essence or nature. — Thus « I » am one substantial essence or nature, as is clear from internal experience. From analogy we may say that every man is simply one in nature or essence, i.e., has only one substantial essence; and the same may be said of every brute, and of every plant. We do not know whether inorganic beings are one or several in nature; v.g., this mass of water, this chemical compound, etc.

c) The plurality of forms in the same mobile being was the common teaching in the Middle Ages, before the time of St. Thomas. Such, indeed, was the teaching of Avicenna, St. Albert the Great, and St. Bonaventure. Scotus supported the teaching of the plurality of forms in living beings: a living being has one form in as much as it is corporeal, and another in as much as it is living.

St. Thomas taught the unity of substantial form in every mobile being, i.e., that there is only one substantial form in any mobile being. His opinion was condemned first in Paris (in 1277) by bishop Étienne Tempier, and later, at the instigation of Robert Kilwardby, at Oxford; but it was generally adopted by later Scholastics.

2° *Proof.* — There can be only one substantial form in a being that has absolute oneness. But every mobile being has absolute oneness. Therefore there is only one substantial form in every mobile being.

Major. — Substantial form gives existence, for it is the act which determines essence, i.e., constitutes it in a determinate species. Therefore, if there were several substantial forms, there would be several existences, and hence several beings, not one being.

243. Substantial forms are like numbers. — For, just as a superior number adds unity to an inferior number, so a superior substantial form adds perfection to an inferior substantial form. Thus, for example, an inorganic being in virtue of its form is a mobile being only, whereas a plant by its form is a *living* being, and a brute by its form is a *sentient* living being.

Nevertheless, material substantial forms are not a priori determinate, as numbers are. But of actually existing substantial forms there are other indefinitely possible substantial forms, just as of determinate numbers there are indefinitely possible fractions ; v.g., between 1 and 2, there are $1\frac{1}{2}$, $1\frac{1}{4}$, etc. The reason is this : material substantial form is educed from the potency of first matter. But first matter is pure potency, i.e., potency that is indefinitely determinable. Therefore substantial forms can be educed indefinitely from the potency of first matter.

244. Permanence of the elements in a compound. — Almost all Scholastics, both ancient and modern, inquire into the question of how chemical elements remain in a compound. Those who support the teaching of the unity of substantial form in every mobile being affirm that the elements do not *actually* remain in the compound, i.e., do not remain with their own proper substantial form, but only *virtually*, i.e., they remain without their properties, and exist in virtue of the substantial form of the whole compound. Others disagree with this opinion. But, in this matter, Scholastics are discussing a pseudo-problem. For they conceive elements as substantial individual particles. But elements, as physicists themselves affirm, are nothing other than metrical parts of something measured. Hence the problem of the permanence of the elements in a compound is understood and dealt with in different ways by the physicist and the philosopher. For, in the case of substantial change, v.g., if a living being becomes a non-living being, the change of the elements can be considered in two ways. First, if the elements are understood formally, the problem is this : are the elements in substantial change changed metrically ? In this case, there is no question whatsoever of the substantial form of the elements. But if the problem is considered philosophically, we may readily reply : the elements are changed in a substantial change, because they become the metrical aspects of another being.

POINTS FOR REVIEW

1. State briefly what is meant by form in its widest meaning.
2. Distinguish between: *a*) extrinsic form and intrinsic form; *b*) subsisting form and informing form.
3. Define accidental form.
4. Why is substantial form called *first* act ?
5. Explain what is meant by the statement: substantial form is the first principle of being.
6. Define material form and immaterial form.
7. Prove the existence of immaterial substantial form.
8. When is a thing potentially contained in another ?
9. Define eduction from matter, and infusion into matter.
10. Explain why there is only one substantial form in every mobile being.

READING

Whenever we state the properties of a body in terms of physical quantities we are imparting knowledge as to the response of various metrical indicators to its presence, *and nothing more.* After all, knowledge of this kind is fairly comprehensive. A knowledge of the response of all kinds of objects — weighing-machines and other indicators — would determine completely its relation to its environment, leaving only its inner un-get-table nature undetermined. — EDDINGTON, *The Nature of the Physical World*, p. 257 (Cambridge), 1933.

The recognition that our knowledge of the subjects treated in physics consists solely of readings of pointers and other indicators transforms our view of the status of physical knowledge in a fundamental way. — *Ibidem*, p. 258.

The Victorian physicist felt that he knew just what he was talking about when he used such terms as *matter* and *atoms*. Atoms were tiny billiard balls, a crisp statement that was supposed to tell you all about their nature in a way which never could be achieved for transcendental things like consciousness, beauty or humour. But now we realise that science has nothing to say as to the intrinsic nature of the atom. The physical atom is, like everything else in physics, a schedule of pointer readings. — *Ibidem*, p. 259.

ARTICLE V

THE SUBSTANTIAL COMPOUND

245. Matter and form are the essential parts of a natural compound. — 1° *Preliminaries.*—*a*) A natural compound is a physical compound. There are two kinds of physical compound or whole : *substantial* and *quantitative.*

A substantial or essential whole is a whole considered as regards its substantial parts, which are matter and form.

A quantitative whole is a whole considered as regards its quantitative parts.

b) The difference between essential or substantial parts and quantitative or integral parts is this :

quantitative parts are parts which, if separated, can singly exist as wholes; v.g., a part of a mass of water separated from the whole mass is a whole ;

substantial or essential parts are parts which always remain incomplete beings. A part can never be a whole ; v.g., neither substantial form nor first matter can be a whole.

c) At present, we are concerned with substantial wholes, i.e., with substantial or essential compounds. And we are investigating whether both matter and form are essential to a substantial compound.

d) Averroes claimed that only form belonged to the essence of a thing, and that matter was merely the subject of essence, as a scabbard is merely the receptacle of a sword, not its constituent. Likewise, Plato said that the soul, which is in the body as a stranger in a hotel, is the whole of man.

2° We shall now prove that *both matter and form are essential parts of a natural compound.*

a) A corruptible and generable being is composed of matter and form as its essential parts. But a natural compound is corruptible and generable. Therefore a natural compound is composed of matter and form as its essential parts.

The *major* is evident. In every generation, a part of the thing is presupposed; and, in every corruption, a part of the thing remains. Hence a corruptible and generable being is essentially composed of a subject which is presupposed and remains, i.e., of matter, and of a perfection which is acquired or lost, i.e., form.

The *minor* is evident from an example. Man, who is a natural compound, is generable and corruptible.

b) Whatever is found in the essential definition of substance belongs to the essence of substance. But both matter and form are found in the essential definition of natural substance. Therefore both matter and form belong to the essence of natural substance(1).

Major. — An essential definition contains essential principles.

Minor. — Natural definitions signify form with sensible matter ; v.g., man is not defined a *rational soul*, but a *rational animal*.

246. Matter and form are immediately united to each other. — 1° *Preliminaries.*—*a*) Union, in general, is that by which several things are reduced to unity.

b) There are three distinct kinds of union between matter and form : *effective* union, *dispositive* union, and *formal* union.

Effective union is the action of an agent producing form in matter.

Dispositive union consists in the dispositions by which matter becomes capable of having and retaining form ; v.g., in living being there is a certain disposition without which a

(1) *De Ente et Essentia*, c. 2. — I, q. 75, a. 4.

body is incapable of retaining its soul ; when this disposition is taken away by sickness, the soul separates from the body.

Formal union is the uniting of form with matter, i.e., that by which matter is rendered formally united to form.

c) It is certain that effective union and dispositive union are distinct from matter and form. Hence our only difficulty concerns formal union. The problem may be presented by the following question : are first matter and substantial form formally united by means of some third thing distinct from themselves, or are they immediately united by their own entities ?

2° We shall now prove that *first matter and substantial form are not formally united by something distinct from themselves, but immediately by their own entities.*

Form is united to matter when it informs and actuates matter. But form essentially and immediately informs and actuates matter. Therefore form is essentially and immediately united to matter.

The *major* is evident from the notions of matter and form, for form is the act of matter.

Minor. — That which is essentially and immediately the act of matter essentially and immediately informs and actuates matter. But form is essentially and immediately the act of matter. Therefore form essentially and immediately informs and actuates matter.

b) Substantial form is the *first* act by which first matter is determined. But, if the union between first matter and substantial form were not immediate, substantial form would no longer be the *first* act by which first matter would be determined : for there would be an intermediate entity, i.e., an intermediate *act*, between first matter and substantial form. Therefore . . .

247. A natural compound is not something distinct from its united parts. — 1° *Preliminaries.*—*a*) A natural compound is a whole nature which results from the union of parts, i.e., of first matter and substantial form.

b) Parts may be understood as divided and separate, as connoting one another, or as united. Here we are considering parts as they are united. The question with which we are concerned is this : is a natural compound a *third* reality that results from its united parts, or the same reality as its united parts ? We reply that a natural compound is not a third reality that is really distinct from matter and form, but that it is matter and form, in as much as they become one nature by being united to each other(1).

2° *Proof.* — *a*) If a natural compound were distinguished from its united parts, it would contain a third entity resulting from the union of first matter and subtantial form. But a natural compound cannot contain a third entity resulting from the union of first matter and substantial form. Therefore a natural compound is not distinguished from its united parts.

The *major* is self-evident, because first matter and substantial form are the first constituent principles of a natural compound.

Minor. — That third actuality which would result from first matter and substantial form would be a form which would perfect and actuate them. But such a form would not be a substantial form, because it would follow substantial form, but would be an accidental form. Therefore one of the constituent parts of a natural compound would be an accidendal form, which is absurd(2).

b) Only first matter and substantial form are found in a natural compound. Therefore a natural compound is not distinguished from its united parts.

Antecedent. — For every substantial entity is either form or matter, or matter and form united to each other : matter

(1) *Suppl.*, q. 79, a. 2, ad 2.
(2) *Contra Gentes*, l. IV, c. 81.

and form are immediately united, without an intermediate entity.

248. The existence of mobile being is really distinct from its essence. — 1° *Preliminaries.*— a) Existence is conceived as the ultimate act by which a thing is placed outside its causes and outside of nothing.

b) Distinction is the lack of identity between two or more things.

Distinction is *of reason*, if it is a distinction between concepts of one and the same thing ; it is *real*, if it exists independently of the consideration of the mind.

It is certain that there is a distinction of reason between essence and existence. But at present we are concerned with whether there is a real distinction between them.

c) Henry of Ghent, Scotus, Suarez, and others, who conceive first matter as imperfect act, hold that the whole existence of mobile being results from two partial substantial existences.

According to them, therefore, there is not a real distinction between the essence and existence of mobile being. The contrary opinion, which is commonly held by Thomists, is certain.

2° We shall now prove that *in mobile being, existence is really distinct from essence*, i.e., *from the natural compound.*

What cannot be identified either with first matter, or with substantial form, or with the compound, is really distinct from the essence of mobile being. But existence cannot be identified either with first matter, or with substantial form, or with the compound. Therefore the existence is really distinct from the essence of mobile being.

Major. — There is no other entity in the essence of mobile being.

Minor. — *a*) *Existence cannot be identified either with first matter or with substantial form.* — Existence which would be identified with first matter, or with substantial form, would be an incomplete and partial existence : for first matter and substantial form are the parts of a compound. But an incomplete and partial existence is absurd : for existence is simple act, and is indivisible. A thing either completely exists, or does not exist at all. Therefore.

b) *Existence cannot be identified with the compound.* — A compound has parts. Existence has no parts, because it is simple, i.e., indivisible.

Corollary. Therefore there are two potencies and two acts in mobile being[1].

Two potencies : first matter is potency (in the order of essence) in relation to substantial form, and the whole constituted essence is potency (in the order of existence) in relation to existence.

Two acts : substantial form is the act of first matter, and is called *formal* act, *essential* act, act *in the order of essence ;* existence is the act of a complete essence, and is called *entitative* act, *existential* act, act *in the order of existence.*

249. The intelligibility of the essence of mobile being is proportionate to the perfection of its substantial form. — A thing is intelligible in as much as it is determinate. But the essence of mobile being is more determinate and is elevated higher above the unintelligibility of first matter in proportion to the greater perfection of its substantial form. Therefore . . .

POINTS FOR REVIEW

1. Explain the distinction between *a*) a substantial physical whole and a quantitative whole, *b*) substantial parts and integral parts.

(1) In rebus compositis est considerare duplicem actum et duplicem potentiam. Nam primo quidem materia est ut potentia respectu formae, et forma est actus ejus; et iterum natura constituta ex materia et forma est ut potentia respectu ipsius esse, in quantum est susceptive ejus. — *De Spiritual. Creat.*, a. 1. — I, q. 7, a. 3, ad 3.

2. Why is matter an essential part of a natural compound?

3. Distinguish between effective union, dispositive union, and forma union.

4. Name the parts of a natural compound, and show whether or not the compound is something distinct from its united parts.

5. Explain why existence cannot be identified with the natural compound.

6. Describe briefly the two potencies found in mobile being.

CHAPTER II

NATURE

Prologue.— In the first chapter, we dealt with principles as the constituents of natural being in the state of becoming, and in the state of actual being. But the principles of natural being can be considered in another way, that is to say, in relation to motion. Under this aspect, a principle is not considered as formal and material, but as the active and passive principle of motion. As such, it is conceived as a *nature*. And since nature is a cause, we shall briefly discuss causes, though such a discussion properly belongs to Metaphysics. After that we shall turn our attention to the study of finality, necessity, and chance. Hence there will be five articles in this chapter.

Nature	Meanings of nature Definition of nature An objection Things that are natures Nature and art Nature and violence
Causes	Definition of cause Division of causes Definition of material cause Definition of formal cause Definition of efficient cause Definition of final cause
Finality in nature	Statement of the question Thesis: Nature acts for an end Scholion Natural agents act for an end in different ways

Necessity in nature	Statement of the question Thesis: A natural agent is not an absolutely necessary cause, but a contingent cause Corollaries Difficulties
Chance and fortune	Statement of the question Thesis: Chance can be found in irrational agents, and fortune in all rational creatures; but, as regards God, there is nothing fortuitous or casual. Corollaries A difficulty

ARTICLE I

NATURE

250. Meanings of nature. — Nature has many meanings.

1° The term nature is used first to signify the generation of living beings, which is called nativity or birth[1]. Hence in this meaning, nature means birth.

2° Since the generation of living beings is from an intrinsic principle, the term nature has been extended to the intrinsic principle of motion.

3° And since the intrinsic principle of motion may be formal or material, both matter and form are called nature.

4° Because the essence of a being is completed by means of form, the essence of a being, which definition signifies, is commonly called nature.

5° Sometimes universal nature is called nature. In this sense, we say: *something exists in nature;* or *all nature is the instrument of God.*

6° Sometimes the term nature is used to designate the *author of nature,* who, nevertheless, is not so much nature as the principle of all nature, i. e., of all things.

In Philosophy of Nature, which is concerned with mobile being, nature is used as signifying the intrinsic principle of motion.

251. Definition of nature. — Nature is defined: *the principle and cause of the motion and the rest of the thing in which*

(1) I, q. 29, a. 1, ad 4.

that principle exists fundamentally and essentially, and not accidentally (1).

1° It is called the *principle and cause,* to indicate that in some things nature is a *passive* principle, and in others is an *active* principle, i.e., a positive principle, not a merely negative principle; and thus it is a cause.

We may also say that substantial nature, with which we are dealing at present, is thus distinguished from *privation* and from the *power of operation.*

Privation is a principle, but not a cause.

The power of operation, which is an accident, is a cause, but is not a radical or fundamental principle of operation.

Therefore nature is called a principle and cause, so that it may be conceived as a positive principle which *causes* motion (and thus it is distinct from privation), and as the first root or source of motion (and thus it is distinct from the power of operation).

2° *Of motion and rest,* that is to say, of motion, or of rest, not of motion and of rest at the same time.

Motion here signifies not merely local motion, but any physical and corporeal motion.

Rest does not signify the absolute lack of motion which is nothing, but the lack of motion with the possession of a term which is attained by motion.

3° *Of the thing in which that principle exists,* in as much as nature is the intrinsic principle of the thing in motion. Thus three things are excluded from the notion of nature.

a) *Artificial things* are excluded : their motion does not originate in a form or intrinsic principle, but in art, which is extrinsic to nature.

b) *The product of violence* is excluded : it is something which originates in some extrinsic power.

---

(1) *Phys.*, l. II, c. 1

c) Excluded too is the efficient causality of the motion of an extrinsic thing, as when fire actively heats something outside itself, or when an animal engenders another animal. For, although the actions by which fire heats something outside itself, and an animal engenders another animal are natural, in as much as they result from nature or are destined for the propagation of nature, nevertheless, nature is formally constituted, not with reference to these actions, but with reference to motion which takes place in that in which nature resides.

4° *Fundamentally* or *first*: thus is excluded a secondary and instrumental principle of motion, which is an accident. Nature is a substance, and therefore the first and radical principle of motion.

5° *Essentially, and not accidentally*: thus is excluded any intrinsic principle of motion which is accidentally united to the subject of motion, as, for example, *when a doctor cures himself*. The doctor is restored to health by a principle found intrinsically in himself. Nevertheless, the doctor who is cured by himself is a sick man. And when a doctor cures himself, the sick man is a doctor accidentally. Hence a doctor is not said to be cured by nature, but by the art that he has within himself, just as other sick persons, who are cured by a doctor, are cured by art.

252. Objection. — There are arts which are intrinsic and essential principles of the motion of those in which they are found; v.g., the art of singing, the art of dancing, etc. Therefore the distinction between nature and art does not derive from nature's being an intrinsic and essential principle of the motion of those in whom it is found.

Antecedent. — Such an art is an intrinsic and essential principle of the motion, as regards the substance of motion or of motion as such, *I deny;* is an accidental principle of motion as regards its mode, that is to say, as regards its artificial direction, *I concede.* And I deny the *consequent.*

Explanation. — Singing and dancing are vital motions which, as such, or as regards their substance, flow from nature. But they are directed by art as regards their mode, in as much as they are artificially regulated. And, from this point of view, they do not derive from a principle that is intrinsic to corporeal nature, but from a principle that is acquired through knowledge, and which has not its root or source in nature. Such a principle is said to be in man intrinsically, because it is inherent in man; but it is extrinsic to nature, i.e., the first principle of motion, and is referred to nature not essentially, but accidentally, because it does not flow from nature.

253. Things that are natures. — *a*) The formality of nature is proper to first matter, i.e., first matter is a nature, because it is the first, substantial, passive principle of motion.

b) But since first matter does not exist except by means of form, the formality of nature is also proper to form. Moreover, the formality of nature more properly belongs to form than to matter, not because form constitutes matter as a passive principle of motion, — first matter of itself is such a principle, — but because matter or nature becomes in act through form[1].

c) In a living being, the formality of nature is proper to substantial form, not only in as much as form is the act of matter or nature, but in as much as form is the first active principle of motion. For a living being not only is moved by another and moves others, but it moves itself. Hence the first active principle of such motion is nature, because vital motion and its principle are in the same subject.

d) The rational soul, even as rational, is properly a nature, because, as such, it is the formal constituent of man, who is a natural being, corporeal, subject to corporeal mobility, and produced by corporeal generation.

The operations of the rational soul, as intellection and volition, though not physical motion, are related to nature, because in this life their exercise is dependent on the senses and the phantasms, i.e., dependent on corporeal motion or movements.

e) A substantial compound whole, if understood as *subsisting*, i.e., as a mobile being, is not a nature, but results from nature, i.e., from matter and form. But if a compound is understood as a complete principle *by which* of mobile being, — as humanity in regard to man, — it may properly be called a nature. For, under this aspect, a substantial compound is the first whole intrinsic principle of motion, and not a partial principle only. The definition of nature properly belongs to the first whole intrinsic principle of motion.

(1) *In Phys.*, l. II, l. 2.

f) The definition of nature is not applicable to angels. For, although angels have natures, in the sense that nature signifies quiddity constituted from essential predicates, they have not that nature which is the principle of physical motion in them, that is to say, the principle of motion that is corporeal, divisible, and imperfect.

254. Nature and art. — 1° Art is defined: *the right conception of external works to be accomplished*[1], that is to say, a habit residing in reason and setting it aright for operation in external matter.

2° Art is distinct from nature : nature is an *intrinsic* principle of motion, whereas art is an *extrinsic* principle [2].

Art may be considered as regards its principle, i.e., as it exists in the intellect, or as regards the form produced by means of it.

Art, as it exists in the intellect, is not an intrinsic principle of motion, for the intellect is exterior to the artifact, and artificially directs or disposes external matter.

As regards the form produced, art is an extrinsic principle of motion, for artificial form is added to nature, but is not natural : *art presupposes nature, and the intellect does not make nature by means of art, unless it is the Divine Intellect.*

255. Nature and violence. — 1° Violence is defined: *that whose principle is outside the thing, and which produces motion without the cooperation of the subject or patient.*

Non-cooperation, i.e., lack of inclination, may be *negative* or *positive*.

It is negative, when there is neither inclination nor resistance.

It is positive, when there is contrary inclination, and so positive resistance.

---

(1) 1-2, q. 57, a. 3. — In scholastic Latin, art is defined with remarkable euphony and succinctness: *recta ratio factibilium*. — Translator's note.

(2) *In Phys.*, l. II, l. 1, and l. 14. — *In Metaph.*, l. XII, l. 3

2° Positive resistance may be *active* or *passive*.

Active resistance obtains when the thing which is moved violently, in virtue of an active principle, resists the mover ; v.g., when a victim actively resists an aggressor.

Passive resistance obtains when the thing which is moved violently is removed from the form to which it is naturally related, in virtue of its passive inclination ; v.g., when matter proximately disposed for a form is removed from the form in virtue of an extrinsic principle.

3° Negative resistance is not sufficient for violence ; positive resistance, active or passive, is required. Hence even first matter can suffer violence.

4° Violence is more opposed to nature than is art. For violence not only is from an extrinsic principle, but it is contrary to the natural inclination of the thing that is violently moved.

POINTS FOR REVIEW

1. Explain what is meant by the term nature as used in Philosophy of Nature. Why is it called a principle and a cause?

2. Of what kind of motion is nature the principle?

3. What is the formal constituent of nature? Is it formally constituted through reference to the motion by which mobile being acts on another?

4. Explain whether or not singing and dancing derive from nature or from art.

5. From what point of view is the form of a living being nature?

6. Explain how art and violence are opposed to nature.

ARTICLE II

CAUSES

256. Definition of cause. — The notion of cause derives from motion, especially by means of internal experience. For conscience provides us with undeniable testimony that we produce realities in ourselves and in other things which depend on our action for their existence ; v.g., when we have an act of intellection, when we experience sensation, or when we produce external works. Moreover, we know very easily from reason that anything new which derives from motion has a cause.

Hence cause may be defined : *the positive principle from which a thing really proceeds as regards dependence in existence.* Hence a cause is a principle on which a thing depends *for existence.*

a) *Principle*, i. e., that from which anything proceeds in any way.

b) *Positive :* thus is excluded a merely negative principle, i.e., a negative term-from-which; v.g., when a statue is made, it is made from a non-statue, i.e., from the privation of the form of a statue.

c) *From which a thing really proceeds :* thus is excluded a principle from which a thing logically proceeds ; v. g., premises from which a conclusion proceeds[1].

d) *As regards dependence in existence :* thus is excluded a principle from which a thing proceeds without dependence in existence ; v.g., the point from which a line begins.

(1) A conclusion proceeds only logically from premises, if argumentation is understood objectively. Nevertheless, the assent of the conclusion really depends on the premises for its existence. Thus understood, the premises really are the causes of the conclusion.

A cause formally consists in a thing's dependence, as regards its existence, on another. This is a real dependence, a real influence of the cause on the production and existence of the effect.

257. Division of causes. — The division of causes derives from act and potency as these *divide* mobile being(1) — mobile being is composed of act and potency. Since mobile being derives from motion, it is constituted from the act and potency on which it depends for its existence or being.

Act is a formal cause, and potency is a material cause.

What is in potency *as regards itself* exists in potency only, and can become in act only *by means of another* which is in act i. e., only under the influence of an agent ; v.g., wood, which can become a statue, does not become a statue except through the agency of a statuary. This kind of cause is called efficient cause.

But every agent intends some determinate effect or end, for otherwise it would not do one thing rather than another : it cannot act except in view of some determinate effect or end. Therefore we have a fourth kind of cause, final cause.

Hence there are four kinds of causes : material cause, formal cause, efficient cause, and final cause. The first two are called intrinsic causes ; the other two, extrinsic causes, as shown in the following outline:

Intrinsic causes	material cause formal cause
Extrinsic causes	efficient cause final cause

258. Definition of material cause. — Material cause is defined by Aristotle(2); *the cause from which a thing is made, since it exists in it.* A material cause is said to exist in the thing produced and to remain in it, to distinguish it from the privation of form from which a thing is made, but which does

(1) 1-2, q. 1, a. 2, c.
(2) *Phys.*, l. II, c. 3.

not remain after the production of the thing ; v.g., a statue is made from the privation of the form of a statue as its term-from-which. But, when the form of the statue is produced, the privation remains no longer. More briefly, material cause may be called *potency receptive of form.*

259. Definition of formal cause. — Formal cause is defined : *the intrinsic ac which determines and specifies material cause.* Since formal cause is a principle which determines and specifies, even an extrinsic principle which determines and specifies, as an *exemplar*, may be reduced to formal cause.

260. Definition of efficient cause. — Efficient cause is defined by Aristotle (1) : *the principle from which motion first flows forth.*

a) This definition has reference to the *order of execution*, and thus efficient cause is distinguished from final cause, from which motion flows in the *order of intention ;* for an agent can act only when it intends an end, i.e., it can act only in view of some determinate end or effect.

b) As the *first* principle from which motion flows, efficient cause is distinguished from material cause and formal cause, which cannot be the *first* principle of change. Material and formal cause do not cause except when they are united ; and they are not united except by efficient cause(2).

Efficient cause has many divisions. For the present it is sufficient that we note its division into principal cause and instrumental cause.

A principal cause is a cause which acts by its own power ; an instrumental cause is a cause which does not act by its own power, but as moved by a principal cause ; v.g., when I write, I am the principal cause of what I write, whereas the pen is the instrumental cause.

---

(1) *Ibidem.*

(2) Joannes a Sancto Thoma, *Cursus Phil.*, t. II, p. 248 (Reiser).

261. Definition of final cause. — Final cause is defined: *that for the sake of which a thing is done.* It is that thing which is sought as the term of the inclination and appetite. Thus every agent acts on account of something for which it has an appetite. Similarly every potency, *since it has reference to act*, i. e., since it is inclined to act, has act as its end.

ARTICLE III

FINALITY IN NATURE

262. Statement of the question. — 1° The thesis on finality in nature is directed against those who affirm that all effects in nature result from the blind necessity of matter.

This thesis is connected with the question of necessity in nature, with which we shall deal in the next chapter. For, if everything results from the necessity of matter, all effects in nature are absolutely necessary.

This question also pertains to the question of Providence. Things which have no knowledge of their end tend to it only when directed to it by a knowing being, as the arrow is directed by the archer ; hence, if nature operates for an end, it must needs be directed to that end by an agent ; and this is the work of Providence(1):

2° Nature is used here to signify all mobile beings, understood not only collectively, but also singly. Hence the thesis must be understood as meaning that all mobile beings act for an end.

3° An end is that for the sake of which a thing is done.

To act for an end is to act with a determinate tendency or inclination towards a thing as an intended term.

4° Almost all physicists deny finality in nature. But Physics of itself is not concerned with finality. Therefore physicists have no right to deny finality, but should pass it over in silence.

Some philosophers, as P. Secchi, S.J., and Herbart, hold

(1) *In Phys.*, l. II, l. 12.

that natural agents act for an end, but do so only under the impulse and extrinsic direction of God.

But, since natural agents truly act in as much as they are in act, they act also for an end to which they are intrinsically related, even though this intrinsic inclination must come from an intellect which relates one thing to another.

263. Statement of the thesis.

THESIS. — NATURE ACTS FOR AN END.

1° Things which happen, always or in a large number of cases, do so for an end. But things which happen naturally do so always or in a large number of cases, as all acknowledge. Therefore everything that happens naturally does so for some purpose, or nature acts for an end.

Major. — Everything that happens does so either from chance, or for an end. But it is impossible that things which happen always or in a large number of cases happen by chance. Therefore things which happen always or in a large number of cases happen for an end.

2° Art acts for an end. But, art imitates nature. Therefore nature acts for an end.[1].

The *major* is evident: art is a habit of the intellect, which apprehends an end as an end.

Minor. — In the case of things done by art and by nature, art imitates nature, as we may see in the case of the restoration of health. For art employs the same means as nature in the restoration of health.

3° Both matter and form are properly called nature. But matter is on account of form, i.e., form is the end of matter, and form is the end of generation. Therefore it follows that becoming and existing for an end are found in natural things[2]. In other words, finality is found in nature.

---

(1) *Ibidem.*
(2) *In Phys.*, l. II, l. 13.

The *major* is clear what has been said already.

Minor. — *a*) Matter is related to form as a determinable thing to its perfection or to the good which it desires. But a good that is desired is an end. Therefore matter is on account of form as on account of an end.

b) Generation is destined to the production of form in a subject, or to the production of a compound which is constituted by form(1).

264. Scholion. — The end to which a natural agent tends is said to be according to the intention of nature. But a distinction must be made between the first intention and the second intention of nature(2).

Nature, according to its first intention, always tends to what is best, and hence it attains its end, sometimes in a few cases, sometimes n many; v.g., nature intends the generation of men of superior intellect, but in many cases men are not endowed with superior intellects. Nature intends the generation of men who have two hands, and it attains this effect in the majority of cases. Similarly, germinal cells, according to the first intention of nature, are destined to produce living beings, but they do so only in a few cases.

According to its second intention, nature, when unable to attain what is best, tends to that of which it is capable, or to things which serve its first intention Thus in the majority of cases nature does not engender men of superior intellect ; and, although this is contrary to the first intention of nature, it is said to be natural. Similarly, nature is said to intend the corruption of things in as much as the corruption of one being serves for the generation of another.

Hence things which are effected in the majority of cases are called natural ; but these are sometimes according to the first intention of nature, sometimes contrary to this first intention, and only according to the second intention. Therefore we must always make a distinction between the first intention and the second intention of nature.

(1) *In Phys.*, l. II, l. 11.
(2) *In IV Sent.*, d. 36, q. 1, a. 1, ad 2.

265. Natural agents act for an end in different ways.— 1° Some natural agents have no knowledge whatsoever of the end towards which they tend; v.g., a stone has no knowledge of the centre to which it tends. Such agents act *executively* for an end, in as much as they elicit actions which tend to an end of which they have no knowledge. Therefore it is more exact to say that they are moved than to say that they move to an end — *magis aguntur quam agunt propter finem.*

2° Other agents apprehend an end as a thing, the goodness of the end, but yet do know the end formally as an end, that is, they have no knowledge of the proportion of the end to the means. It is in this proportion that end formally consists. These agents are knowing agents which have no intellect, as brutes. For it is only an intellect that can have knowledge of the relation or proportion of one thing to another. Such agents act for an end not only executively, but also *apprehensively*, in as much as they tend to an end which they apprehend.

3° Other agents know an end formally as an end, i.e., they have knowledge of the proportion of the means to the end. And they act for an end not only *apprehensively*, but also *directively* or formally, in as much as they are not only directed to an end, but actively direct themselves to an end which they can choose for themselves.

Hence natural agents act for an end in different ways: some act for an end *executively;* others, *apprehensively;* and others, *directively*.

POINTS FOR REVIEW

1. Distinguish between the first intention and the second intention of nature.

2. Explain briefly whether or not corruption is according to the second intention of nature.

3. Explain what is meant by each of the following: to act executively for an end, to act apprehensively and directively for an end.

ARTICLE IV

NECESSITY IN NATURE

266. Statement of the question. — 1° A thing is said to be necessary which cannot not exist, i.e., which cannot be other than it is Therefore necessity obtains when a thing cannot happen to be other than it is. Thus it is necessary that man be a rational animal, because it is impossible for man not to be an animal.

2° A possible or contingent thing is distinguished from a necessary thing But a poss ble thing can have many meanings.

a) First, that 's said to be possible which is not repugnant. This kind of poss ble thing s not opposed to necessary thing, but is a consequence of it. For, a thing, in as much as it is necessary s not repugnant, and therefore is possible ; v.g., God 's a necessary being, and therefore He is a possible being.

b) Again a thing may be called possible, only because it is first in potency and later in act. This k nd of possible being is not opposed to necessary being, because a thing that becomes actual or in act can be necessary.

c) Possible or contingent being, as opposed to necessary being, is a being which has potency for existence and for non-existence(1). Thus a mobile being, as man, has potency for non-existence when it exists, and therefore in not necessary, but contingent. Necessary being and contingent being, as used in the thesis, are used as opposed to each other.

3° We are here speaking of what is necessary and what is contingent in nature And since nature is a cause, our problem is this : is nature determined to produce its effects and to attain its ends in such a way that effects necessarily result from

(1) *Contra Gentes*, l. III, c. 86.

nature as their cause ? In a word, is nature a defectible or an indefectible cause in the production of effects ?

4° *a*) All the philosophers of antiquity, who recognized material cause only, and were unaware of or denied the existence of final cause, affirmed that everything that comes to pass in the world does so of absolute necessity. Their conclusion was correct, for things which are the effect of a material cause are absolutely necessary ; v.g., mobile being, because it is material, is necessarily quantitative, by absolute necessity.

b) Many Scholastics, as Suarez(1), teach that nature is a cause with such oneness of determination, that effects necessarily result from it. If a natural agent fails in its operation, it does so only because of an extrinsic impediment. Therefore they affirm that effects result from a natural cause of *hypothetical necessity*, in as much as they are necessarily produced on the *hypothesis* that there are no impediments.

Aristotle and St. Thomas teach that nature is a cause that is intrinsically contingent, in as much as a natural agent is not so determinate, that effects always and necessarily result from it.

And if a natural agent, because of an extrinsic impediment, does not produce the effects which it is naturally destined to produce, its failure to do so is explained by the fact that it is intrinsically defectible or contingent. For a necessary or in-

(1)... Et ideo dicendum est primo, in ordine ad causam proximam operantem ex necessitate naturae nullum esse effectum contingentem per intrinsecam virtutem talis causae; esse tamen posse contingentem ex imperfectione et defectu talis causae, quae impediri potest ex concursu vel oppositione alterius causae. — *Disputationes Metaphysicae*, Disp. XIX, Sect. X, n. 3 (Vivès).

Hinc tamen majoris claritatis gratia recte distinguitur duplex effectus contingens, scilicet vel intrinsece, vel tantum extrinsece. Priori modo dicitur effectus ab intrinseco contingens, quia manat a causa, quae ex intrinseca vi et potestate potest dare contingentiam effectui. Non quod haec contingentia aliquando sit modus intrinsecus inhaerens ipsi effectui; nihil enim est aliud quam denominatio a sola intrinseca virtute et agendi suae causae; sed quod talis denominatio a sola intrinseca virtute et perfectione propriae causae proveniat. Et haec contingentia tantum est in ordine ad causam liberam. Posteriori autem modo, seu extrinsece dicitur effectus contingens, quando carentia necessitatis quae in illo est, solum *est* ab extrinsecis impedimentis. — *Ibidem*, n. 4.

defectible cause cannot be extrinsically mpeded[1].

5° A contingent thing, as opposed to a necessary thing, may be such in three ways :

contingent to any two ;

contingent in the majority of cases ;

contingent in only a few cases [2].

a) A thing that is contingent to any two is a thing that is potency to opposites ; v.g., the will when not determined by something that is desirable, i.e., that is the object of the appetite. Since nothing acts in as much as it is potency, a thing that is contingent to two cannot be an efficient cause unless it is determined to act, and, in this case, it becomes a cause which is contingent in the majority of cases.

b) A thing is contingent in the majority of cases which produces its effects in the majority of cases, and fails to do so only in a few cases.

c) A thing is contingent in a few cases which rarely produces its effects, as happens in chance and fortune[3].

Nature is contingent in the majority of cases, that is to say, nature does not necessarily and always produce the effects which it is destined to produce, but produces them in the majority of cases, and fails to produce them only in a few cases.

6° Because nature produces its effects in the majority of cases, it may be called a necessary cause whose necessity is not absolute necessity, but physical necessity[4], in this sense : given a natural cause, its effects are necessarily produced in the majority of cases. It is in this way that contingency in

---

(1) Sciendum est etiam quod quidam definierunt esse necessarium, quod non habet impedimentum; contingens vero sicut frequenter, quod potest impediri in paucioribus. Sed hoc irrationale est. Necessarium enim dicitur, quod in sua natura habet quod non possit non esse; contingens autem ut frequenter, quod possit non esse. Hoc autem quod est habere impedimentum vel non habere est contingens. Natura enim non parat impedimentum ei quod non potest non esse; quia esset superfluum. — *In Phys.*, l. II, l. 8, n. 4 (Leonina).

(2) *In Metaph.*, L. VI, l. 2, n. 1183 (Cathala).

(3) *In Phys.*, l. II, l. 8, n. 2.

(4) I, q. 115, a. 6. — Cajetanus, *Comment.* on this article, n. XXII.

the majority of cases is called physical necessity. Hence things which produce their effects in the majority of cases are said to be necessary in the sense that their necessity is physical, but not absolute. Things that produce their effects in only a few cases or rarely, that is to say, casual things or things of chance, are ca.led simply contingent.

We state in the thesis that nature is not an absolutely necessary cause, in as much as it does not always produce its effects, but is a cause that is contingent in the majority of cases, i.e., t is necessary from physical necessity only, in as much as it is intrinsically defectible.

267. Statement of the thesis.

THESIS. — A NATURAL AGENT IS NOT AN ABSOLUTELY NECESSARY CAUSE, BUT A CONTINGENT CAUSE.

1° An agent which can fail in its operation is not a necessary cause, but a contingent cause. But a natural agent can fail in its operation. Therefore a natural agent is not a necessary cause, but a contingent cause[1].

Major. — When an agent is determinate, it is destined to produce determinate effects. But when it is defectible in its operation, it does not produce determinate effects of necessity, but rather produces them only in the majority of cases. Hence it is not a necessary cause, but a contingent cause which produces its effect in the majority of cases.

Minor. — A thing that can fail in its existence can fail in its operation, for operation is proportionate to existence. But natural agents can fail in their existence : they are subject to corruption, because of the first matter by which they are constituted. Therefore a natural agent can fail in its operation.

2° An agent which is changeable and does not always remain the same is not a necessary cause, but a contingent cause.

(1) *Contra Gentes*, l. III, c. 86.

But natural agents are changeable and do not a ways remain the same. Therefore natural agents do not produce their effects from necessity, but produce them only in the majority of cases, or a natural agent is not a necessary cause, but a contingent cause(1).

The *major* is evident, for in order that an agent produce the same effects from necessity, it must remain the same.

The *minor* is true : natural agents are changeable and do not always remain the same, on account of their matter which is in potency to many forms, and on account of their contrariety of forms and powers.

268. Corollaries. — 1° First matter is the first root of contingency in natural beings, both as regards existence and as regards operation. For natural beings, from the fact of their being constituted of matter and form, are corruptible, i.e. contingent as regards existence. In like manner, they are, on account of their first matter, contingent as regards operation. For an agent of necessity produces effects, in as much as it is absolutely determined to produce them. But a natural agent, though determinate because of its form, remains partly indeterminate because of its matter : for form wh ch is finite never completely and totally *de:ermines the potentiality of matter which is pure and indefinite potentiality*(2).

Nevertheless, the complement of contingency derives from an extrinsic cause, whether active or material, which provides an impediment. For a defectible cause fails to produce the effects it is destined to produce because it is impeded from doing so.

269. Difficulties. — 1° Given a sufficient cause, its effect is necessarily produced. But nature is a sufficient cause. Therefore nature necessarily produces its effect.

(1) *Ibidem*.

(2) Unde dicendum est quod possibilitas materiae ad utrumque, si communiter loquamur, non est sufficiens ratio contingentiae, nisi etiam addatur ex parte potentiae activae quod non sit omnino determinata ad unum; alioquin si ita sit determinata ad unum quod impediri non potest, consequens est quod ex necessitate reducat in actum potentiam passivam eodem modo. — *In Periherm.*, l. I, l. 14, n. 9.

Major. — Given a sufficient cause which is indefectible, *I concede;* given a sufficient cause which is defectible, *I deny.*

Minor. — Nature is a sufficient cause which is indefectible, *I deny;* which is defectible, *I concede.*

2° A cause which has oneness of determination is a necessary cause. But nature has oneness of determination. Therefore nature is a necessary cause.

Major. — A cause having such oneness of determination that it cannot be impeded, *I concede;* a cause having oneness of determination that can be impeded, *I deny.*

Minor. — Nature has oneness of determination and cannot be impeded, *I deny;* is a cause that has oneness of determination, but can be impeded, *I concede.*

Nature has oneness of determination in this sense: nature has one principal operation, and its other operations result from it or are referred to it (1).

(1) Joannes a Sancto Thoma, *Cursus Theol.*, t. V, p. 101 (Vivès).

ARTICLE V

CHANCE AND FORTUNE

270. Statement of the question. — 1° All conceive casual and fortuitous events as rare occurrences, things that occur in only a few cases, which are produced by some unknown cause. But since the cause by which anything is produced is an efficient cause, chance, like fortune, may be reduced to an efficient cause.

2° Again, all conceive casual and fortuitous events as accidents or accidental things. Hence chance, like fortune, is not called a proper efficient cause, but an accidental efficient cause.

3° An efficient cause may be accidental in two ways: as regards the cause itself, and as regards its effect.

a) *As regards the cause itself*, when that which is called an accidental cause is joined to a proper cause, as when we say: *the musician is building*. The art of music is not the proper cause, i.e., the cause which is destined to the building of a house as its proper effect, but is an accidental cause, because it is accidentally joined to the proper cause, namely, to the art of building, in the same subject. Accidental cause of this kind is opposed to proper cause in the fourth mode of predication, and is not chance.

b) *As regards effect*, when a cause attains something to which some other effect is joined; v.g., a man digs into the earth to find water, and finds a treasure. The efficient cause is said to be an accidental cause as regards the effect that is joined to the proper effect.

4° An efficient cause may be accidental in two ways as regards the effect.

a) *First*, when a cause attains something to which another effect is joined in the majority of cases or always; in this sense, a person who removes a pillar is the accidental cause of the falling of a stone; for the falling of the stone is joined, by physical necessity, to the removal of the pillar, even though it does not result from the person who removes the pillar, but from gravity.

b) *Secondly*, when a cause attains something to which some other effect is joined only rarely or in only a few cases; v.g., when a tree falls and kills a dog that is running (1).

No one would say that a stone falls by chance or casually when some person removes the pillar that supports it, but all say that a dog is killed by chance by a falling tree. Hence a casual thing, i.e., a thing of chance or a chance occurrence, is one which is joined only in a few cases to what a cause properly produces.

5° That which is joined in a few cases to a thing which a cause attains is not intended by the cause, but results beyond the intention of the cause. Hence chance may be defined: *the accidental cause of things which occur rarely and beyond the intention of its end.*

a) *Accidental cause*, that is to say, a cause not determined to the effects which are produced by chance or casually.

b) *Of things which occur rarely and beyond the intention of its end:* hence two things are required for chance: *a*) that the effects are produced rarely; *b*) that they are not the ends intended by the cause from which they derive (2).

6° Chance, precisely because it produces an effect not intended, fails to attain the end properly intended by a cause.

(1) *In Phys.*, L. II, l. 8, n. 8 (Leonina). — JOANNES A SANCTO THOMA, *Curs. Phil.*, t. II, p. 510 (Reiser).

(2) ... Sciendum est quod non omne quod est praeter intentionem oportet esse fortuitum vel casuale, ut prima ratio proponebat. Si enim quod est praeter intentionem sit consequens ad id quod est intentum vel semper vel frequenter, non eveniet fortuito aut casualiter, sicut in eo qui intendit dulcedine vini frui, si ex potatione vini sequatur ebrietas semper vel frequenter, non erit fortuitum vel casuale; esset autem casuale, si sequeretur ut in paucioribus. — *Contra Gentes*, l. III, c. 6.

Hence for chance there is required a defectible cause, which is impeded by another cause. In other words, in chance there is an accidental concurrence of active causes, as, for example, when a dog runs and a tree falls; or of an active cause and a passive cause, as, for example, when a parent whose powers of generation are in no way defective engenders a monster, because of the indisposition of matter.

An accidental concurrence of this kind is not chance, but the effect of chance. And it is said to be from chance as from an accidental or indeterminate cause, because it has no determinate cause (1).

7° Chance may be given a wide meaning. Thus understood, it has the same relation to chance in the strict sense and to fortune as genus has to species: it is the genus of chance and fortune.

Chance, in its strict or specific meaning, is distinguished from fortune: chance is found in irrational beings, whereas fortune is found in rational beings, i.e., beings endowed with an intellect; v.g., a man is said to be very fortunate, but this is not said of a brute animal, or of a plant.

271. Statement of the thesis.

THESIS. —CHANCE CAN BE FOUND IN IRRATIONAL AGENTS, AND FORTUNE IN ALL RATIONAL CREATURES; BUT AS REGARDS GOD, THERE IS NOTHING FORTUITOUS OR CASUAL.

First part.— *Chance can be found in irrational agents.*— Chance can be found in agents that are intrinsically defectible. But natural agents, that is to say, natural agents not endowed with reason, are intrinsically defectible. Therefore chance can be found in irrational agents.

---

(1) Manifestum est autem quod causa impediens actionem alicujus causae ordinatae ad suum effectum ut in pluribus, concurrit ei interdum per accidens; unde talis concursus non habet causam, inquantum est per accidens. — I, q. 116, a. 6, c.

Major.—Agents that are intrinsically defectible can be impeded by the accidental concurrence of another cause. But such accidental concurrence is from chance, because it has no cause. Therefore...

The *minor* is clear from the foregoing thesis (n. 267).

Second part.— *Fortune can be found in all rational creatures.*—There are two reasons for this: *a)* no rational creature can know everything that can be; *b)* no rational creature has all causes subject to itself.

From the first reason we may deduce that many effects may be produced beyond their intention, because such effects are not known by them; v.g., if God commands an angel to do something, and the accomplishment of this thing results in the conversion of many persons, unknown to the angel.

From the second reason it follows that an accidental concurrence of causes is possible on which a rational creature exercises no influence, i.e., in which it has no part; for such a creature the effect will be fortuitous.

Third part.— *As regards God, there is nothing fortuitous or casual.*—There is nothing that God does not know. Moreover, God's causality extends to all things. Hence every concurrence of causes is known to God, and indeed depends on His causality.

272. Corollaries. — 1° The generation of monsters is not casual as regards God. But it can be either casual or secondarily intended as regards a particular agent. It is casual when it occurs rarely It is secondarily intended, when it occurs in the majority of cases, or when it always occurs. For a particular agent tends, in virtue of its intention, to engender something perfect. But when the agent cannot produce a perfect generation, either because of its own deficiency, or because of the indisposition of matter, it tends, in virtue of its second intention, to produce whatever may be possible, that is to say, a thing engendered with a defect, in as much as the defect is not refused, and thus is in some way attained secondarily (1) Hence a generating agent that has weak active power does not act casually if it engenders a monster in the majority of cases. If, however, its active power is not defective, the engendering of a monster is casual.

2° Chance, as an accidental cause, may be reduced to a proper cause.—This is a common axiom, but it can have a false meaning and a true meaning.

Its false meaning may be expressed as follows: every accidental cause may be reduced to some proximate and particular cause of which the accidental cause is the proper effect. Such a meaning is false, because there are many accidental effects which do not originate from a proper cause; v.g., the whiteness of a musician has no cause.

Its *true* meaning may be stated thus: every accidental cause, or accidental effect, presupposes some proper cause or effect to which it is added. This is the true meaning of the axiom. The finding of a treasure, for example, is joined to the digging into the ground, which is properly intended.

273. A difficulty. — Every effect has a cause. But a casual thing is an effect. Therefore a casual thing has a cause, and therefore chance is not an accidental or indeterminate cause, because an indeterminate cause is not a cause.

Major. — An effect which is essentially one, *I concede;* which is accidentally one, *I deny.*

Minor. — A casual thing is an effect that is essentially one, *I deny,* that is accidentally one, *I concede.*

A casual effect is not intended, and therefore it has accidental unity; v.g., the accidental concurrence of two causes. To better understand this, we should examine the following words of St. Thomas: « . . .Quod iste occidatur a latronibus habet causam per se quia vulneratur; et hoc etiam habet causam per se, quia a latronibus invenitur; sed hoc non habet nisi causam per accidens. Hoc enim quod iste qui negotiatur, ad negotium vadens, inter latrones incidat, est per accidens, ut ex praedictis patet. Unde ejus non oportet ponere aliquam causam. » — *In Metaph.*, L. VI, l. 3, n. 1201 (Cathala).

(1) Joannes a Sancto Thoma, *Cursus Phil.*, t. II, pp. 613-614 (Reiser).

BOOK II

—

Properties of mobile being

Prologue. – If mobile being is considered formally as mobile being, its property or proper passion is physical motion. But physical motion is found only in quantitative being. Hence, first, we shall consider quantity, and, secondly, motion. Therefore there will be two chapters in this book.

CHAPTER I

QUANTITY

Prologue. – First, we shall discuss the essence or formal constituent of quantity. Secondly, we shall treat of place and space, both of which are closely related to quantity. Thirdly, we shall deal with the questions of the compenetration and the multilocation of bodies. Hence there will be three articles in this chapter.

- Formal constituent of quantity
  - Statement of the question
  - Thesis: The formal constituent of quantity consists in the order of the parts in the whole
  - Quantity is distinct from substance
  - Substance of itself is indivisible
  - The substance of mobile being is extended by quantity
  - Division of quantity
  - Parts and indivisibles of continuum
- Place and space
  - Notion of place
  - Notion of space
  - Notion of *where*
  - Notion of posture
  - Notion of habit
- Compenetration and multilocation of bodies
  - Compenetration of places
  - Thesis: Bodies are naturally impenetrable; but by a miracle they can compenetrate one another
  - Multilocation of bodies
  - Thesis: Circumscriptive multilocation is absolutely repugnant, but not mixed multilocation
  - Corollaries

ARTICLE

FORMAL CONSTITUENT OF QUANTITY

274. Statement of the question. — 1° We learn the essence of a thing from external appearances. Hence, to discover the essence of quantity, we must consider what we know experimentally about quantity.

2° We know from experience that quantity has the notes of measure, measurableness, divisibility, impenetrability, filling of place, and extension of parts.

Some Nominalists claim that the essence of quantity consists in its actual filling of place, or in actual divisibility, etc. It is commonly admitted by all that the essence of quantity consists in its being the fundamental root or source of measure, measurableness, divisibility, impenetrability, and the filling of place. This opinion is true. But this explains the essence of quantity only as regards what it s radically, not as regards its formal constituent; v.g., we may say that human nature is the first root of reason, will, and risibility. But, even when this is established, we must continue our inquiry in order to know what the formal constituent of human nature is, i.e., what the formal definition of man is. This investigation will lead us to the conclusion that man is a rational animal.

Similarly, when we know what the results of quantity are, we must continue to seek the formal definition of quantity, i.e., the formal constituent of quantity.

The formal constituent of quantity is the essential constituent of quantity, is that note of quantity which is first and the foundation of all the other notes which are proper to quantity.

3° According to the Thomists, quantity is essentially defined : *the order or the extension of the parts in the whole*, i.e., in relation to the whole.

a) Order, i.e., distinction of the parts.

But distinction is opposed to unity *in one way*, and *in another way* it is opposed to confusion.

Distinction is opposed to unity when it becomes multiplicity by which unity is destroyed.

Distinction is opposed to confusion, when it becomes order, that is to say, when things without order are given the orderly classification proper to them.

Quantity essentially consists in the order or distinction of parts, not in as much as it constitutes parts, but in as much as it destroys the confusion of parts and places part outside of part, uniting them by their extremities.

Thus in man the head, heart, and arms are not merely quantitative parts, but they are also substantial (integral) parts, from which the substantial whole, which is man, results. Hence they are not formally constituted as regards their entity from quantity. Nevertheless, quantity gives these parts an orderly arrangement in as much as it places the heart outside the head, and the arms outside the heart and the head. It is in this *accidental* order or arrangement that quantity formally consists.

b) *Of the parts*, that is to say, of the integral parts, one of which is placed outside another by means of quantity, and which are united only at their extremities.

c) *In the whole*, i. e., in relation to the whole which the parts constitute, and not in relation to something extrinsic, as, for example, place.

275. Statement of the thesis.

THESIS. — THE FORMAL CONSTITUENT OF QUANTITY CONSISTS IN THE ORDER OF THE PARTS IN THE WHOLE.

The formal constituent of quantity is the first of the notes of quantity, and the root of all the other notes that appertain to it. But the order of the parts in the whole, i.e., the extension of the parts in relation to the whole, is the first note of quantity, and is the root of all the other notes that appertain to it. Therefore the order of the parts in the whole, or the extension of the parts in the whole, is the formal constituent of quantity.

Major. — The essential constituent of a thing is its first note, and the root or explanation of all its other notes. But the formal constituent of quantity is the essential constituent of quantity. Therefore . . .

Minor. — *a*) A whole fills a place, because it has parts; *b*) it is impenetrable, i.e., it expels other things from the same place, because it fills a place by means of its parts; *c*) it is divisible into parts, because it has parts ; *d*) it is measurable, because it has extension into parts.

276. Corollaries. – 1° The order of the parts in the whole is the essential definition of quantity. Quantity can be described as it is attained experimentally. From this point of view, it is defined : *that which is known by measure* (1) But measure is the principle or means by which quantity is known. Therefore experimental knowledge of quantity is always relative, that is to say, quantity is not known absolutely, but only by the application of a measure.

There are two kinds of measure by which quantity is known : the measure of numerical quantity, and the measure of dimensional quantity. The former is absolute, and therefore the measurement of discrete things is always made by an absolute measure ; v.g. when we count ten horses. But the latter is relative (2), i.e., is established by convention ; v.g.,

(1) Mensura autem nihil aliud est quam id quo quantitas rei cognoscitur. — *In Metaph.*, L. X, l. 2, n. 1938. — *Ibidem*, L. V, l. 15 (Cathala).

(2) This kind of relativity must not be confused with the principle of relativity of Einstein's physics. The latter has its foundation in the fact that quantity must be defined experimentally by a description of its process of measurement, which cannot be separated from its attendant circumstances. Hence, according to this principle, quantity can vary according to different circumstances, or systems of reference. This conclusion is reasonable, because, on the one hand, continuous quantity experimentally defined is not known absolutely; and, on the other hand, because definitions which differ qualitatively can

a kilogram, a meter. Therefore measurement of dimensional quantity is made by relative measure, i.e., measure established by convention.

2° Theologians commonly teach that the Body of Christ under the species of bread and wine in the Blessed Eucharist has order of its parts in the whole, or, as they say, internal quantity, but not order of its parts in place, or external quantity. Therefore, in the Body of Christ in the Sacred Host, the head is not the neck, the neck is not the chest, etc. On the other hand, since the Body of Christ has no relation to place, it is not diffused or extended under the quantity of bread or wine. Therefore it is wholly in the whole quantity of bread and wine, and wholly in each part of their quantity.

Therefore, when the species are divided into parts, the Real Presence is also multiplied.

277. Quantity is distinct from substance. – 1° *Preliminaries.* — *a*) Here we are concerned with the real distinction of the quantity from the substance of mobile being, that is to say, from the physical compound of first matter and substantial form.

b) The Nominalists (Ockam, etc.) distinguish two kinds of quantity : *accidental* quantity, which is the quantity of accident ; v.g., the quantity of color; and *substantial* quantity, which is identified with corporeal substance.

Descartes and his followers hold that quantity is the very essence or substance of bodies.

Scholastics commonly affirm that quantity is an accident that is really distinct from the substance of mobile being.

c) The real distinction between substance and quantity, though not an article of faith, is certain from the teachings of the Church. The Church has not defined that there is a distinction between quantity and substance, but teaches tha

differ quantitatively also. The principle of relativity of Einstein's physics must be accepted in order to avoid relativism and subjectivism, as they are understood in philosophy; and both are rejected by Einstein.

the substance of bread and wine do not remain in the Blessed Eucharist, but only their accidents or species (1). But we see that the consecrated Host and the consecrated Wine retain their quantity. Hence we must conclude that quantity is an accident, and that it is really distinct from substance.

Aristotle, who had no knowledge of Revelation, teaches that quantity is a predicamental accident, and therefore that it is distinct from substance.

2° We shall now prove that *quantity is really distinct from the substance of mobile being.*

Quantity consists formally in the extension of parts, in as much as parts are placed outside of parts, and are united not as regards the whole of the parts, but only as regards their extremities. But substance does not suffice for such extension and such union ; accident is required Therefore quantity is an accident, and hence really distinct from the substance of mobile being.

Major. — For integral parts, of their very nature, have extension, and therefore one part is not united according to the whole of itself to another part in such a way that it penetrates the other, but rather one part is united to another part as regards its extremity only.

Minor. — The substantial parts of mobile being are first matter and substantial form. But first matter and substantial form are not united to one another by their extremities, but *by penetration*, because form is the act of matter, and matter is potency which is wholly actuated by form. Therefore the extension of parts, which consists in the distinction of parts from one another and their union as regards their extremities, is not a substantial union, but an accidental union (2), and therefore substance does not suffice for the extension of parts, but accident is required.

---

(1) Le Concile de Constance dit: *les accidents* pour indiquer le rapport avec le sujet; le Concile de Trente dit: les *espèces* pour marquer la relation avec les sens. — Hugon, *Les 24 Thèses thomistes.*

(2) Joannes a Sancto Thoma, *Cursus Phil.*, t. I, pp. 545-546.

278. Substance of itself is indivisible. — 1° *Preliminaries.* — *a*) The substance of mobile being would be divisible *of itself*, if before having quantity it had some kind of *entitative* extension. This is the teaching of Suarez and others who, in consequence of their teaching, hold that quantity formally consists in local impenetrability, or in measurableness radically understood. Again, the substance of mobile being would be divisible, if before having quantity it had *integral* substantial parts which were really distinct from one another, as Babenstuber and de Aguirre teach. They affirm that quantity does nothing more than *give order* to integral substantial parts that are already distinct.

b) According to St. Thomas the substance of mobile being, of itself, i.e., before having quantity, is *integrally* simple. i.e., has not parts outside of parts, although it is *essentially* composed of parts, namely, of first matter and substantial form.

c) Integrally simple, i.e, inextensive, may be understood in two ways: *privatively* and *negatively*.

That is said to be *privatively* inextensive which, though completely lacking extension, belongs to the genus of quantity. v.g., a point, which is the term of a line, is completely lacking in extension. A privatively extensive thing has determinate position. Thus the point of one line has position distinct from the position of the point of another line.

A thing is *negatively* inextensive which is entirely outside the genus of quantity, i.e., outside the order of dimension, and has no actual relation to any place. Of itself it is neither in place nor in space, for it abstracts from both.

d) Before the substance of mobile being has quantity, it is privatively inextensive, in as much as it is outside the genus of quantity.

Nevertheless, before the substance of mobile being has quantity, it is not spiritual, because the substance of mobile being has a capacity for quantity, whereas a spirit has no such capacity. Nevertheless, it has a certain mode of spirituality, as has the Body of Christ in the Blessed Sacrament.

2° In the light of the foregoing remarks, we may now set forth two propositions.

1) *The substance of mobile being, before it receives quantity, has no entitative extension.*—If the substance of mobile being had any extension of itself, it would be confused with quantity, for it would have parts united as regards their extremities. But substance and quantity are really distinct (n. 277). Therefore.

2) *The substance of mobile being, before it receives quantity, has no integral substantial parts.* — Integral parts are distinct only by quantity. But, before the substance of mobile being receives quantity, there is no distinction of parts solely by position or order ; for this distinction is the formal effect of quantity. Therefore.

279. The substance of mobile being is extended by quantity. — 1° The Complutenses, the Salmanticenses, and, recently, Domet de Vorges and Mielle contend that the substance of mobile being has no parts under quantity ; v.g., in man the head, the neck, the chest are not parts of substance, but parts of quantity.

b) It is the common teaching of Scholastics that subtance really has different parts under quantity, that is to say, that substance is extended by quantity. Yet it is not extended after the manner of the extension of a thing which of itself belongs to the genus of quantity, as when a small thing is made large, but after the manner of the extension of a thing which of itself is outside the order of dimensions, but which is brought into that order by means of quantity.

c) The parts into which substance is extended may be considered as entities, or as regards their order.

Order or distinction of parts derives from quantity ; but the parts of substance as entities derive from substance, i.e. they are formally substantial, yet are dependent on quantity as a condition. For, just as substance operates only by means of operative power, so it is extended into parts only by means of quantity.

2° We shall now prove that *the substance of mobile being is really extended into parts by quantity.*

The subject into which quantity is received as an accident is really extended into parts. But the substance of mobile being is the subject into which quantity is received as an accident. Therefore the substance of mobile being is really extended into parts of quantity.

Major. — The formal effect of quantity is extension into parts. But the formal effect of an accident is produced in the subject into which it is received. Therefore the subject into which quantity is received as an accident is really extended into parts (1).

280. Division of quantity. — 1° Predicamental quantity is essentially divided first into continuous quantity and discrete quantity.

a) *Continuous* quantity is quantity whose parts are united to one another. It is defined: *quantity whose parts are joined at a common term.*

b) *Discrete* quantity or number is quantity whose parts are actually separate from one another. It is defined : *multitude measured by one.*

Multitude may be understood as the plurality of inextensive beings, and, in this case, it does not pertain to predicamental quantity ; it is called transcendental multitude, because it results from beings as such.

Multitude may also be understood as the plurality of extensive beings; in this case, it is called predicamental quantity, because it includes distinction of parts as regards position, and is measurable ; v.g., ten books.

(1) Etsi corpoream naturam extensio in partes integrales consequitur, non tamen idem est corpori esse substantiam et esse quantum. Substantia quippe ratione sui indivisibilis est, non quidem ad modum puncti, sed ad modum ejus quod est extra ordinem dimensionis; quantitas vero, quae extensionem substantiae tribuit, a substantia realiter differt, et est veri nominis accidens. — *Thesis X* s. Thomae

2° Predicamental quantity is divided into permanent quantity and fluid quantity.

a) *Permanent* quantity is quantity whose parts exist simultaneously ; v.g., the quantity of iron, the quantity of a stone.

b) *Fluid* quantity is quantity whose parts do not exist simultaneously ; v.g., the quantity of time, of motion, of speech.

This division does not derive from quantity, but from something accidental to quantity, and therefore the division is accidental.

281. Parts and indivisibles of continuum. — 1° *Preliminaries.* — *a*) Continuum is quantity whose parts are united in a common term. Here we are concerned with both permanent and fluid continuum.

b) Indivisibles are used here as meaning indivisibles in fluid continuum, and also indivisibles in permanent continuum.

In fluid continuum, indivisibles are *instants* in time, and *changes already made* (mutata esse) in motion.

The indivisibles of permanent continuum are the *point*, the *line*, and the *superficies* or surface.

The point is indivisible in every respect ; the line is indivisible as regards breadth and depth ; the superficies is ind visible as regards depth only.

The problems in regard to continuum may be stated in the questions that follow. *First*, are indivisibles the sole ultimate constituent elements of continuum ? *Secondly*, if continuum is not composed solely of indivisibles, are there parts in continuum which are actual entities, or only potential entities ? *Thirdly*, if the parts of continuum have actual existence, although they are not actually divided or separate, how are the indivisibles distinguished from the parts ?

c) Zeno of Elea (b. 490 B.C.) taught that divisible continuum is composed solely of indivisibles.

Many recent philosophers affirm that the parts of continuum have only potential existence.

2° We may now set forth the following propositions :

1) *Continuum is not composed solely of indivisibles as its ultimate elements.* — A thing that is composed of parts that are indefinitely divisible is not composed solely of indivisibles. But continuum is composed of parts that are indefinitely divisible, for the part of continuous quantity is always continuous quantity. The part of a body is a body, the part of motion is motion, and the part of time is time. Therefore.

2) *In every continuum there are parts which actually exist.* — Parts among which there is order, i. e., among which confusion is destroyed, actually exist. But there is order, i.e., confusion is destroyed, among the parts of continuum, for quantity is the order of parts. Therefore.

3) *The actual parts of continuum are finite in number.* — If the actual parts of continuum were infinite in number, the whole divisibility of cont nuum would be reduced to act. Hence its parts would no longer be divisible, but would be indivisible. Therefore continuum would be composed solely of indivisibles as its ultimate elements But this is repugnant.

4) *In continuum there are actually present both terminating and continuing indivisibles.* — In continuum there is the actual union of the parts of quantity. But one part of quantity is not joined to another part as regards the whole of the parts, i.e., by penetration, but at their extremities, which must not be parts of quantity, but indivisibles. Hence in continuum there are actually present indivisibles by which the parts of quantity are terminated and by which part is joined to part; that is, there are actually present in continuum both terminating and continuing indivisibles.

Therefore indivisibles are realities that are really distinct from parts. They are commonly regarded as modes of parts.

POINTS FOR REVIEW

1. Define formal constituent. What is the formal constituent of quantity?

2. Briefly explain when distinction is opposed to unity, and when opposed to confusion.

3. Explain the following statements: *a*) Experimental knowledge of quantity is relative; *b*) Measure of dimensive quantity is relative.

4. Is it of faith that quantity is really distinct from substance? Explain briefly.

5. Prove that the quantity of mobile being is really distinct from substance.

6. In what sense is substance indivisible before it receives quantity?

7. Explain why substance is extended by quantity.

8. Are the parts of extended substance accidental?

9. Explain why continuum is not composed of indivisibles, and why the parts of continuum have actual existence.

10. Are the parts of continuum infinite in number? Explain.

11. Are indivisibles actually present in continuum? Explain.

ARTICLE II

PLACE AND SPACE

282. Notion of place. — Aristotle defines space: *the first and immobile superficies of an ambient body.*

a) Place is conceived by all as that which contains the thing located. But that which contains the thing located is the first superficies (term) of the body (of the bodies) that immediately contains the located body.

b) It is said to be immobile, *first,* in order that place be distinguished, v.g., from a vessel which contains in a mobile manner : for a vessel contains in a mobile manner, and is moved with its content, whereas place is not moved ; *secondly,* because place is not a superficies of this or that body, but formally *as designating a determinate position in the corporeal universe* Therefore the superficies thus understood remains the same, even though the ambient body moves ; v.g., the water that surrounds a ship anchored in a river is contantly moving around it, but the ship's place remains the same.

283. Notion of space. — Real space results immediately from quantity and is constituted by it. For quantity is essentially the order of parts according to position. The relations of distance and of nearness result from this order. Space formally consists in relation of distance. As the relation of space is considered within one and the same quantity, more or less distant from one extreme to another, from one part to another, we have internal space ; as it is considered as being from one body to another, between one quantity and another, we have external space. Space conceived as a void receptable is merely imaginary space.

284. Notion of « where ». — *Where* is defined: *the accident that results from the circumscription of a body by the circumscription of a place.*

Where, as is clear, is not place, nor is it identified with the quantity or the substance of a body which remain the same, even when its place and *where* do not. Again, *where* is not the mere relation of a located body to place, but is the intrinsic determination of a body that results from place, and therefore is a predicament of a kind all its own.

285. Notion of posture. — Posture is *the accident which results in a corporeal substance from the disposition of the parts of a body in place.* For a body can remain in the same place and retain the same *where*, without always having the same posture. For its parts can have a different disposition ; v.g. a part which had been on the right side can be put on the left, and vice versa.

286. Notion of habit. — Habit (predicamental accident) is defined : *the accident which results in a body from the adjuncts of clothing, arms, or ornaments.*

Therefore habit is not the same as clothing, nor is it a mere relation to clothing, but an accident of a kind all its own in virtue of which a body acquires a new entity, viz., to be clothed, to be armed, to be adorned.

ARTICLE III

COMPENETRATION AND MULTILOCATION OF BODIES

I – COMPENETRATION OF BODIES

287. Statement of the question. — 1° *Origin of the problem.*—We know from faith that *Christ was born* by passing forth through the closed womb of the Blessed Virgin. After the Resurrection the Apostles *saw* Christ entering the cenacle « the doors being *shut.*» Hence the philosopher is confronted with the problem of the possibility of the compenetration of bodies.

2° *Notion of compenetration.* — Impenetrability is the property in virtue of which one body excludes another body from the place which it occupies. Hence compenetration is the simultaneous occupation of the same place (proper, not common) by two or more bodies.

3° *Opinions.* — Durandus thought that the compenetration of bodies was not possible even by the power of God. This opinion is held too by Rationalists and many herectics. All Scholastics hold that bodies are *naturally* impenetrable, but that their compenetration is really possible *by a miracle.*

288. Statement of the thesis.

THESIS. — BODIES ARE NATURALLY IMPENETRABLE ; BUT BY A MIRACLE THEY CAN COMPENETRATE ONE ANOTHER.

First part. — *Bodies are naturally impenetrable.*

a) *Experience.* — This truth is known from experience.

b) *A priori.* — The position of one body outside another is the natural effect of quantity. But impenetrability naturally results from the position of one body outside another. Therefore . .

Second part.— *By a miracle bodies can compenetrate one another.* Everything that is not repugnant is possible, at least by a miracle. But the compenetration of bodies is not repugnant. Therefore by a miracle bodies can compenetrate one another.

Major. — God can do anything that is not repugnant.

Minor. — It is not absolutely repugnant that a thing does not attain its secondary effect. But the order of bodies in relation to place, and consequently impenetrability, is only a secondary effect of quantity, which is defined : *the order of the parts in the whole.* Therefore . . .

II – MULTILOCATION OF BODIES

289. Statement of the question. — 1° Certain Saints, as St. Francis Xavier, etc., have been seen in more than one place at the same time. We know from faith that the Body of Christ is really present at the same time in Heaven and in the Blessed Eucharist. Hence we are confronted with the problem of the possibility of a body's being present in more than one place at the same time, i.e., with the problem of the multilocation of bodies.

2° A thing can be in place *properly* and *improperly.*

A thing is in place *properly, circumscriptively* or *locally,* when its dimensions are measured or circumscribed by the dimensions of the place.

A thing is in place *improperly, incircumscriptively* or *non-locally,* when its dimensions are not measured by the dimensions of the place.

A thing can be in place *improperly* in three ways :

1) *Informatively*, as the spiritual substance (human soul) which informs a body. The human soul has no dimensions whatsoever, and therefore of itself abstracts from place. Nevertheless, it is said to be in place, in as much as the body of which it is the form is in place. 2) *Operatively*, as a spiritual substance which applies its effective power to something located, i.e, in place. Thus God and angels are in place by their operation, i. e., operatively. 3) *Sacramentally*, as the Body of Christ is in the Blessed Sacrament. The Body of Christ is really present under the dimensions of bread and wine. Theologians commonly say that It has Its own internal quantity but not external quantity. Therefore It has not in virtue of Its own quantity, relation to place, i.e., Its dimensions are not measured by the dimensions of bread and wine, but It is in place *after the manner of a substance*, i.e. after the manner of a thing which of itself abstracts from place.

3° Multilocation is the presence of a thing in two or more distinct places at one and the same time.

The foundation of multilocation is the *non-definitive* presence of one thing in one place.

A thing is *non-definitively* in a place, if it can be in another place at the same time.

A thing is *definitively* in a place, if it cannot be in another place at the same time.

4° Multilocation is said to be *circumscriptive*, when a body is circumscriptively in two or more places ; *mixed*, when a body is circumscriptively in one place, and incircumscriptively, i.e., improperly, in another place or places.

5° *Opinions*. — 1) Scotus, Suarez, and many more recent philosophers hold that circumscriptive multilocation is not repugnant. 2) St. Thomas, St. Bonaventure, St. Anselm, and others teach that the circumscriptive multilocation of bodies is absolutely impossible, i.e., it is not possible even by the absolute power of God, but that mixed multilocation is possible.

290. Statement of the thesis.

THESIS. — CIRCUMSCRIPTIVE MULTILOCATION IS ABSOLUTELY REPUGNANT, BUT NOT MIXED MULTILOCATION.

First part — *Circumscriptive multilocation is absolutely repugnant*(1).

1° It is absolutely repugnant that the same body be simultaneously contained and not contained by one and the same place. But a body which would be circumscriptively in one place and circumscriptively in another place at one and the same time would be simultaneously contained and not contained by the first place. Therefore circumscriptive multilocation is absolutely repugnant.

Major. — It is clear from its terms.

Minor. — It would be contained by the first place, for to be circumscribed is the same as to be contained ; it would not be contained by it, for at the same time it would be circumscribed by another place.

2° It is absolutely repugnant that the same body have two numerical y distinct quantities. But a body which would be circumscriptively in two places at the same t me would have two numerically distinct quantities. Therefore circumscriptive multilocation is absolutely repugnant.

Major. — Two quantities are numerically distinct from each other only by their reception into two distinct bodies.

Minor. — It would have one quantity by which it would be circumscribed by one place, and another quantity by which it would be circumscribed by the other place.

Second part. — *Mixed multilocation is not repugnant.*

Mixed multilocation is the presence of the same body *circumscriptively* in one place, and *after the manner of a sub-*

(1) Eadem efficitur quantitate ut corpus circumscriptive sit in loco, et in uno tantum loco de quacumque potentia per hunc modum esse possit. — *Thesis XII* s. Thomae.

stance in another place or other places. But the circumscriptive presence of a body in one place, and its presence after the manner of a substance in other places, is not repugnant Therefore mixed multilocation is no repugnant.

Minor. — The minor is not easily understood, because such presence in two or more places transcends the imagination (1). Nevertheless, we see that substance essentially abstracts from posture, space, and distance. Hence a thing can, at one and the same time, be present *circumscriptively* in one place, and in other places *after the manner of a substance*, without being distant from itself, (for as such it abstracts from distance), provided that there be some foundation for its having relation to different places.

In the Blessed Eucharist this relation results from the conversion of the substance of bread and wine into the substance of the Body and Blood of Christ.

291. Corollaries. — 1) Therefore, if a Saint was seen in several places at the same time, he was present with his *real* body in one place, and with an *apparent* body in the other places.

2) When Christ, after the Ascension, appeared to anyone, v.g., to Paul, He really left Heaven corporally.

3) A body which is in a place circumscriptively is in it *definitively*, and hence it is *naturally* impossible for it to be in another place.

4) A body which is in a place circumscriptively is in it *definitively*, and therefore it could not be in another place circumscriptively even by a miracle, although by a miracle it could be in other places *incircumscriptively* or *improperly*.

(1) Il n'y a pas de contradiction entre ces deux faits que Notre-Seigneur continue d'être au ciel, assis à la droite de son Père, selon sa manière naturelle, et que néanmoins il nous soit présent en plusieurs autres lieux, par sa substance et d'une manière sacramentelle. C'est là un mode d'être que nous pouvons à peine exprimer par des paroles; mais qu'il soit possible à Dieu, *la raison éclairée par la foi nous le fait comprendre*, et nous devons le croire très fermement. — *Conc. Trident.*, sess. XIII, c. 1.

5) Angels have finite power. Hence, when they operate in a place, they are in that place *definitively*, and hence they cannot operate in other places.

6) Since God operates in all th ngs that exist or can exist, He is not in place *definitively*, but *repletively*, i.e., *in an incircumscriptive manner*. For He is *everywhere*.

CHAPTER II

MOTION

Prologue. – Motion is the property of mobile being. The notions of action, passion, and time are closely related to the notion of motion. Hence, first, we shall deal with motion; secondly, with action and passion; and thirdly with time. Therefore there will be three articles in this chapter.

- Motion
  - General notion of motion
  - Proper notion of motion
  - Corollaries
  - What successive motion adds to mutation
  - Predicaments which are terms of motion
  - Unity of motion
  - Difficulties
- Action and passion
  - Notion of action
  - Notion of passion
  - Action and passion are distinct from motion
  - Subject of action
- Time
  - Time as duration
  - Time, eternity, and eviternity
  - Time as measure
  - Presence of time
  - Division of time
  - *When*

ARTICLE I

MOTION

292. General notion of motion. — 1° Motion, *in its widest meaning*, signifies any kind of operation ; v.g., intellection, love. Thus it is that, though God is essentially and absolutely immutable, motion is predicated of Him in as much as He has operation.

2° Motion, *in a wide sense*, is any kind of change. But change is any transition from one thing to another ; v.g., the change that takes place when the intellect acquires knowledge of something it did not know before.

3° Motion, *properly so-called*, signifies change which we perceive in mobile being, i.e., sensible change.

Sensible change of itself may be either sensible or non-sensible.

Change is of itself sensible when it is successive, that is to say, when there is successive progression from one term to another. Such change is sensibly perceived, and is successive motion or *motion in the strict sense*.

Change is not of itself sensible when the change itself is not sensibly perceived, but only the two terms of the change. This occurs in instantaneous change. For instantaneous change is only virtually distinguished from its term-to-which, and therefore is apprehended only by the intellect.

Hence any sensible change is properly called motion. But successive motion, because of its being of itself sensible, is *motion in the strict sense*. Instantaneous motion is not motion in the strict sense, but is called mutation[1].

(1) *In Phys.*, L. V, l. 2. — *De Veritate*, q. 28, a. 1.

293. Proper notion of motion. — Motion, *in its proper sense*, is correctly defined by Aristotle : *the act of a being in potency as such.*

Explanation of the definition. — 1° *From its terms :*

a) *Act :* that by which a thing at first existing in potency later is really determined is act. But a body which at first *can* be moved, and later is moved, really receives determination, v.g., a man who at first is not walking and later walks. Therefore motion is act (1).

b) *Of a being in potency :* act properly belongs to the subject into which it is received. But motion is act received into a subject which is in potency to it; v.g., water becomes hot only if it is first in potency to being heated. Therefore motion is the act of a being in potency.

c) *As such*, i.e., of a being in potency in as much as it is in potency. This is the formal constituent of motion. For act, which is not motion, actuates in such a way that a determinate subject *remains* in its determination. Act, which is motion, actuates in such a way that its subject, in virtue of this very act, tends to some further act ; v.g., cold water which is heated does not become tepid except in as much as it tends to become heated.

Hence motion not only actuates a subject to render it *in act* (in respect to its earlier potency), but also to render it *in potency* (in regard to its later act).

Objection. — The tepidity of water that remains tepid is not motion. But water which remains tepid is in potency to being hot. Therefore hotness, which, in this case, is not motion, is the act of a being in potency as such.

I concede the *major.*

Minor. — Is of itself in potency to being hot, *I concede;* in such a way that in virtue of its tepidity it tends to being hot, *I deny.*

Thus tepidity is the act of water in as much as it is actually tepid, not in as much as it is in potency to being hot.

For water which remains tepid is equally in potency to being hot and to being cold; water which becomes tepid in order that it become hot, in virtue of its tepidity or act, tends, i.e., is placed in potency, to being hot, and hence tepidity is motion.

(1) *In Phys.*, L. III, l. 2.

2° *From the text of St. Thomas* (1) : « . . . Motion is neither the potency of a being n potency, nor is it the act of a being in act, but it is the act of a being in potency ; so that, .n being called *act*, its relation to its former potency is designated, and in its being said to be *a being in potency*, its relation to its later act is designated. Hence the Phi osopher most properly defines motion by saying that motion is *entelechia*, that is, *the act of a being in potency as such* » ( ).

294. Corollaries. — 1° The definition of motion: the act of a being in potency *as such*, is safeguarded also in mutation, that is to say, in instantaneous motion, as, for example, in substantial generation. For two instants of nature can be distinguished in instantaneous motion : *becoming* and *actual existence*. I we consider *becoming* as it is related to *actual existence*, we have the *act of a being in potency as such*. Thus in the production of substantial form which takes place in an instantaneous manner, we can distinguish the instant when substantial form *is being produced*, and the instant when it *has been produced*. When substantial form is being produced, we have motion.

2° The foregoing definition of motion is not verified in immanent actions, i.e., in actions which of themselves are not destined to produce an effect, as *intellection*, *sensation*, *volition*. For motion is the act of a being in potency, precisely in as much

(1) *In Phys.*, l. III, l. 3.

(2) « Movement is . . . the *actus* of a potential being in so far as it is still *in potentia*. » In other words, between the simple aptitude to movement, or *pure potentiality*, on the one hand, and complete actualization which supposes the aptitude fully satisfied, or *potentiality actuated*, on the other, there is an intermediary reality composed of *both* '*act*' and '*power*', and this is movement: it is *actuality* inasmuch as it implies a potency in part realized, and it is *potentiality* inasmuch as the subject, partly actualized, is susceptible of further actuality; it is the actuality of a potential subject, 'actus imperfecti'.

To form an accurate conception of movement we must therefore keep in view a double relation on the part of the subject, namely, with a previous potentiality now become actual, and with an actuality yet acquirable; movement is at once the actualization of a certain potentiality and the capacity for further, more complete actualization; in a word, the *actus* of a *potentia* that is still *in potentia*. — Card. MERCIER, *A Manual of Modern Scholastic Philosophy* (Third English edition, authorized translation), vol. I, pp. 509-510.

as the subject of motion leaves its term-from-which and has not yet attained its term-to-which. Motion ceases with its attaining its term-to-which. But immanent operations are destined to attain their object, and do not cease when their object is attained, but exist, and are more perfect when their object is more perfectly attained Hence such operations are not acts of a being in potency. In other words, the definition of physical motion is not verified in immanent operations.

3° Continuity is essential to motion in the strict sense. Sometimes motion in the strict sense is divided into *continuous* motion and *discrete* motion. But motion in the strict sense, as *discrete*, is nothing other than several interrupted continuous motions, and so it is reduced to the species of continuous motion.

295. What successive motion adds to mutation. — Motion strictly so-called, i.e., successive motion, adds three things to mutation.

First, that it be between positively contrary terms, and not merely between privation and form. For every kind of motion is change. But change obtains between opposites, in as much as in every change there is the forsaking of a term-from-which and the acquisition of a term-to-which. But, in successive motion, there must be some interval, or space to be travelled, between the term-from-which and the term-to-which; for otherwise we have instantaneous change. Therefore the opposition between the terms of motion cannot be *contradictory* or *privative*, as is the opposition between privation and form, between being and non-being, because opposition of this kind is *immediate*. The former kind of opposition must be between two positive terms, i.e., it must be *contrary* opposition.

Secondly, the subject of motion must be complete being in act. Therefore first matter cannot be the subject of motion in the strict sense, although it is the subject of mutation, that is to say, of substantial generation and corruption. The reason is this: the change which takes place in first matter is a change from privation to form, and therefore it is instantaneous. For the principles of substantial generation are three in number:

privation (term-from-which), *form* (term-to-which), and *subject* (first matter).

Thirdly, motion is a *flux* between two terms. For mot on in the strict sense, or successive motion, consists in this flux, whereas mutation is not a flux, but it is an instantaneous transition from non-existence to existence.

296. Predicaments which are terms of motion. — 1° The *proper* term of mot on is that which it first attains. The *accidental* term of mot on is that which it attains by means of another, i.e., by means of that which it first attains; v. g., all substantia generation takes place with previous alteration. Nevertheless, alteration is properly terminated in qualit es, and only mediately, i e., accidentally, in substance.

2° *Substance, relation, action, passion, when, posture*, and *habit* are not properly terms of motion in the strict sense.

a) Substance is not a term of motion, because substantial change formally is a transition from privation to form, and it is in first matter as subject. Therefore change of substance, i.e., substantia generation, cannot be successive because there is no nterval between privation and form.

Carefully observe that, even though the generation of one is the corruption of another, generation does not proceed from the form of something corrupted as its term-from-which, but proceeds from privation to form.

b) Relation is not a term of motion, for relat on results from the positing of its foundation and term. Hence, for a relation, it is sufficient that either the foundation and the term of the re ation be the term of motion, or, if the foundation already exists, that the term of the relation be the term of motion; v.g., one body becomes equal to another when the latter acquires as much quantity as the former.

c) Ne ther action nor passion is a term of motion, because each is itself motion. And motion is not the term of motion, for otherwise there would be an infinite process.

d) The accident *when* is not a term of motion, because it results from time, and time is motion. Hence, if the accident *when* were a term of motion, time would be a term of motion and consequently motion would be the term of motion.

e) Posture and habit cannot be terms of motion, because they are changed by means of local motion, i.e., by means of motion of which the accident *where* is properly the term.

3° There are only three predicaments that can be proper terms of successive motion, namely, the accidents *where*, *quantity*, and *quality*.

In these three predicaments only are found the conditions required for a term of motion in the strict sense:

a) Contrariety between positive terms such as exists between a larger and a smaller quantity, between two qualities, v.g., between heat and cold.

b) Complete being, for the subject of local motion of quantitative motion, and of qualitative motion is complete being.

c) Flux between the term-from-which and the term-to-which: between two places, between a larger and a smaller quantity, and between qualities, there is a certain interval or distance, and thus there can be the flux in which motion consists.

297. Unity of motion. — 1° We may distinguish between three kinds of unity: generic unity, specific unity, and numerical unity of motion.

2° The generic unity and the specific unity of motion derive from the proper term-to-which of motion, because motion is not something apart from things which are produced, but is their becoming. Hence it is reduced to the predicament of the thing which is produced (1).

3° Since there are three proper terms of motion, there are

(1) *In Phys.*, L. V, l. 6.

three supreme genera of motion: *local* motion, motion of *increase* and *decrease*, and motion of *alteration*.

The different species of motion derive from the different species of things which are its proper terms.

4° The numerical unity of motion presupposes the specific unity of its term-to-which, and superadds two kinds of continuity, namely, continuity of time and continuity of subject. For when the subject of motion is changed, the motion is not numerically the same. Likewise, when motion is interrupted by rest as regards time, there is no longer one motion, but there will be many motions or movements [1].

298. Difficulties. — We shall now refute the sophisms of Zeno against the reality of motion.

1) (*The Dichotomy*). — In order that a mobile being travel a determinate distance, it must first cover half the distance, and then half the distance that remains, and again half the distance that remains, and so into infinity. But the infinite cannot be traversed. Therefore a mobile being never travels a determinate distance, i.e., motion is impossible.

Major. — If a mobile being would travel a distance (space) of which the parts are infinite and indivisible, *I concede;* of which the parts are actually finite, *I deny.*

I pass over the minor, but deny the conclusion.

The parts of continuum are not actually infinite, but finite. Therefore a mobile being, *in continuous motion*, does not travel a distance which has actually infinite parts, as Zeno falsely supposes, but a distance which is a whole that has only finite parts.

2) (*The Achilles*). — Achilles, even though he runs very fast, will never overtake the tortoise which began to crawl before he started. For when Achilles reaches the place from which the tortoise started, the tortoise will be at another place farther one; and when Achilles reaches that point, the tortoise will be at another place farther on, and so on without end. Therefore Achilles will never overtake the tortoise, i.e., motion is impossible.

Antecedent. — If Achilles' motion is discrete motion, *I pass over;* if his motion is continuous motion, *I deny.*

The answer in this case is the same as in the preceding case. For Achilles' motion is *continuous motion.* Hence his motion is not interrupted at any point in the race, as Zeno falsely supposes, but continues without interruption.

3) (*The Arrow*). — As long as an arrow is in the same place, it is at rest. But an arrow in flight is in the same place at each instant of its flight. Therefore an arrow in flight is at rest in each instant of its flight, or, in other words, it never moves.

(1) *In Phys.*, L. V, l. 7.

Major. — As long as an arrow is in the same place, as at rest in it, *I concede;* as continuously in motion, *I deny.*

Minor. — At each instant it is in the same place, as at rest, *I deny;* as moving with continuous motion, *I concede.* I deny the conclusion.

The explanation is ever the same. Moreover, we may argue against Zeno in this way: Against a fact no argumentation is valid. But motion is a fact. Therefore any argumentation against the possibility of motion is a sophism. — *In Phys.*, l. VI, l. 2.

POINTS FOR REVIEW

1. Show how motion in the strict sense is distinguished from mutation

2. Explain the following words found in the definition of motion: *of a being in potency as such.*

3. Is substantial generation motion properly so-called? Explain.

4. Enumerate the three conditions required for motion in the strict sense.

5. Whence does motion derive its unity? Explain.

ARTICLE II

ACTION AND PASSION

299. Notion of action. — 1° The notions of action and passion are closely related to the notion of motion. For a thing acts in as much as it moves, and is a patient, i.e., is acted upon, in as much as it is moved.

Action may be understood in a *wide sense* and in a *strict sense.*

Action, in the wide sense, is any operation, and it is defined : *the act of something active, as active*(1), or *the actuality of a power* (2), that is, of an operative power.

2° Action, in the wide sense, is divided into *immanent action* and *transitive action.*

a) Immanent action is action which is not destined to produce an effect, but which remains in the agent as its perfection ; v.g., intellection, sensation, volition.

Immanent action is action in the wide sense, and comes under the predicament of quality, not under the predicament of action. Immanent action is called *metaphysical action.*

b) Transitive action is action which is destined to produce an effect ; v.g., heating, sawing.

Transitive action is predicamental action, and is called *physical action.*

It is with transitive action that we are concerned here.

300. Notion of passion. — As action is the act of the agent, so passion is the act of the patient. Passion, therefore,

(1) *Phys.*, l. III, c. 3 (202 a 23).
(2) I, q. 54, a. 1.

may be defined : *the second act of a passive or receptive power,* or *the accident which constitutes a subject as actually receiving the effect or action of an agent.*

301. Action and passion are distinct from motion. — A thing acts in as much as it moves, and it is a patient, or is acted upon, in as much as it is moved. Therefore it follows that action and passion are not new realities which are added to motion.

Nevertheless, action, passion, and motion are distinct in some ways from one another. For motion of itself is the tendency from the term-from-which to the term-to-which; action is motion as related to the agent from which it originates ; and passion is motion as related to the patient, i.e., to the mobile being into which it is received. In other words, motion of itself is the successive transition from one thing to another ; action is motion as the act of the agent ; passion is motion as the act of the patient. And since motion as the act of the agent, and motion as the act of the patient, is found in different states and with different relations, action and passion are said to be distinguished from motion as its two modes, and from each other as different modes of one and the same entity which is motion.

302. Subject of action. — 1° Action, as we have said, is either immanent, or transitive.

The subject of immanent action presents no difficulty. For immanent action remains in the agent as the perfection of the agent.

Hence it is only with transitive action that there is any difficulty.

2° Transitive action is the actuality of an agent by which the agent produces an effect dependent upon it for its existence. And since the effect is in the patient, we must find out whether the subject of action is the agent, or the patient.

3° In transitive action, there are three things that we may consider.

We may consider :

a) the origin of action in the agent, i.e., action as originating in the agent ;

b) action as the second act of the agent ;

c) the procession of the effect from the agent, i.e., the effect as proceeding from the agent.

4° a) Action has its origin in the agent not by means of an action, but by emanation. For otherwise one action would proceed by means of another action, and this by means of another, and so into infinity. Emanation is defined : *the immediate origin of one being from another, without the mediation of any predicamental action.*

b) Action, as the second act of the agent, is in the agent as in its subject.

c) Action, as it produces its effect, is in the patient ; for the effect is produced in the patient. Hence the difficulty in regard to the subject of transitive action is this : *is action formally action as it is the second act of the agent, or as it produces an effect?*

5° Scotus, Cajetan [1], and certain other Thomists maintain that the agent is the subject of action, because they conceive transitive action formally as the second act of the agent, or as the relation of the agent to the patient.

Marxists, the advocates of Communism in our day, maintain, in a way all their own, that the agent is the subject of action. For they claim that man becomes more and more perfect in proportion to the extent and the perfection of his production. Therefore they conceive transitive action as the perfection of the agent, not the perfection of the patient.

Aristotle [2] and St. Thomas [3] seem to teach that the

(1) *In I*, q. 25, a. 1.

(2) *Phys.*, L. III, c. 3 (202 b 5). — *Metaph.*, L. IX, c. 8 (1050 a 31). — *De Anima*, L. III, c. 2 (426 a 4).

(3) *De Veritate*, q. 14, a. 3. — *De Potentia*, q. 10, a. 1, a. c. — *Contra Gentes*, L. II, c. 1.

subject of transitive action is the patient.

6° To solve the difficulty we must hold with John of St. Thomas ([1]) that transitive action is both in the agent and in the patient according to two distinct formalities, which are interrelated.

Action, as the second act of the agent, is in the agent; but, from this point of view, action is understood as only initiated, or as regards its origin. But action understood as the causality of the agent, i.e., action *in its termination*, is formally in the patient. In other words, transitive action strictly is in the patient, because transitive action strictly exists when the agent produces an effect in the patient. If the agent does not produce an effect, then, strictly speaking, it does not act.

7° We shall now prove that *transitive action strictly is in the patient.*

1) Transitive action produces its effect in the patient. But the subject of action is that in which the effect is produced. Therefore transitive action is in the patient.

Major.—It is clear from the notion of transitive action.

Minor.—Action which is destined to produce an effect exists formally and strictly when it produces the effect and where it produces it.

2) Action which primarily and essentially perfects the patient is in the patient. But transitive action primarily and essentially perfects the patient. Therefore transitive action is in the patient ([2]).

The *major* is clear.

Minor.—The difference between immanent action and transitive action is this: immanent action remains in the agent as the perfection of the agent, whereas transitive action is destined to be the motion or perfection of the patient.

---

(1) *Cursus Phil.*, t. II, pp. 312-314.

(2) I, q. 18, a. 3, ad 3, and q. 54, a. 2. — I-II, q. 3, a. 2, ad 3. — *Contra Gentes*, L. I, c. 100.

POINTS FOR REVIEW

1. Explain how action is distinguished from passion, and how action and passion are distinguished from motion.

2. Name and briefly explain the two formalities found in transitive action.

3. Show how transitive action is in both the agent and in the patient.

ARTICLE III

TIME

303. Time as duration. — By the term time, all understand something which pertains to the duration of things which are subject to change and succession.

But duration is persistence or permanence in existence, i.e., it is continued existence. Therefore duration includes two things: *existence* and its *continuation*.

Mobile and successive things are said to have duration, i.e., to continue in existence in virtue of their continuous flux, in as much as one part ceases and another begins, or as regards *before* and *after*. Therefore their duration includes two things: *a*) the addition of existence to existence which are distinct from each other as the parts of continuum; *b*) the constant production of existence which is superadded to existence, i.e., a cause continually influencing and producing existence (1).

Hence time, as duration, is fluid existence, and may be defined: ***existence continually superadded to existence, as connoting a cause continually producing it.***

304. Time, eternity, and eviternity. – In order that we may have a clearer notion of time, we shall compare it with eternity and eviternity.

Eternity is the duration of a thing which is immutable in its existence and operation, i.e., the duration of God.

Since eternity is absolutely immutable, there can be no potency whatsoever in eternal being.

---

(1) JOANNES A SANCTO THOMA, *Cursus Phil.*, t. II, pp. 369-372 (Reiser).

Eviternity is the duration of a being which is immutable in its existence, but not in its operation; v.g., the duration of an angel (1).

Since eviternity includes mutability, eviternity in a being requires composition of essence and existence, which are related to each other respectively as potency and act. Nevertheless, the essence of a being which is eviternal receives its total existence in the beginning, and retains it immutably; therefore the essence itself is not mutable, nor is it composed of potency and act.

Time is the duration of a being which is mutable in its existence and operation. Therefore the essence of a being which exists in time does not receive its total existence from the beginning, but successively acquires it with change. Therefore it is mutable, and composed of potency and act, i.e., of first matter and substantial form.

305. Time as measure. – Time is successive duration. But such duration is measure and is measurable. Hence time may be defined as measure. Aristotle defines it: *the measure of motion as regards 'before' and 'after'*, i.e., according to an order of anteriority and posteriority.

a) *Measure:* not measure which measures, because otherwise any measure would be time, but measure which is measured, i.e., measured motion or movement.

b) *Of motion*: principally of local motion, because it accompanies all other motions, and is more manifest to the senses and more uniform than other kinds of motion.

c) *As regards 'before' and 'after':* local motion takes place in continuous quantity (magnitude), which has parts outside of parts. Hence, as motion takes place 'before' in one part of quantity, and 'after' in another part, it is measured by time. (Think of how we conceive an hour from the apparent movement of the sun).

Therefore 'before' and 'after' enter the definition of time as they are found in motion in virtue of quantity in which

(1) *In I Sent.*, dist., 9, q. 2, a. 1.

motion take place, not as motion is measured by time. Thus a vicious circle is avoided.

NOTE.—Time, as duration, has real existence as regards its own entity, because it is the duration of motion which really exists. Nevertheless, it is only by reason that it is constituted measure. For the parts of time, as successive, do not coexist. To constitute time as measure, first, reason must unify the parts of successive duration; secondly, it must apply this measure to something measurable.

306. Presence of time. – 1° In time, as in every continuum, there are two elements: *parts* and *indivisibles*. An indivisible of time is an *instant*, just as an indivisible of a line is a point.

2° We shall prove that time is not present in virtue of its part, but only in virtue of its indivisible, i.e., in virtue of the instant. By analogy the same must be said of every successive thing. Any successive thing whatsoever is present only in virtue of its indivisible.

3° *a*) Nothing is present except *now*. But *now* is not a part of time, but only an indivisible of time. Therefore time is not present in virtue of its part, but only in virtue of its indivisible, i.e., in virtue of its instant.

The *major* is clear, for 'before' and 'after' are not present; only *now* is present.

Minor.—*Now* is not divisible into 'before' and 'after.' Hence it is not a part of time, but an indivisible of time.

b) What is successive cannot be present and existing in virtue of its part, but only as an indivisible of itself. But time is successive. Therefore time cannot be present in virtue of its part, but only by means of an indivisible of itself, i.e., by means of an instant.

Major.—The parts of something successive cannot exist at the same time, but one flows after the other. But, if something successive could be present in virtue of a part of itself, successive parts would exist at the same time, for the part of a continuum is divisible into parts. Therefore...

The *minor* is evident.

307. Division of time. – 1° Time is divided into continuous time and discrete time.

Continuous time is the successive duration of uninterrupted motion.

Discrete time is either corporal or spiritual.

Corporal discrete time is the duration of interrupted motion. *Spiritual* discrete time is a plurality of spiritual operations, each of which has its own indivisible duration, because it is not successive. It is this kind of time that is proper to the operations of the angels. We shall not discuss it at present.

2° The principal divisions of time, as measure, are intrinsic time and extrinsic time.

Intrinsic time is the intrinsic duration of motion as measured.

Extrinsic time is the intrinsic duration of any motion that is used to measure the duration of another motion; v.g., the motion of a clock measures the duration of a race, of a piece of work, etc.

308. When. – Just as the accident *where* is not place, so the accident *when* is not time. For, as St. Thomas observes [1], the accident *when* signifies existence in time. But time does not exist in time. Therefore the accident *when* is not time.

The accident *when* is defined: *the accident resulting in a body from the time by which it is measured.* This accident is a determination which a body has from *extrinsic* time by which it is measured.

(1) *Summa Tot. Log.*, tr. IX, c. 1.

The accident *when* is divided into yesterday, today, tomorrow, etc.

POINTS FOR REVIEW

1. Define time as duration.
2. Explain the difference between time, eviternity, and eternity.
3. Is time as measure a being of reason? Explain.
4. Define: corporal discrete time, extrinsic time.

BOOK III

THE ONLY CHAPTER

GENERATION OF MOBILE BEING

Prologue. – In this book, we shall discuss the generation of mobile being. There will be only one chapter in the book. In it we shall deal, first, with generation itself, secondly, with the process of generation, and, thirdly, with the generation of the individual, i.e., the principle of individuation. Therefore there will be three articles in the chapter.

Generation	Notion of generation Terms of substantial generation
Process of generation	Disposition for form Resolution to first matter Previous dispositions and proximate dispositions
Generation of the individual	Statement of the question Opinions Thesis: The principle of individuation, i.e., of the numerical distinction of one individual from another in the same specific nature, is matter signed by quantity. Individuation of the angels, of the soul, and of accidents

ARTICLE I

GENERATION

309. Notion of generation. – 1° Generation, in general, is generation as it abstracts from substantial generation and accidental generation.

Generation, in general, is defined: *the change from non-being to being in a subject.* Hence three things are required for generation: subject, privation, and being or form.

Substantial generation is defined: *the acquisition or the change of a substantial form from its privation in matter.* Generation thus understood is found in living beings and in non-living beings. However, the generation of living beings has a special definition.

2° Corruption is the opposite of generation, and is defined: *the change from being to non-being in a subject.*

3° Generation and corruption are not motions or movements in the strict sense, but rather they are mutations, because they are not between two positive terms (n. 295), but take place between privation and form, and vice versa.

310. Terms of substantial generation. – 1° In generation a new substantial form is acquired, and a new compound results. Hence both substantial form and the new compound are the terms of generation.

2° The compound is the term *which* of substantial generation, and the new substantial form is the term *by which*. For becoming is the way to existence. The compound exists as *that which*, i.e., as a being which exists, whereas substantial form exists only as *that by which*, i.e., as a principle by which mobile being is constituted. Hence only the compound can be the term *which* is produced; and substantial form is the term *by which* the compound is constituted.

The properties which necessarily result from substance are attained by generation as a *secondary term*.

ARTICLE II

PROCESS OF GENERATION

311. Disposition for form. — The corruption of one substance and the generation of another take place by means of an accidental transmutation, by which the proper accidents of the substance to be produced are engendered. By these accidents, matter is rendered disposed for one form, but indisposed for the other. Therefore generation is said to take place by means of the disposition of matter for this or that particular form.

312. Resolution to first matter. — 1° *Preliminaries.* *a*) Resolution to first matter is the stripping matter of all form, both substantial and accidental. This stripping must not be understood as implying that matter remains for some time without any form, for the disappearance of the form of the corrupted being and the appearance of the form of the engendered being take place at the same instant. Hence the only priority there is in the process of generation and corruption is priority of nature.—*b*) Scotus maintained that living being has the form of corporeity, and therefore he taught that, on the disappearance or departure of the soul, the corrupted living being retains this form. Suarez taught that the accidents of a compound which corrupts remain numerically the same, i.e. the same individuals, in the engendered compound. Thomists teach that in every corruption and generation first matter is stripped of all form, both substantial and accidental. Accidents which seem to be the same in the corrupted compound and in the engendered compound, v.g., in a living man and in his cadaver, are not numerically the same, but only similar.

2° *Proof of the Thomistic opinion.—a*) *In substantial gener-*

ation, first matter is stripped of all antecedent substantial form. — There is only one substantial form in any compound. Hence, on the advent of the substantial form of the engendered compound, first matter is stripped of the substantial form of the compound that has corrupted.— *b*) *In substantial generation, first matter is stripped of all antecedent accidental form.* — When the substantial form of the compound which corrupts disappears, all its accidents disappear. For accidents exist in the whole compound as in their subject of inherence, and cannot be supported by first matter that is stripped of all substantial form. First matter is pure potency, whereas the subject of accidents must have actual existence.

313. Previous dispositions and proximate dispositions. — First matter is disposed to receive new form by means of accidental transmutations, which are called dispositions for form.

We make a distinction between previous dispositions and proximate dispositions.

Previous dispositions are produced in the substance to be corrupted, and proximate dispositions in the engendered substance.

Previous dispositions are accidents by which a nearer and nearer approach is made to the proximate dispositions.

Proximate dispositions are proper accidents by which a subject is proximately disposed to receive a substantial form that corresponds to these accidents. Proximate dispositions, as the consummation of previous dispositions, prepare matter for substantial form, and therefore they precede this form «in the order of disposing material cause.» But, «in the order of formal cause», these proximate dispositions are caused by the substantial form of the engendered compound. Therefore, «given the last disposition, form necessarily follows». For, although this disposition precedes, — by priority of nature, not of time — form in the order of disposing material cause, yet form precedes this disposition in the order of formal cause.

ARTICLE III

GENERATION OF THE INDIVIDUAL

OR

THE PRINCIPLE OF INDIVIDUATION

314. Statement of the question. — 1° *Origin of the problem.*—We see that many things are identified in species, but differ numerically or as individuals; v.g., Peter and Paul are numerically distinct, yet they have the same specific nature. Thus we find ourselves confronted with the problem: how is it that many things exist as individuals without a multiplication of their species, or, in other words, why can a substance be multiplied numerically and materially without being multiplied specifically?

2° *Individual* is defined: *that which is undivided in itself and incapable of further division either by formal differentia or by material differentia.*

As undivided, an individual is one, i.e., has numerical unity; as not capable of further division by formal differentia, an individual cannot be divided into different species, as generic essences can; as incapable of further division by material differentia, an individual cannot be communicated to inferiors, as specific essences can. Specific essence, though incapable of further division by formal differentia, is capable of further division by material differentia, for it is capable of multiplication in many subjects; v.g., human nature is multiplied in Peter, Paul, etc.

Individuation is numerical unity. This kind of unity is not predicamental or quantitative unity, but transcendental unity, by which a being is individed in itself and divided from all others; v.g., this being is not that being, and therefore it is divided from it and undivided in itself.

Individual notes are accidents which belong to an individual substance in such a way that taken together they cannot belong to any other individual substance. These notes are seven in number, and are the folowing: *form, figure, place, time, ancestry, native land, and name.*

> Forma, figura, locus, tempus, stirps, patria, nomen,
> Haec ea sunt septem quae non habet unus et alter.

Individuating notes presuppose substance already individuated.

The *principle of individuation* is the first intrinsic and substantial root of numerical unity, i.e., of individuation.

315. Opinions. — 1° There are some, as Suarez, who teach that every being is individuated by itself, and by its own proper entity.

2° Others, as Schopenhauer, teach that the principle of individuation is a collection of accidents. They fail to make a distinction between the principle of individuation and individuating notes.

3° Scotus maintains that the principle of individuation is something extrinsic added to nature, that he calls «*thisness*»; v.g., the principle of individuation of Peter is his «*peterness*».

4° Others, as Avicenna and Averroes, hold that the principle of individuation is substantial form; others, as Soncinas, etc., hold that it is accidental form, as quantity.

5° St. Thomas teaches that the principle of individuation is first matter signed by quantity.

Matter can be signed by quantity in two ways:

first, as it is rendered sensible and manifest to us by means of the quantity which informs the compound in which the matter exists;

secondly, as matter, by means of the compound, is transcendentally related to this quantity rather than to that, as one of the dispositions for form. It is matter thus signed by quantity that is the principle of individuation. Quantity of itself has parts outside of parts. Hence matter, as having a trancendental relation to this quantity, is distinct from matter which is transcendentally related to some other quantity.

According to the opinion of St. Thomas, matter, as having a transcendental relation to this quantity rather than to that, is substantially distinguished from some other portion of matter, and thus it is the first principle of substantial individuation; quantity, as it divides and separates one portion of matter from another portion, is a requisite *condition* that matter be the principle of individuation; the agent which disposes matter for this quantity rather than for that is the extrinsic principle of individuation; and substantial form is the intrinsic principle which actually individuates, yet dependently on first matter signed by quantity.

316. Statement of the thesis.

THESIS.—THE PRINCIPLE OF INDIVIDUATION, THAT IS, OF THE NUMERICAL DISTINCTION OF ONE INDIVIDUAL FROM ANOTHER IN THE SAME SPECIFIC NATURE, IS MATTER SIGNED BY QUANTITY (1).

The principle by which two or more substances of the same species are first distinguished numerically and rendered incommunicable to inferiors is matter signed by quantity. But the principle of individuation, i.e., of the numerical distinction of one individual from another in the same specific nature, is the principle by which two or more substances of the same species are first distinguished numerically and rendered incom-

(1) *Thesis XI* x. Thomae.

municable to inferiors. Therefore the principle of individuation is matter signed by quantity.

The *minor* is clear from the statement of the question. An individual is numerically distinct from every other individual and, as incapable of further division by material differentia, is incommunicable to inferiors.

Major.—The principle by which two or more substances are first distinguished numerically is matter signed by quantity.—For matter which has a relation to *this* quantity is distinct from matter which has a relation to *some other* quantity. Forms which of themselves are the principles of a species, as received into this or that matter, are not distinct as forms and principles of the species, but are merely numerically distinct, because of the matter into which they are received. Thus substances composed of matter and form are not specifically distinct, but materially and merely numerically. Therefore the principle by which two or more substances of the same species are first distinguished numerically is matter signed by quantity.

b) The principle by which two or more substances of the same species are first rendered incommunicable to inferiors is matter signed by quantity.—Substantial forms of the same species are multiplied in as much as they are received into this or that matter, as into distinct subjects. But, since matter is pure potency, it cannot be received into a subject as act, for it is the last subject into which act or form can be received. Therefore substance, once composed of matter and form, is rendered incommunicable to inferiors because of its matter.

317. Individuation of angels, of the soul, and of accidents. — 1° Angels, unlike mobile beings, are not composed of matter and form, but are pure forms. Therefore angels are not individuated by matter, but only by the forms by which they are constituted. Hence one angel is distinct from every other angel not only numerically, but also specifically, for the angelic form is the principle of both numerical and specific distinction in the angel.

2° The human soul is a substantial form which informs matter, and therefore it is individuated by the matter signed by quantity into which it is received.

When, on the death of a man, the human soul is separated from matter, it still retains its individuation, for it retains its transcendental relation to the matter which it previously informed.

3° Accidents are individuated by the substance into which they are received[1].

(1) I, q. 29, a. 1, c., and ad 3.

SPECIAL PHILOSOPHY OF NATURE

INTRODUCTION

318. Notion of Special Philosophy of Nature. – Special Philosophy of Nature is the part of Philosophy of Nature which deals with mobile being endowed with vital motion, i.e., mobile being as animated.

Special Philosophy of Nature is called *Psychology*, or the science of the soul, for the soul is the first principle of all vital motion.

But Psychology does not deal merely with the soul, or merely with phenomena of consciousness, as many philosophers in recent times have maintained, but with all animated mobile being (both as regards the soul, and as regards the body), in the three grades of life, namely, vegetative, sensitive, and rational life.

Psychology, as a part of Philosophy of Nature, is entirely distinct from Experimental Psychology, which, as we pointed out earlier, is a part of Physics.

319. Division of special Philosophy of Nature. — Three kinds of life are found in mobile being, namely vegetative, sensitive, and rational. Special Philosophy of Nature is divided into four books:

Book I : Animated mobile being in general.

Book II: Vegetative mobile being.

Book III: Sensitive mobile being.

Book IV: Intellective mobile being, or man.

BOOK I

Animated mobile being in general

Prologue. In this book, first, we shall consider living being in general, and, secondly, the properties of living being. Hence there will be two chapters in this book.

Chapter I. Living being in general.

Chapter II. Properties of living being.

CHAPTER

LIVING BEING IN GENERAL

Prologue. — In this chapter, we shall study, first, life in general; secondly, the distinction between living being and non-living being; thirdly, the first principle of life, or the soul. Therefore there will be three articles in the chapter.

Life in general	Notion of living being Life in first act and life in second act Kinds of life **Difficulties**
Distinction between living being and non-living being	Statement of the question Thesis: Living being is essentially distinct from non-living being
The first principle of life, or the soul	Statement of the question Thesis: The first principle of life, or the soul, is the substantial form of a living being First definition of the soul Second definition of the soul Four grades of living beings: vegetative, sensitive, locomotive, intellective Heterogeneity of living being

---

ARTICLE I

LIFE IN GENERAL

320. Notion of living being. — The concept of life is known to us from experience, especially from internal experience. Every man knows from experience that he is one substance which is living, in as much as he moves himself; v.g., when he extends his arms, when he walks, when he has sensation, when he exercises an act of his intellect.

Therefore life consists formally in self-motion (automotion), or in active motion from an intrinsic principle.

Living being is defined: *a substance which of its own nature is capable of moving itself* (1).

In this definition,

a) *substance* is understood as one being, i.e., as a being having one nature. Thus a *machine* is not a living being, because it is not one being, but an artificial being;

b) *self-motion* signifies: 1° transitive action which produces a term which remains in the agent; 2° immanent operation which takes place with a transition from potency to act; v.g., the acts of sensation, volition, and intellection in a created being; 3° immanent operation which takes place without a transition from potency to act, as, v.g., an act of intellection in God (2).

321. Life in first act and life in second act. — We name things as we know them. Since we know the essences of things from their properties, we use the names of their proper-

(1) I, q. 18, a. 2, c.
(2) I, q. 18, a. 1, c.

ties to signify their essences. This is the root of the division of life into life in first act and life in second act [1].

a) *Life in first act* is the very substance of a living being. Life thus understood signifies in the abstract what living being signifies in the concrete.

b) *Life in second act* is the operation of a living being, i.e., vital operation, which is self-motion.

322. Kinds of life. — The generic division of life is derived from a consideration of vital motion, i.e., of self-motion [2]. In motion we distinguish three things: 1° the execution of motion; 2° the form which is the principle of motion; 3° the end to which motion tends.

a) Now there is a kind of living being which moves itself only as regards the execution of its motion, but not as regards forms which are the principles of motion, nor as regards the end which is determined for it by nature. This kind of being is *vegetative* living being.

b) There is another kind of living being which moves itself not only as regards the execution of its motion, but also as regards the accidental forms from which its motion results, in as much as it acquires these forms by means of sense knowledge. Beings of this kind are brutes which, on perceiving something, move themselves to desire it. But yet brutes do not move themselves to an end, but rather they are moved by an end, because they act by natural instinct towards an end determined for them by nature. Such living beings are *sensitive* living beings.

c) There is another kind of living being which moves itself both as regards the execution of its motion, and as regards the accidental forms from which its motion results, and also as regards the end, which it freely chooses for itself. This kind of living being is *intellective* living being.

---

(1) I, q. 18, a. 2, c.
(2) I, q. 18, a. 3, c.

Hence there are three kinds of life: vegetative life, sensitive life, and intellective life.

323. Difficulties. — 1° Life is not automotion. a) The motion by which a compressed elastic body tends to regain its former form is automotion. But such motion is not vital motion. Therefore life is not motion from an intrinsic principle.

Major. — It is passive motion, *I concede;* it is active motion by which the body moves itself, *I deny.* I pass over the minor, but deny the conclusion.

Explanation: An elastic body in virtue of its nature has determinate posture in place in virtue of which it is said to be in its natural disposition. If removed from this disposition by an extrinsic agent, it is moved back to it by nature, and then remains at rest. But a living being moves itself the better in proportion to the greater degree it is in its natural disposition.

b) But in no living being is there motion from an intrinsic principle. Therefore life is not automotion.

Motion for which extrinsic exercise is required is not automotion. But vital operation is motion for which exercise from an extrinsic principle is required. Therefore vital operation or life is not automotion.

Major. — Motion which is merely the passive reception of extrinsic exercise, *I concede;* motion for which extrinsic exercise is required, in order that it be actively produced by a living being, *I deny.*

Minor. — Vital operation is merely the passive reception of extrinsic exercise, *I deny;* is actively produced by a living being which receives extrinsic exercise, *I concede.*

2° Life is not operation which remains in the agent. The operation by which a man moves a bat with his hand does not remain in the agent. But this kind of operation is vital operation. Therefore life is not operation which remains in the agent.

Major. — The operation by which a man moves his hand does not remain in the agent, *I deny;* by which he moves a bat, *I concede.*

Minor. — Such operation is vital in as much as a man moves his hand, *I concede:* in as much as he moves a bat, *I deny.*

POINTS FOR REVIEW

1. From what do we derive the three grades of life?
2. Distinguish between the three kinds of life.
3. Define life in first act.
4. In what kinds of operation does automotion consist?

ARTICLE II

DISTINCTION BETWEEN LIVING BEING AND NON-LIVING BEING

324. Statement of the question. — 1° A living being is a being which moves itself from an intrinsic principle, whereas a non-living being is a being which does not move itself, but is moved by another.

2° Essential distinction is lack of identity as regards specific nature.

3° Man's common sense readily makes known to him that living beings are distinct from non-living beings. Everyone knows from internal experience that he is one substance which produces the operations of vegetative, sensitive, and intellective life from an internal principle. Hence he readily knows that any plant, brute, or man in which he sees signs of life are living beings, whereas mobile beings in which these signs do not appear are non-living beings. Therefore man has positive knowledge of life, but only negative knowledge of the negation of life, or of non-living beings.

4° *a*) Scholastics, and philosophers generally, accept the testimony of common sense, and teach that there is an essential distinction between living and non-living being. *b*) Some philosophers, however, do not admit the testimony of common sense. Some make the a priori affirmation that life is an essential characteristic of all beings. This theory is called Pampsychism. Thus the Hylozoists, as Thales and Anaximander in ancient times, and Haeckel in modern times, contend that life is an essential property of all matter. Pantheists teach that the world is one living being. Some materialists deny the existence of life.

325. Statement of the thesis.

THESIS.—LIVING BEING IS ESSENTIALLY DISTINCT FROM NON-LIVING BEING.

A being which moves itself is essentially distinct from a being which does not move itself. But a living being moves itself, whereas a non-living being is a being which does not move itself. Therefore a living being is essentially distinct from a non-living being.(1)

The *minor* is clear from the notions of living being and non-living being.

Major.—In a mobile being which moves itself, substantial form is nature not only as it actuates matter, but also as it is the first principle of motion in the being in which it exists, or as it is the active principle of the motion by which a mobile being moves itself; in mobile being which does not move itself, substantial form is nature only because it actuates matter (n. 253). Hence the substantial form of a being which moves itself is more perfect as a nature than the substantial form of a being which does not move itself. Therefore being which moves itself is essentially distinct from being which does not move itself (2).

(1) I, q. 78, a. 1, c.
(2) Corpora dividuntur bifariam: quaedam enim sunt viventia, quaedam expertia vitae. — *Ex thesi* XIII s. Thomae.

ARTICLE III

THE FIRST PRINCIPLE OF LIFE

OR

THE SOUL

326. Statement of the question. — 1° The soul, according to its nominal definition, is *the first principle of life in the beings which live about us* (1).

a) *First principle of life*, i.e., that from which the operation of life first proceeds.

b) *In the beings which live about us*, i.e., in mobile beings which have vital motion.

2° a) Certain materialists, ancient and modern, hold that all vital activity derives solely from the forces of brute matter. Therefore they teach that the soul is only a body. b) The Phenomenalists, as William James, etc., teach that the soul is an aggregate of phenomena, or a vital force. c) All Peripatetics and Scholastics teach that the first principle of life, i.e., the soul, is the substantial form of a living body.

327. Statement of the thesis.

THESIS.—THE FIRST PRINCIPLE OF LIFE, OR THE SOUL, IS THE SUBSTANTIAL FORM OF A LIVING BEING (2).

The first principle by which a mobile being is constituted a living being is its substantial form. But the first principle of

(1) I, q. 75, a. 1.
(2) In viventibus, forma substantialis, animae nomine designata, *Ex thesi* XIII s. Thomae.

life, or the soul, is the first principle by which a mobile being is constituted a living being. Therefore the soul is the substantial form of a living being.

Major.—That by which a living mobile being is essentially distinguished from a non-living being is its substantial form. But that by which a mobile being is first constituted a living being is that by which it is essentially distinguished from a non-living being. Therefore that by which a mobile being is first constituted a living being is its substantial form.

328. First definition of the soul. — 1° The soul is defined by Aristotle: *the first act of a physical body that has life in potency.*

a) *First act*, to distinguish the soul from accidental form.

b) *Of a physical body*, i.e., of a natural body, not of a mathematical or artificial body.

c) *That has life in potency*, in potency for life in first act, or to live. Thus a body that has life in potency signifies an organic body. For, in order that a body be living, it must have different organs, i.e., heterogeneous parts, as we shall prove later.

Difficulty.—Since the soul is the only substantial form in a living being, its subject is first matter, not a body.

Reply.—The soul may be considered in two ways: *a*) as regards its entity, as it is the principle of corporeity and life; thus understood, it is received into first matter as into its subject; *b*) formally, as it is the principle of life only; in this sense, it is understood as received into first matter to which it gives the form of corporeity, i.e., into a body as into its subject.

2° Sometimes the soul is defined: *the first act of a physical organic* (1) *body that has life in potency.*

In this case: *a*) *physical organic body* signifies living body; and the soul is its act, just as heat is the act of something hot

(1) The word « organic » is added.

(in act); *b*) a body is said to have *life in second act* in potency, i.e., vital operations [1].

329. Second definition of the soul. — The soul is defined, according to its formal effect: *the first principle by which we live, perceive by the senses, move, and understand.*

a) *First principle:* These words indicate that the soul is the first principle of life.

b) *We live,* i.e., we, as living bodies (not merely as men), have the operations of vegetative life.

c) *Perceive by the senses,* i.e., we, as living bodies, have sensations.

d) *Move,* i.e., we, as living bodies, move (ourselves) from place to place, either by walking, or swimming (as fish), or flying (as birds), and not merely by the motion of expansion and contraction (as the oyster) [2].

e) *Understand,* i.e., as we have the operations of intellective life.

Note.—The words «we live, perceive by the senses, move, and understand» in the foregoing definition are not used copulatively, but disjunctively, in this sense: the soul is the first principle by which we live, or perceive by the senses, etc.

330. Four modes of life: vegetative, sensitive, locomotive, and intellective. — 1° The genera of living beings and of souls are derived from the different kinds of operation in self-motion. Therefore we divide living beings into three genera : *vegetative,* which move themselves as regards the execution of their motion only ; *sensitive,* which move themselves as regards the execution of their motion and as regards the form which is the principle of their motion ; *intellective,* which move themselves as regards the execution, the form, and the end of their motion. Similarly, there are three genera of souls : vegetative, sensitive, and intellective.

(1) I, q. 76, a. 5, ad 1.
(2) I, q. 18, a. 3, c.

2° The modes of life, i.e., the grades of living beings, are derived from their greater or lesser perfection within the same class of life, or according to their greater or lesser perfection in the participation of any kind of life. This perfection is known from their operations.

3° *a*) The operations of nutrition and generation appertain to vegetative life. Every vegetative being has these two operations. Hence, though there can be many species of plants, there is only one mode of life proper to vegetative beings ; and this mode or grade of life is called *vegetative.*

b) The operation of the senses appertains to sentient beings. But some animals perceive only things that are united to them. Others perceive things that are distant from them, and consequently they have the power of locomotion by which they tend to things at a distance which they apprehend. Hence the latter have a more perfect participation of sensitive life than the former.

The former class of animals are imperfect animals, and their mode or grade of life is called *sensitive* in general.

The latter are perfect animals, and their mode of life is called *locomotive,* because their more perfect sensitive nature requires that they move (themselves) from place to place, by flying, swimming, or walking. Hence there are two modes of life in the sensitive class : *sensitive* and *locomotive.*

c) There are two operations proper to intellective life : the operations of *understanding* and *willing.* All intellective beings have these two operations ; but they have them more or less perfectly in proportion to their greater or lesser approach to immateriality.

Hence the modes of life, or grades of living beings, in the intellective class are derived from their grades of immateriality.

Philosophy of Nature deals only with mobile intellective beings, not with other intellective beings, as God and the angels. Hence Philosophy of Nature is concerned with four modes of life : *vegetative, sensitive, locomotive,* and *intellective.*

331. Heterogeneity of living being. — 1° A living being is called heterogeneous in as much as it has diverse and dissimilar parts; v.g., the parts of water are homogeneous, because they are similar, and each part of water is water ; but the parts of a living or organic body are heterogeneous, because they are dissimilar.

2° There are two kinds of heterogeneity : *accidental* and *substantial*.

Accidental heterogeneity results from the diversity of accidental disposition which each part has ; v.g., two parts differ in quantity, figure, and color.

Substantial heterogeneity does not result from the fact that each part has its own substantial form, but from the fact that each part of the whole is informed in a different way by the same substantial form.

3° The necessity of heterogeneity in a living being derives from the fact that the soul is united to the body not as a mover to a mobile being, but as its substantial form, by which the body is formally one substance which moves itself [1].

4° We shall prove first that a *living being has heterogeneous parts*.

A living body is formally one substance, and moves itself by passing from potency to act. But a body which is formally one substance, and which moves itself by passing from potency to act, has heterogeneous parts. Therefore a living body has heterogeneous parts [2].

The *major* is clear from the notion of living being.

Minor.—A body which is formally one substance moves itself in as much as it is in act, and is moved by itself in as much as it is in potency. But a body which is formally one substance cannot be in act and in potency at the same time as regards

(1) In viventibus, ut in eodem subjecto pars movens et pars mota per se habeantur, forma substantialis, animae nomine designata, requirit organicam dispositionem, seu partes heterogeneas. — *Thesis VIII* s. Thomae.

(2) *In de Anima*, L. II, l. 1, nn. 230-232 (Pirotta).

the same part. Therefore it must have dissimilar or heterogeneous parts, of which those which are in act move, and those in potency are moved. In other words, because a living body moves itself, it must have diverse parts for its diverse operations. But this is not so in the case of a non-living body: although it has diverse operations, it has not diverse parts for diverse operations, for all its operations are proper to each and every part of it, and therefore it is homogeneous; v.g., if fire heats, all its parts heat; if fire moves upwards, all its parts move; if a magnet attracts iron, all its parts attract it (1).

5° We shall now prove that *the heterogeneity of a living being* is *substantial.*

In a living being, each organic part is the principle and root of proper accidents and operations. But, in order that each part be the principle and root of proper accidents and operations, the heterogeneity of a living being must be substantial. Therefore the heterogeneity of a living being is substantial (2).

The *major* is clear from what has been already said.

Minor.—The soul is the first principle of vital operations. Hence, in order that each part of a compound have its own proper operations, each part must be informed in its own proper way by the soul as substantial form, and therefore each part of the compound is substantially dissimilar to each other part. In other words, the heterogeneity of a living being must be substantial (3).

POINTS FOR REVIEW

1. Prove that the soul is the substantial form of a living being.

(1) Joannes a Sancto Thoma, *Cursus Phil.*, t. III, p. 15 (Reiser).
(2) *De Anima*, q. un., a. 9.— *De Spirit. Creat.*, q. un., a. 4, ad 14.
(3) . . . Licet anima sit forma simplex secundum essentiam, est tamen multiplex virtute, secundum quod est principium diversarum operationum. Et quia forma perficit materiam non solum quantum ad esse, sed etiam ad operandum; ideo oportet quod licet anima sit una forma, partes corporis diversimode perficiantur ab ipsa, et unaquaeque secundum quod competit ejus operationi; et secundum hoc etiam oportet esse ordinem operationum, ut dictum est . . . — *De Anima*, q. un., a. 9, ad 14.

2. What justification is there for saying that the soul is the act of a body rather than the act of first matter? Explain briefly.

3. Explain the statement: *The soul is the first principle by which we live.*

4. Show how the four modes of life, or grades of living beings, are derived.

5. Is the locomotive mode of living derived from locomotive power? Explain.

6. Define accidental heterogeneity and substantial heterogeneity.

7. Explain: *a*) why a living being must have heterogeneous parts; *b*) why the heterogeneity of a living being must be substantial.

CHAPTER II

PROPERTIES OF LIVING BEINGS

Prologue. — There are two kinds of properties in the soul that we may consider: properties in relation to the soul, viz., the divisibility or indivisibility of the soul; and properties in relation to operations and objects, viz., the powers of the soul. In our study of the powers of the soul, we shall find out if they are distinct from the soul, and how they are specified. Hence there will be three articles in this chapter.

Indivisibility of the soul	Statement of the question Thesis: No soul is divisible, even accidentally
Distinction between the soul and its powers	Statement of the question Thesis: There is a real distinction between the soul and its powers Difficulties
Specification of the powers	Statement of the question Thesis: The powers of the soul are specified immediately by their relation to their operations, and mediately by their relation to their formal objects Corollary Division of the powers Difficulties

ARTICLE I

INDIVISIBILITY OF THE SOUL

332. Statement of the question. – 1° All souls are essentially indivisible or simple, for no soul is composed of first matter and substantial form: the soul is substantial form.

2° All souls are of themselves unextended, or quantitatively indivisible, for of itself no soul can have extension; its extension could derive only from something distinct from itself, namely, from quantity. Hence the question arises whether any soul can be accidentally divisible or extended, in as much as it is really extended in virtue of quantity which is received into a corporeal substance, and whether it is divided by the division of quantity, as whiteness is divided by the division of a white surface.

3° It is certain that the human soul, because it is spiritual, has not even accidental extension.

But there is some doubt as regards the souls of plants and animals. The reason for the doubt is this: when plants and certain animals, as worms, are divided, each of their separated parts continue to live. Hence their souls seem to be divisible, and therefore to have extension.

4° Some of the philosophers of antiquity claimed that all souls, even the human soul, were divisible, and therefore had extension.

Scotus (1) and some others held that all souls, except the human soul, were divisible.

Some Thomists affirm that the souls of plants and im-

(1) 4, dist. 44, q. 1.

perfect animals are divisible; others simply affirm that all souls are indivisible.

There is no difficulty in reconciling the last two opinions. Those who hold that the souls of plants and imperfect animals are divisible do not hold that these souls are really divided by the division of a living being, but they merely affirm that, when there is a division of a living being, a new soul is engendered in the part cut off, in which there remains sufficient organization for life (1). Such generation does not take place in the ordinary and natural way, but in an extraordinary and violent manner (2). This opinion is held also by those who contend that all souls are indivisible.

333. Statement of the thesis.

THESIS.—No soul is divisible, even accidentally.

A form which is the principle of the unity of an organized, i.e., organic, body is not divisible, even accidentally. But the soul is a form which is the principle of the unity of an organized or organic body. Therefore no soul is divisible, even accidentally.

Major.—Such a form belongs to all the organized parts taken as a whole, and therefore it informs the whole body in an undivided manner.

The *minor* is clear from the definition of the soul, which is the act of a physical organic body.

POINTS FOR REVIEW

1. Is it true that all souls are essentially simple? Briefly explain your answer.

2. Explain in what sense the soul of a plant and the soul of an imperfect animal may be said to be accidentally divisible.

---

(1) Joannes a Sancto Thoma, *Cursus Phil.*, t. III, p. 53 (Reiser).
(2) Hugon, *Cursus Phil. Thom.*, t. III, p. 65 (Editio 3a).

ARTICLE II

DISTINCTION BETWEEN THE SOUL AND ITS POWERS

334. Statement of the question. – 1° A power (operative), according to its nominal definition, signifies a capacity for acting.

Power and faculty are synonymous terms. But, in their strict meaning, a faculty is a capacity for conscious operation, whereas a power is a capacity for any kind of operation, conscious or unconscious.

The *real* definition of power may be expressed thus: *the proximate principle «by which» of operation in the strict sense.*

a) *Principle «by which»:* the subject *which* operates is excluded.

b) *Proximate*: thus is excluded substantial form, which is the *remote* principle *by which* of operation.

c) *In the strict sense:* thus is excluded *habit*, which is the proximate principle *by which* of *good* or *bad* operations; v.g., the virtue by which the will performs good acts.

2° The soul is the first act of a physical body that has life in potency.

3° Distinction is the lack of identity.

a) Logical distinction, or distinction of reason, is the lack of identity between concepts of one and the same thing.

b) Real distinction is the lack of identity between two or more things, independently of the consideration of the mind.

4° Ockam and other Nominalists, and also the Cartesians deny that the soul and its powers are really distinct.

Scotus claims that the distinction between the soul and its powers is a formal-actual distinction from the nature of the thing.

Scholastics commonly teach that there is a real distinction between the soul and its powers.

335. Demonstration of the thesis. – *Meaning of the thesis:* If powers are considered *radically*, they are distinguished only logically from the soul, for the root of every faculty is the soul.

If powers are considered *formally*, as proximate principles of operation, they are really distinguished from the soul.

THESIS.—THERE IS A REAL DISTINCTION BETWEEN THE SOUL AND ITS POWERS.

1° The soul belongs to the genus of substance; the powers of the soul belong to the genus of accident. But there is a real distinction between substance and accident. Therefore there is a real distinction between the soul and its powers.

Minor.— This is clear from common sense, and is proved in Metaphysics.

Major.—a) The soul belongs to the genus of substance, because the soul is the substantial form of a living body. *b) The powers of the soul belong to the genus of accident.* Operation, which is the proper and specifying act of the powers of the soul, is an accident. But a power, i.e., a potency, whose proper and specifying act is an accident, is itself in the genus of accident. Therefore the powers of the soul belong to the genus of accident.

Major.—Actions come and go, without any substantial change in the subject which operates.

Minor.—A potency is in the same supreme genus as the proper and specifying act to which it is transcendentally related.

2° If the powers of the soul were not really distinct from

the soul, they would always be in act. But the powers of the soul are not always in act. Therefore there is a real distinction between the soul and its powers.

Major.—Because the soul, of its very nature, is an act, in as much as it always constitutes a body as *actually* living (1).

Minor.—Because a living being is not always in operation.

336. Difficulties. — The powers of the soul belong to the genus of substance. Therefore they are not really distinguished from the soul.

1° What is not an accident belongs to the genus of substance. But the powers of the soul are not accidents. Therefore the powers of the soul belong to the genus of substance.

Major. — What is not a predicamental accident, *I concede;* what is not a predicable accident, *I deny.*

Minor. — They are not predicamental accidents, *I deny;* they are not predicable accidents, *I concede.*

The powers of the soul, in as much as they necessarily flow from a living being, are not predicable accidents, but are properties of a living being. Nevertheless, they are predicamental accidents, in as much as they have existence in a subject of inherence.

2° But the powers of the soul are not predicamental accidents. Therefore they are not really distinguished from the soul.

That is not a predicamental accident which is included in the concept of substance. But the powers of the soul are included in the concept of the substance of a living being; v.g., the reason is included in the concept of man, for man is defined: a rational animal. Therefore the powers of the soul are not predicamental accidents.

Major. — What is included in the concept of substance as its constituent, *I concede;* as its result, i.e., as necessarily flowing from substance, *I deny.*

Minor. — As the constituents of substance, *I deny;* as resulting from substance, *I concede.*

When we say: man is a rational animal, rational designates the very nature of man, and includes « the reason » as necessarily flowing from this nature.

3° But the powers of the soul are included in the concept of substance as its constituents. Therefore the powers of the soul belong to the genus of substance.

What supports accidents is substance. But the powers of the soul support accidents; v.g., the intellect supports science. Therefore the powers of the soul are substances.

Major. — What supports accidents as their remote and primary subject, as existing in itself, *I concede;* as their proximate subject, which exists in another subject, *I deny.*

(1) I, q. 77, a. 1.

Minor. — As their primary subject, existing in itself, *I deny;* as their proximate subject, existing in another subject, *I concede.*

4° The powers of the soul are the principles by which we live, perceive by the senses, move, and understand. But the principle by which we live, perceive by the senses, move, and understand is the soul. Therefore the powers of the soul are the soul itself.

Major. — The principles by which we live . . . secondarily and proximately, *I concede;* the principles by which we live . . . primarily and remotely, *I deny.*

Minor. — The principle by which we live . . . secondarily and proximately, *I deny;* the principle by which we live . . . primarily and remotely, *I concede.*

ARTICLE III

SPECIFICATION OF THE POWERS

337. Statement of the question. — 1° Before we discuss the division of powers as regards their genera and species, we must find out their principle of specification. We maintain that powers are extrinsically specified by their relation to their operations and formal objects.

2° The *principle of specification* is that principle which constitutes a nature in its species.

There are two principles of specification : an *intrinsic* principle and an *extrinsic* principle.

a) The *intrinsic principle of specification* is either the specific differentia, or the form (physical) by which a nature is instrinsically constituted.

b) The *extrinsic principle of specification* is that extrinsic thing to which a thing is related *in virtue of its specific essence.*

Everything has its own intrinsic principle of specification, but relative things, whether *predicamental* relations, or things that are *transcendantally related* to another, have also an extrinsic principle of specification. For, in the constitution of their specific essence, they depend on some other thing to which they are related.

3° *Operation* is the second act of an operative power.

4° The *object* of a faculty is the thing the faculty attains.

The object is *material* or *formal.*

The *material* object is everything with which the power deals.

The *formal* object is the aspect under which a faculty attains its material object.

338. Statement of the thesis.

THESIS. — THE POWERS OF THE SOUL ARE SPECIFIED IMMEDIATELY BY THEIR RELATION TO THEIR OPERATIONS, AND MEDIATELY BY THEIR RELATION TO THEIR FORMAL OBJECTS.

A thing which is related to another thing in virtue of its specific essence is specified by its relation to that thing. But the powers of the soul as powers, i.e., in virtue of their specific essence, are immediately related to their operations, and, by means of their operations, to their formal objects. Therefore the powers of the soul are specified immediately by their relation to their operations, and mediately by their relation to their formal objects.

The *major* is clear from the statement of the question.

The *minor* is evident from the notion of a power, and from experience ; v.g., the power of sight is related to vision, and vision to the knowing of colors.

339. Corollary. — The powers are not specified by their operations in as much as these operations are produced from the powers, but in as much as the operations are in the intention of nature, and are the ends for which nature produces such powers.

340. Division of the powers. — 1° A power is always active in relation to *operation*, in as much as it is the active principle of its operation. But in relation to its *object*, a power is *active* or *passive* (1).

An *active* power is a power that acts on its object and changes it ; v.g., a nutritive power.

(1) *De Veritate*, q. 16, a. 1, ad 13.

An active power is specified by its object, as the object is the term of the operation of the power.

A *passive* power is a power which is determined for operation by its object ; v.g., the senses, the intellect.

A passive power is specified by its object, as the object determines it or moves it to operation.

2° The powers of the soul are *organic*, or *anorganic* or *spiritual*.

An *organic* power is a power which exists in a compound, i.e., in a living body, as in its proper subject ; v.g., all the vegetative powers.

An *anorganic* or *spiritual* power is a power which exists in the spiritual soul as in its proper subject ; v.g., the intellect.

3° The powers of the soul are divided into five classes according to their objects [1] For the object of the operation of the soul is :

1) Either a living body in which there are powers. Thus we have the vegetative class.

2) Or an extrinsic thing.

a) An extrinsic thing may be considered as it is destined to exist in the soul through its own likeness, and is : 1. either every sensible body, and thus we have the *sensitive* class ; 2. or being taken in its universality, and thus we have the *intellective* class.

b) Or an extrinsic thing is considered as the soul tends and is inclined to it, 1. as its intended end, and thus we have the *appetitive* class ; 2. as the term of local motion, and thus we have the *locomotive class*.

Therefore there are five classes or genera of powers of the soul: *vegetative*, *sensitive*, *intellective*, *appetitive*, and *locomotive*.

341. Difficulties. — 1° The powers of the soul are not specified by their operations.

(1) I, q. 78, a. 1, c.

Nothing is specified by a thing which is dependent on and posterior to it. But operations are dependent on their powers and posterior to them. Therefore the powers of the soul are not specified by their operations.

Major. — In the order of execution, *I concede;* in the order of intention, *I deny.*

Minor. — Operation as produced, i.e., in execution, *I concede;* operation in intention, *I deny.*

2° Powers are not specified by their objects.

a) If powers were specified by their objects, there would be as many powers as there are objects. But this is false. Therefore.

Major. — As there are material objects, *I deny;* as there are formal objects, *I concede.*

Minor. — Powers are not specified by their material objects, *I concede;* by their formal objects, *I deny.*

b) But powers are not specified by their formal objects. Therefore we are again confronted with the difficulty.

Formal objects are not the specific differentiae of powers. But powers are specified by their specific differentia. Therefore.

Major. — They are not intrinsic differentiae, *I concede;* extrinsic, *I deny.*

Minor. — As by their intrinsic principle of specification, *I concede;* as by their extrinsic principle of specification, *I deny.*

BOOK II

Vegetative mobile being

THE ONLY CHAPTER

Prologue. — In our study of vegetative mobile being, we shall consider the operations and powers of vegetative life. There will be only one chapter in this book, and it will be divided into two articles.

Operations of vegetative life	Operations of vegetative life A living being remains numerically the same under the continuous change of its matter by nutrition and augmentation
Vegetative powers	Number of the vegetative powers Nature of the vegetative powers Vegetative powers and physico-chemical energy

ARTICLE I

OPERATIONS OF VEGETATIVE LIFE

342. Operations of vegetative life. – The operations of vegetative life generally are considered in the cell.

They are of three kinds : nutrition, augmentation, and generation.

1° *Nutrition*, in its material meaning, has several phases, which today are designated by the term *metabolism:* the choosing of food, its transmutation, absorption or intussusception, and assimilation.

Nutrition, in its formal meaning, is assimilation, which is philosophically defined : *the conversion of food that is absorbed into the substance of the being that is nourished.*

2° *Augmentation* is *the operation by which a living substance acquires by nourishment the quantity due to it.*

3° *Generation* of a living being is understood in an active sense as it is in the generator, and in passive sense as it is in the thing engendered.

a) In the generator (active sense), the generation of a living being is defined : *the operation by which a living being produces from its own substance another substantial being similar to itself.*

b) In the being engendered (passive sense), the generation of a living being is defined : *the production of one living being by another living being which is similar to it in nature* (1).

1) *Production of a living being by another living being :*

(1) I, q. 27, a. 2, c.

hence, if a living being were produced by a non-living being (as *efficient cause*), there would not be generation in the strict sense, even though we speak of *sponteneous generation*. The thing engendered is produced from the substance of the generator.

2) *Similar to it in nature*, because generation of itself tends to produce an offspring of the same specific nature as the generator. Hence, if by art a man were to produce a man, there would be no generation, because artificial action of itself does not tend to produce an effect of the same nature as the agent.

343. A living being remains numerically the same under the continuous change of its matter by nutrition and augmentation. – The nutrition and augmentation of a living being result from the loss of its old matter and the assimilation of new matter, so that the whole of the matter of a living body is renewed. Yet a living being remains numerically the same under the continuous change of its matter, because the same substantial form remains, and because the new matter which gradually takes the place of the lost matter is assimilated by the whole and is continuous with it. Nevertheless, since the first matter in a living being does not remain the same, a living being does not remain materially the same.

ARTICLE II

VEGETATIVE POWERS

344. Number of the vegetative powers. — 1° There are three genera of vegetative powers:

a) Nutritive powers, whose end is nutrition.

b) Generative powers, whose end is generation.

c) Augmentative powers, whose end is the acquisition of the quantity proper to a living being.

2° Scholastics and many modern philosophers hold that the augmentative power is not essentially distinct from the nutritive power. The contrary opinion seems at least probable, because the two powers differ :

a) *As regards their object* : the end of nutrition is the conservation of living being, whereas the end of augmentation is the acquisition of due quantity.

b) *As regards their duration :* nutrition lasts for the whole of life ; augmentation ceases after a certain period of life.

345. Nature of the vegetative powers. — 1° *Preliminaries.* — *a*) All Antivitalists deny the existence of vital powers in vegetative living being. They claim that the operations which appear, v.g., in a plant, are merely the results of a special disposition of elements which is found in an organic body. Therefore their opinion is called organicism. *b*) Certain Vitalists, even though they teach that a vegetative living being has a soul, contend that it has no special vital powers that are distinct from the energy which is found in a non-living body. Such is the teaching of Mercier, Marcellus a Puero Jesu, etc. *c*) Aristotle, St. Thomas, and many modern philosophers teach that a vegetative living being has special vital operative powers, which cannot be identified with the energy of a non-living being.

2° *Proof of the teaching of Aristotle.* — If a vegetative living being has vital operation which surpasses the operation of a non-living being, it has special vital powers. But a vegetative living being has vital operation which surpasses the operation of a non-living being. Therefore a vegetative living being has special vital powers.

Major. — Because a power is specified by its operation.

Minor. — A vegetative living being has automotion, which surpasses every non-vital operation.

346. Vegetative powers and physico-chemical energy. — Some Vitalists bold that in living being tnere is an opposition or battle between the vital powers and physico-chemical energy, so that the former operate for the conservation of living being, and the latter tend to its destruction. Such is the teaching of Stahl, Bichat (1), and the medical men of the Montpellier school. This opinion is called exaggerated vitalism.

2° Aristotle, St. Thomas, and many others teach that vegetative powers produce their operations and effects by means of active and passive qualities, as, for example, by heat,

(1) « Bichat, au commencement de ce siècle, a attaché le prestige de son nom à cette conception ultraspiritualiste de la vie. A l'encontre de ceux qui prétendent établir une identité entre les phénomènes des corps vivants et ceux des corps inorganiques, Bichat pose en principe que les propriétés vitales sont absolument opposées aux propriétés physiques, de sorte qu'au lieu de passer dans le camp des physiciens et des chimistes, il reste vitaliste avec Stahl et l'école de Montpellier.

« Comme eux, il considère que la vie est une lutte entre des actions opposées; il admet que les propriétés vitales conservent le corps vivant en entravant les propriétés physiques qui tendent à le détruire. Quand la mort survient, ce n'est que le triomphe des propriétés physiques sur leurs antagonistes. Bichat d'ailleurs résume complètement ses idées dans la définition qu'il donne de la vie: la vie est l'ensemble des fonctions qui résistent à la mort, ce qui signifie en d'autres termes: la vie est l'ensemble des propriétés vitales qui résistent aux propriétés physiques. » — CLAUDE BERNARD, *La Science Expérimentale*, Paris, 1878, pp. 160-161.

so that the effects are wholly produced by means of these qualities, but as directed by the vital powers. According to this teaching, active and passive qualities are qualities that belong to elements.

Some philosophers, as Maritain ([1]), who identify active and passive qualities with physico-chemical energy ([2]), hold the same opinion. This teaching is called *animism* or *moderate vitalism*.

3° It seems to us that there is another way of solving the problem. In the first place physico-chemical energy cannot be identified with a power, as it is understood in philosophy ; it is rather physical matter in motion, as measured by a physicist. Therefore, in the second place, we have no need to find out the relation between physico-chemical energy and the vegetative powers. It is sufficient for us to state that the philosopher and the physicist consider vegetative life under entirely different aspects. The philosopher deals with powers, the first principle of life, and substantial change ; the physicist does nothing more than measure *metrically* the phenomena of vegetative life. Hence the philosopher and physicist speak of vegetative life in entirely different ways.

(1) « Les énergies physico-chimiques sont regardées dans cette conception comme les instruments du principle *psychique* qui use d'elles pour produire des effets (j'entends l'auto-conservation et l'auto-construction de l'organisme vivant) dont elles seraient incapables à elles seules: en telle sorte que tout se fait par ces énergies, mais pas par elles seules, et que la science est fondée à regarder tous les phénomènes de la vie comme pouvant (matériellement et instrumentalement) être analysés au point de vue physico-chimique, mais sans que cette analyse puisse jamais épuiser leur réalité propre, et sans que ses progrès limitent le domaine du vital, qui n'est pas « juxtaposé » au physico-chimique, mais auquel le physico-chimique est instrumentalement « subordonné ». — *Vues sur la Psychologie Animale*, par Hans Andre, etc. Paris, 1930, p. 172, notes par Jacques Maritain.

(2) It is not clearly evident that active and passive qualities, as used by St. Thomas, can be identified with physico-chemical energy.

BOOK III

Sentient mobile being

Prologue. — Sentient mobile beings have knowledge. Appetite results from knowledge. Moreover, the nature of the sensitive soul is manifested from its knowledge and appetite. In this book, we shall consider, first, knowledge in general; secondly, sensitive knowledge ; thirdly, the sensitive appetite ; and fourthly, the sensitive soul. Hence there will be four chapters in this book.

CHAPTER I

KNOWLEDGE IN GENERAL

Prologue. — In our study of knowledge in general, we shall consider, first, the root of knowledge; secondly, the impressed species, which is a principle required for knowledge; thirdly, the expressed species, which is the term of knowledge; and fourthly, the act of knowledge. Hence there will be four articles in this chapter.

Root of knowledge	Statement of the question Thesis: Immateriality is the root of knowledge The grades of knowing beings correspond to the degrees of their remoteness from matter.
Impressed species	Statement of the question Thesis: The impressed species is generally required for knowledge The impressed species informs in two ways
Expressed species	Statement of the question Thesis: The expressed species is often required for knowledge
Act of knowledge	Statement of the question Thesis: The act of knowledge is not a transitive, but an immanent action The production of the expressed species is not an operation that is really distinct from the act of knowledge Corollary

ARTICLE I

ROOT OF KNOWLEDGE

347. Statement of the question. — 1° Everyone knows from internal experience what knowledge is.

First, knowledge is a vital operation by which a knowing subject attains, seizes, and draws to itself the determinations, notes or forms of the thing known. For an indeterminate thing as such is not knowable.

Secondly, the forms of the thing known which are attained by the knowing subject do not become the forms of the latter, but remain the forms of the former, because the knowing subject possesses them *objectively*, that is, possesses them as the forms of the thing which it knows.

Philosophers, as a result of internal experience, clearly describe knowledge as follows: to know is *to have the form of another as of another*, or, in other words, to know is *to be another, in as much as it is another*.

Explanation. In the *physical* order, a nescient subject receives and has the form of another merely subjectively, as act in potency, so that it has it as its own; and from the union of subject and form is constituted a third thing which is physically distinct both from the form, and from the subject without the form. Thus wax receives the form of a seal, and it has it as its own; and from the union of the form of the seal and the wax there is constituted *sealed wax*.

In the order *of knowledge*, the knowing subject and the thing known remain physically distinct; and the form of the thing known is attained by the knowing subject, and it exists in the knowing subject not as its own, but objectively as the form of another.

Thus wax which has the form of a seal as its own is sealed wax. But a knowing subject that has the form of another as of another *is another in as much as another*.

2° Immateriality may be understood in two ways: *a*) in a strict sense, as subjective and intrinsic independence of matter, i.e., as spirituality ; b) in a wide sense, as elevation beyond the potentiality of first matter.

Here immateriality is used in the wide sense.

3° The root of knowledge can have two meanings : *a*) the principle from which knowledge flows ; or *b*) the condition necessary and sufficient for the acquisition of knowledge.

The root of knowledge, as used in the thesis, is the condition necessary and sufficient for knowledge.

348. Statement of the thesis.

THESIS. — IMMATERIALITY IS THE ROOT OF KNOWLEDGE.

The amplitude of nature is the root of knowledge. But the amplitude of nature derives from immateriality. Therefore immateriality is the root of knowledge [1].

Major. — A knowing being is distinguished from a nescient being thus : a nescient being has only its own form, whereas a knowing being is capable of having, besides its own form, the form of another as of another. Hence it is clear that a knowing being as such has a nature of greater amplitude than a nescient being has, or the amplitude of nature is the root of knowledge [2].

Minor. — First matter, as pure potency, denotes imperfection, indetermination, and restriction of perfection. Hence the amplitude of nature results from elevation beyond the potentiality of matter, i.e., from immateriality.

(1) Immaterialitatem necessario sequitur intellectualitas. — *Thesis* XVIII s. Thomae.

(2) I, q. 14, a. 1.

349. The grades of knowing beings correspond to the degrees of their remoteness from matter.—Since immateriality is the root of knowledge, it is clear that the grades of knowing beings correspond to the degrees of their remoteness from matter. These grades, in ascending order, are as follows : 1° *the brute :* the brute is in a way delivered from the imperfection of first matter by its substantial form, which, though not spiritual, is more perfect than the substantial form of the plant, and thus is capable of knowledge ; 2° *man :* man has a spritual substantial form which is united to this first matter ; 3° *the angel :* the angel has no first matter, but has potency, because the essence and the existence of the angel are distinguished as potency and act ; 4° *God :* God is pure act and excludes all potentiality (1).

(1) *Ex thesi* XVIIl s. Thomae.

ARTICLE II

IMPRESSED SPECIES

350. Statement of the question. – 1° In latin, species signifies, among other things, a beautiful or formed being. Therefore species receives its name from form. The name species is also used to designate the determination or form which is required in knowledge. The form required in knowledge is an intentional or representing form. Hence species, as it is used here, signifies any intentional form whatsoever, that is to say, a form which determines a cognitive power, and which formally represents something else.

2° Species is either *impressed* or *expressed.*

We shall deal with the expressed species in the next article.

The impressed species is the species which is impressed in a cognitive power by an object. It is defined : *the likeness of form which takes the place of an object, and determines a cognitive power to produce knowledge.* Hence the impressed species constitutes with the cognitive power the principle of knowledge, and hence knowledge derives from a power and an object.

The impressed species is *sensible,* when it is in one of the senses ; *intelligible,* when it is in the intellect.

3° Galen, Plotinus, and Porphyrius among the philosophers of old, and Durandus among Scholastics deny the existence of the impressed species. Philosophers such as Fichte, Schelling and Hegel, who deny the existence of things, and regard the knowing subject as the sole source of all knowledge, logically hold the same opinion.

4° In the thesis, we state that the impressed species is

generally required for knowledge. God does not require the impressed species for knowledge. Moreover, neither an angel, nor a seperated soul requires an impressed species to know itself. Similarly, the impressed species is not required in the beatific vision, for, according to the teaching of theologians, the divine essence of itself actuates the created intellect.

351. Statement of the thesis.

THESIS. — THE IMPRESSED SPECIES IS GENERALLY REQUIRED FOR KNOWLEDGE.

1) *Experience* [1]: in the external and internal senses.

a) *External senses.* — Sound, even though within the range of our hearing, is not perceived as soon as a blow is struck at some distance from us. Similarly, a colored object, even though within the range of our vision, is seen only dimly if it is far away from us, but it is seen more clearly when it is brought nearer to us. Hence, in order that the external senses have knowledge, something more than the mere presence of their objects is required : the senses must be determined by their objects. But since the end of this determination is knowledge, the determination must be not only physical, but intentional, i.e., must belong to the order of knowledge. This intentional determination, i.e., determination in the order of knowledge, is the impressed species.

b) *Internal senses.* — The internal senses have knowledge of things that are not present to them, and in dreams. Hence, in order that they know such things, they must be determined by a likeness of the things which take the places of the things. Otherwise the internal senses would not have knowledge of *these* things rather than *those,* that is, would not have knowledge of certain definite things.

2° *Reason.* — Knowledge depends on both an object and on a cognitive power. But knowledge cannot in general depend on both an object and on a cognitive power, unless there

(1) JOANNES A SANCTO THOMA, *Cursus Phil.*, t. III, p. 181 (Reiser).

is an impressed species. Therefore an impressed species is generally required for knowledge.

Major. — Since knowledge has a particular object as its term, it must proceed from a power which determinately tends to an object which is its term. Hence it cannot proceed from a power only, which is indeterminate as regards objects, but must proceed also from an object.

Minor. — Knowledge is a vital operation, and therefore it cannot proceed from an object as it exists outside the cognitive power ; it can proceed from it only as it exists in the cognitive power. But generally an object is in a cognitive power only by its likeness, i.e., by its impressed species. Therefore . . .

352. The impressed species informs in two ways. — An impressed species informs a cognitive power in two ways : *entitatively* or *materially*, and *cognitively* or *immaterially*. An impressed species informs a cognitive power *entitatively* or *materially*, in as much as it is an accidental form received into a potency as its act, and constitutes with it another thing ; an impressed species informs a cognitive power *cognitively* or *immaterially*, in as much as it is the form of another as of another, gives the power an immaterial determination, and makes it the object in first act. Hence it is as an accident, not as a species, that an impressed species gives entitative determination to a cognitive power.

POINTS FOR REVIEW

1. Define: species in general, intentional species, impressed species.
2. Is the impressed species the term of knowledge? Explain briefly.
3. Explain why an impressed species is generally required for knowledge.

ARTICLE III

EXPRESSED SPECIES

353. Statement of the question. — 1° All knowledge tends to an object as its term ; but sometimes knowledge cannot have an object that is physically present as its immediate term. Therefore in this case the knowing subject must form in itself a likeness of the thing known, and in this likeness it contemplates the object. This likeness is called the *expressed species* : *species* because it is the intentional form of the being ; *expressed,* because it is expressed by the knowing subject in its act of knowledge.

2° Expressed species is defined : *the intentional likeness of the object which is produced in the act of knowledge, and in which the knowing subject comtemplates the object known.*

The expressed species is not *that from which* the object is known, so that the knowing subject knows the expressed species by one act, and the object by another act ; but it is *that in which* the knowing subject immediately attains its object.

The impressed species is the principle of knowledge ; the expressed species is its term (in which).

3° The expressed species is *sensible* or *intelligible,* as it is the term of sensitive or intellective knowledge.

The intelligible expressed species is called *the subjective concept, the formal concept,* or *the mental word.*

4° An expressed species is not required in knowledge of the external senses, nor in knowledge of an internal sense (common sense), which attain their object as physically present.

An expressed species is produced in God not from necessity, but from the superabundance of His knowledge ; and this expressed species is the Word, the Second Person of the Blessed Trinity, the image of the Father, and the figure of His substance.

354. Statement of the thesis.

THESIS. — THE EXPRESSED SPECIES IS OFTEN REQUIRED FOR KNOWLEDGE.

The expressed species is required for knowledge, if the cognitive faculty does not attain its object as physically present. But often the cognitive faculty does not attain its object as physically present. Therefore the expressed species is often required for knowledge.

Major. — If the cognitive faculty is not terminated by its object as physically present, it must be terminated by it as intentionally represented by the expressed species.

Minor. — *a*) Often we contemplate an object that is not physically present to us, as, v.g., in knowledge of the imagination ; *b*) or if the object is present, a cognitive faculty, as the intellect, attains it by abstracting from its actual existence, because it considers it in its state of universality.

POINTS FOR REVIEW

1. State briefly why a species is described as expressed.
2. When is an expressed species called intelligible ?
3. Is the expressed species the principle or the term of knowledge ?
4. Explain briefly when and why an expressed species is required.

ARTICLE IV

ACT OF KNOWLEDGE

355. Statement of the question. — 1° We know from what has been already said that often an expressed species is produced in the act of knowledge. We are now concerned with the problem of the relation between the act of knowledge and the production of the expressed species.

2° Suarez and his disciples hold that every act of knowledge of its very nature produces an expressed species. Therefore, according to this opinion, *a*) knowledge is a predicamental action, i.e., an action that produces a term; *b*) knowledge consists essentially in a representation.

3° Thomists insist upon the necessity of an expressed species not because of the act of knowledge, but because of the object, either because it is not physically present, or is not proportionate to the cognitive power. Therefore, according to Thomists, *a*) knowledge of its very nature is a strictly immanent operation, i.e., an operation which does not consist in the production of a term, but which is essentially a perfection of the agent ; *b*) although knowledge sometimes produces an expressed species or representation of the object, yet it does not consist essentially in being a representation, nor in the production of a representation, but is the act of having a form immaterially, i.e., of being the object known by means of a representation.

356. Statement of the thesis.

THESIS.— THE ACT OF KNOWLEDGE IS NOT A TRANSITIVE, BUT AN IMMANENT ACTION.

An action which sometimes produces no term whatsoever, and which, when it does produce a term, is not of its nature designed for the production of a term, is not a transitive, but an immanent action. But the act knowledge is an action which sometimes produces no term whatsoever, and which, when it does produce a term, is not of its nature designed for the production of a term. Therefore the act of knowledge is not a transitive, but an immanent action.

The *major* is evident.

Minor.—*a*) *The act of knowledge sometimes produces no term whatsoever.* In knowledge of the external senses (and the common sense) no expressed species is produced, for, as experience testifies, the object is attained as physically present, not as intentionally represented.

b) *The act of knowledge, even when it does produce a term, is not of its nature designed to produce a term.* For, when a species is produced, the act of knowledge does not cease, but continues, and, moreover, it is then that it properly takes place as the contemplation of the object. Hence the act of knowledge is not produced for the sake of the expressed species, but rather the expressed species is produced on account of the act of knowledge.

357. The production of the expressed species is not an operation that is really distinct from the act of knowledge.— 1° *Preliminaries.* *a*) An expressed species is produced both in the act of knowledge of some of the senses, and in the act of knowledge of the intellect. The production of the expressed species or mental word by the intellect is called a *diction.* *b*) Scotus seems to affirm that the production of the mental word or *diction* is an operation that is really distinct from the act of knowledge. Thomists deny this.

2° *Proof.*— The production of the term (in which) of the act of knowledge is not really distinct from the act of knowledge. But the production of the expressed species is the production of the term (in which) of the act of knowledge. Therefore [1].

(1) *Contra Gentes*, l. IV, c. 2.

358. Corollary. — Therefore the act of knowledge is formally an immanent operation that belongs to the predicament of quality; yet it is at the same time virtually and supereminently a transitive action,in as much as sometimes it accidentally produces a term.

CHAPTER II

SENSITIVE KNOWLEDGE

Prologue.—In this chapter, we shall deal, first, with the subject of the sensitive powers; secondly, with reflexion on sensation; thirdly, with the external senses; and fourthly, with the internal senses. The division of the chapter is as follows:

Subject of the sensitive powers	Statement of the question Thesis: The subject of the sensitive powers is not the soul alone, but the compound of soul and body Corollaries
Reflexion on sensation	Statement of the question Thesis: No sensitive power can reflect either on its own act or on itself by a distinct act of reflexion; but it can attain its own act by concomitant reflexion Corollary
External senses	Definition of the external sense Object of the external senses Sensation and perception Number of the external senses Superior senses and inferior senses Seat of external sensation
Internal senses	Notion of the internal sense Number of the internal senses Common sense Phantasy or imagination Estimative faculty Sensitive memory Organ of the internal senses

ARTICLE I

SUBJECT OF THE SENSITIVE POWERS

359. Statement of the question. — 1° A sensitive power or faculty is a *proximate principle-by-which of sensation as such.*

Sensations are the acts of seeing, hearing, tasting, touching, imagining, etc.

2° The sensitive powers, as vital powers and accidental acts, are produced together with the sensitive living being, and hence the essence of its soul is their intrinsic first principle (1). It is under this aspect that they are called powers of the *soul.*

3° We are at present concerned with the problem of whether the sensitive powers exist in the soul alone, or in the compound of soul and body, as their subject.

The subject of the powers is that (substance) in which they inhere as accidents. The compound of soul and body is a sensitive living being composed of a soul and first matter, or, in other words, it is a mobile being as informed by a sensitive soul.

4° Many philosophers, as Plato, the Cartesians, Rosmini, and many others of recent times, who do not hold that the soul is the substantial form of the body, teach that the soul alone is the subject of the sensitive powers.

Scholastics commonly teach that the sensitive powers exist in the compound of soul and body as their subject.

360. Statement of the thesis. — The thesis is of great importance, for, if the soul alone is the subject of the sensitive

(1) I, q. 77, a. 6.

powers, the sensitive soul of the brute exists not only as a principle *by which*, but as a principle *which*, and therefore does not depend on matter for its existence, and is spiritual and immortal.

THESIS.—THE SUBJECT OF THE SENSITIVE POWERS IS NOT THE SOUL ALONE, BUT THE COMPOUND OF SOUL AND BODY.

Every sensitive power is organic. But the subject of an organic power is not the soul alone, but the compound of soul and body. Therefore the subject of the sensitive powers is not the soul alone, but the compound of soul and body[1].

The *minor* is clear from the fact that an organ is a part of the compound of soul and body.

Major.—a) Experience. For we see and hear by means of organs. *b) Reason.* A power whose proper object is a corporeal thing as corporeal is itself corporeal or organic, because a power corresponds exactly to its object. But the proper object of a sensitive power is a corporeal thing as corporeal; for when we have knowledge of a thing by our senses we know it as an object with a determinate extension, color, figure, etc. Therefore...

361. Corollaries. — 1° Therefore, a fortiori, vegetative powers are organic and do not exist in the soul alone as subject, but in the compound of soul and body.

2° Therefore an organ is not only an indispensable condition of sensation, but, when informed by a sensitive power, it is the proximate efficient cause of sensation.

3° The sensible species must be carefully distinguished from physical, chemical, and physiological determinations, which are produced by an object in an organ (2).

(1) Duplicis ordinis facultates, organicae et inorganicae, ex anima humana per naturalem resultantiam emanant; priores ad quas sensus pertinet, in composito subjectantur. — *Ex thesi* XVIII s. Thomae.

(2) Modern philosophers, who do not treat of sensation in a philosophical manner, agree with this. « L'apparition de la sensation consécutivement à l'excitation, est inexplicable. Si l'on admet que l'excitation reste, comme l'excitant, un phénomène essentiellement mécanique, de même nature pour tous les sens, on ne peut, en effet, comprendre comment il en peut résulter ces phénomènes si différents entre eux et du mouvement qui sont les odeurs, les pressions, les sons, les couleurs, etc., tels que nous les sentons. » — *Traité de Psychologie*, par GEORGES DUMAS, etc., t. I, édit. 1, p. 394.

ARTICLE II

REFLEXION ON SENSATION

362. Statement of the question. — 1° Reflexion is defined: *the attention of a knowing subject to its own acts.* Since the knowing subject experiences its own act by such attention, reflexion is also called *consciousness.*

2° Reflexion is improper or proper.

Improper reflexion is reflexion by which a knowing subject, by means of the act of one of its powers, directs its attention to the act of another power; v.g., when a man, by means of his intellect, considers that he knows something by means of the senses.

Proper reflexion is reflexion by which a knowing subject reflects, by the same power by which it has knowledge, on its own act and knows (or is conscious) that it knows, i.e., has knowledge.

3° Proper reflexion is either concomitant reflexion (in actu exercito) or reflexion by a distinct act (in actu signato) (1).

Concomitant reflexion is reflexion by which a cognitive power *by the same act* knows something and perceives that it knows it.

Reflexion by a distinct act is reflexion by which a cognitive power *by a new act* reflects upon an act it already has and considers it.

4° All admit improper reflexion in the senses, for the inter-

---

(1) *Reflexio exercita* and *reflexio signata*, though sometimes translated *exercised reflexion* and *signified reflexion*, are, we think, more accurately rendered *concomitant reflexion* and *reflexion by a distinct act.* — Translator's note.

nal sense knows the act of the external sense. But proper reflexion offers a difficulty.

There are a few who hold that the sense reflects upon its own act by a distinct act of reflexion.

Some maintain that the sense in no way reflects upon its own act.

Others contend that the sense reflects on its own act only by concomitant reflexion (in actu exercito).

363. Statement of the thesis.

THESIS.—NO SENSITIVE POWER CAN REFLECT EITHER ON ITS OWN ACT OR ON ITSELF BY A DISTINCT ACT OF REFLEXION; BUT IT CAN ATTAIN ITS OWN ACT BY CONCOMITANT REFLEXION.

First part.—*No sensitive power can reflect either on its own act or on itself by a distinct act of reflexion.*—A sensitive power that could reflect on its own act and on itself by a distinct act of reflexion would have to be acted upon by itself. But no sensitive power can be acted upon by itself. Therefore no sensitive power can reflect either on its own act or on itself by a distinct act of reflexion.

Major.—Sensation is knowledge. But knowledge is produced only when the power is acted upon by its object. Therefore...

Minor.—A sensitive power is dependent in its operation on a corporeal organ and a corporeal mode. But no corporeal thing can act upon itself as regards the whole of itself, for all corporeal things operate with their extension (i.e., as extended) and depend on quantitative contact. But quantitative contact cannot be contact of a thing with itself, but must be contact of one thing with another, whether a part with a part, or a whole with a whole. Therefore...

Second part.—*A sensitive power can attain its own act by concomitant reflexion.*—A sensitive power, in knowing an object, knows that it has knowledge of it, and thus, by the same act, has some knowledge of its own act.

364. Unconscious sensation. — Is unconscious sensation possible? Some deny its possibility, because they hold that sensation of its very nature is conscious, so that unconscious sensation is repugnant. But it should be pointed out that some sensation takes place with very little attention, and as such may be called unconscious.

POINTS FOR REVIEW

1. Distinguish between: *a*) proper reflexion and improper reflexion; *b*) concomitant reflexion and reflexion by a distinct act.

2. Is concomitant reflexion proper reflexion? Explain.

3. Explain why the senses cannot act upon themselves.

ARTICLE III

EXTERNAL SENSES

365. Definition of external sense. – The external sense is defined: *a cognitive organic faculty which attains its object without the mediation of other senses.*

The intellect and the internal senses presuppose the knowledge of the external senses, in order that they may know their object; the external senses immediately attain by physical contact an object presented to them.

366. Object of the external senses. – There are two classes of sense objects, i.e., of sensibles: proper and accidental.

1° A *proper sensible* is a sense object that is really attained by the sensitive power. It is subdivided into *immediate* sensible and *mediate* sensible.

a) An *immediate* sensible is the immediate object of a sense. Sense objects of this kind are called *secondary sensible qualities* by modern philosophers since the time of Galileo and Descartes, and they are color, sound, odor, taste, heat, etc.

b) A *mediate* sensible is an object which is really attained by the sensitive power, not immediately, but by means of an immediate sensible; v.g., an extended object is known by the sense of sight, but as *colored.*

The mediate sensible is also called *common* sensible, because it can be attained by several senses. Common sensibles are called *primary sensible qualities* by modern philosophers, and they are *quantity* and the adjuncts of quantity, as *motion, rest, figure, posture.*

2° An *accidental sensible* is an object which is not attained by a sensitive power, but yet is joined to a proper sensible.

a) *A sense does not of itself attain it,* for otherwise it would be a proper sensible.

b) *It is joined to a proper sensible,* in this sense: when the proper sensible is attained by one of the senses, the accidental sense object is immediately attained by another cognitive faculty of the sentient subject; v.g., when we see a colored object, our intellect immediately apprehends this colored object as a *being.* The accidental sensible is in some way attained by the sensitive power, as subject of the proper sense object.

3° The accidental sensible can be such in two ways:

a) in regard to a determinate sense; v.g., a man who sees food can, by means of his imagination, apprehend its taste. In this case, taste is accidentally visible.

b) in regard to all the senses, in as much as something that is joined to a proper sense object can be apprehended only by the intellect. In this sense, all the first notions of the intellect, as the notions of being, the good, the true, substance, life, etc., are accidental sensibles. Of themselves they are intelligible only, i.e., objects of the intellect, not of the senses.

367. Sensation and perception. – The distinction between sensation and perception, as used by modern philosophers, results from the distinction between proper sense object and accidental sense object.

Sensation is the knowledge of a sense as it attains a proper sense object.

Perception is the knowledge by which a sentient subject unites accidental sensibles to proper sensibles which it knows (1).

(1) Reproduced attributes tied together with presently felt attributes in the unity of a *thing* with a name, these are the materials out of which my actually perceived table is made. — William James, *Psychology, Briefer Course*, p. 313.

Generally simple sensation is found only in an infant; in adults, it is accompanied by perception.

368. Number of the external senses. – We cannot penetrate the specific natures of the objects of the external senses; v.g., we do not know the specific differentiæ by which heat and color are distinguished from each other. And since every faculty is specified by its object, we cannot demonstrate philosophically the specific distinction of the external senses. Nevertheless, we can set forth the division of the external senses, as it appears from experience (1).

The external senses are classified as follows:

1° *Sight*, whose immediate object is color;

2° *Hearing*, whose immediate object is sound;

3° *Smell*, whose immediate object is odor;

4° *Taste*, whose immediate object is savor;

5° *Touch*, which is a generic sense that has several species (2). The sense of touch is distributed throughout the nervous system, and is found in all the other senses. The species of the sense of touch are the following:

a) *touch specifically understood*, whose immediate object seems to be differences of pressure exercised by external bodies on the sentient subject;

b) *sense of temperature*, whose immediate object seems to be the difference between the external temperature and the temperature of the sentient body.

Many modern psychologists claim there are other senses: the *muscular sense*, which perceives muscular contractions and expansions; the *cinesthesic sense*, i.e., the sense of hunger, thirst,

(1) S'agit-il de définir chacun des sens externes dans sa spécificité, nous manquons de notions ontologiques suffisantes. Est-il impossible de rapporter à la même faculté la connaissance de la saveur et celle de l'odeur? Pour répondre à cette question, il faudrait savoir d'une connaissance ontologique entièrement déterminée, c'est-à-dire spécifique, ce que c'est que la saveur et ce que c'est que l'odeur, et cette connaissance nous fait défaut. — YVES SIMON, *Introduction à l'ontologie du connaître*, p. 51, 1934, Desclée, De Brouwer et Cie, Paris.

(2) I, q. 78, a. 3. — *In De Anima*, c. 15, lect. 22.

and fatigue; the *sense of pain*, and the *sense of orientation*. We do not deny the possibility of these senses. However, it is not evident that they are distinct from the senses already enumerated.

Thus the muscular sense seems to be reducible to the sense of *touch* as applied to the different parts of the organism, in as much as these parts touch one another and exercise pressure on one another.

In like manner, the *cinesthesic* sense and the sense of pain (1) seem to be identified with the sense of touch, in as much as it perceives pressure that is disagreeable to it.

The sense of *orientation* seems to be reducible to external senses, v.g., to sight and touch, but as they receive the aid of an internal sense called the common sense.

369. Superior senses, and inferior senses. – The external senses may be divided into superior senses and inferior senses.

The *superior senses* are those senses which are related to their object in a purely objective manner, as sight and hearing.

The *inferior senses* are those senses which are related to their object in a manner not purely objective, but to some extent subjective, in as much as they perceive their object as affecting the knowing subject. Such are the senses of taste, of smell, of temperature, and of resistance.

370. Seat of external sensation. — It is a much disputed question whether external sensation is completed in the peripheral organs, v.g., the eye, ear, etc., or in the brain.

1° *Opinions.*—*a*) Descartes (because he held that the brain is the seat of the sensitive soul) and nearly all modern psychologists hold that external sensation is completed in the brain. Such is the opinion of many neo-scholastics, as Frobes, De La Vassière, etc.

(1) Dolor est secundum passionem corporalem, ... et ideo incipit a laesione corporis, et terminatur in apprehensione tactus, propter quod dolor est in sensu tactus ut in apprehendente. — *De Veritate*, q. 26, a. 3, c. and ad 9.

This opinion is not greatly at variance with that of Aristotle and St. Thomas, who held that the organ of external sense, v.g., of sight, is in the vicinity of the brain (1).

b) Some scholastics maintain that external sensation is completed in the peripheral parts of the organism. Such is the opinion of Farges, Urraburu, Remer, Gredt, etc.

2° *Judgment of the problem.*—The problem is of little importance in rational psychology (2), and perhaps its solution is not possible.

POINTS FOR REVIEW

1. Distinguish between: *a*) the external senses and the internal senses; *b*) proper sense object and accidental sense object; *c*) immediate sensible and common sensible.

2. Name the common sensibles.

3. State briefly the difference between sensation and perception.

4. Give the divisions of the generic sense of touch.

5. To what sense may the cinesthesic sense be reduced ? Explain.

5. Explain the distinction between the superior and the inferior senses.

---

(1) ... Sensitivum animae dicitur potentia sensitiva, quae, quia est principium sensibilis operationis animae quae per corpus exercetur, oportet esse in aliqua determinata parte corporis; et sic principium visionis est interius, juxta cerebrum, ubi conjunguntur duo nervi ex oculis procedentes. — *De Sensu et Sensato*, lect. 5, n. 64.

« Organum odoratus dicitur esse in loco, qui est circa cerebrum. » — *Ibid.*, n. 69.

(2) Many scholastics, as Farges, Remer, Gredt, etc., claim that the opinion that affirms that external sensation is completed in the brain favors idealism. But this is not evident, since Aristotle and St. Thomas, who were not idealists, held that the organs of sight and smell are in the vicinity of the brain.

ARTICLE IV

INTERNAL SENSES

371. Notion of internal sense. — The internal senses are defined: *organic faculties whose knowledge presupposes external sensation.*

The external senses attain an object presented to them by physical contact; the internal senses deal with an object already known by the external senses.

372. Number of the internal senses. — The arguments used to determine the number of the internal senses are only probable, and therefore we find that there is much disagreement in regard to the number of these senses. Scotus and Suarez hold that there is only one internal sense; the Conimbrenses maintain that there are two; Pesch claims that there are three; Averroes and St. Thomas say there are four; Avicenna and St. Bonaventure assert that there are five; and St. Albert the Great supports the opinion that there are six internal senses.

St. Thomas holds that there are four internal senses in a perfect animal, but not necessarily four in an imperfect animal [1].

The opinion of St. Thomas, which we regard as the most probable, is the one we adopt.

373. Common sense. — Common sense is not used here to signify an opinion held by all people, but rather to designate an internal sense.

1° *Existence of the common sense.*—The common sense exists, if sentient beings can distinguish between their external

(1) I, q. 78, a. 4. — *De Anima*, q. un., a. 13.

sensations and between the objects of the external senses. But sentient beings can distinguish between their external sensations and between the objects of the external senses. Therefore the common sense exists.

Major.—a) *If sentient beings can distinguish between their external sensations.*—The external senses cannot reflect by a distinct act of reflexion on their sensations, and therefore they cannot distinguish between these sensations. Therefore the distinction between their sensations must be made by an internal sense, which is called the common sense. b) *If sentient beings can distinguish between the objects of the external senses.* An external sense, v.g., sight, cannot distinguish between its own object and the object of another sense, v.g., of hearing, which it cannot attain. Therefore, if sentient beings can distinguish between the objects of the external senses, there exists an internal sense, i.e., the common sense, which not only attains these objects, but distinguishes between them.

Minor.—a) It is evident from internal experience.—We perceive our sensations *in the concrete*, and by sense knowledge distinguish between the objects of the external senses. b) The truth of the minor is shown also by external experience.—An animal raises its ear to hear, directs its gaze towards a thing to see it, etc. Hence an animal distinguishes between its sensations, and between the objects of the external senses.

2° *Definition of the common sense.*—In the light of what has been said, the common sense may be defined: *an organic faculty which immediately perceives and distinguishes external sensations, and mediately all sense objects when they are present.*

3° *Act of the common sense.*—The act by which the common sense perceives external sensations is called *sensitive consciousness;* in a wide sense, the faculty itself is sometimes called sensitive conscience.

4° *The common sense and sensible species.*—a) An *impressed species* is produced in the common sense by the sensation of the external senses, which is its immediate object. b) The common sense does not require an expressed species for its knowledge, because its object is immediately and even physically present.

374. Phantasy or imagination. — The phantasy is an internal sense, and is also called the *imaginative* faculty because of the *images* of things which it produces.

1° *Existence of the phantasy.*—The phantasy exists, as an internal sense that is really distinct from the common sense, if a sentient being retains and conserves the species of sensible things. But a sentient being does retain and conserve the species of sensible things. Therefore the phantasy exists, as an internal sense that is really distinct from the common sense.

Major.—Since the principle of reception and the principle of conservation are really distinct in material things [1], the internal sense and conserves the species of sensible things is distinct from the common sense, which receives them when they are present.

Minor.—It is clear, for animals are moved by sense objects that are absent from them; v.g., they seek prey far removed from them. The immediate testimony of the human consciousness also confirms this.

2° *Definition of the phantasy.*—The phantasy or imagination is defined: *an organic faculty which has knowledge of things known by the external senses and the common sense, even in their absence.*

3° *The phantasy and sensible species.*—*a*) An *impressed species* is produced in the phantasy, by means of the common sense, from a thing perceived by the external senses. *b*) An *expressed species*, called a *phantasm*, is required for knowledge of the phantasy, because the phantasy can abstract from the physical presence of its object.

(1) Thus water easily receives wood, but it does not retain it well, because wood can easily be removed from water; iron, on the contrary, receives wood only with difficulty, but it retains it well, because wood once received into iron is not easily removed from it.

NOTE.—A phantasm, in a wide sense, is also the name given to an expressed species of any internal sense, and is simply called an *image* by modern psychologists.

4° *Functions of the phantasy.*—The phantasy has three functions: *a*) it receives and conserves the species of sensible things; *b*) it reproduces them in the absence of the things they represent; *c*) in man especially, it forms new images from the images it already has.

375. The estimative faculty. — The estimative faculty is an internal sense, and is really distinct from the common sense and the phantasy.

1° *Existence of the estimative faculty.*—The estimative faculty exists, if a sentient being perceives intentions not known by the other senses, i.e., something concrete not perceived by the external senses, the common sense, or the phantasy. But a sentient being does perceive sensations not perceived by the external senses, the common sense, or the phantasy. Therefore the estimative faculty exists.

The *major* is clear.

Minor.—It is clear from experience that a sentient being, v.g., an animal, perceives intentions which the external senses do not perceive, and which in consequence neither the common sense nor the phantasy perceives; v.g., a sheep, on seeing a wolf, flees not because the color of the wolf is deleterious to the eye, but because the sheep recognizes the wolf as a natural enemy, i.e., perceives the noxious character of the wolf. In like manner, a bird gathers straw not because it is pleasing to any of the external senses, but because its utility for nest-building is perceived.

2° *Definition of the estimate faculty.*—In the light of what has been said, the estimate faculty may be defined: *an internal sense by which a sentient being perceives in an external thing represented by the external senses intentions not perceived by the external senses*, i.e., it perceives the character of the *external thing as noxious or beneficial not to the senses, but to the nature of the individual or species.*

3° *The estimative faculty and impressed species.*—An impressed species is produced in the estimative faculty by a sensible object, by means of previous external and also internal sensation.

4° *The estimative faculty in man.*—The estimative faculty in man, because of its conjunction with the intellect, is called the *cogitative* faculty or the *particular reason:* *a*) because, in man, the estimative faculty perceives singular things as beneficial or noxious to man's nature not only immediately, but by some kind of reasoning or comparison (¹), whereas, in the animal, it perceives singular things as beneficial or noxious only by natural instinct and immediate experience; *b*) because, whereas in the brute the estimative faculty apprehends an individual only as a principle or a term of some action or passion, in man, because of its alliance with the intellect, it apprehends an inividual as a nature (²); v.g., a sheep recognizes a particular lamb, not in as much as it is this particular lamb, but in as much as the lamb is its suckling; and a particular herb, not as this particular herb, but as its food; the estimative faculty in man, on the contrary, recognizes a particular man as such.

376. Sensitive memory. — Man has two kinds of memory, viz., intellective and sensitive. It is with his sensitive memory, which is an internal sense, that we are concerned for the present.

(1) I, q. 78, a. 4. — Cette faculté se trouve également chez l'homme, plus parfaite, en raison de son voisinage avec l'intelligence: elle prend alors le nom de *cogitative* (co-agitare) parce que les appréciations concrètes ne résultent plus, comme chez l'animal, de prédispositions instinctives innées mais de raisonnements concrets du particulier au particulier sur des objets individuels, sans intervention d'idées ou de lois universelles ... Elle se manifeste dans la connaissance tout empirique, incapable de se justifier scientifiquement, faite d'intuitions divinatrices qu'ont, par exemple, la mère de son enfant, le mécanicien ou le cycliste de leur machine à faire marcher, le rebouteur de l'organisme, l'artiste de son œuvre: c'est la faculté maîtresse des gens débrouillards, c'est elle qui donne le savoir-faire pratique sous toutes ses formes. — COLLIN, *Manuel de Phil. Thom.*, t. I, p. 305, ed. 6.

(2) *In De Anima*, l. III, l. 13.

1° *Existence of the sensitive memory.*—The faculty of sensitive memory exists, if sentient beings conserve unperceived intentions. But sentient beings conserve unperceived intentions. Therefore the faculty of sensitive memory exists.

Major.—Because in material things the principle of reception and the principle of conservation are really distinct.

Minor.—*a*) From intentions of this kind an animal recalls something as noxious or beneficial; v.g., such is the case when a birds goes in search of straw. *b*) The past as such is an unperceived intention, in as much as it implies a relation between two states of concrete knowledge (the past and the present).

2° *Definition of sensitive memory.*—The sensitive memory may be defined: *an organic faculty which conserves unperceived intentions*, or *an internal sense which apprehends singular sensible things as previously perceived or known by the estimative faculty.* Hence a sentient being recalls two things at the same time: *a*) the sensation of the object; *b*) the object itself as already perceived.

3° *Sensitive memory and sensible species.*—*a*) By means of the estimative faculty, an impressed species is produced in the memory by the external senses, the common sense, and the phantasy; *a*) an expressed species is required for knowledge on the part of the memory.

4° *Functions of the sensitive memory.*—The following are the functions of the sensitive memory: *a*) the conservation and reproduction of species; *b*) the recognition of a singular thing as previously known; *c*) localization in the past. The conservation and reproduction of species are also common to the memory and the phantasy; but the recognition of a singular thing as previously known and its localization in the past are functions proper to the memory.

The *recognition of an object* takes place: *a*) When a sentient being represents intentionally to itself an object as already known in some particular circumstances (1). In this case, the sentient being clearly distinguishes between an object as *recalled* from an object simply *imagined*. *b*) When a sentient being knows an object that is physically present, and apprehends it as already known.

Localization of the past takes place when the sentient being determines the time of the occurrence of the event which it recalls (2).

In the case of the proximate past, localization can be made quite easily by a computation of the events which took place between the present moment and the proximate past; but localization is more difficult in the case of the remote past. Generally a sentient being localizes an event between two other events that it recalls.

5° *Memory and reminiscence.*—In man the sensitive memory has a special act called *reminiscence*, for in man the memory not only spontaneously recognizes a thing as soon as it is recalled, as happens also in the case of animals, but, under the command of the will and the direction of the intellect, it seeks things that have escaped the memory.

377. Organ of the internal senses. — The internal senses are located in the brain. The special location of each of them in it is difficult to determine.

POINTS FOR REVIEW

1. Name the internal senses. Do all agree that the internal senses are four in number?

(1) Ainsi, quand j'imagine la tour Eiffel, je me la représente mentalement d'une façon objective; quand je m'en souviens, je me rappelle en fait que je l'ai vue, je me revois moi-même la contemplant d'un tel point de vue, dans telles circonstances de temps, de lumière, etc., avec telles dispositions; suivant la formule de Royer Collard, « on ne se souvient pas des choses, on ne se souvient que de soi-même », c'est-à-dire des choses qu'en tant qu'incorporées à notre passé mental perçues auparavant par nous et telles que nous les avons perçues. — COLLIN, *op. cit.*, p. 345.

(2) Nous nous représentons naturellement le temps comme une ligne en profondeur (troisième dimension) sur laquelle les événements s'éloignent successivement à partir du moment présent. « Localiser » un souvenir consiste donc à déterminer la place relative occupée sur cette ligne par l'événement que nous nous rappelons. — COLLIN, *ibid.*, p. 347.

2. Prove the existence of the common sense, and describe its proper act.

3. Prove the existence of the phantasy, and state its functions.

4. Define unperceived intention.

5. Define estimative faculty, and state why it is called the cogitative faculty.

6. Prove the existence of the sensitive memory, and enumerate its functions.

7. What is reminiscence?

CHAPTER III

SENSITIVE APPETITE

Prologue. — Since the sensitive appetite is an elicited appetite, first, we shall speak of the elicited appetite, and afterwards, we shall deal with the sensitive appetite itself. The movements of the sensitive appetite are called *passions*. Therefore there will be three articles in this chapter.

Elicited appetite	Statement of the question Thesis: Every cognoscitive being has an elicited appetite, which is a faculty really distinct from the cognitive faculties
Sensitive appetite	Statement of the question Thesis: Every sentient being has a concupiscible appetite and an irascible appetite, which are really distinct powers Corollary
Passions of the soul	Passions of the body Passions of the soul Explanation of the passions of the soul Division of the passions All the passions can be reduced to love Organ of the passions of the soul.

ARTICLE I

ELICITED APPETITE

378. Statement of the question.—1° In general, an appetite is an *inclination to a good.*

The appetite is natural or elicited.

The *natural* appetite is the transcendental relation of a thing to a good suitable or proportionate to it; v.g., the appetite of first matter for form.

The *elicited* appetite is the inclination of a cognoscitive being to a good as apprehended.

2° A faculty is defined: *the proximate principle* (*by which*) *of operation as such.* A faculty is an accident that is really distinct from the thing of which it is a property.

379. Statement of the thesis.

THESIS.—EVERY COGNOSCITIVE BEING HAS AN ELICITED APPETITE, WHICH IS A FACULTY REALLY DISTINCT FROM THE COGNITIVE FACULTIES.

First part.—*Every cognoscitive being has an elicited appetite.*—1° *Experience.*—Our consciousness testifies that we have inclinations that follow knowledge. And we know from external experience that other men and animals have similar inclinations.

2° *A priori.*—Every form is followed by an inclination. But a cognoscitive being has not only a natural form by which it is constituted in its natural existence but also an intentional form by which it is constituted cognoscitive. Therefore a cognoscitive being has an inclination or appetite which follows an intentional form or knowledge (1).

Major.—*a*) *Experience.*—In nature we see that different forms, or natures, follow different inclinations. *b*) *A priori.*—Every nature has its own end, which is itself, or something other than itself. Hence, in the first case, a nature, once constituted by its form, is inclined to itself, i.e., rests in itself; in the second case, it is inclined to another.

Second part. *The elicited appetite is a faculty.* An appetite whose act is vital operation is a faculty. But the elicited appetite is an appetite whose act is vital operation. Therefore the elicited appetite is a faculty.

Minor. For when a cognoscitive being has knowledge of something, it moves itself vitally— it is not moved by nature, —to the thing known (2).

Third part.—*The elicited appetite is a faculty that is really distinct from the cognitive faculties.*—Faculties which have different modes of tending to their objects are really distinct. But the elicited appetite and the cognitive faculties have different modes of tending to their objects. Therefore the elicited appetite is a faculty that is really distinct from the cognitive faculties.

The *major* is clear, because all vital operations proceed proximately from faculties.

Minor.—The appetite tends to an object as it really exists in itself; a cognitive faculty tends to an object in order to draw it to itself — the object known is in the subject knowing. Hence the act of the appetite is the movement of a being that tends to a thing, whereas the act of a faculty results rather from the movement of the thing to the knowing subject (3).

(1) I, q. 80, a. 1. — Étienne Gilson, *Le Thomisme*, Paris 1923, pp. 184-200. — Sertillanges, *S. Thomas d'Aquin*, pp. 194-209, édit. 42.
(2) *De Veritate*, q. 22, a. 3, c.
(3) I, q. 81, a. 1, c.

ARTICLE II

SENSITIVE APPETITE

380. Statement of the question. — 1° The elicited appetite follows knowledge. Since knowledge is of two kinds, intellective and sensitive, there are two kinds of appetite: the rational appetite or the will, and the sensitive appetite.

The sensitive appetite is defined: *an organic faculty by which a sentient being is inclined to a good known by the senses.*

2° The sensitive appetite is divided into the concupiscible appetite and the irascible appetite (1).

The concupiscible appetite, which derives its name from the Latin word *concupiscentia*, is defined: *an organic faculty by which a sentient being is inclined to pursue what is suitable according to the senses, and to avoid what is harmful ;* v.g., the appetite by which a dog seeks its prey.

The irascible appetite, which derives its name from the Latin word *ira*, is defined : *an organic faculty by which a sentient being resists anything that is an impediment to its acquisition of a good, or anything which is harmful ;* the appetite by which a dog resists a robber who attempts to steal its prey(2).

381. Statement of the thesis.

THESIS.—EVERY SENTIENT BEING HAS A CONCUPISCIBLE APPETITE AND AN IRASCIBLE APPE-

(1) SERTILLANGES, *op. cit.*, pp. 199-205.

(2) La classification part de ce fait que l'objet peut être bon ou mauvais. A l'objet connu qui est bon répondra une tendance vers l'objet; à l'objet connu qui est mauvais répondra une réaction d'éloignement, d'écart. Mais il peut se présenter des obstacles à cette recherche du bien et à cette fuite du mal. Il faudra donc doubler l'appétit simplement concupiscible de l'appétit irascible qui ne s'exerce pas directement sur le bien ou le mal de l'animal, mais sur les difficultés à atteindre le bien ou à repousser le mal. — *Psychol. Expér.*, DE LA VASSIÈRE, pp. 211-212, édit. 5.

TITE, WHICH ARE REALLY DISTINCT POWERS.

First part.—*Every sentient being has a concupiscible appetite and an irascible appetite.*— 1° *Experience.*—We know from our own experience that animals not only seek things that are good and useful from the point of view of the senses, but that they resist anything that impedes their acquisition of a good, and also anything that may do them harm.

2° *A priori.*—Every form is followed by an inclination. But, as we observe in bodies, a natural form is followed by an inclination both for the attainment of things that are beneficial, and for the resistance of things that are noxious. Therefore, in like manner, an intentional form in a sentient being must be followed by these two inclinations.

Second part.—*The concupiscible appetite and the irascible appetite are really distinct powers.*—Appetites whose formal objects are distinct are really distinct powers. But the concupiscible appetite and the irascible appetite have formal objects that are distinct. Therefore the concupiscible appetite and irascible appetite are really distinct powers.

Major.—Because powers are specified by their formal objects.

Minor.—The formal object of the concupiscible appetite is good as suitable *from the point of view of the senses;* the formal object of the irascible appetite is good as *attainable only with difficulty and labor.*

382. Corollary. — The concupiscible appetite follows the knowledge of the phantasy and of the common sense ; the irascible appetite follows the knowledge of the estimative faculty, which alone can attain a good that is suitable or beneficial from the point of view not only of the senses, but of nature.

ARTICLE III

PASSIONS OF THE SOUL

383. Passions of the body. — A distinction must be made between the passions of the body and the passions of the soul (1).

The passions of the body imply two things : *a*) an agreeable or disagreeable modification of the body ; *b*) the apprehension of this modification by the sense of touch, according to the earlier philosophers; according to modern psychologists, by special senses, as the sense of pain ; v.g., *bodily pain* results from an injury to the body. Similarly, *bodily delight* results from the union of the body with a suitable or beneficial object.

The passions of the body are called affective sensations by modern psychologists, and they may be defined : *affective states which have, as their immediate antecedent, organic modification.*

384. Passions of the soul. — The passions of the soul are defined : *movements of the sensitive appetite which result from sense knowledge of good or evil, and which are accompanied by some bodily change* (2).

a) *Movements of the sensitive appetite :* this is the formal element of a passion of the soul.

b) *Which result from sense knowledge of good or evil :* every movement of the sensitive appetite presupposes sense knowledge.

c) *Accompanied by some bodily change :* this is the material element of a passion, and also the reason why the acts of the

(1) *De Veritate*, q. 26, a. 2, a., and a. 4, ad 4 and ad 5.
(2) I, q. 20, a. 1, ad 1. — I, q. 22, a. 2, and a. 3.

sensitive appetite are called *passions*. For, on the one hand, an act of the sensitive appetite is always accompanied by a bodily change [1]; on the other hand, this change is properly called a *passion*, because the change is accompanied by motion or movement in the strict sense.

Modern psychologists use the word *passion* to signify *any dominant inclination*; v. g., a passion for money. *Passions*, as understood by Scholastics and Descartes, are called *emotions*, or *feelings*; and these they define in almost the same way as Scholastics define passions : *affective states which have as their immediate antecedent a state of conscience or consciousness, or rather an act of knowledge.*

385. Explanation of the passions of the soul. – 1° Scholastics explain the passions of the soul as follows : we have *a*) first, sensitive knowledge in the brain ; *b*)secondly, the movement of the sensitive appetite in the brain ; *c*) thirdly, the transmission of this movement into the body, wherein it produces bodily change.

Modern psychologists offer a similar explanation, called the *cerebral theory* : first, we have an affective movement in the brain, and, secondly, an organic change produced from the transmission of this movement into the body.

2° According to the *peripheric theory* (James, Lange, Sergi), the passions of the soul, or rather the emotions, are explained thus : we have *a*) first, knowledge or a state of consciousness ; *b*) secondly, organic (muscular) reaction ; *c*) thirdly, emotion ; v.g., a man loses some money, later sheds tears, and then becomes sad. This theory is not common today, and seems to confuse a passion of the body with the passions of the soul.

---

(1) La passion remue la chair et le sang plus que la pensée, plus que le vouloir intellectuel, plus que l'acte de vision sensible. Les passions atteignent la chair et le sang, les font passer par toutes les transes du spasme et de l'extase, elles jouent sur les nerfs et sur les muscles, sur le cerveau et le cœur comme sur un instrument vivant et vibrant, les hymnes de l'amour, du désir, de la joie, de l'ivresse. — *Les Passions*, Janvier, 1ère Conf.

386. Division of the passions. – Scholastics teach that there are six passions of the concupiscible appetite, and five of the irascible appetite.

1° The following are the passions of the concupiscible appetite : love, hatred, desire, flight, joy, sadness.

Love is the inclination to good as simply apprehended.

Hatred is the aversion for evil as simply apprehended.

Desire is the inclination to good apprehended as absent, but possible.

Flight is the aversion for evil apprehended as absent, but possible.

Joy is the resting in good that is apprehended and possessed.

Sadness is the suffering caused by the interior apprehension of evil.

2° The following are the passions of the irascible appetite : hope, despair, courage, fear, and anger.

Hope is the movement to a good apprehended as difficult, but possible of attainment.

Despair is the recession from good apprehended as impossible of attainment.

Courage is the movement to evil apprehended as terrible and imminent, but superable.

Fear is the recession from evil apprehended as terrible and immiment, but not superable.

Anger is the vehement inclination to fight or to inflict evil on an enemy.

The foregoing are the principal passions ; and to them may be added mixed passions, as envy, which is sorrow because of another's good in as much as it is an impediment to one's own good, etc.

387. All the passions can be reduced to love. — Love is complacency in good. From this complacency results, rest, or joy, in the appetite, if the good is possessed ; and desire, if the good is absent [1]. Similarly a movement of aversion for evil results from this complacency. Hence the following movements of the sensitive appetite, or passions, result from complacency in good, i.e., from love :

1° in the concupiscible appetite :

with reference to evil as opposed to good	hatred
" " " possible good	desire
" " " possible evil	flight
" " " good possessed	joy
" " " evil suffered	sadness

2° in the irascible appetite:

as regards good difficult of attainment	if possible	hope
	if impossible	despair
as regards evil difficult to overcome	if superable	courage
	if insuperable	fear
as regards something that is an impediment or that inflicts evil that must be vindicated		anger

388. Organ of the passions of the soul. — The organ of the sensitive appetite and consequently of the passions is the brain. The heart, which the philosophers of old regarded as the organ of the sensitive appetite, is merely the organ that manifests the passions, especially the passion of love.

(1) BOSSUET, *La Connaissance de Dieu et de Soi-même*, c. 1, n. 6.

CHAPTER IV

SENSITIVE SOUL

Prologue. — In our discussion of the sensitive soul, there are three things that we must consider : first, its existence ; secondly, its nature ; thirdly, its generation and corruption. Hence this chapter will contain three articles :

Existence of the sensitive soul	Statement of the question Thesis: Animals have a sensitive soul, which is united to their body as its substantial form The sensitive soul is the only substantial form in an animal
Nature bf the sensitive soul	Statement of the question Thesis: The sensitive soul is not subsistent, but exists only as the principle by which the animal exists and lives
Generation and corruption of the sensitive soul	Statement of the question Thesis: The soul of an animal is engendered and corrupts not directly, but accidentally Corollaries

ARTICLE I

EXISTENCE OF THE SENSITIVE SOUL

389. Statement of the question. — 1° The sensitive soul is the first principle by which a being exists, lives, and has sensation.

2° An animal [1] is a living being which manifests not only vegetative life but also sensitive life, but not intellective life ; v.g., a horse.

3° The thesis has two parts.

In the first part we affirm that animals have a sensitive soul. This is opposed to the teaching of Descartes, who held that animals are mere artificial machines, and is opposed also to the teaching of certain modern physiologists, who deny that animals have sensation.

In the second part, of the thesis, we affirm that the sensitive soul is united to the body as its substantial form. This teaching is opposed to the opinion of Tongiorgi, Palmieri, and others, who refuse to accept the doctrine of hylomorphism on the composition of mobile being.

390. Statement of the thesis.

THESIS. — ANIMALS HAVE A SENSITIVE SOUL, WHICH IS UNITED TO THE BODY AS ITS SUBSTANTIAL FORM.

First part. — *Animals have a sensitive soul.* — A living being that has sensation has a sensitive soul. But all animals

(1) The term *animal* is used here in a specific sense, as equivalent to *irrational animal.* — Translator's note.

have sensation. Therefore animals have a sensitive soul.

Major. — Sensation, as true knowledge, is an operation of a higher order than any operation of vegetative life. Therefore it must have as its first principle a soul that is specifically superior to the vegetative soul, i.e., it must have a sensitive soul as its first principle.

Minor. — *a*) Animals have organs that are entirely similar to those by which man experiences sensation. *b*) The movements of an animal are manifested as the movements of an appetite which follows sensation. Indeed, an animal moves in such manner as to appear to move in order to know and discover whether such and such a thing is suitable and beneficial to it or not.

Second part. — *The sensitive soul is united to the body as its substantial form.* The sensitive soul and the body constitute one principle of operation, i.e., one nature. But they cannot constitute one nature, if the sensitive soul is not the substantial form of the body. Therefore the sensitive soul is united to the body as its substantial form.

Major. — Things whose operation is *numerically* the same constitute one nature ; for every nature has its own operation, so that, if nature is multiplied, operation also is multiplied. But sensation is an operation that is numerically one, and it is produced not by the soul alone, but by the animated body.

Minor. — If the sensitive soul were not the substantial form of the body, it would have its own complete nature in itself.

391. The sensitive soul is the only substantial form in an animal.—An animal has one nature, i.e., is essentially one being. But there can be only one substantial form in a mobile being which has one nature, or which is essentially one. Therefore . . .

Therefore the sensitive soul is the substantial form by which an animal is constituted a mobile, vegetative, sensitive being. In other words, the sensitive soul, though formally sensitive, gives an animal the perfections of vegetative life and of corporeity.

ARTICLE II

NATURE OF THE SENSITIVE SOUL

392. Statement of the question. — 1° We are concerned in this article with the question of whether the sensitive soul, i.e., the soul of the animal, is subsistent.

A subsistent form is a form which has its own proper existence, and thus can exist without matter ; v.g., the human soul, which can exist when separated from the body.

Since a subsistent form does not depend on matter for its existence, it is a spiritual form.

A non-subsistent soul does not exist, nor can it exist, as a being *which*, but only as a principle *by which* a being is constituted as living.

2° The thesis is a refutation of the teaching of Plato, who, holding that the sensitive soul of itself has its own sensation, conceived it as being a spiritual form ; and a refutation too of the teaching of Tongiorgi and Palmieri, who, because of their rejection of the doctrine of hylomorphism, maintained that the soul of an animal is a complete substance.

393. Statement of the thesis.

THESIS. — THE SENSITIVE SOUL IS NOT SUBSISTENT, BUT EXISTS ONLY AS THE PRINCIPLE BY WHICH AN ANIMAL EXISTS AND LIVES [1].

1° The soul of a living being whose proper operation is

(1) « Vegetalis et sensibilis ordinis animae nequaquam per se subsistunt ... sed sunt tantummodo ut principium quo vivens est et vivit ... » — *Thesis XIV* s. Thomae.

sensation is not subsistent, but exists only as the principle by which a living being exists and lives. But the proper operation of the sensitive soul, i.e., of the soul of an animal, is sensation. Therefore the sensitive soul is not subsistent, but exists only as the principle by which an animal exists and lives (1).

Major. — The mode of existence of a thing is similar to its mode of operation. But sensation is not an operation proper to the soul, but is an operation of the compound (of body and soul), since sensation is organic.

The *minor* is clear from the foregoing thesis.

2° If the sensitive soul were subsistent, an animal would have an intellect. But an animal has no intellect. Therefore the sensitive soul is not subsistent, but is only the principle by which an animal exists and lives.

Major. — If the sensitive soul were subsistent, it would be spiritual, and therefore would be the principle of the spiritual cognitive faculty, i.e., of the intellect.

Minor. — *a*) *Lack of speech.* — Animals, though endowed with organs suited for speech and with the inclination to manifest their affections, do not speak, i.e., do not manifest *universal concepts* and *judgments*, but manifest only *sensitive affections*, v.g., by tears.

b) *No intellectual progress.* — The history of animals shows no progress in the arts and sciences, such as man has attained by his intellect. Any progress made by animals is determinate and unilinear, and is explained by the evolution of sensations and by associations that are purely empirical.

d) *Experiments.* — No experiments that have been made prove that any animal has an intellect, for the results of these experiments can always be explained by purely empirical association that results from practice or habit. Thus, for example, a dog that holds up a card on which the word *food* is written, in order to beg for food, acts thus as a result of an

(1) I, q. 75, a. 3. — *Contra Gentes*, l. II, cc. 80 and 82, and l. IV, c. 39.

association between the sensation of this particular card and the sensation of hunger. In like manner, monkeys that use branches of trees to reach fruit in an orchard do so as a result of an association that is purely empirical.

ARTICLE III

GENERATION AND CORRUPTION OF THE SENSITIVE SOUL.

394. Statement of the question. — 1° Generation is the transition from non-existence to existence that results from the union of form with matter ; and corruption is the transition from existence to non-existence that results from the separation of form from matter [1].

2° A thing is engendered directly when, by the union of form with matter, it acquires existence which it has as a being which exists, or as proper to itself. A thing corrupts directly when, by the separation of form from matter, it loses existence which it has as a being *which* exists, or as proper to itself.

Since a compound of matter and form exists as a being *which* exists, it is engendered and corrupts directly.

3° A thing is engendered or corrupts accidentally, when, existing only as a principle *by which* (physical principle) in a compound which is engendered and corrupts directly, it acquires or loses existence when the compound is engendered or corrupts.

4° The thesis is directed against all who hold with Tongiorgi and Palmieri that the soul of an animal comes into existence by creation, and ceases to exist by annihilation.

395. Statement of the thesis.

THESIS. — THE SOUL OF AN ANIMAL IS ENGENDERED AND CORRUPTS NOT DIRECTLY, BUT ACCIDENTALLY [2].

(1) *Contra Gentes*, l. II, c. 55.
(2) *Thesis* XIV s. Thomae.

First part. — *The soul of an animal is engendered and corrupts.* — Every non-subsistent substantial form is engendered and corrupts. But the soul of an animal is a non-subsistent substantial form. Therefore the soul of an animal is engendered and corrupts.

Major. — *a*) *Every non-subsistent substantial form is engendered.*—A form that is educed from the potency of matter is engendered. But every non-subsistent substantial form is educed from the potency of matter, since it is a material form. Therefore . . .

b) *Every non-subsistent substantial form corrupts.* — A form that loses its existence by the transmutation of matter corrupts. But every non-subsistent substantial from, because it exists only when united to matter, loses its existence by the transmutation of matter, i.e., when matter acquires a new form. Therefore . . .

The *minor* is evident from the preceding article.

Second part. — *The soul of an animal is engendered and corrupts not directly, but accidentally.* — A non-subsistent substantial form is engendered and corrupts not directly, but accidentally. But the soul of an animal is a non-subsistent substantial form. Therefore the soul of an animal is engendered and corrupts not directly, but accidentally.

Major. — A non-subsistent substantial form has not its own existence, but exists only when united to matter, i.e., by the existence of the compound. Hence it cannot be engendered, nor can it corrupt, except when the compound is engendered or corrupts, i.e., it is engendered and corrupts accidentally.

395. Corollaries. - 1° Therefore the sensitive soul, like every material substantial form, is educed from the potency of matter.

2° Therefore the vegetative soul, which is a material form, is engendered and corrupts accidentally.

BOOK IV

Intellective mobile being

OR

Man

Prologue. — Intellective mobile being or man has two proper faculties : the intellect and the will. After we have studied these two faculties, we shall discuss the nature of the intellective soul. Finally, having studied the nature of the intellective soul, we shall deal with the problem of the origin of man. Hence there will be four chapters in this book.

Chapter I. The intellect.

Chapter II. The will.

Chapter III. The intellective soul.

Chapter IV. The origin of man.

CHAPTER I

THE INTELLECT

Prologue. - First, we shall consider the intellect; secondly, we shall study its object. After that, we shall deal with the origin of the intelligible species, the mental word, and the first thing known by the intellect. Therefore there will be five articles in this chapter.

Nature of the human intellect

1) The spirituality of the human intellect:
   - Statement of the question
   - Thesis: The human intellect is a spiritual faculty
2) Is the human intellect a passive power?
   - Statement of the question
   - Thesis: The human intellect is a passive power
   - The human intellect has need of being determined by an impressed intelligible species
   - In the beginning, the human intellect is similar to a blank tablet on which nothing is written
   - The human intellect, as formally cognitive, is called the possible intellect by Aristotle

Object of the human intellect

1) Formal object of the human intellect:
   - Statement of the question
   - Thesis: The common formal object of the human intellect is being
2) Adequate object of the human intellect:
   - Statement of the question
   - Thesis: The adequate object of the human intellect is being in general
   - The possible intellect is a single faculty, but is given different names according to its different acts
   - Conscience
3) Proportionate object of the human intellect:
   - Statement of the question
   - Thesis: The proper object of the human intellect, in the state of union, is the abstracted quiddity of a

Object of the human intellect	sensible thing represented in the phantasy Origin of intellective knowledge in the state of union The human intellect, in the state of union, is incapable of intellection without the aid of phantasms Knowledge of material singular things How the intellect knows singular things in its reflexion on phantasms Analogical knowledge of spiritual things Knowledge of the soul The soul does not know its essence and its existence in the same way The soul habitually knows itself through its essence
Origin of intelligible species	Statement of the question Thesis: The human soul must have an active intellect which abstracts intelligible species from the phantasms The active intellect and the possible intellect are really distinct faculties Causality of the phantasms and of the active intellect Functions of the active intellect Difficulties
Mental word	1) Existence of the mental word: Statement of the question Thesis: The human intellect produces a mental word within itself in all natural intellection Requisites of intellection Diction and intellection are not really distinct Intellection is essentially a metaphysical action, which only virtually produces the mental word Necessity of the mental word 2) The mental word as a formal sign: Statement of the question Thesis: The mental word is the formal sign of the thing known by the intellect Scholia
First thing known	Statement of the question Thesis: The first thing known by the human intellect is being concretized in sensible quiddity Scholia

ARTICLE I

NATURE OF THE HUMAN INTELLECT

I

SPIRITUALITY OF THE HUMAN INTELLECT

397. Statement of the question. - 1° The human intellect is described : *a cognitive faculty by which man apprehends universals, judges, and reasons.*

The existence of this faculty is attested by internal experience, and is denied by no one.

2° A faculty is defined : *the proximate principle (by which) of operation as such.*

3° A spiritual faculty is a faculty that is intrinsically and subjectively independent of matter.

Since the subject of a spiritual faculty is not the compound of matter and form, but the soul alone, it is called an anorganic faculty.

4° *Materialists* (*rigid*) reduce the intellect to physicochemical forces of matter. This is the tenet of Democritus, Epicurus, Lucretius, the Stoics, Hobbes, Helvetius, D'Alembert, and many others.

Sensists teach that the intellect is not essentially different from one of the senses, and therefore that it is an organic faculty. Such is the opinion held by Locke, Berkeley, Hume Condillac, Ribot, Wundt, and James

Spiritualists, as Anaxagoras, Plato, Aristotle, Plotinus, all Scholastics, and the Cartesians teach that the intellect is a spiritual faculty.

398. Statement of the thesis.

THESIS. — THE HUMAN INTELLECT IS A SPIRITUAL FACULTY.

1° A faculty whose operation is spiritual is a spiritual faculty. But the operation of the human intellect is spiritual. Therefore the human intellect is a spiritual faculty (1).

Major. — Because every faculty is specified by its operation.

Minor. — Spiritual operation is operation that is concerned with spiritual objects. But the operation of the human intellect is concerned with spiritual objects : we apprehend wisdom, truth, relations, beings of reason, and God Himself. Therefore (2).

2° An organic faculty cannot know universals. But the human intellect can know universals. Therefore the human intellect is not an organic faculty, but is a spiritual faculty (3).

Major. — An organic faculty can have the form of another only in an extended manner, and therefore it can know only singular and concrete things : for a thing that has extension is concrete and singular.

Minor. — *Evident from introspection :* we perceive from internal experience that we have two kinds of knowledge : sensitive knowledge, by which we apprehend objects as singulars; and intellective knowledge, by which we apprehend universals ; v.g., if we speak of color, we perceive that we have a sensible representation which corresponds to some color, as

(1) Est igitur facultas ab organo intrinsece independens. — *Thesis* XVII s. Thomae.
(2) *Contra Gentes*, L. II, c. 66.
(3) *Ibid.*

red, or white, etc., and which can have infinite variety; but we have something more than this sensible representation: we have the universal concept of color which, ever remaining the same, can be attributed to all colors.

3° An organic faculty is injured by the excellence of its object. But the human intellect is not injured, but is perfected, by the excellence of its object. Therefore the human intellect is not an organic faculty, but is immaterial.

Major. — Sight is injured by color that is too bright hearing by sound that is too loud, etc.

Minor. — The intellect is not injured, but rather is perfected, by highly intelligible objects.

II

IS THE HUMAN INTELLECT A PASSIVE POWFR ?

399. Statement of the question. 1° A faculty is called active in relation to its operation. But a faculty can be active or passive in regard to its object.

An active faculty is a faculty that acts on its object and changes it. Thus all the powers of the vegetative soul are active.

A passive faculty is a faculty that is actuated by its object [1].

2° All who teach that the intellect is alone responsible for the production of knowledge teach at least implicity that the human intellect is an active power. Such is the tenet of Kant, Fichte, Schelling, Hegel, etc.

400. Statement of the thesis.

THESIS. — THE HUMAN INTELLECT IS A PASSIVE POWER.

(1) *De Veritate*, q. 16, a. 1, ad 13.

An intellect which is not a passive faculty is infinite. But the human intellect is not infinite. Therefore the human intellect is a passive faculty (1).

Major. — Knowledge obtains in as much as the knowing subject has the forms or perfections of another as of another, i.e., of an object. But the object of the intellect is universal being, i.e., all things. Therefore an intellect which is not a passive faculty has in itself the perfections of all things, and it does not receive these perfections by being informed by an object, and therefore is in itself infinite.

401. The human intellect has need of being determined by an impressed intelligible species. — An impressed intelligible species is the vicarious form of an object by which the intellect is actuated and determined to know that object. Since the human intellect is a passive power, it must needs be determined by an object. But it cannot be determined or informed by an object as it physically exists. Hence it must be determined mediately, i.e., by means of a vicarious form, or by an impressed intelligible species.

402. In the beginning, the human intellect is similar to a blank tablet on which nothing is written. — Every created intellect, because it is finite, is a passive faculty, and therefore may be compared to intelligible objects, as potency to act (1). But potency has a twofold relation to act. There is a kind of potency that is always perfected by act ; and there is another kind that is not always in act, but passes from potency to act.

We may distinguish two grades of created intellect. The angelic intellect is more perfect than the human intellect, because the angel is a spiritual form which does not exist in matter. Therefore the angelic intellect is always in the act of its intelligible objects. The human intellect is the lower grade of created intellect, because it is the faculty of a substan-

(1) I, q. 79, a. 2. — *Contra Gentes*, L. II, c. 59. — *De Veritate*, q. 16, a. 1, ad 13.
(1) I, q. 79, a. 2, c.

tial form, i.e., of the soul, which exists in matter. Therefore it is in potency in relation to its intelligible objects, and, in the beginning, is similar to a blank tablet on which nothing is written.

This is clearly manifest from the fact that in the beginning we are intelligent only in potency, but afterwards become intelligent in act.

403. The human intellect, as formally cognitive, is called the possible intellect by Aristotle. — The intellect, as formally cognitive, is a passive faculty, and is in potency to all things. It is called the *possible intellect* (from the Greek-δμυατὸν) by Aristotle, and not the *passive intellect*, both because the intellect, as a spiritual faculty, has no passion in the proper meaning of the term, i.e., bodily passion, and because in the time of Aristotle there were some who called the sensitive appetite the passive intellect, and others who gave this name to the cogitative power or particular reason (1).

(1) I, q. 79, a. 2, ad 2.

ARTICLE II

OBJECT OF THE HUMAN INTELLECT

I

FORMAL OBJECT OF THE HUMAN INTELLECT

404. Statement of the question. — 1° The formal object of the intellect is the formality which the intellect as such attains in any knowable thing, i.e., in any material object whatsoever.

2° Being is the formal object of the human intellect, not in as much as the intellect knows only being in general, but in as much it knows a thing only in as much as it is a being. Hence the human intellect can know all the differentiæ and determinations of being, because and in as much as they are beings, just as the sight, which knows things in as much as they are colored, can know all the differentiæ of a colored object (its whiteness, redness, etc), because and in as much as it is colored.

3° Being is the common formal object of the human intellect, in as much as it is the common formal object of any intellect, or the formal object of the human intellect in as much as it is an intellect. Besides this common formal object, the human intellect, in the state of union with the body, has a proper formal object, which is a kind of restriction of the common formal object.

405. Statement of the thesis.

THESIS. — THE COMMON FORMAL OBJECT OF THE HUMAN INTELLECT IS BEING.

1° *From the three operations of the human intellect* (1). — *a*) In simple apprehension, the idea or concept always represents what the object is, i.e., its quiddity. Moreover, since the idea perfectly represents an essence, it represents it as the source of the being of properties (2).

b) In judgment, we affirm that two objective concepts are identified or are not indentified in the same being, by the copula verb, *is*; v.g., *man is white* signifies : man and white are the same being.

c) In reasoning, the intellect always proceeds in virtue of the principles of identity or contradiction, principles which are the supreme laws of being.

Therefore being is the formality or objective concept that the intellect attains in its three operations, and therefore being is the common formal object of the intellect.

2° *From the immateriality of the intellect.* — The common formal object of a faculty which can know all things is being. But the human intellect can know all things. Therefore the common formal object of the human intellect is being.

Major. — Being is the common formality under which all things are contained and can be attained.

Minor. — Immateriality is the root of knowledge, so that capacity for knowledge is proportionate to immateriality. But

(1) « Selon moi, la faculté distinctive de l'être intelligent, est de pouvoir donner un sens à ce petit mot *est.* » J.-J. Rousseau, *Profession de Foi du vicaire savoyard.* — Cf. also Collin, *op. cit.*, t. I, pp. 351-352, édit. 6a. — Garrigou-Lagrange, *Le Sens Commun*, pp. 42 ss., édit. 3a.

(2) Mettez un sauvage en présence d'une locomotive, faites-la marcher devant lui, laissez-lui le loisir de l'examiner et d'examiner d'autres machines semblables. Tant qu'il ne fera que les voir courir, tant qu'il se contentera d'en considérer les pièces diverses, il n'en aura qu'une connaissance sensible et particulière, ou si vous voulez une image commune accompagnée d'un nom, comme celle que pourrait avoir un perroquet. Mais s'il est intelligent, un jour il comprendra qu'il faut qu'il y ait là une force motrice que la locomotive produit ou qu'elle applique . . .; s'il parvient à comprendre que c'est par la dilatation de la vapeur emprisonnée que cette force motrice est obtenue, il entendra *ce que c'est* qu'une locomotive (quod quid est) et il s'en formera un concept spécifique. Les sens ne voyaient que des éléments matériels, une masse de fer noire, disposée d'une façon singulière. L'idée montre quelque chose d'*immatériel:* la raison d'être de cette disposition, et de l'agencement de ces pièces variées. — Vacant, *Etudes comparées sur la philosophie de saint Thomas d'Aquin et celle de Scot*, t. I, p. 134.

the human intellect is spiritual, and so is absolutely immaterial. Therefore the human intellect has an absolute capacity for knowledge, i.e., it can know all things.

II

ADEQUATE OBJFCT OF THE HUMAN INTELLECT

406. Statement of the question. — 1° The adequate object of the human intellect is everything which the human intellect can know either by its own power or by a superadded power. There is a distinction between the adequate object and the proportionate object of the intellect. The proportionate object is defined : the object which the human intellect can know by its own power ; v.g., God as seen in the beatific vision comes under the adequate object, but not under the proportionate object of the human intellect.

2° The distinction between the adequate object and the proportionate object of the human intellect derives from the that fact in every created intellect there is a distinction between its capacity and its proper power.

The adequate object derives from and corresponds to the capacity of the intellect, considered as a passive power ; the proportionate object derives from and corresponds to the power of the intellect, as informed by its connatural species.

3° The adequate object of the human intellect is being in general, i.e., any being whatsoever : sensible beings, immaterial creatures, God as known from created things, and God as known in the beatific vision. Although this vision surpasses the connatural power of the human intellect, it does not surpass its passive capacity.

407. Statement of the thesis.

THESIS — THE ADEQUATE OBJECT OF THE HUMAN INTELLECT IS ANY BEING WHATSOEVER.

1° The adequate object of a cognitive faculty whose common formal object is being is any being whatsoever. But the human intellect is a cognitive faculty whose common formal object is being. Therefore the adequate object of the human intellect is any being whatsover [1].

Major. — The capacity of a faculty extends to everything to which its formal object extends, i.e., the capacity of a faculty is measured by its formal object.

2° The adequate object of a spiritual cognitive faculty is any being whatsoever. But the human intellect is a spiritual cognitive faculty. Therefore . . .

Major. — A spiritual cognitive faculty is absolutely immaterial, and therefore it is absolutely cognitive ; in other words, it can know all beings, as we have already stated.

408. The possible intellect is a single faculty, but is given different names according to its different acts. — Every power is specified by its formal object. Therefore a faculty which has several objects which are formally the same is not multiplied, but remains one and the same faculty. But the formal object of the possible intellect is everything which is being as such. Therefore the possible intellect is not multiplied according to the differentiae of beings ; in other words, the possible intellect is a single faculty [2].

The intellect receives different names according to its different acts ; it is called *memory, reason, inferior reason, superior reason, speculative intellect, practical intellect.*

1° *The memory* is the intellect as it conserves intelligible species [3]. If the memory is understood as being a faculty whose object is the past as the past, it is not the *intellective* memory, but rather the *sensitive* memory, which apprehends singular things. For the past as the past is a singular thing, because it signifies existence at a determinate time.

(1) Adaequatum intellectionis objectum est communiter ipsum ens. — *Thesis* XVIII s. Thomae.
(2) I, q. 79, a. 7.
(3) *Ibid.*, a. 6.

2° *The reason* is the intellect as it proceeds from one known truth to another, in order to acquire new knowledge [1]. When man arrives at the knowledge of an intelligible truth by proceeding from thing to another, he is properly called a rational animal.

3° The reason is divided by St. Augustine into the *superior reason* and the *inferior reason* [2].

The superior reason is the reason as directed to eternal things, for the purpose of beholding them and of taking counsel from them. It beholds them in as much as it speculates on them in themselves ; and it takes counsel from them in as much as it learns rules of acting or conduct from them.

The inferior reason is the reason as it is concerned with temporal things.

The superior reason and the inferior reason are not distinct powers, but one and the same faculty ; they are distinguished only by the functions of their acts, and according to their different habits. Wisdom is attributed to the superior reason, and science to the inferior reason [3].

4° *The speculative intellect* is the name given to the intellect as it knows truth for the sake of the knowledge of truth.

The *practical intellect* is the name given to the intellect as it directs knowledge to work, i.e., it directs its knowledge to some practical end.

The intellect is called speculative or practical according to its end, but it is only one faculty. An act of the practical intellect presupposes an act of the will ; v.g., an act of the intellect concerning means presupposes the act of willing an end. An act of the speculative intellect does not presuppose an act of the will; v.g. an act of intellect concerning an end. Since an end is proposed to the will by the speculative intellect, and since an end is the first principle of action, the speculative

(1) I, q. 79, a. 7.
(2) *De Trin.*, c. 12.
(3) I, q. 79, a. 9.

intellect is called the first rule of all action (1). Thus we understand how everything practical is radicated, i.e., has its foundation in the speculative.

409. Conscience. — Conscience, according to its etymology, implies the relation of science to something. For conscience means *science with another*, and to have consciousness, i.e., to be conscious, means *to know something at the same time.*

Hence it is evident that conscience, as the very name implies, is not a power, but an act (2).

By conscience we judge that a thing ought to be done or ought not to be done, or we judge that something done has been well done or has not been well done. This kind of conscience is called *moral conscience*, and a discussion of it belongs to another part of philosophy. By conscience we perceive that we are doing or are not doing something. This kind of conscience is called *psychological conscience,* as distinguished not only from *moral conscience*, but also from *ontological conscience*, by which we return to an object already known, i.e., from recogitation of the same object. Hence psychological conscience is *that conscience by which a person returns to an act, considers it as present, in the concrete, and perceives it as its own.*

a) *as present*, because the perception of a past act is the work of the memory ;

b) *in the concrete*, because conscience perceives not the bare act, but the act as it effects the subject, i.e., the subject with its act (3);

c) *perceives*, because the conscience attains the act as a fact, but does not inquire into the nature and cause of the act, for this is the work of the reason as such.

---

(1) *In Politicorum*, l. VIII, l. 2.
(2) I, q. 79, a. 13.
(3) *De Veritate*, q. 10, a. 8. In hoc aliquis percipit se animam habere, et vivere et esse, quod percipit se sentire et intelligere.

III

PROPORTIONATE OBJECT OF THE HUMAN INTELLECT

410. Statement of the question. - 1° The proportionate object of the human intellect is that object that the human intellect can attain by its own proper power.

The proportionate object is divided into principal or proper object, and secondary object.

The *proper object* is the first proportionate object, i.e., the formal object. It is defined : *the first object which the intellect knows by its own power.*

The *secondary object* is *an object which the intellect knows, but not as its first object.*

We say that the intellect knows both the proper object and the secondary object by its own proper power, because it really, and not merely accidentally, attains them; in other words, these objects are not attained solely by another faculty of the intelligent subject. We say that the proper object is *first* known, because it is attained directly ; but we say that the secondary object is *not first known*, because it is attained indirectly, i.e., by means of the proper object ; v.g., God, as He is known from sensible things, is the secondary object of the human intellect.

2° In the thesis, it is stated that, in the state of union, the proper object of the human intellect is the abstracted quiddity of a sensible thing represented in the phantasy.

a) *The state of union* is the state of the present life in which the soul is united to the body, and it is distinguished from the state of separation of the soul from the body, and from the state of elevation in the life of the blessed, i.e., in Heaven.

b) By the term *quiddity* we understand not only predicamental substance, but also accidents and modes.

c) The quiddity of a sensible thing is called *abstracted* in as much as it is stripped of all material conditions, i.e., from time, place, and other sensible conditions, from which spiritual things abstract.

d) The *phantasy*, used here in a wide sense, designates the three higher internal senses, i.e., the imagination, the cogitative faculty, and the sensitive memory.

3° The Platonists, Cartesians, and Ontologists teach that the first thing known by the human intellect is either separated ideas, or the essence of the soul, or God.

The teaching of Aristotle, St. Thomas and Thomists generally is set forth in the thesis that follows.

411. Statement of the thesis.

THESIS. — THE PROPER OBJECT OF THE HUMAN INTELLECT, IN THE STATE OF UNION, IS THE ABSTRACTED QUIDDITY OF A SENSIBLE THING REPRESENTED IN THE PHANTASY.

1° What is first and foremost attained by the human intellect, in the state of union, is the abstracted quiddity of a sensible thing represented in the phantasy. But the proper object of the human intellect, in the state of union, is what is first and foremost attained by it in this state. Therefore the proper object of the human intellect, in the state of union, is the abstracted quiddity of a sensible thing represented in the phantasy (1).

The *minor* is the definition of proper object.

Major. — It is evident from experience. — *a*) When the phantasy is impeded or disturbed, v.g., by a lesion of the brain, in sleep, in the state of drunkenness, the intellect is impeded or disturbed.

(1) Proprium vero intellectus humani objectum in praesenti statu unionis, quidditatibus abstractis a conditionibus materialibus continetur. — *Thesis* XVIII s. Thomae.

b) We always form within ourselves pictures or phantasms of things that we know. Similarly, when we wish to explain something to another, we make use of pictures : we suggest pictures or phantasms to him by means of sensible examples.

c) The only way in which we can have knowledge of things that are not represented in the phantasy is by comparing them to things that we know by the senses. Thus a man who is blind from birth has only an analogical concept of colors, and this he has by means of sensible qualities of which he has phantasms ; v.g., thus he conceives the color red as a loud sound.

Similarly, we can conceive immaterial things only by comparing them to material things of which we have phantasms, as is very evident from philology. For things that are highly immaterial are signified by words that primarily signify sensible things ; v.g., the Latin word *Deus* (God) is derived from the root *div*, which signifies *to be bright, to shine ;* likewise, the Latin word *anima* (soul) is derived from the Sanscrit root *an*, which signifies *to breathe.*

These examples clearly show that the human intellect first and foremost attains the quiddity of a sensible thing represented in the phantasy. Experience shows too that this quiddity is attained as abstracted, for singular essences are hidden from us.

2° The proper object of a cognitive faculty is a knowable thing that is proportionate to it. But the knowable thing that is proportionate to the human intellect, in state of union, is the abstracted quiddity of a sensible thing represented in the phantasy. Therefore the proper object of the human intellect, in the state of union, is the abstracted quiddity of a sensible thing represented in the phantasy.

Major. — Because the knowing subject becomes the knowable thing, i.e., the thing known.

Minor. — Just as the human intellect in the state of union, as an immaterial faculty which informs a sensitive body, is a thing that has no corporeity, but yet exists in a sensitive body, so too the abstracted quiddity of a sensible thing represented in the phantasy is a thing that has no corporeity, but yet exists in a sensitive body, i.e., in a material thing represented by the phantasy [1].

3° The object which the human intellect first attains in virtue of the union of the soul to the body is its proper object. But the object which the human intellect first knows or attains in virtue of the union of the soul to the body is the abstracted quiddity of a sensible thing represented in the phantasy. Therefore the proper object of the human intellct, in the state of union, is the abstracted quiddity of a sensible thing represented in the phantasy.

Major. — Since the inferior exists on account of the superior (the body on account of the soul), the soul is naturally united to the body, in order that it may acquire its proper perfection by means of the body ; and its proper perfection is either its existence or its operation. But the soul is not naturally united to the body in order that it may acquire its existence, because it has its own proper existence. Therefore it is naturally united to the body, in order that it may acquire that perfection which is intellection, or, in other words, that it may know its own proper object.

Minor. — The intellect does not require a body to serve as an organ of its intellection, but only in as much as a body or phantasy furnishes it with sensible things from which the quiddities are abstracted.

412. Origin of intellective knowledge in the state of union. — All knowledge of the human intellect, in the state of union, has its origin in the senses. This proposition is nothing more than a corollary of the thesis, and it must be understood as follows [2]: *a)* The knowledge of the intellect presupposes the knowledge of the phantasy, from which it

(1) *De. Mem. et Rem.*, l. I. — I, q. 12, a. 4, c.
(2) *De Veritate*, q. 10, a. 6, ad 2.

receives its proper object, and consequently the knowledge of the external senses. *b*) The senses do not apprehend in sensible things all that the intellect knows ; the senses do not go beyond the knowledge of exterior accidents, whereas the intellect reaches the very quiddity of a thing. *c*) From its knowledge of the abstracted quiddity of a sensible thing, the intellect proceeds, by means of reflexion and reasoning, to the knowledge of its secondary objects ; v.g., from sensible things, the intellect can arrive at a knowledge of God.

Corollary. — The human intellect, in the state of union, depends objectively on the senses, because they furnish it with the material in which it attains its object. This objective dependence does not exclude the intellect's subjective independence of matter, i.e., its spirituality.

413. The human intellect, in the state of union, is incapable of intellection without the aid of phantasms.— The intellect has recourse to the phantasms both in the acquisition of knowledge and in the use of knowledge already acquired, and in its knowledge of sensible things and of spiritual things. This is so because the human intellect knows nothing except by means of its proper object ; and its proper object, in the state of union, is the quiddity of a sensible thing represented in the phantasy.

414. Knowledge of material singular things. — 1° The material singular can be known in two ways.

First, it is attained as a certain quiddity, or the ultimate metaphysical grade.

Secondly, it is attained as a thing modified by singular and material conditions, i.e. as a material singular.

Under its first aspect, a material singular, like all quiddities, is attained by the intellect.

Under its second aspect, a singular quiddity is opposed to an abstracted quiddity, i.e., a metaphysical universal, and is known both by the senses and by the intellect. This is evident from the fact that the intellect forms propositions whose subject and even predicate represent singulars ; v.g., *Peter is white, Peter is not Paul.*

2° We are concerned at present with the question of how the intellect knows a material singular, as a thing modified by or existing under material conditions.

Scotus [1] held that the intellect directly knows material singulars.

St. Thomas and his disciples hold that the human intellect, in the state of union of the present life, knows material singulars only indirectly. Consequently the human intellect has direct knowledge of universals only.

3° The direct knowledge of the intellect is opposed to its reflex knowledge.

Direct knowledge is knowledge that does not require reflexion of the intellect either on itself or on the acts of another cognitive faculty.

Reflex knowledge is knowledge that requires reflexion of this kind.

The human intellect, in the present state of union, indirectly knows material singulars by reflexion not upon its own act, but upon the phantasms.

4° We shall prove first that *the human intellect, in the state of union, directly knows only universals.*

An intellect whose proper object is a quiddity abstracted from its material conditions directly knows only universals. But a quiddity abstracted from its material conditions is the proper object of the human intellect in the present state of union. Therefore the human intellect, in the present state of union, directly knows only universals, and can know material singulars only indirectly [2].

(1) *In IV*, dist. 45, q. 3. — *I*, dist. 3, a. 4. — *De Anima*, q. 22.

(2) Per has species directe universalia cognoscimus; singularia sensu attingimus, tum etiam intellectu per conversionem ad phantasmata. — *Thesis* XX s. Thomae.

The *minor* is evident from the preceding thesis.

Major.—An object which is not intelligible cannot be known by an intellective faculty. But only a universal is an intelligible object of an intellect whose proper object is a quiddity abstracted from its material conditions: for an object is rendered intelligible only in so far as it abstracts from its material singularity and is rendered a universal [1]. Therefore.....

5° Now we shall prove that *in the present state of union, the human intellect indirectly attains material singulars by reflexion upon the phantasms.*

An intellect that knows universals by reflecting on phantasms indirectly knows material singulars by reflexion upon the phantasms. But, in the present state of union, the human intellect knows universals by reflecting on phantasms. Therefore...

Major.—This is clear from the fact that the intellect knows a universal in the singular which the phantasm represents.

Minor.—The proper object of the human intellect, in the present state of union, is the abstracted quiddity of a sensible thing represented in the phantasy.

415. How the intellect knows singulars in reflexion upon the phantasms. — 1° All Thomists hold that material singulars are known indirectly by the human intellect, but some disagree on whether the human intellect knows them in a *confused* or in a *distinct* manner.

2° Distinct knowledge is knowledge by which we attain a thing by distinguishing it from other things.

Confused knowledge is knowledge by which we attain a thing in general, without distinguishing it from other things.

3° Cajetan [2] teaches that the human intellect has only

(1) Joannes a Sancto Thoma, *Cursus Phil.*, t. III, p. 325 (Reiser).
(2) *In I*, q. 86, a. 1.

confused knowledge of material singulars. Francis Silvester of Ferrara (Ferrariensis) [1] and John of St. Thomas [2], on the contrary, hold that the intellect has distinct knowledge of material singulars.

According to the latter opinion, a universal, of which the human intellect has direct knowledge, connotes a singular as its term-from-which. The intellect, in directing its attention to this connotation, attains the material singular distinctly, though indirectly.

This opinion seems to be the truer of the two, because the intellect, in forming propositions about singulars, distinguishes one from another. Thus, when it forms the proposition: *Peter is not Paul*, it makes a distinction between Peter and Paul.

416. Analogical knowledge of spiritual things. — 1° Spiritual things are things which are subjectively and intrinsically independent of matter; v.g., an angel, God.

2° In the state of union, the human intellect knows spiritual things by analogy: it knows them not as regards their proper and positive nature, but only in an imperfect manner, by comparison to sensible things. This analogical knowledge proceeds *by way of negation*, in as much as we eliminate from spiritual things the imperfections of material things, v.g., extension, division of parts, etc.; and *by way of excellence*, in as much as we attribute the perfections of material things to them in an eminent manner.

3° Plato and all Ontologists hold that we know immaterial substances in themselves.

Averroes maintains that man, at the end of this life, can attain to a knowledge of separated substances.

St. Thomas teaches that, in the present state of union, we can know spiritual things only imperfectly, by comparison to sensible things. We know spiritual things directly, but not by

(1) *In Contra Gentes*, L. I, c. 65, n. 8.
(2) *Cursus Phil.*, t. III, pp. 328-329 (Reiser).

reflexion. We know them not immediately, but mediately, i.e., by means of the quiddities of sensible things.

4° We shall prove that *the human intellect, in the present state of union, knows spiritual things only imperfectly and by analogy* (1).

An intellect which knows spiritual things by comparing them to sensible quiddities knows them only imperfectly and by analogy. But the human intellect, in the present state of union, knows spiritual things only by comparing them to sensible quiddities. Therefore the human intellect, in the present state of union, knows spiritual things only imperfectly and by analogy (2).

Major.—Sensible quiddities, as material, are not proportionate to spiritual things, but, indeed, are very different from them.

Minor.—In the present state of union, a sensible quiddity is the proper object of the human intellect, and a spiritual thing is its secondary object. Hence spiritual things are known only by means of sensible quiddities, and by comparison to them.

417. Knowledge of the soul. — 1° Knowledge of the soul may refer either to knowledge of the existence of the soul (whether it exists) or to knowledge of the essence of the soul (what it is). Here we deal with both questions.

2° Knowledge of the soul may be either actual or habitual. We are concerned with the question of whether the soul *actually* knows itself through its own essence.

3° The question of whether the soul is known through its own essence may be understood in two ways: first, in as much as its essence is a known object; secondly, in as much as its essence is the principle by which the soul knows itself. It is

(1) Ad cognitionem vero spiritualium per analogism ascendimus. — *Thesis* IX s. Thomae.

(2) I, q. 88, a. 2. — *Contra Gentes*, L. II, c. 45. — *De Anima*, q. unica, a. 10.

with this second aspect of the question that we are concerned for the moment: can the soul know itself through its essence (1) ?

4° St. Augustine holds that through itself the soul can have knowledge of itself and of all incorporeal things (2).

The Cartesians, who maintain that the essence of the soul consists in thought, teach that the human soul knows itself through its own essence. They hold that the first principle of all intellective knowledge is the knowledge of the thinking subject (I think, therefore I am).

Thomists teach that the soul, in the present state of union, knows itself not through itself, but through its acts.

5° We shall prove that *the soul, in the present state of union, does not actually know itself through its own essence.*

If the human soul knew itself through its own essence, it would always actually know itself, and error in regard to its essence would be impossible. But the soul, in the present state of union, does not always actually know itself, and there are many errors in regard to the essence of the soul. Therefore the soul, in the present state of union, does not actually know itself through its own essence (3).

Major.—*a*) *The soul would always actually know itself.*—A knowing subject which is actually determined to know always knows in act. But if the soul knew itself through its own essence, it would always be actually determined to know itself: for the essence of the soul is always actually present to itself. Therefore...

b) *Error in regard to the essence of soul would be impossible.*—A knowing subject which is perfectly determined to know an object cannot err in regard to it, as is evident. But, if the human soul knew itself through its own essence, it would be perfectly determined to know itself. Therefore error in regard to the essence of the soul would be impossible.

(1) *De Veritate*, q. 10, a. 8.
(2) *De Trin.*, IX, 3, 3.
(3) *Contra Gentes*, L. III, c. 46.

Minor.—It is evident from experience that the soul, in the state of union, does not always actually know itself. Moreover, experience shows the possibility of many errors in regard to the essence of the soul, for some maintain that the soul is a body, others hold that it is a force, etc.

418. The soul does not know its existence and its essence in the same way. — The soul knows both its existence and its essence through its own acts.

a) The soul knows its existence experimentally and immediately through its own acts. When a man perceives that he is exercising any vital operation, as an act of intellection, of sensation, etc., he perceives that he has a principle of intellection, of sensation, etc., which is his soul.

b) The soul can know its essence either confusedly and obscurely, or clearly and distinctly. The soul attains its essence confusedly and obscurely by attaining its existence: for a man who attains his existence in some obscure way also attains his essence.

The souls knows its essence clearly and distinctly only from its object and acts, after a diligent and careful inquiry into them (1).

419. The soul habitually knows itself through its essence. — 1° *Preliminaries* *a*) A knowing subject has *habitual* knowledge when it is proximately disposed to have actual knowledge. Habitual knowledge is distinct from *actual* knowledge, i.e., knowledge by which a knowing subject actually knows or considers; and from merely *potential* knowledge, i. e., knowledge by which a knowing subject has only a potency that is remotely disposed for the act of knowledge.

b) There are *two kinds* of habitual knowledge: the first is knowledge that exists as a habit or disposition, which is an accident that is really distinct from the cognitive power; the second is knowledge superadded to the cognitive power without

(1) I, q. 87, a. 1, c.

any disposition. It is in the second sense that the soul has habitual knowledge of itself through its essence.

2° *Proof.*—The soul habitually knows itself, if without a superadded habit it is capable of an act of knowledge of itself. But the soul is capable of an act of knowledge of itself, without a superadded habit. Therefore...

The *major* is evident from the preliminary remarks.

Minor.—No habit is required in order that the soul perceive that it exists and that it adverts to what takes place within itself; for this nothing more is required than the essence of the soul, which is present to the mind: from it proceed acts in which it is itself actually perceived (1).

POINTS FOR REVIEW

1. Distinguish between the adequate object and the proportionate object of the human intellect; and state what is the adequate object.

2. Explain briefly why the speculative intellect is called the first rule of all action.

3. Explain the difference between: *a*) superior reason and inferior reason; *b*) proper object and secondary object of the human intellect.

4. Define: state of union, abstracted quiddity of a sensible thing.

5. Explain the proposition: All knowledge of the human intellect has its origin in the senses.

6. Can the human intellect, in the state of union, have direct knowledge of material singulars? Explain and prove your answer.

7. Define reflex knowledge. What are its divisions?

8. What is mediate knowledge?

---

(1) *De Veritate*, q. 10, a. 8.

ARTICLE III

ORIGIN OF INTELLIGIBLE SPECIES

420. Statement of the question. – 1° The problem of the origin of intelligible species is the problem of the origin of ideas. The problem may be stated thus: the human intellect is a spiritual faculty; but sensible objects, because they are material, cannot produce spiritual species such as are the species which determine the intellect. What, therefore, is the origin of the spiritual species that determine the intellect?

2° Those who, like Democritus, hold that the intellect does not differ from the sensitive power, maintain that our knowledge is produced by a mere impression brought about by sensible things. (1).

Those who hold that the human intellect is an immaterial power claim that intellectual knowledge is not produced by a mere impression made on the intellect by sensible things, but that another cause is required. There are three opinions: *the opinion of infused ideas* from without, *the opinion of innate ideas*, and *the opinion of species acquired* by means of the active power of the soul, which abstracts species from sensible things.

3° Plato, Avicenna (2), St. Augustine, the Ontologists, and the Traditionalists hold the first opinion.

a) Plato claimed that subsisting separated ideas exist independently of sensation, and that these ideas, as exemplars, are participated as entitative forms in matter to constitute sensible being, and, as intelligible forms in the intellect, for knowledge.

b) Avicenna rejected Plato's teaching on the existence of

(1) I, q. 84, a. 6, c.
(2) I, q. 84, a. 4, c.

separated ideas, and claimed that man, on having phantasms presented to him, receives intelligible species from some subsisting immaterial substance, as, v.g., from an angel.

c) St. Augustine, who was imbued with the teachings of Plato, maintained that the human soul knows immutable and eternal truths by a divine illumination. The Ontologists, as Malebranche and Gioberti, hold that the human intellect is immediately united to God and to the divine ideas, and therefore is determined, without the medium of a created form, for the act of knowledge. The Traditionalists (De Bonald, Lamennais) maintain that God gave the treasury of truths to our First Parents, and that posterity receives them by tradition. The mitigated Traditionalists, as Bonnetty and Ventura, restrict this teaching to the clear and distinct knowledge of God, of the spiritual soul, and of moral obligations.

4° Descartes and Leibniz hold the second opinion. Descartes asserts that all ideas are innate (1). Leibniz teaches that the soul has an innate confused knowledge which contains all ideas, and that these ideas become clearer and more distinct by means of sensation.

5° Aristotle, St. Thomas, and in general all Scholastics hold the third opinion, and teach that intelligible species are acquired by the intellect. And, since sensible objects cannot produce intelligible species, which are immaterial, they maintain that there is an active power in the soul which abstracts these species from the phantasms. This active power is called the active intellect.

Therefore the active intellect may be defined: *an active and immaterial faculty which abstracts the intelligible species from the phantasms.*

---

(1) Descarted divides ideas into *properly innate ideas, adventitious ideas,* and *fictitious ideas.*

Properly innate ideas are the ideas which the mind forms without the intervention of sensation. Adventitious ideas are the ideas which it forms on the occasion of sensation. Fictitious ideas are the ideas which it forms from ideas it already has. GILSON, *Discours de la Méthode*, texte et commentaire, pp. 327-328, 1930 (Vrin).

6° The first opinion, which explains the origin of ideas by claiming that they derive from a spiritual and extrinsic agent, may not be admitted, because the knowledge of sensible things is a connatural operation of the soul. Every agent has within itself power sufficient for its own operation. Hence the human soul must not receive its ideas from an extrinsic agent.

The second opinion affirms the existence of innate ideas; and it too must be rejected. For, if the human soul had innate ideas, its union with the body would be in vain.

Therefore we must adopt the opinion of Aristotle and St. Thomas.

421. Statement of the thesis.

THESIS.—THE HUMAN SOUL MUST HAVE AN ACTIVE INTELLECT WHICH ABSTRACTS INTELLIGIBLE SPECIES FROM THE PHANTASMS.

In the state of union, intellective knowledge is derived from sensible things. But intellective knowledge cannot be derived from sensible things, unless the human soul has an active intellect which abstracts intelligible species from the phantasms. Therefore the human soul must have an active intellect which abstracts intelligible species from the phantasms (1).

The *major* is evident from what has been already said.

Minor.—The intellect, as a formally knowing faculty, i.e., the possible intellect, is a passive power, which is reduced from potency to act by its object. But nothing can be reduced from potency to act except by a being in act. Therefore, in order that a sensible thing, which as a material thing is not actually intelligible, determine the intellect, it must be made actually intelligible by an active faculty of the soul which

(1) Cognitionem ergo accipimus a rebus sensibilibus. Cum autem sensibile non sit intelligibile in actu, praeter intellectum formaliter intelligentem, admittenda est in anima virtus activa, quae species intelligibiles a phantasmatibus abstrahat. — *Thesis* XIX s. Thomae.

abstracts intelligible species from their material conditions; and this faculty is called the active intellect (1).

422. The active intellect and the possible intellect are really distinct faculties. – 1° *Preliminaires.*—It is the common teaching of Thomists that there is a real distinction between the active intellect and the possible intellect; but this distinction is not admitted by Scotus, Suarez, Arriago, and Lossada.

2° *Proof.*—A faculty that is active and that produces intelligible species is really distinct from a faculty that is purely passive and receptive as regards intelligible species. But the active intellect is a faculty that produces intelligible species, whereas the possible intellect is purely passive and receptive as regards intelligible species. Therefore...

423. Causality of the phantasms and the active intellect. – The phantasms and the active intellect *effectively* concur in the production of impressed intelligible species. The active intellect is the principal cause, and the phantasms serve as the instrumental cause, subordinate to the principal cause. The intelligible species is immaterial, because it is produced by the active intellect; and is the likeness of the quiddity of a sensible thing known by the senses, because the phantasm is its instrumental cause (2).

424. Functions of the active intellect. – 1° *It illuminates the phantasms.*—Just as material light renders bodies actually visible, so too does the active intellect render the phantasms actually intelligible. It is for this reason that it is said to illuminate the phantasms. Hence it is often called a *light*, or a natural light of the intellect. (3).

2° *It abstracts the intelligible species (impressed) from the phantasms.*—The abstraction of the active intellect differs from that of the possible intellect: the latter is a *considerative* abstraction, i.e., a consideration by which the possible intellect

(1) I, q. 79, a. 3.
(2)) *De Veritate*, q. 10, a. 6, ad 7.
(3) I, q, 85. a. 1, ad 4

has knowledge of one thing, and omits others; the former is a *productive* abstraction, i.e., a production, by which the active intellect, aided by the phantasms, produces the intelligible species (1).

3° *It strengthens the possible intellect.*—It assists in uniting the possible intellect with its act: it actuates the possible intellect with the intelligible species (2).

4° *It makes first principles evident.*—It does this, not because the active intellect abstracts first principles and produces them in the possible intellect, but because the possible intellect, determined by the impressed intelligible species produced or abstracted by the active intellect, apprehends first concepts, and immediately formulates first principles from them. (3).

425. Difficulties in regard to the existence of the active intellect.— 1° No faculty exists in us of which we are not conscious. But we are not conscious of the existence of the active intellect. Therefore we have no active intellect.

Major. — Of which we are not either immediately or mediately conscious, *I concede;* immediately only, *I deny.*

Minor. — Mediately, *I deny;* immediately, *I concede.*

It is not repugnant that we know the existence of a faculty in us only through reasoning.

2° An intellect that has no intellection is repugnant. But the active intellect has no intellection. Therefore the active intellect does not exist.

Major. — A formally cognitive intellect which has no intellection is repugnant, *I concede;* an intellect which exercises only a causal influence on intellection is repugnant, *I deny.*

Minor. — The active intellect is formally cognitive, *I deny;* exercises only a causal influence on intellection, *I concede.*

POINTS FOR REVIEW

1. State the teaching of Democritus, Plato, and Avicenna on the origin of ideas or intelligible species.

2. Explain briefly why the theory of innate ideas is inadmissible.

3. What is the active intellect? Is it really distinct from the possible intellect? Is it a cognitive power?

4. Give the definition of the active intellect.

(1) I, q. 85, a. 6.
(2) *De Veritate*, q. 9, a. 1, and q. 10, a. 13.
(3) *De Anima*, q. un., a. 4, ad 6.

ARTICLE IV

MENTAL WORD

I

EXISTENCE OF THE MENTAL WORD

426. Statement of the question. – 1° The mental word is nothing other than the intelligible expressed species. It is also called *conception* or *concept of the mind*, *idea* (1), *notion*, *intention*, and *mental term*.

The mental word is defined: *the intentional likeness of an object begotten by the possible intellect in its act of knowledge, which is the intrinsic term of intellection.*

a) *Begotten by the possible intellect:* the mental word is produced by the possible intellect already determined by the intelligible impressed species, and is a kind of spiritual birth.

b) *Which is the intrinsic term of intellection:* the mental term is thus distinguished from the object, i.e., extrinsic term, which is expressed by the word.

2° The mental word is distinct from the *oral word*, which is the word that signifies the concept of the intellect; and from the *imagined word*, which is the likeness of the oral word existing in the phantasy.

3° It is the common teaching of Scholastics that the mental word is produced in all human intellection. Rosmini teaches that it is formed only in reflex intellection.

Thomists teach the intellect does not form the mental word in the beatific vision. Suarez disagrees with this teaching.

(1) An idea, in the strict sense of the word, is the concept of an artificer.

427. Statement of the thesis.

THESIS.—THE HUMAN INTELLECT PRODUCES A MENTAL WORD WITHIN ITSELF IN ALL NATURAL INTELLECTION.

1° *Experience.*—The spoken word signifies neither the intellect itself, nor the intelligible impressed species, nor the act of the intellect, but the conception of the intellect through which the intellect knows an object. But the conception of the intellect is the mental word. Therefore (1).

2° *A priori.*—A cognitive faculty which is not determined to attain its object as present or absent, or which does not attain its object when present as it exists in reality, produces an expressed species within itself. But, in its natural intellection, the human intellect is not determined to attain attains its object as present or absent, and does not attain its object according to the mode in which it exists in reality. Therefore the human intellect produces an expressed species, i.e., a mental word, within itself in all natural intellection.

Major.—An intellective faculty which attains its object in this way must attain it as intentionally represented. But such an intentional representation of an object is an expressed species. Therefore...

Minor.—It is evident that the human intellect is not determined to attain its object as present or absent; and if it attains it as present, it abstracts, divides, and composes it according to relations which are not distinct in reality, and therefore it does not attain it according to the mode in which it exists in reality.

428. Requisites of intellection. – 1° According to the opinion of St. Thomas, four things are required by the human intellect for its act of knowledge: a power, an intelligible impressed species, an act of intellection, and a word or concept.

(1) *De Potentia*, q. 8, a. 1.

2° Moreover, the Thomistic opinion holds that these four things are really distinct. The proof of the opinion is as follows: Things which can be separated, or of which one is the cause of the other, are really distinct, But the power, the intelligible impressed species, the act of intellection, and the word either can be separated, or are related to one another as causes to effects. Therefore they are really distinct.

Minor.—Sometimes the species and power are separated, for a power can exist without a species which we acquire. The act of knowing is distinct from the species and power, both because the species and power are the causes of intellection, and because sometimes our intellective knowledge is not actual, even though we possess the power and species. The mental word is distinct from the power, the intelligible impressed species, and the act of intellection, because it is the term of intellection.

429. Diction and intellection are not really distinct. – 1° *Preliminaries.*—*a*) Diction is the production of the mental word by the possible intellect.

b) Suarez makes no distinction between intellection and the mental word, and holds that the mental word is a quality produced by its own true and proper action, distinct from intellection.

c) Scotus maintains that intellection and diction are distinct actions.

d) Thomists teach that diction and intellection are not really distinct.

2° *Proof.*—Diction is the production of a word which expresses and manifests a thing, not in any way whatsoever, but as known by the intellect. But a thing cannot be rendered actually known by the intellect except by an act of intellection of the possible intellect. Therefore it is only by the act of intellection that the intellect can produce the word, or, in other words, diction and intellection are not really distinct.

430. Intellection is essentially a metaphysical action, which only virtually produces the mental word. — 1° *Preliminaries.*—*a*) A metaphysical or immanent action is an action which of itself is not destined to produce an effect, but whose function consists in its perfecting the agent and remaining in it as its second act.

b) Predicamental or transitive action is distinct from metaphysical action, for the former is destined to produce a term either within or outside the agent.

c) Although intellection of itself, i.e., essentially, is a metaphysical action, yet as diction it is virtually a predicamental action; and therefore there is a distinction of reason, but not a real distinction, between intellection and diction.

2° *Proof.*—Intellection is essentially a metaphysical action, if it is destined to perfect the agent, but not to produce the word as an effect. But intellection is destined to the perfection of the intellect, not to the production of the word. Therefore intellection is a metaphysical action, which only virtually produces the word.

The *major* is clear from the preliminary remarks.

Minor.—Intellection is the ultimate perfection intended by the intellect, and consists not in the production of an effect, but in the *attainment* of truth; and, when it does produce a mental word, intellection is not related to it as to an effect, but rather it relates the word to itself: for, when a mental word is produced, the intellect remains in contemplation of it, and, indeed, it is then that contemplation properly takes place.

NOTE.—It is evident from the foregoing remarks that intellection formally consists in *operation which is the ultimate act of the knowing subject in relation to its object.*

431. Necessity of the mental word. — *a*) Philosophers, such as Suarez, Molina, Vasquez, etc., who hold that all actions are predicamental, or productive of a term, maintain that the mental word is necessitated by the very nature of intellective knowledge: the act of knowledge is an operation, and therefore necessarily produces a term.

b) Thomists hold that intellection is a metaphysical action, and they give two reasons for the necessity of the mental word: 1) it is required by the object, in order that it be rendered present to the intellect, if it is absent from it; or, if it is physically present, in order that it be rendered sufficiently immaterial and spiritual as a known term in the intellect; *b*) it is required by the richness of the intellect, in as much as the intellect tends to manifest and speak its object to itself in a representation.

Thus, in God, the Word, the Second Person of the Most Holy Trinity, proceeds from the richness of the divine intellection.

II

THE MENTAL WORD AS A FORMAL SIGN

432. Statement of the question. — 1° A sign in general is defined: *that which represents something other than itself to a cognitive faculty.*

2° The sign is instrumental or formal.

An *instrumental* sign is a sign which, from previous knowledge of itself, leads to the knowledge of something other than itself; v.g., a statue of Mercury is an instrumental sign of Mercury.

A *formal* sign is a sign in which the thing represented is immediately known, without previous knowledge of the sign. Every expressed species is a formal sign.

3° Descartes and many modern philosophers teach that only the mental word or, as they say, the idea, is directly known, and they think that the philosopher must prove that this representation or idea corresponds to the external thing.

All Thomists hold that the mental word is a formal sign,

and therefore that the intellect immediately and directly knows the thing represented in the mental word.

433. Statement of the thesis.

THESIS.—THE MENTAL WORD IS THE FORMAL SIGN OF THE THING KNOWN BY THE INTELLECT.

The intrinsic term of intellection, by which a thing is rendered known and present to the intellect, is the formal sign of the thing known by the intellect. But the mental word is the intrinsic term of intellection, by which a thing is rendered known and present to the intellect. Therefore the mental word is the formal sign of the thing known by the intellect (1).

Major.—Such a term does not lead first and directly to knowledge of itself, but to knowledge of the thing of which it is the representation or sign.

Minor.—The mental word renders a thing present and proportionate to the intellect, as actually known terminatively.

434. Scholia. — 1° The concept may be called the *instrument by which* (2) the intellect knows a thing: it is not the medium known which is the instrument and the external medium, but is the internal medium in which the intellect knows within itself; in other words, it is the formal sign.

2° The concept may also be called *that which* the intellect knows (3), not as the extrinsic thing known, but as that in which is contained the thing known within the intellect. Thus by the same act of knowledge both the concept and the thing

(1) *Quodl.*, 4, a. 17. — *De Veritate*, q. 4, a. 1 ad 7. — *Contra Gentes*, L. II, c. 11.

(2) Intellectus intelligit aliquid dupliciter, uno modo formaliter, et sic intelligit specie intelligibili qua fit in actu, alio modo sicut instrumento quo utitur ad aliud intelligendum, et hoc modo intellectus verbo intelligit, quia format verbum ad hoc quod intelligat rem. — *Quodl.*, 5, a. 9, ad 1.

(3) *De Veritate*, q. 4, a. 2, ad 3.

conceived are directly attained; it is not from the knowledge of the concept, as concept of the thing known, that knowledge of the thing conceived is attained.

The instrumental sign is the thing known in this sense: it is *that which* is known extrinsically, the external thing from the knowledge of which knowledge of the thing signified is attained. And although it can be attained by the same act of knowledge as that by which the thing signified is attained, yet, even in this case, the intellect knows the thing signified from the instrumental sign as from the thing known, because the instrumental sign does not render the thing signified formally known within the intellect (1).

POINTS FOR REVIEW

1. Define mental word.

2. Enumerate the requisites of intellection, and prove that they are really distinct from one another.

3. Distinguish between diction and intellection.

4. Is the mental word necessary in intellection? Give reasons for your answer. Is the mental word *that which* is known? Explain.

5. What is a formal sign?

(1) JOANNES A SANCTO THOMA, *Cursus Phil.*, t. I, p. 705 (Reiser).

ARTICLE V

FIRST THING KNOWN

435. Statement of the question. — 1° Human knowledge is in the senses, and in the intellect. Knowledge that is the senses is prior, in the order of acquisition, to knowledge that is in the intellect. In this article, we are concerned with the first thing known by the intellect, not with the first object attained by the senses.

2° Certain philosophers, as Durandus, hold that the first thing known by the intellect is a singular thing, because it is through the senses that an object is most capable of moving the intellect. This opinion may not be admitted, because it is only by reflexion that the intellect can know singulars.

3° Scotus teaches that the first thing known by the intellect is the specific nature of a singular thing, as abstracted from the singular, because, as he points out, it is the object which the intellect can abstract most easily.

4° Thomists teach that the first thing known by the intellect is the quiddity of a material thing under its most common and most confused aspect, which is that of being. It is, as Cajetan teaches, being concretized in sensible quiddity, i.e., being applied to sensible quiddity. Being, as the first thing known by the intellect, is not being known by *positive* abstraction, i.e., abstraction by which the intellect distinguishes being from its inferiors, i.e., from generic and specific predicates (1); but it is being known by *negative* abstraction, that it so say, being as the most common notion under which is contained in a confused manner all predicates which can belong to a thing.

(1) Therefore being as the first thing known by the intellect is not being as being, or being metaphysically understood.

This is an easier kind of abstraction than positive abstraction: negative abstraction is almost equivalent to simply knowing that a thing exists.

436. Statement of the thesis.

THESIS.—THE FIRST THING KNOWN BY THE HUMAN INTELLECT IS BEING CONCRETIZED IN SENSIBLE QUIDDITY.

The most imperfect and confused notion under which the proper object of the human intellect can be attained is being concretized in sensible quiddity. But the human intellect, which proceeds in a manner that is connatural to it, first attains its proper object under its most confused and indeterminate aspect. Therefore the first thing known by the human intellect is being concretized in sensible quiddity.

The *major* is clear, because that notion or aspect of a thing is most imperfect and confused by which we are least able to discern and distinguish the predicates that belong to it. But this notion can be none other than that of being, for in it no distinction is made even between substance and accident. Therefore...

Minor.—An intellect which proceeds from potency to act first attains its object under its most indeterminate and confused aspect, because it acquires its perfection little by little by passing from a state of imperfection to a state of perfection. But the human intellect connaturally proceeds from potency to act. Therefore...

437. Scholia. - 1° The human intellect, in the state of union, evolves, i.e., acquires and perfects its knowledge, by three acts, namely, simple apprehension, judgment, and reasoning. For, since the intellect acquires its perfection little by little by passing from a state of imperfection to a state of perfection, it does not all at once apprehend all the predicates of a thing, but gradually seizes upon them: when it has apprehended one thing, it passes on to another which it immediately (judgment) or mediately (reasoning) unites with the first thing it apprehended.

2° The concepts formed in simple apprehension and judgment are distinct, because the objects represented in each of these operations are distinct. In simple apprehension, the nature or quiddity of a thing is represented; in judgment, a thing is shown to be or not to be, and consequently truth is expressed.

Reasoning does not seem to produce a concept distinct from that produced in judgment.

CHAPTER II

THE WILL

Prologue. — In this chapter, first, we shall prove the existence of the will; secondly, we shall compare the intellect with the will; thirdly, we shall deal with the problem of free will. Then, in appendixes, we shall discuss the indifference of the will towards good and evil, and the deliberate acts of will.

Existence of the will	Statement of the question Thesis: Man is endowed with a will, which is a spiritual faculty whose formal object is good in general Difficulties
Comparison of the intellect and will	Statement of the question Thesis: The intellect is absolutely more perfect than the will; but the will is relatively more perfect than the intellect Corollaries Difficulty
Free will	Statement of the question Adversaries of liberty Thesis: Man is endowed with free will Election and the last practical judgment How the will always chooses the greater good Objects of liberty Difficulties
Indifference towards good and evil	Statement of the question Thesis: Indifference towards good and evil, and hence the power of sinning, is not of the essence of liberty
The complete deliberate act of the will	Integrant parts of the complete deliberate act of the will Explanation of the partial acts

ARTICLE I

EXISTENCE OF THE WILL

438. Statement of the question. 1° Our internal experience manifests to us that we have a will. In the thesis, we prove *a priori* the existence of the will, and at the same time we show that the will does not precede the intellect, but follows it (1).

2° Because it follows the intellect, the will is a spiritual faculty.

The formal object of the will, i.e., the formality or aspect under which the will attains all things, is good in general, or universal good. Therefore, *first*, the will cannot desire a thing under the aspect or formality of evil; *secondly*, the will can desire all things that in any way participate goodness, whereas the sensitive appetite desires only particular good (2).

3° The thesis that follows is intended as a refutation of the teaching of those who subordinate the intellect to the will, and refuse to admit the value of speculative knowledge. Such is the tenet of almost all modernists.

The thesis is directed also against some nominalists who claim that the will desires evil as such.

439. Statement of the thesis.

THESIS.— MAN IS ENDOWED WITH A WILL, WHICH IS SPIRITUAL FACULTY WHOSE OBJECT IS GOOD IN GENERAL.

(1) Intellectum sequitur, non praecedit voluntas. — *Thesis* XXI s. Thomae.

(2) I, q. 82, a. 5, c. — *De Veritate*, q. 25, a. 3.

First part.—*Man is endowed with a will.*—The will follows the intellect. But man is endowed with an intellect. Therefore man is endowed with a will [1].

Major.—Every form is followed by an inclination, because everything tends towards its form, or perfection, if it does not possess it; and if it does possess it, it rests in it. But the intellect, in as much as it is a knowing faculty, is constituted in act by the intelligible form by which it apprehends a thing. Therefore the intelligible form which actuates the intellect is followed by an inclination to the good apprehended by the intellect; and this inclination we call the will [2].

The *minor* is evident from what has been already said.

Second part.—*The will is a spiritual faculty.*—An appetite that pursues a good presented to it by the intellect is a spiritual faculty. But the will is a faculty that pursues a good presented to it by the intellect. Therefore the will is a spiritual faculty.

Major.—Such an appetite is a faculty, because it has vital operation; and it is a spiritual faculty, because its object is a universal.

The *minor* is evident.

Third part.—*The formal object of the will is good in general.*—The will pursues the good apprehended by the intellect. But the intellect knows good as universal, or good in general.

440. Difficulties. — 1° An intelligible form is not followed by an inclination to the good apprehended. Therefore the will does not follow the intellect.

An intelligible form is followed by an inclination to the form itself, and not to the good apprehended. But the intellect is constituted as actually knowing by an intellible form. Therefore an intelligible form is not followed by an inclination to the good apprehended, i.e., the will does not follow the intellect.

Major. — An inclination follows an intelligible form, as it is only an accidental entity, *I deny;* as it represents a thing in itself, or a good, *I concede.*

(1) I, q. 19, a. 1.
(2) JOANNES A SANCTO THOMA, *Cursus Phil.*, t. III, pp. 378-379 (Reiser).

Minor. — It is constituted as formally knowing by an intelligible form, as it is an accidental entity, *I deny;* as it represents a good distinct from itself, *I concede.*

The intellect determined by an intelligible species is followed by an inclination, not to the intelligible form itself in as much as it is an intentional species, but to the object apprehended. An intelligible form does not constitute the intellect as knowing in as much as it is an accidental entity, but in as much as it represents an object. Therefore an appetite which follows the intellect thus informed ought not pursue the entity which is the intentional species, but rather the object represented, as it is represented as suitable and proportionate, because an inclination follows a form, in as much as the form represents something suitable to it so that it may be desired.

2° The formal object of an appetite whose operations are specified by evil cannot be good. But certain operation of the will are specified by evil; v.g., flight from evil. Therefore . . .

Major. — Whose operations are strictly specified by evil, i.e., by evil as the object of desire, *I concede;* whose operations are specified by evil, in as much as evil is the privation of the good which is desired, *I deny.*

Minor. — Certain operations are specified by evil, in as much as evil is the privation of the good which is desired, *I concede;* otherwise, *I deny.*

3° The formal object of an appetite which is inclined to evil is not good. But the will is inclined to evil; v.g., in the case of sin, of suicide, etc. Therefore.

Major. — To evil as such, *I concede;* to evil under the aspect of good, even if only apparent, *I deny.*

Minor. — To evil under the aspect of evil, *I deny;* to evil under the aspect of good, even if only apparent, *I concede.*

Sin is desired only in as much as it is here and now desired as a particular good, an apparent good. In like manner, suicide is desired only in as much as a man desires to be free from the evil which is opposed to the good desired.

ARTICLE II

COMPARISON OF THE INTELLECT AND WILL

441. Statement of the question. — 1° One power can be absolutely or relatively more perfect than another.

A power is *absolutely more perfect* than another, when it is such by its nature.

A power is *relatively more perfect* than another, when it is such in regard to something accidental.

Thus, in the order of beings, man is more perfect than the lion: he is more perfect in virtue of his nature; but the lion is relatively more perfect than man, from the point of view of his physical strength.

2° Plato, St. Augustine, St. Bonaventure, and Scotus hold that the will is absolutely more noble than the intellect. This teaching is supported by Kant, Schopenhauer, Secrétan, Renouvier, etc. *b*) Aristotle, St. Thomas, Suarez, and Vasquez maintain that the intellect is absolutely more perfect than the will, but that the will is relatively more noble than the intellect.

442. Statement of the thesis.

THESIS.—THE INTELLECT IS ABSOLUTELY MORE PERFECT THAN THE WILL; BUT THE WILL IS RELATIVELY MORE PERFECT THAN THE INTELLECT.

First part.—*The intellect is absolutely more perfect than the will.*—1° It is absolutely more perfect to have the perfection of a thing in oneself than to be inclined to the thing as it is in itself. But the intellect knows in as much as it has in itself the perfection of the thing known; and the will desires in as much as it tends to a thing as it is in itself. Therefore the intellect is absolutely more perfect than the will (1).

2° The nature of a faculty is determined by its formal object. But the formal object of the intellect is absolutely more perfect than the formal object of the will. Therefore the nature of the intellect is more perfect than the nature of the will, i.e., the intellect is absolutely more perfect than the will.

The *major* is evident, for the perfection of a faculty derives from the perfection of its formal object.

Minor.—The more abstract and universal an object is, the more perfect it is: abstraction results from remotion from matter or imperfection. But the object of the intellect is more abstract than the object of the will; good, which is the object of the will, includes within itself a relation of suitability to the appetite, but being, which is the object of the intellect, abstracts from this relation of suitability. Therefore...

Second part.—*The will is relatively more perfect than the intellect.*—One power is said to be relatively more perfect than another power, if its perfection is considered as deriving, not from its formal object, but from its relation to this or that thing. But the will, in its relation to spiritual things which are superior to the soul, is more perfect than the intellect. Therefore the will is relatively more perfect than the intellect (2).

Major.—It is accidental to a power that it attains this or that thing; v.g., it is by accident that the power of sight attains this or that colored object.

Minor.—The perfection of a power is greater according as it attains a superior thing in a more perfect manner. But the will attains spiritual things which are superior to the soul,

(1) *De Veritate*, q. 22, a. 1.
(2) I, q. 82, a. 3. — *De Veritate*, q. 22, a. 11. — *In III Sent.*, dist. 37, q. 1, a. 4.

i.e., things higher and nobler than the soul, in a more perfect manner than does the intellect: the will attains them as they are in themselves; the intellect attains them as they exist in the intellect, that is to say, it attains or knows them by analogy, i.e., by comparison to material things. Therefore the will, in its relation to spiritual things which are superior to the soul, is more perfect than the intellect.

443. Corollaries. — 1° In this life, it is more perfect to love God than to know Him; or, in other words, in this life the love of God is better than the knowledge of Him. 2° But, in Heaven, where God is known as He is in Himself, the act of knowing God is more perfect than the act of loving Him: *This is eternal life: that they may know Thee, the only true God* (Jn. XVII, 3). 3° In this life, the knowledge of things that are inferior to the soul, i.e., less noble than it, exist in the intellect in a more perfect manner than in themselves.

444. Difficulties. — The perfection of a faculty is in proportion to the perfection of its object. But the object of the will, which is good, is more perfect than the object of the intellect, which is being: for good includes being, and adds to it actual existence and the relation of suitability to an appetite. Therefore . . .

Major. — In proportion to the perfection of its object considered formally, *I concede;* its object considered materially, *I deny.*

Minor. — The object of the will is more perfect, if it is considered formally, *I deny;* if considered materially, *let it go.*

The intellect, in virtue of its formal object, attains good in a more perfect manner than does the will. The will only attains a good as concretely moving and as existing; the intellect attains both the quiddity of a good, and its existence, by means of its formal object which is being.

ARTICLE III

FREE WILL

445. Statement of the question. — 1° Free will, or liberty, is, according to all, the opposite of necessity.

Necessity implies two things: fixity or immutability, and thus it is the opposite of chance, or contingency and fallibility; determination to one thing (i.e., one object or one direction) together with the inability of being determined to more than one thing; it is thus the opposite of liberty.

Liberty, therefore, consists in the lack of determination to one thing, or in indifference towards several things.

2° There are two kinds of indifference: passive indifference or indifference of potentiality, and active indifference or indifference of power.

Passive indifference results from the imperfection of the agent. It is not conducive to action, but an obstacle to it, for it leaves the agent without determination. This kind of indifference is found in all natural agents, and is not of the essence of liberty.

3° *Active* indifference derives from the perfection of the agent. There are two kinds of active indifference.

a) The first kind is that active indifference which exists as a mode of universality in acting, in as much as a cause is able to produce not one effect only, but several effects. This kind of active indifference is found even in necessary causes, and does not pertain to liberty; v.g., the sun can produce many effects.

b) The second kind is that active indifference in virtue of which an agent can act or not act, and cannot be placed under obligation to act. This kind of active indifference belongs to the very essence of liberty (1).

An agent is able to act or not act, not only because it has power over its own act, but also because it has dominative power over that by which it is moved. And since the mover, in the case of an act of the will, is the judgment of the reason, it follows that there is required for liberty the dominative power of the will over the judgment by which it is moved.

Therefore liberty, or free will, is defined: *the active indifference in virtue of which the will has dominative power over its own act, because it has that power over the judgment by which it is moved, in as much as it can change this judgment.*

Or more briefly: *the power of choosing between goods proposed as desirable by a mutable judgment,* i.e., proposed by a practical judgment that the will can change (2).

Animals have no liberty, for their judgment is determined by natural instinct. (3)

446. Adversaries of liberty. — 1° Fatalists, according to whom everything that comes to pass happens from absolute necessity, especially in virtue of some superhuman cause. This superhuman cause is *a)* either fate (common fatalism), *b)* or the divine substance, of which all mundane things are merely the necessary evolution (pantheistic fatalism), *c)* or God Himself, Who determines the will to one thing (theological fatalism or determinism, — Calvin, 1509-1564).

2° Determinists, according to whom every act of the will

---

(1) Joannes a Sancto Thoma, *Cursus Phil.*, t. III, p. 387 (Reiser).

(2) Voluntas ... inter bona quae judicio mutabili appetenda proponuntur, libere aligit. — *Thesis XXI* s. Thomae.

(3) We have defined liberty as immunity from determination from within. Sometimes liberty is used to signify immunity from determination from without, and is divided thus: *a)* exterior liberty, or, as it is called nowadays, physical liberty which, v.g., a man lacks in prison; *b)* civil liberty, by which a man is allowed to seek his rights in society; *c)* political liberty, by which a citizen is allowed to have a part in the government of society; *d)* religious liberty, or liberty of conscience, by which a man is allowed to profess his religion publicly.

is necessarily determined by some natural cause ([1]).

Determinism may be physical, physiological, social, or psychological.

a) *Physical* or *mechanical determinism* holds that the will is a corporeal force, and therefore that its act, like any other mechanical operation, is physically or mechanically determined.

b) *Physiological determinism* teaches that all acts of the will are determined by physiological changes in the human body.

c) *Social determinism* maintains that the will receives its determination from the influence of society.

d) *Psychological determinism* teaches that the will is always determined by the strongest motive, by the greatest good offered to it (Leibniz).

447. Statement of the thesis. — The Council of Trent (Sess. 7, can. 5) declared that it is an article of faith that man is endowed with liberty, i.e., free will ([2]).

THESIS.—MAN IS ENDOWED WITH FREE WILL.

---

(1) Le fatalisme affirme que tout arrive parce que tout doit arriver. Les déterministes, adversaires modernes du libre arbitre, disent davantage. Au lieu de s'en tenir à quelque vague et arbitraire affirmation sur la fatalité des événements, ils examinent les causes qui peuvent influer sur la marche du monde, et notamment sur la volonté, et prétendent démontrer par cette analyse que la cause détermine toujours tout événement au point d'exclure en toute rigueur un choix libre de la part de la volonté. — *Dictionnaire Apologétique de la Foi catholique*, article « Déterminisme ».

(2) As the Catholic Church declares in the strongest terms the simplicity, spirituality, and immortality of the soul, so with unequalled constancy and publicity she ever also asserts its freedom. These truths she has always taught, and has sustained them as a dogma of faith; and whensoever heretics or innovators have attacked the liberty of man, the Church has defended it and protected this noble possession from destruction. History bears witness to the energy with which she met the fury of the Manicheans and others like them; and the earnestness with which in later years she defended human liberty in the Council of Trent, and against the followers of Jansenius, is known to all. At no time, and in no place, has she ever held truce with *fatalism*. — LEO XIII, Encyclical Letter *Libertas Praestantissimum*, 20 June, 1888.

1° *Internal experience.*—At three different moments, we perceive from our internal experience that we have free will: *before an action*, when we deliberate; *during the action*, when we perceive that we can cease to act; *after the action*, when we know that we were able not to have performed it (1).

2° *Testimony of all peoples.*—All peoples testify that man is free. But this testimony is true. Therefore...

Major.—Among all peoples, man is considered as master of his own acts: laws are made which man is bound to observe, counsels are formulated for the direction of man's conduct, penalties are imposed for the violation of justice, etc.

Minor.—The testimony of all peoples is true, because it concerns a matter which is easily known by conscience (2).

3° *A priori.*—An agent whose appetite follows a judgment which of its nature is indifferent is endowed with free will. But man is an agent whose appetite or will follows a judgment which of its nature remains indifferent in regard to particular goods. Therefore man is endowed with free will in regard to particular goods (3).

Major.—If an appetite follows a judgment which of its nature is indifferent, it is not determined by that judgment, but has dominative power over it, in as much as it can accept or not accept it, and therefore it remains free.

Minor.—Man passes judgment on particular goods by his intellect which, as a spiritual faculty, can reflect upon its own judgment, and can compare particular goods with the notion of universal good. But such a judgment is of its nature indifferent, because particular goods, in as much as they are com-

(1) Un homme qui n'a pas l'esprit gâté n'a pas besoin qu'on lui prouve son franc arbitre, car il le sent; et il ne sent pas plus clairement qu'il voit ou qu'il vit, ou qu'il raisonne, qu'il se sent capable de délibérer et de choisir. — BOSSUET, *Connaissance de Dieu et de soi-même*, c. 1, XVIII.

(2) La persuasion commune de se sentir responsable, l'usage ordinaire de faire des lois, de punir, de récompenser, tout cela montre assez que tout le monde se sait libre; nier cette vérité c'est presque se mettre en dehors du genre humain; c'est soutenir une doctrine paradoxale. — MATTIUSSI-LEVILLAIN, *op. cit.*, p. 246.

(3) *De Veritate*, q. 24, a. 2. — I, q. 83, a. 1. — *De Malo*, q. 6, a. 1.

pared with universal good, can be considered as non-goods or evils, if they fail to fulfill the conditions of universal good. Therefore... [1].

448. Election and the last practical judgment. — Since the will follows the intellect, it does not choose, i.e., accept one thing in preference to another, unless the intellect judges that this good ought to be chosen here and now. This judgment is called the last practical judgment from which election or choice results. But since the judgment of the intellect is of its nature indifferent, the intellect cannot elicit its last determinate judgment, unless the will applies or directs it to make this determinate judgment.

Therefore there is a mutual causality between the intellect and the will in election. The last judgment, either as *extrinsic formal cause*, or as *final cause*, directs the will; and the will, as *efficient cause*, applies the intellect to make a determinate judgment.

From this we may make the deduction that the will infallibly follows the last practical judgment : for this judgment is the last only because the will has already chosen it, i.e., determined it as the last. Moreover, we see how the will has dominative power over this judgment, and therefore is free : it is the will that determines this judgment as the last [2].

449. How the will chooses the greater good. — 1° A distinction must be made between good speculatively apprehended and good practically apprehended.

A good that is speculatively apprehended is a good considered in an abstract manner, i.e., considered independently of the dispositions or circumstances in which the knowing subject is found.

---

(1) The argument from reason in regard to particular goods may be stated thus: I wish good. But this particular good is here and now good (in as much as it is a participation of good), and not good (in as much as it fails to fulfill the conditions of universal good). Therefore I can choose this good or not choose it, in as much as I consider it as a good, or as a non-good.

(2) Sequitur proinde electio judicium practicum ultimum, et quod sit ultimum voluntas efficit. — *Thesis* XXI s. Thomae.

A good that is practically apprehended is a good considered in a practical manner, i.e., as a good considered in relation to the dispositions or circumstances of the knowing subject.

2° The will does not always choose the good that is speculatively apprehended as the greater. But it always chooses the good that is practically apprehended as the greater, because it chooses one good rather than another because that good affects it more than does the other : the good chosen has a greater attraction for the will because of its being more proportionate to the dispositions of the will.

3° Although the will always chooses the good that is practically apprehended as the greater, it does so freely. For the good that is practically apprehended as the greater is a good which is here and now more suited to the disposition of the subject. If this disposition is mobile, the subject can always remove it, and consequently can also refuse to consent to the practical judgment made in accordance with it. But if the disposition is immobile, i.e., cannot be changed or removed, liberty no longer exists.

450. Objects of liberty. — 1° Liberty is divided into liberty *as regards specification*, and liberty *as regards exercise.* Necessity has a similar division.

Necessity as regards specification obtains when an object can be attained only by a particular species of act ; v.g., when an object is necessarily loved and cannot be an object of hatred.

Necessity as regards exercise obtains when a subject is so disposed that it is not able not to act.

Liberty of specification, on the contrary, obtains when an object can either be loved or be an object of hatred. Liberty of specification is called *liberty of contrariety.*

Liberty of exercise, or *liberty of contradiction*, obtains when a subject can at will act or not act, perform an action or omit it.

3° In the light of the foregoing remarks, we may set forth the following propositions :

a) *Man, even in this life, does not enjoy liberty of specification or contrariety in regard to good in general, or happiness in general, for such happiness is the formal object of the appetite for good*, i.e., *of the will.* In other words, man cannot hold happiness in general as an object of hatred. This is evident from the fact that good in general is the object from which the will receives its specification. Hence every act of the will is necessarily specified by good in general.

b) *Man enjoys liberty of exercise in regard to all particular goods, and also in regard to infinite good known by analogy to creatures.* This is clear from the fact that liberty is the faculty of choosing between particular goods. Although infinite good is in itself the highest good, as known by means of creatures, it does not appear in a positive manner as it is in itself, but only by means of creatures. Therefore it is good presented in a limited manner, which, in practice, may be considered as a limited or imperfect good.

c) *Man does not enjoy liberty of exercise in regard to God when clearly seen*, i.e., as known in Himself. God clearly seen appears as the highest good, and therefore cannot be considered as a non-good by the intellect.

451. Difficulties. — 1° Against the testimony of conscience.

a) In order that man have conscience, i.e., be conscious, of his liberty he must have conscious knowledge not only of his act, but of the faculty by which he can act otherwise than he does. But man has not conscious knowledge of this faculty. Therefore man cannot be conscious of his liberty. (Such is the teaching of Stuart Mill (1).

Major. — Conscious knowledge of the faculty either in itself, or from its act, *I concede;* in itself only, *I deny.*

Minor. — Has not conscious knowledge of the faculty in itself, *I concede;* from its act, *I deny.*

A faculty, as a potency, is known only from its act. But, when through conscience we perceive that the act which we perform is free in as much as we can, at any moment, cease from performing it, we perceive that we are able not to perform it, or that we have the faculty by which we can act otherwise.

(1) *Examination of Hamilton's Philosophy*, 6th ed., p. 580.

b) We are conscious that we are free, because we do not know the cause which necessarily determines the act of our will. Therefore the testimony of conscience in regard to liberty is an illusion. (Such is the argument of Spinoza).

Antecedent. — Only because we do not know the cause necessitating the act of the will, *I deny;* because we have positive consciousness that we have dominion over certain acts of the will, *I concede.*

I deny the consequent.

2° Objections of Determinism.

a) The same cause in the same circumstances produces the same effects. But if the will were free, it would produce different acts in the same circumstances. Therefore the human will is not free. (Such is the argument of Kant).

Major. — A cause which is necessarily determined to one thing, *I concede;* a cause which is not necessarily determined to one thing, *I deny.*

Minor. — The will is necessarily determined to one thing, *I deny;* is not necessarily determined to one thing, *I concede.*

b) A faculty which is determined by an object is not free. But the human will is determined in its action by its object. Therefore the human will is not free.

Major. — A faculty which is necessarily determined by its object, *I concede;* which is only sufficiently determined by its object, *I deny.*

Minor. — Is necessarily determined by universal good, *I concede;* by a particular good, *I distinguish:* necessarily, *I deny;* only sufficiently, *I concede.*

c) But the will is necessarily determined by a particular good. Therefore the will is not free.

The intellect is necessarily determined by a particular truth. But the relation of the will to a particular good is similar to the relation of the intellect to a particular truth. Therefore the will is necessarily determined by a particular good.

Major. — By an evident particular truth, *I concede;* by a particular truth that is not evident, *I deny.*

Minor. — As the intellect to an evident particular truth, *I deny;* to a truth that is not evident, *I concede.*

A particular truth, when it is evident, is always and necessarily true. It is for this reason that it necessarily determines the intellect. A particular good has the aspect of a non-good, i.e., it is a non-good in as much as it is not universal good. Hence it does not necessarily attract the will.

POINTS FOR REVIEW

1. Define: active indifference, and passive indifference.

2. Explain what is meant by active indifference which exists as a mode of universality in acting.

3. From what does an agent's active power of acting or not acting result?

4. Define free will, and give an a priori proof of its existence.

5. From what point of view does the will always choose the greater good? Explain.

6. Distinguish between liberty as regards specification and liberty as regards exercise.

APPENDIX I

INDIFFERENCE TOWARDS GOOD AND EVIL

452. Statement of the question. — 1° The active indifference of the will has reference to its performing or not performing an act, and in this case we have liberty of exercise or contradiction ; or it has reference to the objects by which the act is specified, and in this case we have liberty of specification.

Liberty of specification is either liberty as regards disparate objects, and is called liberty of disparate specification ; or it is liberty in regard to contrary objects, and in this case is known as liberty of contrary specification.

Indifference to good and evil, or the power of sinning, pertains to liberty of contrary specification.

2° There are many nowadays, especially those who style themselves Liberals, who teach that liberty essentially implies the power of good and evil. Hence, according to such persons, civil society is bound to grant its citizens liberty in the matter of good and evil. In like manner, every man has the right of publicly professing any religion he wishes, and no civil law may interfere with this inalienable right.

453. Statement of the thesis.

THESIS. — INDIFFERENCE TOWARDS GOOD AND EVIL, AND THEREFORE THE POWER OF SINNING, IS NOT OF THE ESSENCE OF LIBERTY.

1° *Nature of liberty.* — The fact that man has dominion over his own acts is sufficient for the essence of liberty. But liberty of exercise, in virtue of which a man can act or not act, is sufficient for this dominion. Therefore liberty of contrary specification, and a fortiori indifference towards good and evil, or the power of sinning, is not of the essence of liberty.

2° *Object of liberty.*—Indifference towards good or evil is not of the essence of a power which is essentially inclined to good, but rather is a defect in such a faculty. But liberty is a power which is essentially inclined to good. Therefore indifference towards good and evil is not of the essence of liberty, but rather is a defect of liberty.

The *major* is evident from the very terms used in that premise.

Minor. — Good is the object of the will, and therefore the will tends to evil only when evil is apprehended under the guise of good.

3° *Confirmation from the comparison of the intellect and will.* — Just as it does not pertain to the perfection of the intellect, but rather is a defect, to adhere to falsity, so too it is a defect of liberty to tend towards evil.

THE COMPLETE DELIBERATE ACT OF THE WILL

454. Integrant parts of the complete deliberate act of the will. — In the complete process of the deliberate act of the will, specification pertains to the intellect, whereas motion pertains to the will. Thomists teach that the complete process of the complete deliberate act is composed of twelve partial acts, of which six are acts of the intellect, and six are acts of the will.

The following is an outline of these twelve partial acts :

Acts of the intellect		*Acts of the will*
	As regards the end	
1° Apprehension of good		2° Simple volition
3° Judgment proposing the end		4° Intention of the end
	As regards the means	
5° Counsel		6° Consent
7° Last practical judgment		8° Election
9° Command		10° Active use
11° Passive use		12° Enjoyment (as regards the end)

455. Explanation of the partial acts. — Since the will is the inclination to a known good, first there is required the *apprehension of good* in the intellect. Immediately there arises in the will indeliberate complacence in the good presented, or *simple volition.*

In virtue of its simple volition, the will determines the intellect to judge whether the good is capable of attainment. If it judges in the affirmative, we have the *judgment proposing the end.* This judgment is followed by the *intention of the end* in the will.

As a result of the intention of the end, the will determines the intellect to inquire into or deliberate concerning the means to the end, i.e., determines it to *counsel.* The counsel is a practical syllogism whose conclusion is a practical (indifferent) judgment, proposing not one means, but several.

Corresponding to the counsel of the intellect is the *consent* of will, i.e., approbation of the utility of the means.

In virtue of this consent, the intellect is determined to its *last practical judgment* concerning the one determinate means that must here and now be chosen. This is followed by the *election* of the will.

When the election has taken place, the intellect moves to the *command* by which the execution of the means chosen is intimated : *do this.* Corresponding to the command of the intellect is the *active use* of the will, i.e., the act by which the will determines the other powers to make use of the means.

The *passive use,* or passive application, in the powers subject to the will (in the intellect, senses, and motive power), corresponds to the active use.

The application of all the means is followed by the *enjoyment* of the will, which is the happy possession of and delight in the end.

CHAPTER III

INTELLECTIVE SOUL

Prologue. — In this chapter, we shall discuss the following problems : first, the subsistence of the human soul ; secondly, the immortality proper to the soul as a subsisting being ; thirdly, the union of the intellective soul and the body. Therefore, there will be three articles in this chapter.

Subsistence of the intellective soul
- Statement of the question
- Opinions
- Thesis: The intellective soul is subsistent
- The intellective soul is essentially and integrally simple
- Difficulties

Immortality of the intellective soul
- Statement of the question
- Opinions of adversaries
- Thesis: The intellective soul is intrinsically immortal
- Scholion
- Difficulties

Union of the intellective soul and the body
- Statement of the question
- Opinions
- Thesis: The intellective soul is so united to the body that it is the body's one and only substantial form; and by it man is constituted as man, animal, living being, body, substance, and being
- The intellective soul endows man with every essential degree of perfection
- The intellective soul communicates to the body the act of existence by which it exists
- Numerical multiplication of intellective souls
- Mode of presence of the soul in the body
- Corollaries

ARTICLE I

SUBSISTENCE OF THE INTELLECTIVE SOUL

456. Statement of the question. — 1° The intellective soul, i.e., the soul of man, is the first principle by which man lives, perceives by the senses, and has intellective knowledge.

2° The human soul is subsistent, since it is a substantial principle that has its own proper existence independently of the body or matter. It is thus distinct from the sensitive soul and the vegetative soul, which are material, and consequently have not their own proper existence, but exist by means of the existence of the compound. In other words, the intellective souls exist as a *being which*, whereas the sensitive soul and the vegetative soul exist only as a *principle by which* the subsisting compound is constituted.

3° Since the human soul is subsistent, it is also spiritual, for it is a form that is intrinsically independent of matter in its existence, and consequently in its operation.

457. Opinions. — 1° Materialists and Sensists, by the very fact of their refusal to admit a distinction between the intellect and the senses, deny the subsistence and spirituality of the soul.

2° Phenomenalists and Actualists, as Hume, Taine, Wundt, and W. James, who do not admit of the existence of the soul as of a permanent substance, distinct from the flux of acts and passions, arrive at the same conclusion.

3° All Scholastics hold that the intellective soul of man is subsistent. This teaching has the support of Plato, Aristotle, and most of the great philosophers outside the School.

458. Statement of the thesis.

THESIS. — THE INTELLECTIVE SOUL IS SUBSISTENT.

The first principle of spiritual faculties and operations is subsistent. But the intellective soul is the first principle of spiritual faculties and operations. Therefore the intellective soul is subsistent (1).

Major. — *a*) As the first principle of faculties and operations, which are accidents, the intellective soul is a substance : for all accidents are radicated in substance. *b*) As the first principle of spiritual operations, it is a substance which has its own proper existence, i.e., is subsistent : for a thing operates in the way it exists, that is to say, operation manifests the nature of its principle. But spiritual operation is operation which is intrinsically independent of a body. Therefore the first principle of spiritual operations has existence which is not dependent on a body, or on matter, and therefore it is subsistent (2).

Minor. — The intellective soul is the first principle of intellection and volition. But intellection and volition are spiritual operations which proceed from anorganic faculties, as we have already proved. Therefore . . .

459. The intellective soul is essentially and integrally simple. — 1° *Preliminaries.* *a*) Simplicity must not be confused with spirituality. Spirituality excludes intrinsic dependence on matter, whereas simplicity excludes only composition of parts. Thus, for example, the sensitive soul is simple, but not spiritual. *b*) The intellective soul is essentially simple since it is not composed of first matter and subtantial form ; it is integrally simple, for it is not composed of homogeneously opposed parts, i.e., it does not admit of quantitative composition. *c*) Essential and integral simplicity do not exclude either composition of substance and accidents or composition of essence and existence in the intellective soul.

(1) Per se subsistit anima humana . . . — *Thesis* XV s. Thomae.
(2) I, q. 75, a. 2.

d) St. Bonaventure teaches that the soul is composed of a certain spiritual matter and form.

2° *Proof.* — *a*) *The intellective soul is essentially simple.* — The intellective soul, like every other kind of soul, is a form, and therefore an act. But an act is essentially simple, because of its very nature it excludes potency, and therefore cannot be composed of form and first matter. Therefore . . .

b) *The intellective soul is integrally simple.* — This is clearly evident, for, as a spiritual substance, it excludes all extension.

460. Difficulties. — 1° A substance which depends on matter in its operation is not spiritual. But the human soul depends on matter in its operation. Therefore the human soul is not spiritual, nor is it subsistent.

Major. — Which subjectively and intrinsically depends on matter in its operation, *I concede;* objectively and extrinsically, *I deny.*

Minor. — The soul depends subjectively and intrinsically on matter, *I deny;* objectively and extrinsically, *I concede.*

2° But the soul subjectively depends on matter. Therefore the difficulty remains.

The human soul evolves and grows old with the body, and is subject to the influence of its dispositions of sickness and health. But this cannot happen unless the soul is subjectively dependent on the matter of the body. Therefore . . .

Major. — As regards the faculties of vegetative and sensitive life, *I concede;* as regards the intellective faculties, *I distinguish:* as regards the entity of these faculties, *I deny;* as regards the use of them, in the present state of union, in as much as the soul depends objectively on organic conditions, *I concede.*

Minor. — Unless the soul depends objectively on matter, *I concede;* subjectively, *I deny.*

3° Children are often similar to their parents in regard to intellect and will. But this would not happen if the soul were spiritual. Therefore the human soul is not spiritual, nor is it subsistent.

Major. — On account of organic dispositions on which the intellect and will depend objectively, *I concede;* on which they depend subjectively, *I deny.*

Minor. — If the soul were spiritual and also objectively dependent on matter, *I deny;* if it were not even objectively dependent on matter, *I concede.*

ARTICLE II

IMMORTALITY OF THE INTELLECTIVE SOUL

461. Statement of the question. — 1° Immortality is the inamissibility of life. Life (in first act) is lost when a living being corrupts.

Corruption is the transition from existence to non-existence that results from the separation of parts. There are two kinds of corruption : *direct* (per se) *corruption* and *indirect* (per accidens) *corruption*.

Direct corruption is the corruption that is proper to a compound whose parts are separable ; v.g., the body corrupts when first matter and substantial form are separated.

Indirect corruption is the corruption which is proper to a *material* form, which corrupts with the corruption of the compound in which it exists as a principle *by which* ; v.g., when a house is destroyed, its form is destroyed indirectly.

2° There are three kinds of immortality : *a*) *Essential* immortality, which is proper to God, in Whom essence and existence are identified. *b*) *Natural* immortality, which is proper to creatures, in which essence and existence are distinct from each other, but which do not receive intrinsic natural potency to non-existence. *c*) *Gratuitous* immortality, which is given by God strictly as a gift to a naturally corruptible being ; v.g., the immortality with which Adam was endowed in the state of innocence.

The intellective soul is endowed with natural immortality, i.e., it is intrinsically immortal.

462. Opinions of adversaries. — Materialists, all Sensists, and Pantheists deny the immortality of the human soul.

463. Statement of the thesis. — According to the Fifth Lateran Council [1], the thesis is an article of faith.

THESIS. — THE INTELLECTIVE SOUL IS INTRINSICALLY IMMORTAL.

1° A living being which cannot corrupt either directly or indirectly is intrinsically immortal. But the intellective soul cannot corrupt either directly or indirectly. Therefore the intellective soul is intrinsically immortal [2].

The *major* is evident. A living being which cannot corrupt in any way whatsoever by its very nature ever remains in existence, that is to say, is immortal.

Minor. — *a) The intellective soul cannot corrupt directly.* a being which is essentially simple cannot corrupt directly. But the intellective soul is essentially simple. Therefore . . .

b) The intellective soul cannot corrupt indirectly. A being which does not depend on a body for its existence cannot corrupt indirectly, when the body corrupts. But the intellective soul does not depend on a body for its existence, because it is spiritual. Therefore . . .

2° A living being which has a natural desire to exist forever naturally must ever remain in existence. But the intellective soul has a natural desire to exist forever. Therefore the intellective soul naturally must ever remain in existence, i.e., it is intrinsically immortal.

Major. — Otherwise a natural desire would be in vain, i.e., nature would incline a being to something that is nonexistent.

Minor. — The desire of every knowing being is proportionate to its knowledge : for any form whatsoever is followed by a proportionate desire. But the human or intellective soul

(1) Damnamus et reprobamus omnes asserentes animam intellectivam mortalem esse.

(2) I, q. 55, a. 6. — I-II, q. 81, a. 6. — *Contra Gentes*, L. II, cc. 78, 79, 82 et passim.

knows existence in an absolute manner, abstracted from time. Therefore the human soul naturally desires existence abstracted from time, i.e., it desires to exist forever (1).

3° *Moral argument.* — In any well regulated State, it is the duty of the ruler to reward the good and punish the wicked. But the whole universe is, as it were, a State whose ruler is God. Therefore God makes provision in the universe for the reward of the good and the punishment of the wicked. But very often this does not come to pass in this life. Therefore man's soul must continue to exist after this life, in order to receive its reward or punishment ; and hence it follows that the human or intellective soul is immortal (2).

4° This is confirmed by the universal testimony of mankind, for all peoples, either on account of natural desire or on account of the moral argument, admit the immortality of the soul.

464. Scholion. — Since the soul is composed of essence and existence, absolutely speaking, it could be annihilated in as much as God would not conserve it in its existence ; but such annihilation is impossible, because God conserves all things in their existence, according to the mode of their nature. Therefore He conserves incorruptible things in their existence forever.

---

(1) Dans les êtres capables de quelque connaissance, le désir est en proportion de cette connaissance. Le vivant qui n'a que des sens, et une âme sensitive, ne va plus loin que l'impression reçue *hic* et *nunc*, et là se borne son désir. Mais le vivant doué d'une âme intelligente connaît l'être d'une manière absolue et selon toute l'étendue de la durée. Son désir ne peut être moins vaste que sa connaissance. Voilà pourquoi toute nature intelligente désire naturellement être toujours. — MONSABRÉ, *Conf.* 1888, p. 92.

(2) Il faut croire les législateurs et les traditions antiques, et particulièrement sur l'âme, lorsqu'ils nous disent qu'elle est totalement distincte du corps ..., que le moi de l'homme est véritablement immortel, et que c'est que ce que nous appelons l'âme, et qu'elle rendra compte aux dieux comme l'enseigne la loi du pays, ce qui est également consolant pour le juste, et terrible pour le méchant. — PLATON, *Des Lois*, XII.

A pagan philosopher of the second century: Les chrétiens ont raison de penser que ceux qui vivent saintement seront récompensés après la mort et que les méchants subiront des supplices éternels: ce sentiment leur est commun avec le monde entier. — Cited by ORIGEN, *Contra Celsum*.

Moreover, the annihilation of the human soul is repugnant : *a*) to the wisdom of God, for, if God were to annihilate the soul, He would destroy a nature which He constituted as intrinsically immortal ; *b*) to the goodness of God, for, if God annihilated the soul, He would torture creatures with a desire for immortality which He would never satisfy (1) ; *c*) to the justice of God, because, if God failed to conserve the soul in its existence forever, He would not adequately reward virtue and punish vice.

Hence God cannot annihilate the human soul (2).

465. Difficulties. — Against the first argument. 1) A form which demands determinate dispositions in a body is corruptible on the corruption of the body. But the human soul demands determinate dispositions in the body. Therefore the human soul is corruptible on the corruption of the body.

Major. — Which demands determinate dispositions, in order that it exist absolutely, *I concede;* that it actually inform the body, *I deny.*

Minor. — It demands determinate dispositions, in order that it actually inform the body, *I concede;* that it exist absolutely, *I deny.*

2) But the human soul is united to the body in order that it exist absolutely. Therefore the difficulty remains.

In man there is only one existence, i.e., the existence of the whole man, which is at the same time the existence of the soul. But, on the corruption of the body, the existence of man ceases. Therefore, on the corruption of the body, the existence of the soul ceases.

Major. — There is one existence, and this existence is communicated to man through the soul, in such a manner that it retains this existence even when it does not communicate it to the body, *I concede;* in such a manner that the soul does not retain this existence when it does not communicate it to the body, *I deny.*

(1) Dieu est juste, il ne peut se faire le bourreau de sa créature, la remplir de désirs qui jamais ne seront assouvis, la pousser violemment vers un terme qu'elle ne doit jamais atteindre. Pourquoi cet universel besoin du bonheur qui tourmente nos pauvres cœurs si la vie humaine se termine au tombeau ? Entre la naissance et la mort, avons-nous été quelquefois satisfait ? Hélas ! les plaisirs éphémères de ce monde n'ont fait que tromper la divine langueur de nos âmes, les joies mêmes de la vérité et de la vertu ont été constamment troublées par de basses exigences, assombries par l'incessantes contradictions ! Notre nature est ainsi organisée qu'elle veut, qu'elle espère nécessairement le vrai sans ombre, le bien sans mélange, le repos actif de toutes ses facultés dans la paix, et l'on veut que Dieu la jette impitoyablement dans la nuit, le vide, le néant éternel. C'est atroce et par conséquent c'est incroyable. — MONSABRÉ, *Conf.*, 1875, conf. 17.

(2) Quand on voit le malheur de la vertu, et la prospérité du crime, c'est un besoin profondément senti que celui d'un ordre de choses a venir: car on ne voit point que l'auteur de la nature ait soumis à un semblable désordre aucune autre partie de cet univers. — CUVIER, *Histoire des mammifères.*

Minor. — The existence of man ceases in such a way that the soul does not retain this existence, *I deny;* in such a way that the soul retains this existence, *I concede.*

The human soul is a spiritual substantial form; therefore of its very nature it has *existence,* which it communicates to the body.

3) But it is repugnant that the soul exist separated from the body. Therefore the difficulty remains.

It is repugnant that the soul exist in a state in which it cannot operate. But the human soul cannot operate when separated from the body. Therefore it is repugnant that the human soul exist separated from the body.

Major. — In which it can exercise no operations, *I concede;* in which it cannot exercise certain operations, *I deny.*

Minor. — The soul separated from the body can exercise no operations, *I deny;* cannot exercise the operations of vegetative and sensitive life, *I concede.*

The soul, when separated from the body, can exercise the operations of intellective life.

4) But the human soul, when separated from the body, cannot exercise the operations of intellective life. Therefore the difficulty remains.

The soul can know nothing without the aid of the phantasms. But the soul, when separated from the body, has no phantasms. Therefore the human soul, when separated from the body, cannot exercise the operations of intellective life.

Major. — In the present state of union, *I concede;* in the state of separation, *I deny.*

I concede the minor.

Against the second argument. — The natural desire for immortality is not a sign of immortality. Therefore . . .

1) Animals have a natural desire of existing forever. But animals are not immortal. Therefore the natural desire of existing forever is not a sign of immortality.

Major. — Animals have an instinct by which they continually tend towards their self-preservation, *I concede;* an elicited desire by which they desire everlasting existence as known to them, *I deny.*

I concede the minor.

The human soul of its very nature has knowledge of everlasting existence, and consequently in an elicited manner naturally desires to exist forever.

2) But an elicited desire of immortality is not a sign of immortality. Therefore.

In an elicited manner, we naturally desire the immortality of the body. But our bodies are not immortal. Therefore . . .

Major. — We naturally desire the immortality of the body in virtue of the nature of the body, *I deny;* in virtue of the nature of the soul, *I concede.*

The desire for immortality derives from the apprehension of everlasting existence, an apprehension that is proper to the soul, and therefore it is a sign of the immortality of the soul only.

3) But the desire for immortality is not natural. Therefore . . .

What is natural cannot be refused. But the desire for the immortality of the soul can be refused. Therefore such a desire is not natural.

Major. — It cannot be refused by a free act that is in conformity to nature, *I concede;* by a free act which is opposed to nature, *I deny.*

Minor. — It can be refused by a free act that is in conformity to nature *I deny;* by a free act that is opposed to nature, *I concede.*

The desire for immortality in the human soul is not called natural in, the sense that, if immortality is presented to it, it necessarily desires it, but in the sense that, when the human soul apprehends absolute existence, in virtue of its very nature it desires such existence. But a free act can be exercised which is opposed to this natural appetite.

Against the moral argument. — 1) The moral argument has no force, unless God is the ruler of the world. But this has not been proved. Therefore.

Minor. — This cannot be proved, *I deny;* this can be proved, *I concede*.

And this is sufficient for the validity of the moral argument.

2) The moral argument is a proof, if virtue in itself is not a sufficient reward of itself, and if vice in itself is not a sufficient punishment of itself. But virtue is in itself a sufficient reward of itself, and punishment is in itself a sufficient punishment of itself. Therefore . . .

I deny the minor.

This is evident from experience: the labor, sufferings, etc. connected with the practice of virtue sometimes far exceed the pleasure that derives from virtue, v.g., in the case of death on account of virtue; on the other hand, remorse, etc. which accompany vice, sometimes are not proportionate to the pleasure that derives from it.

ARTICLE III

UNION OF THE INTELLECTIVE SOUL AND BODY

466. Statement of the question. — 1° It is clear that the human soul, even though it is spiritual, is united in some way to the body. We are concerned for the moment with the *mode of union* between the intellective soul and the body. We may state that the intellective soul is united to the body in such a way as to be its substantial form.

2° The second problem with which we are confronted is that of the proper subject of the intellective soul. Some teach that a being that is essentially one, i.e., has only one nature, can have many substantial forms that are subordinate to one another. According to this opinion, first matter is not the immediate subject of the intellective soul, but only its mediate subject, i.e., is its subject by means of intermediary forms, so that the proximate subject to which the intellective soul is immediately united as form is a body already perfected, according to some, by the form of corporeity or, according to others, by the sensetive soul (1).

We maintain, on the contrary, that the intellective soul is united to the body as its *one and only* substantial form, and therefore that by it man is constituted as man, animal, living being, body, substance, and being. In other words, we affirm that the immediate subject of the intellective soul is first matter, and we state too that the only substantial form and the only soul that can exist *in man* is the intellective soul.

467. Opinions. — 1° The following deny that the intellective soul is the substantial form of the body.

(1) *De Spir. Creat.*, q. unica, a. 3.

a) *Plato*, who holds that intellective soul is united to the body as a mover to the thing that it moves ;

b) *Peter of John Olivi*, O.F.M., who maintains that in the human soul, there are three distinct formal principles : vegetative, sensitive, and intellective ; and he contends that the human soul is not immediately the form of the body, in as much as it is intellective, but as it is vegetative and sensitive ;

c) *Descartes*, who describes the union of the soul with the body as accidental ;

d) *Malebranche*, who supports the theory of Occasionalism, in as much as he affirms that the movements of the body are only an occasion for God to act immediately upon the soul, and the acts of the soul are an occasion for Him to act on the body ;

e) *Leibniz*, who thinks that the body and soul act only immanently, without dependance on each other, but that they act in this way in virtue of a harmony preestablished from the beginning so that their actions would be in perfect concert ;

f) *Recent experimental psychologists*, who deny the substantiality of the soul and its distinction from the body, in as much as they hold that *the physical*, i.e., our physical life (bodily movements and operations), and *the psychic*, i.e., our psychic life (affections, sensation, etc.), constitute, without a permanent subject, two parallel series that are independent of each other.

2° *Scotus* teaches that the intellective soul is the form of the body. But he contends that in man there is, besides the intellective soul, the form of corporeity, and hence that the intellective soul is not received immediately into first matter, but into the body already perfected by its substantial form.

468. Statement of the thesis. — The Church, in condemnation of the teaching of Peter of John Olivi, defined that the rational or intellective soul is of itself and essentially the form of the human body, so that any opinion to the contrary is heretical. This definition was given at the Council of Vienna, and was later confirmed by the Fifth Council of the Lateran, under Pope Leo X (2).

THESIS. — THE INTELLECTIVE SOUL IS SO UNITE TO THE BODY THAT IT IS THE BODY'S ONE AND ONLY SUBSTANTIAL FORM; AND BY IT MAN IS AND CONSTITUTED AS MAN, ANIMAL, LIVING BEING, BODY, SUBSTANCE, AND BEING.

First part. — *The intellective soul is so united to the body that it is its substantial form.* — 1° The first principle of man's intellective operation is so united to his body that it is its substantial form. But the intellective soul is the first principle of man's intellective operation. Therefore the intellective soul is so united to the body that it is its substantial form (3).

Major. — Nothing acts except in so far as it is in act, and it acts according to the mode of its existence, i.e., its operation is proportionate to its existence. But mobile and corporeal being is primarily in act by its substantial form. Therefore the first principle of the intellective operation of man, who is a mobile and corporeal being, is so united to his body as to be its substantial form.

The *minor* is the nominal definition of the intellective soul.

2° The principle from which man derives his proper species is so united to his body as to be its substantial form. But the intellective soul is the principle from which man derives his proper species. Therefore the intellective soul is so united to the body as to be its substantial form.

Major. — Every being derives its species from its proper form.

---

(1) DENZINGER, *Enchiridion*, n. 481.
(2) *Ibid.*, n. 738.
(3) I, q. 76, a. 1.

Minor. — The nature of a thing is shown by its operation ; and man's proper operation is intellection. Hence the intellective soul, which is the first principle of this operation, must be the principle from which man derives his proper species.

Second part. — *The intellective soul is so united to the body that it is its one and only substantial form ; and by it man is constituted as man, animal, living being, body, substance, and being.*

1° If man is a being that is strictly one, i.e., has only one nature, the intellective soul is so united to the body as to be its one and only substantial form ; and by it man is constituted as man, animal, living being, body, substance, and being. But man is a being that is strictly one. Therefore the intellective soul is so united to the body that it is its one and only substantial form ; and by it man is constituted as man, animal, living being, body, substance, and being.

Major. — In order that a mobile being be strictly one, its substantial form must immediately inform its first matter as pure potency, for a being that is strictly one cannot be constituted from two beings in act ; furthermore, it can have only one substantial form, because any additonal form informs a subject already in act, and therefore is accidental, v.g., the form of whiteness which informs a subject already in act. Hence, if man is a being that is strictly one, i.e., has substantial unity, the intellective soul is united to the body as its one and only form ; and by it man is constituted as man, animal, living being, body, substance, and being.

Minor. — It is evident from internal experience : when a man perceives his existence, his life, his sensation, and his intellection, he perceives that it is he himself who exists, lives, and exercises the operations of sensation and intellection.

2° If something were constituted as a being, a substance, a body, a living being, an animal, and a man by various forms, then either all these things, (being, substance, etc.)

would be accidentally predicated of one another, or body, living being, animal, would be predicated of man as properties. But each of the two alternatives is false. Therefore by the same form man is constituted a man, an animal, a living being a body, a substance, and a being, or, in other words, there is only one substantial form in man, and that is his intellective soul (1).

Major. — Things (i.e., predicates) which are derived from various forms are predicated of one another accidentally if the forms are not essentially related to one another, as when we say that something white is sweet ; or, if the forms are essentially related to one another, a predicate derived from a later form is predicated as a property of the earlier form, as when we say that a body with a surface is colored. Therefore . . .

Minor. — *a*)Man is not accidentally an animal, a living being, a body, a substance, and a being. *b*) On the other hand, animal, living being, etc. are not predicated of man as properties, because otherwise every animal and every living being would be a man, and man would enter into the definition of animal and living being, just as man is found in the definition of risible being, v.g., when we say : a risible animal is a man.

469. The intellective soul endows man with every essential degree of perfection (2). — This assertion is evident from the thesis. For by one and the same intellective soul man is constituted as man, animal, living being, body, substance, and being. Just how this happens may be readily seen from a study of the differences of forms. For the forms of things differ from one another as regards degrees of perfection. Hence a more perfect form can effect by itself all that can be effected by two or more inferior forms ; for example, if the form of an inanimate body gives material and corporeal perfection, the form of a plant gives these perfections and the perfection of life as well ; the sensitive soul gives all this and in

(1) I, q. 76, a. 3.
(2) *Thesis* XV s. Thomae.

addition sensitive perfection ; and the rational soul adds rational perfection to the perfections given by the sensitive soul.

Since the intellective soul endows the human body with all the perfections that the inferior forms can give and adds its own proper perfection, it is said to possess *formally-eminently* the grades of perfection of the corporeal, vegetative, and sensitive forms.

470. The intellective soul communicates to the body the act of existence by which it itself exists. — 1° *Preliminaries.* — *a*) Existence is the property of form, because neither first matter nor the compound are in act except by form. *b*) But existence is the property of form in two ways : as the formal constituent of its existence, i.e., as the principle *by which it exists*, or as its subject, i.e., as the principle *which exists.* *c*) Non-subsisting substantial form is only the principle *by which* of existence. In other words, existence is not received into non-subsisting form, but rather into the compound, so that non-subsisting substantial form is only the principle-by-which of existence.

But, since the intellective soul is a subsisting substantial form, it has not existence as a principle *by which* only, but has it also as a being *which.* Therefore by itself it communicates to the body the act of existence by which it itself exists (1).

2° *Proof.* — A subsisting substantial form which is united to the body communicates to it the act of existence by which it itself exists. But the intellective soul is a subsisting substantial form which is united to the body. Therefore the intellective soul communicates to the body the act of existence by which it itself exists (2).

The *minor* is evident from what has been already said.

Major. — Every form is prior to its compound by priority of nature. Therefore a substantial form that first subsists according to priority of nature first has existence in itself, and

(1) *Thesis* XV s. Thomae.
(2) I, q. 76, a. 1, ad 5. — *Comm.*, Cajetan.

afterwards communicates that existence to the compound or body (1).

471. Numerical multiplication of intellective souls. - 1° *Preliminaries.* — *a*) We are here concerned with the problem of the *numerical multiplication* of intellective souls. Intellective souls are multiplied as bodies are multiplied; in other words, there are as many intellective souls are there are human bodies, or men.

b) This assertion is against the teaching of Averroes, who affirmed the existence of one intellect which belonged to all men.

2° *Proof.* — Substantial forms are numerically multiplied according to the multiplication of bodies. But the intellective soul is the substantial form of the human body. Therefore intellective souls are multiplied according to the multiplication of human bodies, i.e., there are as many intellectives souls as there are human bodies (3).

472. Mode of presence of the soul in the body. — 1° *Preliminaries.* — *a*) The intellective soul exists in the human body. But the question arises : is it in the whole body or in some part of it? *b*) Plato maintained that the soul exists in the brain ; the Stoics held that it resides in the heart ; Descartes taught that it is located in the pineal gland : and others assigned it to other parts of the body.

Aristotle and all Scholastics teach that the intellective soul is wholly in the whole body and wholly in every part of the body according to the totality of its essence, but not according to the totality of its power.

c) To understand the scholastic opinion, we must know that there are three modes of totality corresponding to the three modes of division. A whole is that which is divisible into parts. There is one kind of whole which is divisible

(1) Joannes a Sancto Thoma, *Cursus Phil.*, t. III, p. 228 (Reiser).
(3) I, q. 76, a. 2.

into quantitative parts, as a whole line, a whole body ; another kind, which is divisible into logical and essential parts, as a thing defined is resolved into the parts of its definition, and a compound into matter and form ; and a third kind, which is divisible into the parts of its power, i.e., into different powers.

d) Totality of quantity can in no way be attributed to the intellective soul, because it is spiritual. But we may attribute to it totality of essence as regards logical and essential parts ; and totality of power, because the intellective soul is the principle of various powers.

2° *In the light of the foregoing observations, we may now set forth the proof of the Scholastic opinion.*

a) *The intellective soul is wholly in the whole body and wholly in every part of the body according to the totality of its essence.* — The intellective soul is the substantial form of the body. But the substantial form is wholly in the whole body and wholly in every part of the body according to the totality of its essence. Therefore . . .

Minor. — Substantial form according to its essence is the perfection not only of the whole compound, but also of every part of it.

b) *The intellective soul is not wholly in the whole body and wholly in every part of it according to the totality of its power.* — *a*) It is not wholly in the whole body according to the totality of its power, because the intellective soul has spiritual powers. *b*) It is not wholly in every part of the body according to the totality of its power, i.e., with all its faculties, because its power of sight is in the eye, of hearing in the ear, and similarly its other powers are in determinate organs.

473. Corollaries. — 1° Since the intellective soul is the substantial form of the body, it is so united to one body that it cannot be united to another. Therefore metempsychosis, i.e., the successive existence of the same soul in several bodies, is repugnant.

2° The intellective soul is individuated by its relation to this determinate body. And since the soul corresponds exactly to the subject into which it is infused, souls differ substantially in perfection according to the perfection of the dispositions of the bodies which they inform.

3° Therefore the innate diversity of quality in human intellects derives from the diversity of disposition of human bodies.

CHAPTER IV

ORIGIN OF MAN

Prologue. — We have already studied the questions of the nature of the human soul and its union to the body. There now remains our for consideration the problem of man's origin. There are two phases to this problem : the origin of man's soul, and the origin of his body. Therefore there will be two articles in this chapter.

Origin of the intellective soul	Statement of the question Thesis: The intellective soul is created by God The intellective soul is created when it can be infused into a sufficiently disposed subject Moment of the infusion of the soul into matter Man is engendered by his parents
Origin of the body of the first man	Statement of the question Opinions Thesis: God, or some other spiritual cause, immediately and naturally disposed first matter for the reception of the soul of the first man, by the evolution of the species Divine operation in the formation of the body of the first man Scholia Materialistic evolutionism and spontaneous generation Difficulties

ARTICLE I

ORIGIN OF THE INTELLECTIVE SOUL

474. Statement of the question. -- Many opinions have been offered as the explanation of the origin of the human soul.

1° Certain philosophers of antiquity were of the opinion that the human soul is a part of God [1]. Thus the Manicheans, unable to rise above their imagination, held that God is a body which is the principle of other bodies. And since they conceived the soul to be a principle, they asserted that it is a part of that body which is God.

Others, as Varro and the Stoics, conceived God as something incorporeal, but yet the form of a body. They maintained that the human soul is a part of that whole soul which is God, just as man is a part of the whole world.

2° *Traducianism* asserts that the human soul is engendered by the parents, either by means of a corporeal seed (Tertullian), or by a spiritual seed (Saint Augustine, who expressed this opinion as doubtful).

3° *Transformism* holds that the human soul originates through the transformation of one species into another.

Rosmini teaches that the parents engender only the sensitive soul, and that this soul becomes intellective on the appearance of the idea of being which God manifests to it. The opinion proposed by Rosmini was condemned in Rome, 14 Dec. 1887.

---

(1) I, q. 90, a. 1.— *In II Sent.*, dist. 17, q. 1, a. 1.— *Contra Gentes*, L. II, c. 83.

4° *Creationism* maintains that the human soul is created. There are two forms of creationism.

a) Some creationists, as Frochschammer, hold that the parents, in virtue of some power communicated to them by God, create the soul when they engender.

b) Others teach that the soul is immediately created by God. This is the Catholic opinion.

5° *a*) It is evident that the human soul cannot be a part of God, because God is absolutely simple and the most perfect being. Hence He cannot have parts, nor can He be the form of the body, as some of the ancients maintained : for the form of the body is imperfect and incomplete.

b) The human soul cannot be engendered from a corporeal seed, because the human soul is spiritual. Similarly, the human soul cannot originate through the transformation of one species into another, nor by the transformation of the sensitive soul into the intellective soul. Indeed, every change of form is dependent on a transmutation of matter ; but the human soul, in virtue of its spirituality, is independent of matter, and therefore is produced independently of matter.

c) The human soul cannot be engendered from a spiritual seed, because that seed would be a part cut off from the spiritual soul of the generator ; but this is impossible, for a spiritual soul cannot be divided into parts.

d) The human soul cannot be created by the parents, because no created cause can create, even as instrumental cause.

Therefore we must conclude that the human soul is immediately created by God.

475. Statement of the thesis.

THESIS. — The intellective soul is created by God.

A subsisting form is created by God. But the intellective

soul is a subsisting form. Therefore the intellective soul is created by God (1).

The *minor* is evident from what we said earlier.

Major. — Since becoming is the way to existence, the mode of the production of a thing corresponds to the thing's mode of existence. But a subsisting form is intrinsically independent of a subject. Therefore a subsisting from is produced independently of a subject, i.e., it is produced from nothing ; in other words, it is created by God.

476. The intellective soul is created when it can be infused into a sufficiently disposed subject. — 1° *a*) We assert that the creation of the intellective soul and its infusion into a subject take place at the same time. But the creation of the soul and its infusion into matter are distinct : creation has reference to the principle from which the soul has its existence ; infusion has reference both to the principle from which the soul has its existence, and to the matter which it perfects (2). *b*) A sufficiently disposed subject is first matter made determinate by its last disposition, by which it becomes adapted for the reception of the human soul. *c*) Our teaching is contrary to that of the Platonists, Origin, and Leibniz, who hold that souls exist before their union with the body (3).

2° *Proof.* — 1) Things are created by God in their natural perfection. But the intellective soul has not the perfection of its nature apart from the body, but exists in its natural perfection when it is united to sufficiently disposed matter. Therefore the intellective soul is not created apart from the body, but is created when it can be infused into a sufficiently disposed subject (4).

Minor. — The intellective soul is not of itself the complete species of any nature, but is a part of human nature.

---

(1) I, q. 90, a. 3, c.
(2) *Thesis* XV s. Thomae.
(3) *In II Sent.*, dist. 32, q. 2, a. 1, ad 1.
(4) *De Potentia*, q. 3, a. 10.

2° Intellective souls are created by God as numerically distinct in the same species. But intellective souls cannot be created as numerically distinct in the same species unless they are infused into sufficiently disposed matter. Therefore the intellective soul is created when it can be infused into sufficiently disposed matter, i.e., into a sufficiently disposed subject.

The *major* is evident : intellective souls are specifically the same, though numerically distinct.

Minor. — Intellective souls are acts that are specifically the same. But acts specifically the same are multiplied numerically only when they are received into different subjects that are adapted to receive them. Therefore . . .

477. Moment of the infusion of the soul into matter. There are two opinions. According to the opinion commonly held today, the intellective soul informs the body at the very moment of conception, i.e., it is infused into the body at the very moment of conception. The other opinion is that of St. Thomas and of many Scholastics, who teach that the foetus is first informed by the vegetative soul, secondly by the sensitive soul, and thirdly by the intellective soul.

The second opinion, though not generally admitted today, seems to us to be the more probable, and, indeed, seems certain. For, in the order of generation, the imperfect always precedes the perfect ; or potency which passes to act attains imperfect act before it attains perfect act (1).

478. Man is engendered by his parents. — Although parents are not causes of the intellective soul, which is created by God, yet they are the causes of the union of the intellective soul to matter, for they so dispose matter that of necessity it receives the soul. Therefore parents are said to engender offspring or man, because they cause the offspring to become a sharer of the human species (2).

(1) I, q. 118, a. 2.
(2) *De Potentia*, q. 3, a. 9.

ARTICLE II

ORIGIN OF THE BODY OF THE FIRST MAN

479. Statement of the question. — 1° Two things are evident from what has been already said : *a*) the human soul is created and infused into sufficiently disposed matter by God ; *b*) matter is disposed by the natural generator, in order that is may receive the human soul and may become a sharer of its existence.

Another problem in regard to the origin of man remains for our consideration : by what agent was matter disposed for the reception of the human soul of the first man ? It is quite evident that it was not disposed through the agency of another man as generator.

In the thesis, we state that first matter was disposed for the reception of the human soul either by God, acting not only as universal cause but as a particular cause, or by some other spiritual cause.

2° Having established that the body of the first man was produced either by God or some other spiritual cause, we find ourselves confronted with the problem of how matter was disposed for the reception of the soul of the first man. This problem may be expressed in the following alternative question : was matter disposed gradually and successively by God or by some other spiritual cause for the reception of the human soul of the first man *through the evolution of the species*, or was it disposed *without the evolution* of the species, v.g., by the formation of the body of the first man from some inorganic body ?

3° In *Genesis*, II, 7, we read : *And the Lord God formed man of the slime of the earth . . .* There are two observations to be made in regard to this text.

First, it pertains to the theologian to decide whether this text must be accepted in its literal sense, and, in particular, whether the slime of the earth must be understood as signifying some inorganic body.

Secondly, since God is omnipotent, He could have formed the body of the first man either from matter disposed in some way by the evolution of the species, or from matter not so disposed (1). But the problem of the philosopher is not what, in the light of God's omnipotence, could have taken place, but rather what, in view of the exigencies of nature, and, in particular, of first matter, must have taken place. Moreover, the philosopher must refrain from recourse to a miracle as the explanation of the production of things, when this production can be explained without a miracle.

4° If God formed the body of the first man from some inorganic being, two miracles took place : one on the part of the agent, and another on the part of the matter (2).

There was a miracle on the part of the agent, because first matter was not disposed for the reception of the soul of the first man by a natural generator, but immediately by God. But, in this case, there is no miracle in the strict sense, but only in a wide sense. For, admitting the creation of inferior beings, man must have been made as the principal part of the universe ; and his body could only have been formed either immediately by God (3), or by some other spiritual cause.

(1) Ad tertium dicendum, quod de limo terrae corpus primi hominis formatum est virtute divina, cujus est statim ad perfectum adducere cum voluerit. — *In II Sent.*, dist. XX, q. 2, a. 1, ad 3.

(2) Ad quartum dicendum, quod formatio hominis de limo terrae fuit miraculosa quantum ad agens et quantum ad materiam. — *In III Sent.*, dist. III, q. 2, a. 2, ad 4.

(3) Ad secundum dicendum, quod nec etaim creatio animarum vel justificatio impiorum proprie miracula debent dici: quia quamvis praeter rationes seminales agentes ad perfectionem effectus, non tamen sunt praeter eas disponentes: dispositio enim corporis ad receptionem corporis (animae?) et praeperatio voluntatis ad susceptionem gratiae, est per virtutem creaturae collatum. Si tamen sine tali praecedente praeperatione vel anima infunderetur vel gratia conferretur, utrumque mireculum dici posset, ut patet in formatione primi hominis et in conversione Pauli. — *In II Sent.*, dist., XXVIII, q. 1, a. 3, ad 2.

Ad primum dicendum, quod creatio, proprie loquendo, non est opus miraculosum, quia deficit una conditio miraculi: quamvis enim causam occultam habeat, tamen non est in re unde aliter fieri deberet: immo esse rerum naturali quodam ordine a primo ente producitur, quamvis non per necessitatem naturae. — *Ibidem*, ad 1.

There was a miracle on the part of the matter, because the body of the first man was formed from non-natural matter, i.e., from naturally non-proportionate matter (1).

Hence the only question with which we are concerned at present is this: was a miracle, from the point of view of the matter, necessary in the formation of the body of the first man? Our answer to this question is in the negative. We maintain that, in consideration of the laws of nature, first matter could have been naturally disposed either by God, or by some other spiritual cause, to receive the soul of the first man.

5° To understand this, we must note that the body of the first man had its origin not through creation, but through generation, i.e., through the transmutation of first matter. That generation was not univocal, since it was not effected by an agent similar to it in species; but it was equivocal, because it was effected by a superior agent, namely God (2), or some other spiritual cause.

This process of generation was gradual, i.e., from the imperfect to the perfect (3). Such is the case, because first matter which is a nature (n. 253), is not of itself disposed for any form whatsoever, and does not naturally and without succession of time receive its own greater perfection, but it is disposed gradually by inferior forms for the reception of superior forms

(1) Ad hoc enim quod generatio aliqua naturalis dicetur, oportet quod fiat ab agente naturaliter, ex materia naturali ad hoc proportionata. Quodcumque autem horum defuerit, non potest dici generatio naturalis, sed miraculosa, si virtute fiat supernaturali. Agens autem naturale, cum sit finitae virtutis, non potest ex materia non naturaliter proportionata effectum producere: agens vero supernaturale, cum sit infinitae virtutis, potest ex utraque materia operari, naturali scilicet et non naturali; et ideo duobus modis contingit esse miraculum. Uno modo quando usque agens est naturale, neque materia proportionata ad talem formam, ut patet in formatione hominis de imo terrae. — *In III Sent.*, dist. III, q. 2, a. 2.

(2) *De Potentia*, q. 7, a. 7, ad 7.

(3) Posset etiam dici, quod via generationis ab imperfectioribus ad perfectiora pervenitur, et hoc ordine quod quae imperfectiora sunt, prius ordine naturae producuntur. In via enim generationis quanto aliqud perfectius est, et magis assimilatur agenti, tanto tempore posterius est; quamvis sit prius natura et dignitate. Et ideo, quia homo perfectissimum animalium est, ultimo inter animalia fieri debuit, et non immediate post corpora coelestia, quae cum corporibus inferioribus non ordinantur secundum viam generationis . . . — *De Potentia*, q. 4, a. 2, ad 33.

([1]); v.g., first matter, as its exists under the form of an animal, is more disposed for the reception of the human soul than it is as it exists under the form of a plant, and more disposed as it exists in a perfect animal than as it exists in an imperfect animal.

Since first matter is naturally inclined to the human soul as to the most perfect form it can possess, it must have been disposed for it either by God, or by some other spiritual cause, according to the laws of nature, little by little: it must have been disposed gradually, i.e., by passing successively from an imperfect form to a more perfect form through the process of the evolution of the species ([2]). If first matter was not disposed for the human soul by the evolution of the species, then it was so disposed by a miracle, which must be accepted as of faith, but which cannot be demonstrated by reason.

480. Opinions. — 1° *Materialistic Evolutionism* denies the existence of God, the creation of the world, the creation and spirituality of the human soul, and teaches that an inorganic being evolves, without the influence of a superior cause, by the

(1) In actibus autem formarum gradus quidam inveniuntur. Nam materia prima est in potentia primum ad formam elementi; sub vero forma elementi existens, est in potentia ad formam mixti, propter quod elementa sunt materia mixti; sub forma autem mixti considerata, est in potentia ad animam vegetabilem, nam talis corporis anima actus est. Itemque anima vegetabilis est in potentia ad sensitivam, sensitiva vero ad intellectivam; quod processus generationis ostendit. Primo enim in generatione est foetus vivens vita plantae, postmodum autem vita animalis, demum vero vita hominis. Post hanc autem formam, non invenitur in generalibilibus et corruptibilibus posterior forma et dignior. Ultimus igitur generationis totius gradus est anima humana, et in hanc tendit materia sicut in ultimam formam. Sunt ergo elementa propter corpora mixta, haec vero propter viventia, in quibus plantae dunt propter animalia, animalis propter hominem: homo enim est finis cujuslibet generationis. — *Contra Gentes*, l. 3, c. 22.

(2) Primo, quia secundum utrosque (scilicet secundum Augustinum et alios sanctos) in prima rerum productione materia erat sub formis substantialibus elementorum: ita quod materia prima non praecessit duratione formas substantiales elementorum mundi. Secundo, quia secundum utrorumque opinionem in prima rerum institutione per opus creationis non fuerunt plantae et animalia in actu sed tantum in potentia, ut ex ipsis elementis per virtutem Verbi possent produci. — *De Potentia*, q. 4, a. 2, c.

Ad vigesimum tertium patet responsio ex dictis: quia corpus humanum non fuit productum in actu in illis sex diebus, sicut nec corpora aliorum animalium, sed tantum secundum rationes causales, quia Deus in ipsa creatione indidit ipsis elementis virtutem, seu rationes quasdam, ut ex eis virtute Dei, vel stellarum, vel seminis possent animalia produci. — *Ibidem*, ad 23.

successive evolution of the species until it becomes the human compound. This opinion may not be adopted; and it is entirely incompatible with the teaching of faith.

2° *Fixism* holds that in the beginning God produced each of the different species from inorganic matter. These species are fixed, and remained unchanged for the future.

481. Statement of the thesis.

THESIS—GOD, OR SOME OTHER SPIRITUAL CAUSE, IMMEDIATELY AND NATURALLY DISPOSED FIRST MATTER FOR THE RECEPTION OF THE SOUL OF THE FIRST MAN BY THE EVOLUTION OF THE SPECIES.

First part. — *God, or some other spiritual, cause disposed first matter for the reception of the soul of the first man.* — The body of man could only have been produced either immediately by a spiritual cause (i.e., God or some other spiritual cause), or by a natural generator, which is man. But no natural generator existed before the formation of the body of the first man. Therefore the body of the first man was produced by a spiritual cause, i.e., God, or some other spiritual cause, immediately disposed first matter for the reception of the soul of the first man.

Major.—An agent is similar to its effect. Hence the human body cannot be produced by an inferior compound, as is evident. Therefore we must conclude either that the human body can be formed only from another human body, i.e., from the seed of man through the process of generation, or that it can be formed by a spiritual cause. For, although a spiritual cause is absolutely immaterial, it can dispose matter for the reception of form.

The *minor* is evident.

Second part.—*A spiritual cause naturally disposed first matter for the reception of the soul of the first man.*—A spiritual cause naturally disposed first matter to receive the soul of the first man, if this kind of disposition corresponded to the natural aptitude of first matter. But this kind of disposition did correspond to the aptitude of first matter. Therefore a spiritual cause naturally disposed first matter for the reception of the soul of the first man.

Major.—Although the operation of a spiritual cause was not natural in as much as it derived from a supermundane cause, nevertheless, it was natural from the point of view of the first matter which was changed by this operation (1).

Minor. — This is evident from the fact that first matter is naturally inclined to the human soul as to the most perfect form which it can possess. And, in the formation of man, it could be disposed for this form only by the action of a spiritual cause.

Third part. — *A spiritual cause disposed first matter for the soul of the first man by the evolution of the species.* A spiritual cause disposed first matter for the soul of the first man either by a miracle, or by the evolution of the species. But we must refrain from recourse to a miracle as the explanation of the disposition of first matter for the soul of the first man when there is no necessity for a miracle. Therefore a spiritual cause disposed first matter for the soul of the first man by the evolution of the species.

Major. — If a spiritual cause did not dispose first matter for the soul of the first man by the evolution of the species, it disposed it by a non-successive change. But the non-suc-

(1) Non tamen est negandum motum coelestem esse naturalem. Dicitur enim esse aliquis motus naturalis, non solum propter activum principium, sed etiam propter pessivum; sicut patet in generatione simplicium corporum, quae quidem non potest dici naturalis ratione principii activi. Movetur enim id naturaliter a principio activo cujus principium activum est intra natura enim est principium motus in eo in quo est. Principium autem activum in generatione simplicis corporis est extra. Non est igitur naturalis ratione principii activi, sed solum ratione principii pessivi, quod est materia, cui inest naturalis appetitus ad formam naturalam. Sic ergo motus coelestis corporis, quantum ad activum principium non est naturalis, sed magis voluntarius et intellectualis; quantum vero ad principium passivum est naturalis, nam corpus coeleste habet naturalem aptitudinem ad talem motum. — *Contra Gentes*, L. III, c. 23.

cessive change of first matter is not according to the nature of prime matter, and therefore is a miracle. Therefore . . .

482. Spiritual operation in the formation of the body of the first man. — 1° If God immediatly formed the body of the first man, God acted not only as the first cause, but as a particular cause.

2° In the act of disposing first matter for the reception of the soul of the first man, a spiritual cause acted immediately as the sole principal cause, even though it used natural agents as instruments.

3° God constituted the human body formally as human not by the evolution of the species, but by an act of creation. For the human body is constituted as formally human by means of the intellective soul, which is immediately created by God. Hence the human body is formally constituted as human by the creative action of God, by which He produces the intellective soul and infuses it into matter.

483. Scholia. — 1° We established in a general way in the thesis that the species had their origin through a process of evolution. The work of discovering the peculiar and determinate processes by which this evolution took place belongs to experimental science. Thus only experimental science can determine with some degree of probability the particular animal which, by a change of accidents, was disposed for the human compound.

Therefore, in dealing with the problem of evolution, we must not confuse the philosophical solution with the scientific solution of that problem. The philosophical solution does not resolve the scientific problem, just as, for example, recourse to the divine will does not provide a *physiological* explanation of a disease of the body. In like manner, the scientific solution does not solve the philosophical problem. The philosopher, as philosopher, may not contradict the theories of science, except in so far as experimental scientists give, as too often they do, a strictly philosophical meaning to their theories.

Again, we must make a distinction between the experimental elements and the philosophical elements found in the teaching of St. Thomas. He offers a theory in regard to the heavenly bodies by which he attributes to them a universal influx in acts of generation. This is not a philosophical theory, but a physical theory, and one that may not be admitted. But we must hold fast to all that he affirms in virtue of philosophical principles.

2° We are not permitted to say that man evolved or descended from an animal, except in the following sense : some spiritual cause constituted the first man by making use of matter already naturally disposed in some most perfect animal.

The fixists hold that the body of the first man was formed from a much inferior compound, i.e., from an inorganic being. We teach that the body of the first man, as regards the disposition of its matter, was formed from an animal as from a more noble term-from-which. We teach, in a word, that God created the first man by making use of matter already disposed, such as existed in a very perfect animal.

3° No part of the animal formally remains in man, for, on the one hand, resolution to first matter takes place in every substantial generation, i.e., first matter is stripped of all form, substantial and accidental (n. 312); and, on the other hand, man receives his animality from his intellective soul, which is formally-eminently vegetative and sensitive. Therefore we may not say that the soul of the first man was infused into an animal, and thus that man was made from an animal and an intellective soul, as some unlettered persons think.

4° Evolution correctly understood manifests in a wonderful manner the power of God and the dignity of man, and at the same time it safeguards the unity of the human species.

It manifests the power of God, Who not only created man, but also made nature a *cause* in the production of so sublime a work.

The dignity of man is acclaimed, because man is made the end of all creation, and of all inferior beings. Therefore, when the number of the elect will be complete, there will be no more generation, and this visible universe of ours will be renewed, for *the fashion of this world passeth away* (1).

The unity of the human species is safeguarded, because, once the first man was produced, and woman was formed from him, there existed in the terrestrial world a sufficient cause — a man and a woman — capable of naturally disposing first matter for the human soul, or, in other words, capable of engendering in the strict sense other men in the likeness of their nature.

5° Faith teaches us that the first man was elevated to a supernatural state both as regards his body and as regards his soul, for he was endowed with impassibility, immortality, etc.

Theologians commonly teach that man was created in this state. Two conclusions follow from this : *a*) man was created in a special manner, for, in forming him, God acted not only as the author of nature, but also as the author of the supernatural order ; *b*) since the body of the first man was a work in some way supernatural, the problem of man's origin cannot be completely solved under the light of natural reason, but only from divine Revelation.

484. Materialistic evolutionism and spontaneous generation. — 1° Materialistic evolutionism teaches that inanimate matter, by its own power, evolves from an inorganic grade to a vital grade, and then to the human species.

2° Therefore materialistic evolutionism teaches spontaneous generation, i.e., the generation of living being from non-living being, solely by the forces of matter, and without any influence whatsoever of a superior cause.

3° Both materialistic evolutionism and spontaneous generation are metaphysically repugnant, because an inferior cause, acting as principal cause, cannot produce an effect more noble than itself.

(1) *I Cor.*, VII, 31.

4° Nevertheless, the evolution of the species and the origin of a living being from a non-living being are, as we have already pointed out, possible through the causality of a spiritual cause.

485. Difficulties. — 1° If there is an evolution of the species, forms change. But forms are indivisible. Therefore there is no evolution of the species.

Major. — The compound changes, *I concede;* the forms change, *I deny.*

Let the minor go.

Material forms are not subsistent. Therefore they do not change in generation, but merely corrupt accidentally when the compounds in which they exist change.

2° If there is an evolution of the species, nature tends to its own destruction. But every nature tends to its own conservation, not to its own destruction. Therefore there is no evolution of the species.

Major. — Of itself or accidentally, *I concede;* of itself only, *I deny.*

Minor. — A corruptible nature does not tend of itself to its own destruction, *I concede;* accidentally, in as much as in virtue of its first matter it tends to a higher form, *I deny.*

The indefinite multiplication of individuals is contrary to the very notion of end, for the indefinite can never be actuated; hence it is rather a *towardness to something.* From this it is evident that all natural beings which are completely corruptible, as regards their whole and as regards their part, can in no way pertain to the essential perfection of the universe in its final state. All species of material living beings, as animals and plants, which could attain perpetuity only by their numerical multiplication, pertain only to the perfectible condition of the universe and to time. Their conservation cannot be an end. Therefore, if they seek their conservation as an end, it must be said that this desire is contrary to nature. Hence, if they seek their conservation, this must be considered as a means to something else (1). Yet since all natural things desire perpetuity not in order that they become something else, but in order that something else be produced, they tend to man as to the attainment of their end, to man who as an individual has perpetuity; hence only man can be the intrinsic end of nature.

The following text of St. Thomas is often cited by fixists: « There exists in all things the natural desire of conserving their own existence; but this would not be conserved, if they were changed into other natures. Hence no being of a lower order can desire the grade of a higher nature; just as a donkey does not desire to be a horse; because, if a thing were promoted to the grade of a superior nature, it would no longer be itself » (2).

A being that is corruptible as regards its whole and as regards its part certainly desires its own conservation as its proper and proximate end. But, since the conservation of corruptible things is impossible in the individual, and indefinite in the species, it cannot possibly be desired as an ultimate end.

A corruptible being is a part of a whole, i.e., of the universe. As a

(1) *Contra Gentes,* l. 4, c. 97. — *De Potentia,* q. 3, a. 5.
(2) I, q. 63, a. 3.

part, it tends to the good or end of the whole. Its corruption can follow not directly, but indirectly from such a tendency or inclination.

More briefly, a corruptible being tends to its own conservation according to the manner of its existence, that is to say, as a being essentially related to another as its end. Therefore, if a donkey does not desire to be a horse as its proximate end, nevertheless is tends to its own conservation only in order that it may serve another end.

3° A new species is created or engendered. But a new species cannot be engendered. Therefore a new species is created, or, in other words, creationism must be admitted, and the evolution of the species rejected.

Major. — Either by creation or by equivocal generation, *I concede;* by univocal generation, *I deny.*

Minor. — It cannot be engendered by univocal generation, *I concede;* by equivocal generation, *I deny.*

In univocal or proper generation, the being which engenders is of the same species as the being which is engendered, for generation is defined: the origin of a living being from a non-living being in likeness of nature, effected by a conjoined principle. But it is evident that a new species cannot be produced by this kind of generation.

In equivocal generation, a living being is naturally produced by the reduction of matter to form, under the influx of a superior principal cause, which is either God or an angel.

The possibility of equivocal generation is often affirmed by St. Thomas (1).

4° The evolution of the species may be admitted only if it is confirmed by certain facts, and if the origin of the species can only be explained by an evolutionist theory. But the evolution of the species is not confirmed by certain facts, and the origin of the species can be explained by a non-evolutionist theory. Therefore the evolution of the species may not be admitted.

Major. — If the evolution of the species is not proved by philosophical principles, *let it go;* if it has already been proved by philosophical principles, *I deny.*

Minor. — The evolution of the species has not been confirmed in an absolutely certain manner by facts, *I concede;* has not been confirmed nor indicated by facts, and the origin of the species can be explained *scientifically* by a theory which is non-evolutionist, *I deny.*

---

(1) The following excerpts from the writings of the Angelic Doctor manifest his mind in this matter:

I, q. 70, a. 3 ad 3: Corpus coeleste, cum sit movens motum, habet rationem instrumenti, quod agit in virtute principalis agentis. Et ideo ex virtute sui motoris, qui est substantia vivens, potest causare vitam.

De Potentia, q. 6, a. 6, ad 10: Corpora coelestia citamsi non sint animata, moventur a substantia vivente separata, cujus virtute agunt, sicut instrumentum virtute principalis agentis; et ex hoc causant in inferioribus vitam.

In II Sent., dist. XVIII, q. 2, a. 3, ad 3: Cum motus sit actus motoris et mobilis, oportet quod in motu non tantum relinquatur virtus corporalis ex parte mobilis, sed etiam virtus quaedam spiritualis ex parte motoris; et quia motor est vivens nobilissima vita ideo non est inconveniens, si motus caelestis, inquantum est in eo intentio et virtus motoris, per modum quo virtus agentis principalis est in instrumento, est causa vitae materialis, qualis est per animam sensibilem et vegetabilem.

To understand the solution of the objection, the following points must be kept in mind: *a*) Philosophy does not depend on experimental science for its conclusions, although the philosopher must proceed most carefully if the teaching of experimental science is in contradiction to the teaching of philosophy. *b*) Since a scientific theory is always imperfect, i.e., is perfectible, it cannot furnish that absolute certitude such as is found in the demonstrations of philosophy and mathematics; therefore it is not extraordinary that no scientific theory is of such a nature that no other theory can be devised that could explain the origin of the species and the facts confirming and indicating the evolution of the species. *c*) But yet only an evolutionist theory can explain *scientifically* the origin of the species. Fixism explains nothing scientifically, but rather affirms the impossibility of any scientific explanation, for philosophical reasons. In the thesis, we said that such reasons do not exist, and we proved philosophically the natural necessity of evolution.

END OF PHILOSOPHY OF NATURE

GLORY BE TO GOD THE FATHER.

Alphabetical Index

(Numbers refer to sections)

R

S